Wagons, Gold and Conflict

Wagons, Gold and Conflict

Captain Alfred Davenport's Adventures
in the Trans Mississippi West

John G. Wilder

Copyright © 2022 by John G. Wilder.

Library of Congress Control Number:		2022900308
ISBN:	Hardcover	978-1-6698-0617-2
	Softcover	978-1-6698-0616-5
	eBook	978-1-6698-0615-8

All rights reserved. No part of this book may be reproduced or transmitted in any form or by any means, electronic or mechanical, including photocopying, recording, or by any information storage and retrieval system, without permission in writing from the copyright owner.

Any people depicted in stock imagery provided by Getty Images are models, and such images are being used for illustrative purposes only. Certain stock imagery © Getty Images.

Print information available on the last page.

Rev. date: 01/28/2022

To order additional copies of this book, contact:
Xlibris
844-714-8691
www.Xlibris.com
Orders@Xlibris.com
835507

To
Sheila Maher Wilder

Contents

Preface xiii

Part I   Early Years

Chapter 1   Summer 1830 1
Chapter 2   Young Alfred Travels in New York 7
Chapter 3   New York's Erie Canal 14
Chapter 4   Arrival in Ohio 20
Chapter 5   Ohio, 1830–1843 25
Chapter 6   A Wet Beginning 33
Chapter 7   Sandhills and Sagebrush 41
Chapter 8   Platte, Sweetwater, and the Snake 49
Chapter 9   Oregon, 1844 56
Chapter 10   Sandwich Islands and the Hudson's Bay Company 67

Part II   California, 1846–1847

Chapter 11   Arrival in California..73
Chapter 12   The Surprise... 80
Chapter 13   Osos..85
Chapter 14   The Californian Republic 89
Chapter 15   The California Battalion...97
Chapter 16   Fremont Takes the Battalion South 102
Chapter 17   San Juan Bautista to Santa Barbara..............................105
Chapter 18   Kearny Arrives in California... 111
Chapter 19   Alfred Leaves the Battalion 117
Chapter 20   Alfred Returns East, 1847 121

Part III Gold Rush, 1849–1861

Chapter 21	Alfred Joins the '49ers	131
Chapter 22	Sacramento	141
Chapter 23	Hangtown	145
Chapter 24	San Francisco, Autumn 1849	151
Chapter 25	Gold Fields, 1850	159
Chapter 26	Northern Mines, 1851–1852	166
Chapter 27	Northern Mother Lode in 1853	174
Chapter 28	Nevada City, 1854–1855	179
Chapter 29	Southern Mines, 1856–1857	184
Chapter 30	1858: A Request from Fremont	189
Chapter 31	Mariposas	192

Part IV Civil War

Chapter 32	Missouri, 1861	203
Chapter 33	The Mountain Department, Western Virginia	214
Chapter 34	Mountain Department: Early 1862 Shenandoah Valley	222
Chapter 35	Shenandoah Valley, May–June 1862	229
Chapter 36	Cross Keys and Port Republic	234

Part V Quartermaster Department

Chapter 37	Alfred's New Assignment	241
Chapter 38	Alfred Visits Western Hospitals	249
Chapter 39	A Brief Trip East	255
Chapter 40	Mississippi River	263
Chapter 41	New Orleans	268
Chapter 42	Military Detective and a New Assignment, 1865–1866	273
Chapter 43	Louisiana, Florida, and Alabama	278
Chapter 44	Winding Down	282

Part VI Army Warrant

Chapter 45	Kansas	289
Chapter 46	Eureka, Kansas, 1868–1875	294

Chapter 47   Kansas, 1876–1879 305
Chapter 48   Alfred Returns to California 308
Chapter 49   Alfred in Kansas and Ohio, 1880–1886 313

Special Thanks 315
Sources 317
Bibliography 319
Chapter Notes 335
Index 353

Illustrations

Map and Profile of the Erie Canal 12
Lockport, New York, Canal Town Scene 13
Map: Ohio's Canals, Circleville, and Ohio Courthouse 24
Map: Oregon Trail, 1843 32
Emigrants on the Great American Desert, Nebraska, and Fort
Laramie, Wyoming 40
Arriving at an Evening Camp on the Oregon Trail 48
Hudson's Bay Company Trading Post 69
Map: Bay of San Pablo and San Francisco Bay 84
Map: The Conquest of California, June 1846–January 1847 96
Map: Northern California Gold Mining Locations 140
Benton Dam, Merced River, and Murderer's Bar 191
Map: Civil War Campaigns in Missouri, 1861 200
Fremont's Body Guard Led by Major Zagonyi, Springfield, Missouri 215
Map: Fremont's Route in the Shenandoah Valley of Virginia
Spring, 1862 230
Pontoon Bridge on the March 235
Naval Combat off Fort Wright, Mississippi River, May 6, 1862;
Timber-Clad Gunboat 262
U.S. Navy Hospital Ship and Hospital Tree at Fair Oaks 263
Map: Site of Chickasaw Bayou Battle, Civil War Mississippi
River Campaign, 1863 264
Map: Fort Pickens, Florida, Pensacola Bay, and the Gulf of Mexico 279
Texas-Kansas Cattle Trails 295
Portraits: John Charles Fremont, Fitz Henry Warren, Jerome C.
Davis 314

Preface

In late spring 1843, Alfred Davenport arrived in Saint Louis, finding he had missed the last wagon train for Oregon. In 1844, he partnered with frontiersman James Clyman, joining Nathaniel Ford's wagon train departing from Westport, Missouri, for Oregon City. Alfred quickly adapted to life on the trail. His hunting provided meat for food-short westbound emigrants. Tall and quick witted, Davenport faced confrontation head-on, using his head and strength to handle obstacles. When thrown into situations he could not control, Davenport chose the best methods to survive immediate dangers. He faced record floods in Kansas and Nebraska, near starvation on western deserts, and hostile Indians in the Columbia River basin.

Soon after Alfred arrived in California in May 1846, the Mexican government demanded removal of all Americans. Alfred eagerly joined a ragtag group of settlers who captured the Mexican Army's northern garrison in Sonoma in an action known as California's Bear Flag Revolt. He joined California's volunteer battalion of mounted riflemen created by explorer John Charles Fremont, whose efforts ended with Mexico's expulsion from California. Davenport returned East with Fremont in 1847, racing back to California in 1849 to join the gold rush. Alfred shared with us the hard life of searching for gold in California's Sierra Mountains, the growth pains of Sacramento and San Francisco, and the turbulent life in California during this era. In 1858, Fremont selected Davenport to supervise the construction of a dam on the Merced River to provide power for gold mining operations before choosing him to manage his famous Pine Tree Mine.

When the Civil War began in 1861, Davenport joined the U.S. Army in Missouri as a captain in Fremont's special cavalry, the Body Guard. In 1862, Captain Davenport served as a special messenger on Fremont's staff in Virginia's Mountain Department, participating in the Shenandoah Valley campaign. In 1863, assigned to the Army Quartermaster Department, Alfred visited military hospitals in the war's western theater in the Mississippi and Ohio River valleys, where he reported on hospital development and construction for the Quartermaster Department's Washington headquarters. While visiting Memphis, Tennessee, he visited wounded soldiers from Ohio's 114th Infantry Regiment (recruited at Camp Circleville, Ohio), assisting disabled soldiers writing letters to their families. Later, the Quartermaster Department assigned Captain Davenport to the customhouse in occupied New Orleans, where he discovered that the Union's occupational government was plagued by corruption. He resigned from customhouse duties to supervise the construction of a military hospital in the Greenville area of New Orleans, built for men serving in the army's colored cavalry.

He ended his military service with quartermaster posts in Pensacola, Florida, and Mobile, Alabama. Davenport moved to Kansas, discovering new railhead towns serving Texas cattle drovers and an influx of emigrants clamoring for newly opened Indian lands. He became a real estate investor.

The nineteenth century produced scores of unrecognized men and women like Capt. Alfred Davenport whose strong set of values, hard work, and personal contributions, though largely unrecognized, created the country we enjoy to this day.

Part I

Early Years

Chapter 1

Summer 1830

Led by Samuel, head of the Davenport family, Alfred quickly boarded a sleek sailing ship bound to New York City from Liverpool, England. The morning was August 16. Racing to catch an ebb tide, the captain hoped to clear Mersey River before the tide turned; however, light air was slowing the ship's departure. Soon tides would work against the forward progress of the ship. The captain hailed a launch needed to pull his vessel to the open sea, much to the thrill of young Alfred. Puffing and spouting black soot and dust, a steam launch approached the bow where a man threw a line to a waiting crew member who secured the launch's line to the ship. Slack in the line was taken up. Alfred, fascinated by the whole process, was excited to see his towed ship moving faster when pulled by the launch than under sail power. Quickly, they moved past the mouth of the Mersey, leaving behind the English countryside.

The packet was now in open water, causing the launch to slow; lines were cast off, and the great sailing ship was underway, moving by the power of the wind. A ship's bell rang, telling the Davenports that dinner was served in the galley. They quickly went below. His mother, father; elder siblings, George and Anne; and younger sister, Harriet, enjoyed their first meal aboard ship.

Alfred, a typical ten-year-old, was casting aside the comforts of childhood. His head was full of questions, probing and scrutinizing his world. He still accepted instruction from his parents and teachers, but advice and suggestions from an elder sister and his elder brothers were often jettisoned or rejected. Taller than his contemporaries, he had light brown hair, blue eyes, and a large frame with strong shoulders and arms and agile hands. School was an enjoyment for Alfred. He constantly questioned what he saw and heard, the sign of a bright, quick learner.

Later in the day, an hour before sunset while on deck, watching the crew perform their chores, Alfred asked a myriad of questions about the working of the ship, specifically what made a ship increase its speed. A friendly member of the crew pointed out how the strength of the wind made a ship move. Fresh winds brought more speed to a ship and chop to the sea.

Whitecaps soon appeared on wave tips, painting the ocean with foamy white spray. Clouds raced to block the sun; a distant horizon turned black. Suddenly, the captain standing next to the helmsman on the quarterdeck yelled out, "All hands!" Immediately, sailors, the cook, the steward, the ship's carpenter, and everyone in the crew raced to the deck, scampering up ratlines, pulling in sails, lashing them to yardarms.

The first mate came to Alfred, who had been joined by his father, telling them they must return to their cabins and secure themselves in their bunks. "A big blow was approaching ship." It would not be safe on deck nor out of their cabins. Alfred and Samuel hurried below. The family was safe and secure in their bunks when heavy winds struck the ship.

Canvas was down and made fast when the leading edge of a violent storm with winds of sixty knots and higher gusts pushed the ship over on its side. The helmsman and first mate struggled with the ship's wheel. They used all their strength to turn the wheel and bring the ship into an upright position, heading her into the wind. A once placid sea with moderate waves had become twenty-five- to thirty-foot mountains of moving water. The packet ship would climb a wave and hesitate at its crest before plunging down the back side of the wave, dropping into a trough, hesitating like a runner catching his breath, before it caught the next wave climbing out of the abyss. Powerful winds and surging waves continued until the storm blew itself out.

Inside the Davenports' small cabin, the storm took its toll. At first, the children were scared. Their fears were addressed by their parents, who had a calming effect, when suddenly the youngest, Harriet, developed a pale, ashen color. She blurted out she was going to be sick. In seconds, it was all over. Alfred and the others avoided seasickness until the sight and smell of a vomiting family member brought on their own malady. Everyone became sick. George, a teenager, began questioning, "Why did we leave the comforts of home? Was this the sign of perils ahead? Would we survive the long journey to New York?"

Education was important to Alfred's father, whose schooling permitted him to enjoy a long and successful career in Her Majesty's service as a crown surveyor. He was able to provide for his family's needs, acquire a few luxuries, and accumulate savings. Some of his most important aspirations were for each of his sons to receive an education and for the family to become landowners. The development of England's industrialized society created a need for surveyors to construct canals, bridges, roads, and newly developing railroads. The first thirty years of the nineteenth century saw most major roads in England and Scotland surveyed and rebuilt to designs created by the prominent engineers Telford and Macadam. Improvements permitted the speed of stagecoaches to reach eight to ten miles per hour, about twice their speed before reconstruction. Inns along the roads became desirable places for travelers to stop, serving robust meals and offering decent accommodations. This was known as the golden era of coach travel.

A wide variety of social and economic changes took place in England between 1780 and 1830. Rural villages contained tracts of open land used by small farmers who collectively enjoyed plow and grazing rights through the ages. They were given access to small plots or strips of land for their personal use. Parliament's Enclosure Act of 1801 was a plan to consolidate land and make it more productive. The results removed plow and grazing rights from peasants and small farmers, forcing them off the land. The displaced migrated to industrial centers, seeking employment in growing industries—textiles, pottery, and manufacturing.

Samuel's career moved his family to towns where a surveyor was needed. He resided in Norwich, Eccleshill, Stafford, and other industrial towns located in central England. He learned the benefits of land ownership by England's upper classes. Owning land became one of his lifetime ambitions. He did not have the resources to acquire a sizable tract of land in England but learned that inexpensive land could be purchased in the United States. Farmland in new states of America (located west of the Allegheny Mountains) could be acquired for $1 per acre.

Samuel retired from surveying at age fifty-two. A family decision found Samuel and his wife, Harriet, following their dream to leave England and immigrate to America, where they would become landowners. Two older boys, Harry and Charles, both in their twenties, would remain in England to complete their education. The family would move to a farm purchased in "the Interior" as Americans called the land west of the Allegheny Mountains.

The best help Samuel and Harriet could offer their children during the tumultuous first few days at sea was to tell them to close their eyes and sleep, assuring them the ship was well built, designed to survive North Atlantic storms. Rough weather creating a wild ride through an angry Irish Sea plagued the ship for several days. Storms were over when the ship passed Ireland's Cape Clear lighthouse on the island's southwestern point of land. The weather improved; Alfred adjusted to the gentle roll of the ship, finding her rocking motion a comfort as she plowed westward toward America. His appetite for food and desire to learn more about sailing returned to normal.

During the wee hours of night before the sun spread its rays above the eastern horizon, the day after the storm ended, Alfred was awakened by a strange scraping sound, something new. He rose and dressed, creeping slowly up the companionway to the deck, noticing the scraping becoming louder. His discovery upon arriving topside was one of astonishment. Everything—the deck, rails, cabins, spars, and rigging—had turned white. An explanation was given by the steward. Ocean spray from the recent storm coated all surfaces of the ship, depositing water containing fine crystals of salt. When water evaporated, salt crystals remained. The sounds were from the ship's crew using a special soft stone known as a holystone to scrape away salt.

Alfred quickly adjusted to shipboard routines. A bell located near the companionway was rung frequently to make announcements. Included were a change in the ship's watch, shipboard activities, or summoning all on board for announcements from the captain. (A watch was typically four hours when the captain or his designated appointee was officer of the deck.) Bells rang at seven in the morning to announce breakfast, dinner at one, and supper at six. A ship's bell could be heard from anywhere—in passenger cabins midship, at crew quarters forward, or in the captain's quarter aft. When breakfast was finished, Harriet and Samuel used the galley as a classroom for their children.

Samuel's skill as a surveyor provided him with an opportunity to teach his boys a few navigation lessons. He summoned them to the quarterdeck at noon, where the captain used a sextant to measure the altitude of the sun over the horizon. The data gathered by the captain and plotted on a chart measured the approximate distance they had traveled since leaving Liverpool.

Days of light to moderate winds permitted Alfred to visit the quarterdeck, where he learned about sailing. The helmsman explained the name and function of each of the ship's three masts, their sails, and how they worked together. Sounds emitting from the ship were intriguing—the creaking of the ship's wheel as it guided the ship on her course, groans from rigging as fresh puffs of wind filled sails, and the splashing of the sea as the vessel cut through ocean waves. On a calm day when wind eluded his ship and the ocean was as calm as a millpond, Alfred asked if he could climb with a sailor up the crow's nest perched on top of the tallest mast far above the deck but was told this was not permitted by the captain.

The ten-year-old traveler befriended the steward and first mate, who answered his questions about life and lore aboard ship. They taught him a wide and varied vocabulary of nautical terms and chanteys; not all, he was told, were appropriate for his mother's ear. A donkey's breakfast was the name of a mattress in the crew's quarters constructed of cheap rough cloth stuffed with straw. The staple of the crew's diet was the so-called Cape Cod turkey, a serving of boiled and salted cod. He watched men mend sails and repair frayed lines they called "Irish pennants" or watched the ship's carpenter making daily rounds and small repairs. New knowledge picked up from his shipboard "teachers" made Alfred feel he was a real sailor.

Davenports were waiting for a Sunday church service led by the captain when a young sailor returning down from a yardarm misstepped, tumbled, and fell to the deck. The captain called for the ship's doctor. Much to Alfred's surprise, the ship's carpenter came forward. Many nineteenth-century ship medical needs were provided by the captain or carpenter. The injured sailor was examined and found to have no broken bones.

Afternoon rest time was mandatory for Alfred and Harriet. George and Anne read or entertained themselves. After nap time, the family played games to break the boredom of endless days at sea, which began to weigh on the children. Backgammon, whist, chess, or checkers became competitive contests played by the family.

After long days at sea, a surprise meeting for all passengers was called by the captain. Mornings were now foggy; the air was cool. Rumors spread among passengers. They were nearing iceberg alley, where a dreaded unseen mountain of ice could rip a hole in the bottom of the ship, sending her to the depths of the ocean in a matter of minutes. Confirming approaching dangers, the captain announced a change of course, heading south, to avoid suspected ice fields. He reported they were approaching the North American continent. The ocean turned dark green; the ship was entering the Gulf Stream. A combination of cold North Atlantic water joining warm tropical water from the Gulf of Mexico created fog. Most days, a bright morning sun cleared fog away by noon.

Meals were changing. Fresh meat was replaced with salted meat. Several crates holding pigs and fowl, food for the ship's larder, washed overboard during heavy storms in the Irish Sea. Chicken, eggs, and fresh pork were no longer on the menu. Food choices would soon improve dramatically, for they were approaching their destination, New York City.

One sunny, bright morning, Alfred took his usual trip to the quarterdeck. A flock of wild geese flew toward the ship, honking like a pack of hounds in full cry. The helmsmen told Alfred they were Gabriel Hounds. Legend tells they are the souls of deceased unbaptized children wandering in space until judgment day, a favorite sailor's tale.

Appearing on the starboard side of the ship, the helmsman pointed to a long green strip of land. It was Long Island, New York, the first view of America. Later in the day, a steam launch approached the ship. The captain hove to, stopping the ship's forward motion, allowing a launch to come alongside. A man from the launch boarded the ship. He was a pilot who would take the helm guiding the ship through Hell Gate, a narrow passage leading into New York Harbor. She would be placed in a berth on New York's East River. The journey across the Atlantic Ocean had taken six weeks.

Chapter 2

Young Alfred Travels in New York

The excitement of arriving in New York bordered on a frenzy for Alfred and his brother George. The boys were restless and fidgety, sparring and poking at each other, calling each other names. Each wanted to be first to put his foot on American soil, but a few details needed to be completed before going ashore. A doctor from the port of New York must come aboard and certify the health of all passengers and crew before anyone could leave the ship. Samuel had to clear customs. Personal belongings and trunks stored in the ship's hold were to be taken ashore. Both sons channeled their energy into helping their parents prepare to leave the ship but quickly became impatient with the slowness of the tasks at hand. It seemed like an eternity had passed when Samuel declared he was ready to take his sons ashore. The girls and their mother remained on board, finishing their packing chores.

The boys raced to the ship's gangplank, each bolting toward the South Street Seaport pier. George claimed to be the first onshore. Alfred refuted this, saying he was faster and first. Their father settled the issue, exclaiming the race was a tie. Alfred was quick to notice that the South Street Seaport had more ships and much more activity than seen in Liverpool. The quay was filled with ship bows extending in a line over a mile in length. Walking was not easy, for the walkway was crowded with stevedores, sailors, and merchandise.

The variety of assembled ships delighted the boys. A large ship with an ornate bow sprit of a partially naked lady caused the boys to chuckle with laughter. Teams of freight wagons vying for space to load or unload merchandise obscured paths to nearby streets. Most intriguing was a variety of packets, the sleekest ships in port. One packet stood out from all the others. It was new. You could see your image reflected from bright black paint and sparkling varnished wood. Its highly polished brass fittings were sharper and brighter than those on any other ships in the harbor.

The travelers soon discovered New York's renowned Fulton Fish Market. Founded in 1822, it had grown to become the port's largest and most active market. Samuel asked the boys if they were hungry. What a silly question to ask a ten- and thirteen-year-old boy. They stopped at a small café where Samuel ordered a plate of oysters on the half shell. The boys were told each must try an oyster. Neither one could believe what they saw; "ugly, slimy, horrible" was the reaction, yet each opened his mouth with great trepidation, nervously swallowing a live mollusk. A thoughtful father ordered a second course, this time a bowl of fish chowder. The boys devoured their chowder, each clamoring for a second bowl.

Exploration continued with a walk past a row of buildings called the Schermerhorn Row filled with merchants serving the maritime trade. Cooperage, sail lofts, equipment, and materials needed to rig a ship; chemists; a print shop; and warehouses were some of the many stores along the route. Stores generated questions about maritime businesses for the boys, who had little knowledge of the shipping industry. The three left the seaport following Wall Street to the center of the island until the street ended at Trinity Church. They continued in a westerly direction, coming to a large body of water called the North River, named by the Dutch in the early seventeenth century, later renamed the Hudson River. The shore was lined with over a dozen docked steamboats.

Samuel inquired about passage on a boat that would take the family to Albany. He secured a place on a vessel leaving the next morning. Boarding was to be completed by four o'clock. Departure was scheduled at first light. Sunrise was a little past six. Steamboats did not sail at night, avoiding unseen navigational hazards hidden by darkness.

Alfred was thrilled to start a riverboat adventure. He would travel aboard a sleek white steamboat 145 feet long, powered by giant paddle wheels located on each side of the ship. High above the top deck, he noticed a small enclosed glass room containing a large wheel manned by the ship's pilot, who would guide the boat to Albany. The next day's trip would take thirteen hours.

A quiet and dark New York City night found the Davenport family arriving at the North River steamboat docks brightly lit by gaslights. The scene was lively, animated, and noisy. Crews of workers toiled and struggled loading freight and wood aboard the lower deck of each boat. Throngs of people stood in queues, waiting to board their appointed vessel. A ship's bell rang, announcing it was time for travelers in the Davenport queue to begin boarding. Passengers surged up a narrow gangplank, each seeking a good seat on the top deck. Harriet and her two daughters went aft to the ladies' cabin. Samuel and the boys moved forward to the men's cabin. They settled into seats where they would remain during the journey.

A shrill steam whistle emitted three blasts as the crew struggled to bring the ship's heavy gangplank onto the deck. Anchor lines were retrieved from pilings on the shore. Clanging pistons and thumping sounds arose from deep inside the boat. Two bells rang, and the deck began to shake. Slowly, the boat began to slide backward. A pair of steam-driven tugboats saddled up to each side of the boat, gently nudging her to the middle of the river, her bow facing north. One bell rang, and the engine stopped. Giant paddle wheels slowly turned, propelling the boat upstream. Speed increased, engines throbbed, and the deck shook and vibrated as the boat picked up speed. A pleasant breeze began to flow over her bow. Lights encountered at the boarding area were soon left behind, plunging the vessel into a graying predawn light. Stars illuminating the night receded. A new dawn, the Davenports' first day in America, was slowly emerging.

Alfred stood next to the leeward rail, watching the city slowly recede from view. Large flocks of geese aroused from nocturnal slumber departed from protected coves along the river's shore. Great honking sounds called their flocks together while they gathered in the sky, forming giant Vs for the journey south as part of their annual fall migration. Shorebirds left nests, starting daily routines, seeking the morning's breakfast. An occasional splash broke the surface of the river created by a solitary fish seeking a tasty insect. The eastern sky changed from gray to pink, followed by orange and yellow, lighting palisades—tall granite cliffs lining the river's western shore.

A pair of tall black chimneys located amid ship emitted thick plumes of dark black smoke. Alfred asked his father how the ship's propulsion system worked. "Below each chimney a firebox heated giant boilers generating steam. Steam drove pistons transferring power to a connecting rod, shaft, and paddle wheels located on each side of the ship. Turning wheels propelled the steamboat through the water." The process fascinated Alfred and George, who wanted to see how each component in the propulsion system worked.

Samuel and the boys decided to view the equipment on the lower deck. It was crowded with piles of wood needed to fuel fireboxes. Barrels of cargo, pallets of goods, horses, and mules were crammed into spaces on the deck. Squeezed among freight were deck travelers roughly dressed and tough looking, a stark contrast to the finely dressed travelers on the upper deck. Some earned passage by wooding. The steamboat stopped every two hours to bring aboard wood for fireboxes. Wooding passengers earned passage by loading logs at fuel stops. Deck passengers stayed in any space they could find, crowding next to animals, interspersed among cargo or near the ship boilers. Boiler explosions, broken steam pipes, shifting cargo, stampeding panicked animals, or the risk of being forced overboard faced deck passengers. The boys' view of the ship's propulsion equipment was cut short by the ship's engineer, who shooed them away, sending them back to the safety of the upper deck.

The first ferry stop was Yonkers. Before touching the dock, the boat's engineer opened a steam valve, allowing boiler pressure to drop while the boat was idle. The noise of escaping steam startled some passengers, who feared the boat was in some sort of peril. Four men jumped ashore as the boat drifted to a stop. They raced to a stack of wood, handing logs to waiting shipboard companions. In five minutes, the whistle blew, signaling that all should be aboard; the steamboat was departing.

North of Greenburgh (Dobbs Ferry), the river became a three-mile-wide lake known as Tappan Zee. *Tappan* was the name of a branch of the Algonquin Indians who were the original inhabitants of the area. *Zee* was Dutch for "sea." Early settlers thought the wide river was an inland sea. Steamboats were not the only merchant vessels plying the Hudson. Sailing vessels carrying freight were abundant. Most popular was the single-mast, gaff-rigged Hudson River sloop. About 106 feet long, they were shallow-draft, centerboard, Dutch-designed boats. They handled well in strong tides, shallow water, and fluky winds. On windy days, a fully loaded sloop could beat steamboats on the run from Albany to New York.

Bright sunshine and crisp, clear skies provided beautiful vistas of the Hudson River valley. The river narrowed as the boat approached Stony Point's lighthouse on its west bank. Autumn was in the air. Farmers along the waterway were harvesting and gathering crops. The countryside was beginning to change from a blanket of green to magnificent colors of yellow, orange, and red. North of Stony Point was Storm King Mountain, Bear Mountain, and West Point. West Point was established as a Revolutionary War fortification by Gen. George Washington. It became the United States Military Academy in 1802.

The river narrowed, flowing into an *S* curve at this location a little more than a quarter of a mile wide, snaking around the cliffs below the military academy. Beyond was Newburgh, an important stop for passengers and freight shipments and a location to load additional wood for the ship's fireboxes. Newburgh was the northern limit of tidal water known as brackish water, a mixture of fresh and salt water. Beyond this location, one found fresh water in the Hudson River.

Waiters rang bells, calling everyone to dinner. Passengers raced to a single long, narrow table set up in the main salon. Women arrived first and were seated. Next came the men. They found platters of boiled beef, pork, sliced cabbage, and bacon swimming in vinegar. Butter, bread, and wedges of cheese accompanied the platters. Beer was the beverage of the day. Platters were not passed. Each person grabbed what food he could find in front of his place. No one spoke a word; everyone was silent. Demands were not made of waiters. In fifteen minutes, the meal was over, the salon table deserted. Meals were included in the price of upper deck passage. You ate what was provided; there were no menus. Passengers returned to their seats. Back in their seats, away from the dining salon, comments came forward about the meal. They ranged from "It was good" and "I've had better" to "It was horrible" or an occasional "I was robbed."

North were the towns of Poughkeepsie and Hudson, major stops for transferring people and freight. Along the western horizon, Alfred could see the Catskills, the highest mountains he had ever seen. The tallest was Slide Mountain, rising to 4,190 feet. Alfred told his father he would like to climb the mountain to see the view from the peak. Samuel replied, "A little way ahead is Albany, the end of the day and our riverboat trip."

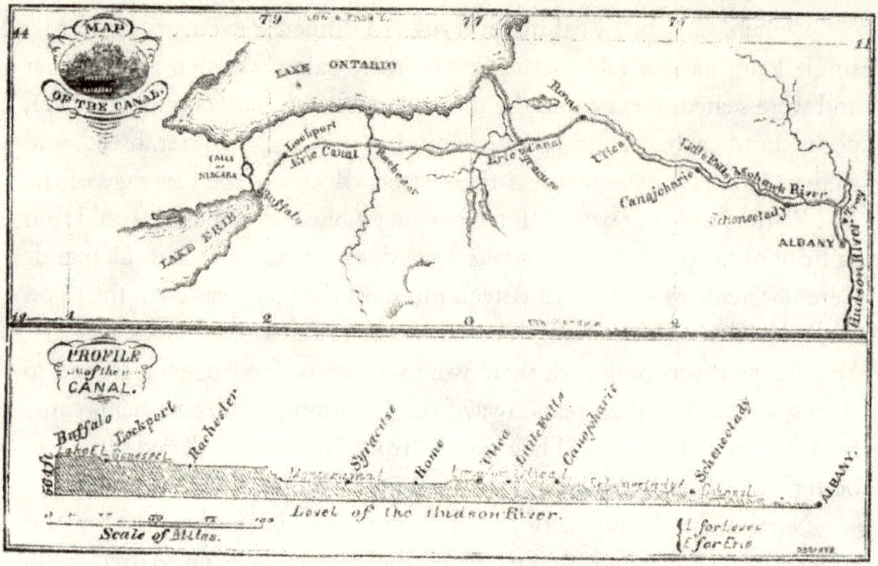
MAP OF THE CANAL
LAKE ONTARIO
Lockport
Erie Canal
Buffalo
LAKE ERIE
Rome
Utica
Mohawk River
Canajoharie
Schenectady
ALBANY
PROFILE of the CANAL.
Buffalo
Lockport
Rochester
Syracuse
Rome
Utica
Little Falls
Canajoharie
Schenectady
ALBANY
Level of the Hudson River.
Scale of Miles.
L for Level
E for Erie

Lockport on the Erie Canal

Chapter 3

New York's Erie Canal

The view from six to seven feet above the land is certainly not spectacular like a hilltop or mountaintop view. Alfred, standing on a rooftop of a boat floating across New York State, felt that the vista was exciting. The family left Albany, New York, embarking on a six-day, 363-mile journey to Erie Canal's western terminus on Lake Erie at the city of Buffalo. Forty passengers were squeezed aboard a 60-foot-long boat traveling day and night. The boat was pulled by three horses at the end of a 200-foot towline.

A teenage boy called a "hoggy" drove the animals, impressing the Davenport boys, for they were city lads knowing little about horses. They learned horses were rotated every 12 to 15 miles from a stable maintained in the bow of the boat. Horses pulled at a speed of 4 miles per hour. The boat, a packet boat, was built for passengers. Boats designed to carry freight were called line boats with speed limited to 2 miles per hour. When a line and a packet boat approached a lock, the packet was first to proceed through the lock because packets had the right-of-way over a line boat. Alfred confronted the crew with questions about the boat. He was told the small cabin sitting on the aft deck was home for the captain and his wife. This explained laundry fluttering in the breeze from the rear of the boat.

A short distance from the boat's starting point, the first of twenty-seven locks located in the 15 miles' canal stretch between Albany and Schenectady was reached. Alfred watched as the boat slowed, entering a tall chamber lined with cut limestone blocks. A line boat was waiting for

Alfred's boat to clear the lock before proceeding ahead. Alfred's boat halted at a gate located at the forward end of a walled chamber. Gates behind the boat were closed by a lock tender barking orders at the boat's deckhand, who answered in a similar vitriolic tone. A call was shouted for mooring lines to be changed. The deckhand and tender's conversations became heated, each hurling insults at the other to the point where a full-fledged argument erupted. Alfred expected the two men to begin exchanging punches, starting a fistfight. Tempers cooled while water flowed into the lock. In the end, the canalboat rose to a new level, front gates were opened, and the journey resumed. The captain was not idle when his boat was in a lock. He made rounds, collecting tolls, each fare depending on the length of a passenger's trip.

The beauty of central New York was enjoyed by the Davenports as their boat passed rolling farmlands, orchards, forests, small villages, towns, and people living near the canal. Carriages, wagons loaded with freight, drovers herding animals, and others crossed many of the bridges under which the boat passed on its journey west. On one bridge, a preacher wearing a top hat and cutaway coat stood on a box with a Bible in his hand, shouting at anyone one who would listen, "Repent! Repent! Save your soul! Follow the ways of the Lord!"

Height of bridges over the canal was a concern because clearance for boats passing beneath bridges was tight. A warning of "Low bridge!" was shouted at passengers. Anyone on deck needed to avoid a bridge. Slamming into a bridge could be fatal.

Midday produced a call to dinner. Alfred could not see how forty people could fit into the boat's small cabin. He descended into a smoky room filled with the odor of tobacco spittle and foul air. A long table stretched the length of the cabin. Benches along each wall served as chairs for the table. The table was loaded with fixings, travelers' food, not unlike the one on the steamboat. Women and children sat first, followed by men, who silently began to devour the fixings.

Alfred was in awe of one man's dining habits. He used a broad-bladed knife to spear a slice of meat; holding it in the air, he thrust it deep into his mouth. Samuel commented, "The man had a strange and possibly dangerous way to eat meat." A two-pronged fork next to his plate was largely ignored. The Davenport children were not excited about American food, missing their mother's home cooking, especially meat pies, swedes with other root vegetables, and a wonderful dessert favorite, spotted dick.

School lesson began after dinner in the cabin, taught by Alfred's parents. Some travelers remained below, playing backgammon or cards or reading one of the books found in the boat's small library.

Canalboat captains clamored for a level of respect given to sea captains. They dressed to look the part, resulting in their being known as "nautical dandies." Captains called stops along the canal "ports." A port was a small settlement containing a lock tender and a shanty where he would sleep, take his meals, and store supplies of medicines and liquors to sell to travelers. Taverns and commercial buildings began developing near canal ports. You were a "canaller" if your livelihood came from the canal. This group included the boat captain, deckhand, cook, helmsman, and hoggy. Other canallers worked on land as lockkeepers, toll collectors, repair crews, bridge operators, surveyors, and canal bank watchers. A bank watcher patrolled 10-mile sections of the canal, looking for leaks or a break in the canal bank.

Alfred enjoyed the boat crew. They were young and spirited and liked to gamble. In their spare time, they bet on racing caterpillars, cockroaches, bedbugs, or frogs in contests held on the deck of the boat. Onshore, they attended cockfights and dogfights. Crew members sang songs and chanteys and enjoyed telling tall tales to entertain boat passengers. Children were warned of haunted bogs through which boats passed at night where ghosts could be encountered. A twitching broom at the entrance of the ship cabin signaled that a witch was on board. When this occurred, a new broom would be attached to the bow of a boat to ward off witches.

Nighttime was a new experience for Alfred and his family. A large red curtain separated men's and women's cabins, women in the front, men in the rear. Settees became beds. Two levels of canvas bunks were installed above each settee. Passengers squeezed into tiny sleeping places. Air quality was foul, deteriorating as night progressed, compounded by a rank odor of unwashed bodies and spent tobacco juice. Strategically placed spittoons failed to contain discarded tobacco juice, resulting in smelly, wet, and slippery floors. Tobacco chewing was the norm in America, yet men would never smoke tobacco in front of women, for it was considered bad etiquette. Snoring was a major nocturnal issue. Puffing, wheezing, and rattling sounds filled small crowded canalboat cabins. The annoyance drove many outside to sleep on the cabin roof in a search for limited peace and quiet.

A sleepless night was forgotten when the boat arrived at Utica the next day. Six weeks of braving the Atlantic Ocean, a hurried trip up the

Hudson River to Albany, and a race to catch a canalboat exhausted the Davenport family. Young and old welcomed a stay in Utica for a few days before resuming their journey.

The foothills of the Adirondack Mountains, north of Utica, were full of brilliant fall colors, painting an impressive sight for the senior Davenports. They were impressed by the town's rolling hills, comfortable houses, paved streets, churches, and public buildings. It reminded them of towns located in England's Midlands. Samuel was tempted to stay in Utica and call it home, but he desired cheaper farmland in new states west of the Allegheny Mountains, specifically rural central Ohio. Success of the Erie Canal created land speculation. Farmland was more expensive in New York near the canal. They would continue their journey to the Midwest. His eldest son, Harry, and wife, Sarah, remained in England. They decided in 1832, upon arriving in Utica, to make the town their home.

A portion of the canal between Utica and the Seneca River at Salina (Syracuse) was over flatland. The section was a 69½ miles' stretch where passengers enjoyed a comfortable uninterrupted pace free of delays caused by passage through locks. The boat passed many eastbound line boats loaded with agricultural products including flour, wheat, and maize. Samuel questioned his captain about the shipping costs of agricultural products and the canal's impact on New York commerce. Year 1830 saw the cost of shipping wheat from western New York state to New York City drop to one-tenth of the rate charged before 1825's opening of the canal. The canal brought prosperity to upstate New York. Real estate values in towns near the canal were on the rise. New factories, mills, and warehouses were seen along the route. Commerce created by the canal was greater than what the canal builders had anticipated.

The spirit of rural America touched passengers crossing the Empire State on the Erie Canal. Peaceful days passed as the Davenports slowly meandered among green pastures and fields filled with sheaves of harvested corn waiting to be collected and stored in nearby barns. Men were seen harvesting wood from the many groves of trees scattered among open fields. Pigs and geese approached the canal, near but not close enough to be touched. Cattle lazily grazed on rolling pastures. Alfred observed on several occasions that the canal plunged travelers into dense dark forests where trees and thick vegetation pushed against the towpath, blocking out sun, creating a tunnellike feeling. A clear, crisp, cloudless morning after a rainstorm on the third day after Utica brought a chill to the air. Summer was gone; cooler weather lay ahead.

The scenery changed after the boat passed the town of Syracuse, reaching the great Montezuma Swamp. Swarms of mosquitoes attacked travelers, striking any exposed skin. Passengers raced below to the cabin to escape the massive clouds of stinging, biting insects. This section of the canal had been extremely difficult to construct. Muck, sand, and clay located under 10 inches of water had to be excavated. Spring rains and resulting high water caused construction to be halted until water levels subsided. It had been reported that over one thousand workers died of swamp fever (malaria) during the construction through the swamp. Construction workers were paid $12 per month, shared a room in a shanty, and supplied with food and whiskey. Irish emigrants provided the greatest number of workers in the Montezuma Swamp.

Alfred seemed undeterred by mosquitoes, staying on deck to view the swamp's abundance of wildlife. Migratory waterfowl seemed to be everywhere. An occasional blue heron was seen strolling on a bank, waiting for a boat to pass so it could begin hunting for fish frequently caught in the canal's shallow waters. Bald eagles, an owl, a muskrat family, and several deer were identified for Alfred by a member of the boat's crew. He remained on deck for another anticipated event.

New York's Seneca River did not have an aqueduct for canalboats to cross in 1830. The boat stopped at a gate on the river's edge. Towlines were carried across the river on an adjoining bridge while gate tenders opened and closed gates to facilitate crossing. A 10-foot-deep ditch had been dug on the river bottom to accommodate canalboats during times when river water levels were too low to carry a boat. Crossing the Seneca River was smooth without problems.

An early nineteenth-century engineering marvel lay ahead; a great aqueduct crossed the Genesee River in Rochester, New York. Samuel, with his engineering and surveying knowledge, explained construction details to all who were interested, especially his sons. Aqueduct designs originated in ancient Rome. Eleven arches made of sandstone and limestone blocks supported the canal's waterway over the river. Stone blocks were cemented together with a recently developed mortar compound made from finely powdered limestone and clay, not unlike compounds used in England for canal and bridge construction. Rochester's 802-foot-long aqueduct traversing the Genesee was built high above the river. Towpaths were located on each side of the aqueduct.

A sixty-foot-high hill, part of the Niagara Escarpment, stood in the canal's path before it reached Lake Erie. Canal engineer Nathan Roberts solved the problem by designing a series of five double locks spaced end to end to carry boats over the impediment to the surface of the lake. The locks were each 90 feet long, 15 feet wide, and 12 feet deep. Locks were separated by a terraced walkway 30 feet wide. Double locks permitted the simultaneous movement of boats in opposite directions at the same time. This was a nineteenth-century engineering marvel. Alfred learned the name of this strange canal location, Lockport.

The next leg of the journey was a nine-hour steamboat trip on Lake Erie to Cleveland, Ohio, the northern end of the yet to be completed Ohio and Erie Canal. Early the next morning, Samuel and Harriet surprised their children. Their trip to Cleveland would be delayed. The family was taking a side trip to see Niagara Falls. Americans, travelers from Europe, and others visiting Niagara were awed by the power and intensity of the falls. The size and scope of the falls was unimaginable. Reactions varied; the Davenports were dumbstruck. Great rivers of green water thundered over cliffs, plunging over 160 feet, splashing on boulders, creating clouds of spray and mist that filled the air. Everyone in the family was speechless. Some visitors described their experience as a poetic, religious, or mystic event. Alfred became very quiet, lacking his normal flow of youthful questions, when he first looked on the falls.

Chapter 4

Arrival in Ohio

Alfred was mystified. He was told he would be traveling on a steamboat and was directed to a vessel not unlike the one he sailed from Liverpool to New York. The bow and stern were familiar, containing two masts rigged with sails. The difference was amidships. A tall black metal chimney rose from the center of the ship's deck. Giant paddles were mounted on the outside in the middle of each side of the boat. The boat design created many questions from Alfred. Was this a sailboat or a steamboat? Why would a steamboat be rigged for sailing? He was told there were two reasons. Sails could be used if steam equipment broke down or if winds were strong and favorable sailing would be faster than steam propulsion.

The boat was designed with two classes for passengers, cabin and deck. Samuel decided his family would travel as deck passengers, joining other emigrants for a nine-hour journey to Cleveland. He would pay one-third the fare charged for cabins located on the aft part of the deck. Each family would need to bring their own food and beverages for the trip. A canvas top covered deck passengers for protection from sun and rain. Lower deck space was reserved for machinery, wood for firing boilers, and small amounts of freight; no passengers were allowed.

Alfred's boat departed before sunrise from Buffalo, New York, sailing to Cleveland, Ohio. Arrival was late afternoon, in time to have supper at an inn where they would spend the night. It would be their first night in the American Interior as land west of the Allegheny Mountains was known. The Davenports' visit to Cleveland introduced Samuel, Harriet, and their children to a new world of social customs and practices unknown in England.

The senior Davenports were aware of American social and class distinctions practiced in Eastern and Southern United States. Class distinctions ceased to exist in the Interior. Men had no valets nor personal attendants. Beards were unshaved and untrimmed, hair was unkept, and shoes were not shined. Household servants could not be found. A young woman preferred to go hungry rather than work as a domestic servant. Farmworkers were expected to dine with the family for whom they worked and be treated as a family member, or they would leave the farm. An educated man who became a doctor or judge or held an elected office might own a farm and farm the land. A chosen occupation had little bearing on one's status in the community. Strange dining habits, speed eating, repugnant use of chewing tobacco, and communal use of towels and combs were hard to accept by Alfred's parents, especially his mother.

The Davenports would never forget their night in Cleveland. Samuel arranged for two rooms to be let for his family for the night, one for the women and one for the men. Soon after the men got to sleep, a strange man entered their room and climbed into their bed. Beds were in short supply in the Interior and in many areas of the country. It was customary for an innkeeper to sell space in a bed for up to three travelers. The practice was accepted by the local population. The Davenports were horrified. No amount of haggling with the innkeeper could remove an unwanted stranger from their midst.

The next morning, Alfred boarded a boat on the Ohio and Erie Canal. The trip started in Cleveland, ending near Newark, Ohio. Remaining sections of the canal would be completed when the canal reached the Ohio River in 1832. Canal trenches were frequently lined with limestone, and locks were constructed of limestone covered in wood. Submerged wood would swell, creating a watertight barrier. The Ohio and Erie Canal cost $10,000 per mile to build. Construction workers were provided food, whiskey, and a place to sleep. Pay was thirty cents a day. Northern portions of the canal were drained and remained dry from November to April to stop damage from winter's ice. By 1830, the canal brought a surge in economic benefits to areas served. New towns along the canal route were established; one of the most notable was Akron.

Newcomerstown and Coshocton were other important canal stopping points. Originally, these two towns were home to Delaware (also known as Lenape) Indians, part of the Algonquin nation. The tribe had been forced west of the Alleghenies to Ohio territory by the Treaty of Easton in 1758. Removal continued when Ohio Indians lost most of their Ohio lands with the Treaty of Greenville in 1795. During the War of 1812 between England and the United States, Indians allied with the English, attacking settlements and farmsteads in Ohio from locations in southern Canada. Tecumseh, the Indian chief and leader, was killed in an unnamed battle in 1813. Hostilities ceased when the U.S. government acquired the Wyandot reservation in Upper Sandusky, moving Indians to Oklahoma.

One canal community was founded by a special interest religious group. In 1817, religious dissenters, the Society of Separatists, from Wurttemberg, Germany, purchased five thousand acres of land south of Cleveland with funds borrowed from the Society of Friends (Quakers) in Philadelphia, Pennsylvania, naming their commune Zoar. They paid off the loan and earned a cash surplus with funds raised by digging seven miles of the canal crossing their property.

Canal workers were paid in cash, replacing a barter system on the frontier. Workers had money to spend. Products from eastern cities such as glass, cloth, coffee, and tea were suddenly available and affordable west of the Allegheny Mountains, brought to consumers by the canal. The canal system opened new markets in the East for Ohio farm products. Ohio's agricultural products reached national markets. Wheat selling for twenty-five cents a bushel in Ohio in 1826 rose to national market levels of seventy-five cents after the canal was completed in 1833. Costs to ship grains for eastern markets dropped to 10 percent of precanal costs.

Samuel noted the contrast of canal communities in Ohio versus those seen along New York's canal. New Ohio towns were smaller, offering fewer services and amenities than those found along New York's canals. The Davenports left the canal near Newark, taking an overland route by coach west to Circleville, Ohio.

People living in Ohio and throughout the West chose not to walk, a popular habit in England and many parts of Europe. If you walked in America, it was thought you were poor. Long distances between settlements or towns in the Interior made walking unpopular and impractical. People traveled in wagons, carts, or carriages or on horseback or mules. They chose any available mode of transportation. Wealth was not measured by the size of your house or farm, rather by the number of horses, wagons, or carriages one owned. Alfred's journey ended at a 320-acre farm located in Walnut Township, Pickaway County, Ohio, a few miles north of the town of Circleville. It was known as the Burton Farm.

Courthouse, Circleville, Ohio

Chapter 5

Ohio, 1830–1843

The journey south from Cleveland had been an eye-opener. The canal did not cross flat prairie lands as described by land promoters. It wandered through a landscape of rolling hills, following three river systems: Cuyahoga, Tuscarawas, and Licking Rivers. Early settlers long the canal route were subsistence farmers. Thick forests provided timber for simple log homes built on small plots of land. The task of clearing land for crops was a difficult and time-consuming struggle. Hired labor was not available. A farmer cleared his land by felling or notching trees, leaving stumps or dead trees, among which corn could be planted. He owned an ox and a milk cow and raised hogs and chickens. Vegetables were raised near his cabin. Hunting provided additional protein for his diet.

Alfred's father was surprised to see numerous plots of land containing rotten stumps and dead trees. The ugly sight astonished Davenport and other emigrants from Europe. Cheap land had its downside. Settlers, often dreamers and wonderers, remained several years in one location and then packed up their families, heading West to look for better opportunities and cheaper land in newly opened states. Abandoned farmsteads with dilapidated structures could be seen from the canal. By 1830, many small plots were consolidated into larger tracts of land consisting of several hundred acres available to emigrants, people from the eastern states, and Revolutionary War veterans who wanted to settle on large farms of several hundred acres.

Walnut Township was located on the eastern edge of Pickaway County.

The county seat was Circleville. Pickaway derived from Piqua, a Shawnee Indian tribe formerly camped on the Pickaway Plains, a lush grass plain of grass located three and a half miles south of Circleville. The county and town were established in 1810. Circleville was so named because it was located inside a circular Indian fortification (some thought it a religious monument) built by prehistoric Indians whom the locals named Mound Builders. No record of the ancient people who built the ring and its adjacent square as well as other large mound formations located throughout the Scioto River valley had ever been discovered. An octagonal county courthouse was built in the center of the town's circle. Streets radiated out of the center of the circle like spokes of a wheel.

Agriculture was the leading business in Ohio, made possible by the construction of the canals, giving farmers access to eastern markets. The national road entering Ohio from Wheeling, Virginia (West Virginia after 1863), through Zanesville, Columbus, and west through Indiana to the Kaskaskia River in Vandalia, Illinois, contributed to Ohio's growth. Branches of the road served Circleville and other towns.

Alfred and his family had much to learn after moving to central Ohio. They left behind life in England's industrial Midlands, where mills, potteries, and manufacturing thrived, part of the growing England's Industrial Revolution. The Davenports would no longer live in crowded, smoke-filled cities, which they exchanged for fresh air and open land. They would miss goods and services, merchants and stores found in England's industrial towns. Circleville's population in 1830 was 1,136. It would grow 105 percent to 2,329 in 1840 largely due to the Ohio and Erie Canal.

Life on the farm was hard and challenging. Winters could be very cold; summers were hot. Wood for heating and cooking came from forests on the farm. Cattlehides were processed into leather and taken to a shoemaker where every family member was fitted with a last from which a shoemaker would make a person's shoes. Most clothes were made at home. Food was produced on farms. Everyone in the family worked to supply food. They sowed seeds for garden vegetables in the spring while raising cattle, hogs, and chickens. In the autumn, they gathered nuts and berries from wild trees and vines, harvesting and preserving vegetables, fruit, and meat needed throughout long winters.

Business serving farmers, doctors, attorneys, and the county courts were available in town. Reports from 1825 stated that Circleville lacked a grocery store; there were no furniture or hardware stores. Dry goods were expensive. Before canals, merchandise was brought, weather permitting, by teamsters hauling large wagons from eastern cities over the Allegheny Mountains to Ohio.

Big changes occurred after the Ohio and Erie Canal was completed from Lake Erie to the Ohio River in 1832. By 1837, a wide variety of new businesses had developed and grown due to the canal. One purchased in Circleville glassware, earthenware (pottery), and queensware (fine china) at better dry goods stores. Whiskey was cheap, as low as twenty cents a gallon. When a farmer visited a neighboring farmer's house, he would be offered a drink of whiskey. If he refused, he was considered rude. Banks issued paper currency; however, much business was done by trading and barter. Wheat, corn, dressed hogs, beef, and eggs traded at national market prices, shipped East by canal freight boats. One thing missing was a bookstore. Books needed to be purchased in Chillicothe, the nearest town south of Circleville, or in Columbus, the state capital, located twenty-nine miles north of town.

Streets in 1837 were dirt. On busy late summer days when streets were filled with traffic, dust was so thick that you could not see from one side of the street to the other. Wagons loaded with large tanks of water drawn from the canal or Scioto River drove through town sprinkling water on streets to dampen dust. Merchants or homeowners paid for this service. Failure to pay for a watered street in front of his business gave the impression that a merchant was not a successful businessman. Wet months saw streets turn into a sea of mud. Main Street was the lone street paved in gravel. It had a crown in the center permitting water to run off during storms. When the circle was squared starting in 1838, new streets built in a rectangular grid were graded and covered in gravel, eliminating mud and dust.

Pigs were another story. Circleville, like other Ohio towns, had pigs. Pigs were everywhere, snorting, rooting, and sleeping, encouraged by residents who dumped garbage into streets. One city was called "Porkopolis." We know it as Cincinnati. Pork was the most readily available item on a traveler's dinner plate. Early houses had a parlor located on the front of the house next to the street with a door opening to a narrow yard. Hot summer evenings found residents moving parlor chairs to the yard to avoid the room's heat. Frequently, their quiet evening was disturbed by grunting visiting porkers. When this occurred, it was said people had "pigs in the parlor." Cows were also visitors. They were known to wander into town, strolling along streets during the day, returning to familiar farms at day's end.

Alfred soon learned his role in helping with farm chores. He gathered wood for cooking and heating the family house. The farm's smokehouse needed hickory, apple, cherry, and oak. Cows had to be milked twice a day. All animals received food and water twice a day. The Davenport boys performed appointed chores, went to school, and assisted their father with farm labor. The girls helped their mother with inside activities: cooking, laundering clothes, sewing, making butter, and preserving and storing food.

The family quickly settled into their new life and routines. They were happy to have long days of travel, rough weather, cramped quarters, and questionable food as distant memory. Alfred was especially pleased when some of his old favorites emerged from his mother's kitchen—pork pie, oxtail soup, Davenport fowl (a boiled chicken with giblet stuffing), bubble and squeak, toad-in-the hole, and apple fritters.

Schools in Ohio were private academies funded by parents. The Davenport children's schoolhouse was located on township land provided by the state. Monday through Friday from late autumn after harvest until spring planting, Alfred and his siblings walked two miles to school in all types of weather, rain or snow, hot or freezing cold days. Classes were held in a one-room log cabin with a stone fireplace and windows covered with greased paper to provide light for the room. Benches constructed from split logs provided seating. Younger children sat in the front of the room. Taller older children sat in the rear. Students studied spelling, grammar, arithmetic, writing, and reading. A teacher would alternate weeks boarding with a student's family. Textbooks were the Bible and a geography book. The Davenport family loved and acquired books. *Gulliver's Travels*, Irving's *Life of Washington*, *The Ohio Gazetteer*, Madison's *United States Constitution*, and books by local author Caleb Atwater were part of their library.

On June 30, 1831, Alfred's twenty-three-year-old brother, Charles, arrived from England. Charles had finished school where he had studied medicine. He planned to help the family develop a profitable farming operation; medicine would be a sideline. New buildings were needed on Samuel Davenport's farm. George, Charles, Alfred, and Samuel discussed designs for new structures. Alfred was particularly interested in building details. His father took the time to answer his son's many questions about the design and construction of a large barn. The farm needed space to shelter and feed animals; a milking parlor; spaces to store grains, hay, and farming equipment; and a small apartment for a hired hand.

Local custom dictated that neighbors would provide labor in building or raising a barn. Lumber would be cut and prepared for the day's work. Men would gather to assemble a barn. When work was completed and a barn had been raised, cider and whiskey appeared. Ladies served a large spread of food for everyone to enjoy. Other difficult tasks on a farm requiring intensive labor were shared by members of the farming community. Hog processing was an example. Hogs would be brought into an enclosed yard, slaughtered, cleaned, and cut. Roasts, chops, sausage, and other meat products were created. Pork hide was set aside for further processing.

Ladies had their own projects. Women and their daughters from neighboring farms gathered for activities such as a wool cleaning party where freshly sheared wool was spun and dyed in preparation for weaving into cloth. Quilting bees were popular and held regularly.

Saturday nights were reserved to be enjoyed by the entire family. A special treat for Davenport children was popcorn smothered with butter accompanied by sweet cider or milk. Sunday breakfast was special. Harriet served her family pancakes floating in maple syrup, accompanied by sausages and oatmeal with cream. The family would leave the farm after breakfast to attend an Episcopal church service.

Alfred's farm responsibilities grew as he became older, stronger, and taller: clearing stones from the fields, cutting brush, assisting with planting and harvesting crops, and—his least favorite—removing spent straw and manure from the barns. In the winter, he helped Charles and George saw blocks of ice from the farm pond, load a sleigh, and take the ice to the farm's icehouse, where it was stored in sawdust for use next summer. His chores, farm labor, and school meant he had limited time for leisure activities. In summer months, when his schedule permitted, he would go fishing in the canal or the Scioto River. Autumn was hunting season. Samuel would take the boys to hunt rabbits, turkey, or deer. He hunted with a prized double-barreled shotgun acquired in England for his move to Ohio.

Charles befriended Caleb Atwater author of *A Description of the Antiquities Discovered in the Western Country*. Atwater's book described the location, size, and construction of prehistoric Mound Builder sites in Ohio's Scioto River valley. Charles and Alfred enjoyed visiting sites with Atwater. Ancient mounds were found near Circleville, Chillicothe, and

Newark, Ohio. Springtime found Alf and George walking over newly plowed fields where Indians had once lived. They discovered arrowheads, spear points, ax-heads, and other Indian artifacts from freshly plowed soil. Many were found on a farm Charles had purchased on Pickaway Plains.

On Saturday, January 31, 1835, Charles Davenport married Martha Wilkes at Saint Philip's Episcopal Church in Circleville. The next year, 1836, Samuel—the head of the family—died at the age of fifty-eight. Alfred was sixteen years old. He had begun reading and learning guides and pattern books needed for a carpenter's apprentice. Three years later when he was nineteen, his mother died. In 1840, his younger sister, Harriet, married Joseph Smith Wilkes, owner of a successful warehouse, shipping, and lumber business in Circleville. Alfred lived with siblings after his mother's death. He continued carpentry apprenticeship, becoming a master carpenter, working part time at his brother-in-law's lumberyard.

Year 1843 was monumental for Alfred Davenport. He decided to leave Circleville and fulfill a long-term dream to see the American West, traveling to Oregon. Shortly after the completion of the family farm's spring planting, he began a journey that would change his life. He left for Saint Louis, taking a steamboat on the Ohio River from Portsmouth, Ohio, traveling as a deck passenger. His fare was half the cost fare of cabin-class passage. Food was not included in passage; he needed to bring his own. Once on board, he discovered that the kitchen would sell him a meal for twenty-five cents. Wood, cargo, and animals were loaded onto the deck, followed by passengers squeezing into available space.

Alfred quickly mingled with fellow travelers. He met emigrant families, revivalist preachers, politicians, gamblers, and assorted con men. He learned that the passenger ratio was four deck-class passengers for each cabin-class passenger. Sleeping was impossible. Traveling on a steamboat could be dangerous. Deck-class travelers faced threats of exploding boilers, steam from broken pipes, shifting cargo and tumbling wood piles, panicked stampeding animals, or being squeezed off the boat into the river. They endured loud sounds emitted from clanging, banging, puffing machinery day and night. Men from the ship's crew shoveled animal manure, spent tobacco juice, and tobacco plugs from the lower deck into the river once a day. Steamboats stopped every four hours for wooding, the loading of wood for the ship's boilers. Wood would be gathered from preplanned stops along the shore or from purveyors who brought skiffs loaded with wood to a stopped boat. Alfred saw an opportunity to reduce his fare by loading wood at wooding stops. He was no stranger to work in a wood lot, having grown up in a farm. He discovered hard work helped him sleep among din and chaos of deck travel. Major stops were Cincinnati and Louisville. Each town brought a new crowd of gamblers aboard, working the crowd to fleece the gullible of hard-earned dollars.

Alfred watched excitement grow as Saint Louis came in sight. Passengers pushed and shoved as the boat approached the quay. More than dozen jumped or were pushed off the boat into the swirling, muddy Mississippi River. Alfred immediately began a search for a wagon train or caravan to join for his greatly anticipated western journey. He soon discovered western travelers departed farther west from Independence, Missouri, a three- to four-day boat trip up the Missouri River. Disappointed, he learned more bad news. It was too late to start west. Travelers who departed this late in the year might find themselves stranded in the Rocky Mountains by winter storms. Most stranded travelers did not live to see the next spring.

Choices for the future were clear. Saint Louis needed skilled carpenters, especially in steamboat construction. Alfred would work and add to his savings. He would travel to Oregon in April 1844.

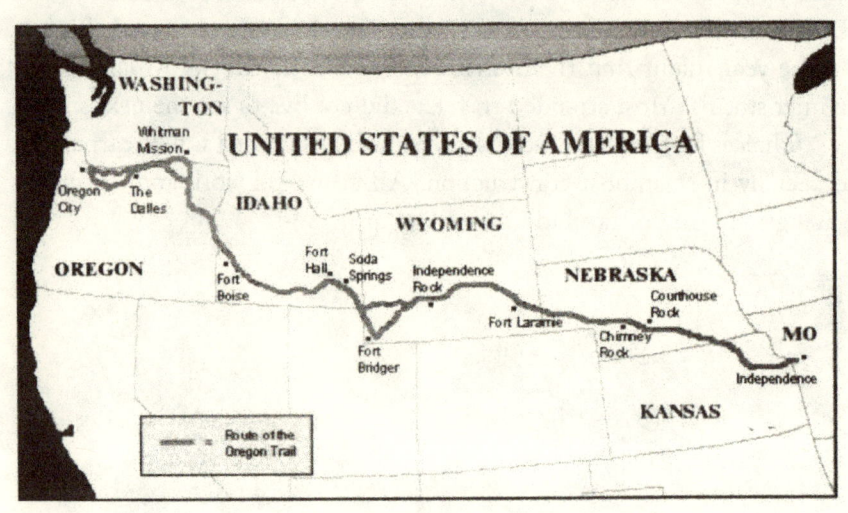

Oregon Trail, 1843

Chapter 6

A Wet Beginning

A frown of apprehension crossed Alfred's brow. Dangerous situations did not usually faze him, but rocky, jerky movements of his steamboat since leaving Saint Louis on the Missouri River concerned him. Excessive spring rains added to mountain snow runoff in 1844, flooding the turbulent and muddy Missouri River with a violent surging current three times faster than normal. Alfred elected to travel cabin class, for he had been warned that freight, animals, and people had been washed overboard from the lower deck during recent trips to Independence. The trip was exceedingly dangerous even for experienced steamboat captains. Submerged, hidden trees and snags were a constant threat. Uncharted sandbars and a newly cut channel were a challenge to the best river pilots.

Alfred was standing at a rail late in the day when the boat shuddered and stopped, slamming into a hidden sandbar. A firm grip on the deck rail kept him from being thrown forward; others were not so fortunate. A wide stretch of water was seen on each side of the boat. She seemed to be in midchannel but was stopped dead on a new, unseen, and uncharted sandbar. Thanks to a skilled captain, with help from a rapidly moving current, the steamboat—with engines in reverse—backed away from the obstruction. Immediately, crew men increased soundings, helping the pilot locate a safe passage as the boat resumed its journey toward Independence. Night fell; the captain found an inlet to dock his boat. Invisible water hazards made travel too dangerous for steamboats after dark. Alfred's captain, like others plying the Missouri that spring, was confident of his skills in the most trying of circumstances. He owed money for his boat, needed revenue from emigrant travelers, and was willing to ignore river dangers to provide service to Westport, Independence, Saint Joseph, and other Missouri River locations.

Alfred landed in early May at Independence, a town that had grown overnight to over a thousand people. Shops were crowded; streets were full of active people busily preparing for a western journey. Draft animals, mules, and oxen were selling for higher prices than they would command in the East. Wagons were being repaired, strengthened, and outfitted with supplies needed for a six-month journey to Oregon.

Independence's celebratory atmosphere was filled with all types of characters. Shawnee and Kansa Indians with painted bodies mingled with Mexicans sporting brightly colored pants and broad hats. Mountain men dressed in rough-looking buckskins, rivermen, Negro slaves, peddlers, and preachers roamed the streets, adding to the commotion of the town. Lively activity reminded Alfred of a Midwestern county fair. He spent the next several days finding a group to join for his journey to Oregon. Emigrants, he soon learned, were young, energetic, tough, and idealistic. Their parents had successfully endured hardships, opening new lands west of the eastern mountains, passing to their offspring a legacy of restlessness that dominated their pioneer spirit.

Davenport met Col. Nathaniel "Nat" Ford, a forty-eight-year-old former Missouri sheriff who was moving to Oregon with his wife, Lucinda, and his three slaves. Ford selected Moses "Black" Harris, who had led several groups to Oregon, as guide for his wagons. James Clyman, a well-known frontiersman and mountain man, would join the 1844 caravan as a pilot. Clyman, with Thomas "Broken Hand" Fitzpatrick and Jedediah Smith, rediscovered the South Pass through the Rocky Mountains located in western Wyoming while trapping in 1824. It became the major northern pass through the Rocky Mountains that Ford used to reach Oregon. Alfred liked Ford and was impressed with Clyman. He chose to travel in Clyman's group. Soon after leaving Independence, members of the wagon train elected their captain or leader. Their choice was Col. Nathaniel Ford.

Located at the Great Nemaha Indian Subagency twenty miles from Saint Joseph, Missouri, Cornelius "Neal" Gilliam, a captain in the Black Hawk and Seminole Wars, assembled a wagon train of 323 people heading for Oregon. Tall, physically fit, and headstrong, he was an ordained minister and a former sheriff. He called his caravan the Independent

Colony and was elected its "general." The general divided his "brigade" into four divisions. Captains of each company were Robert Morrison, William Shaw, Allen Saunders, and Richard Woodcock. Gilliam departed on May 20. The next day, one of Cornelius's sons, Martin, was married to Elizabeth Asabill in a ceremony led by Oregon-bound preacher Rev. Edward E. Parish.

The Independence newspaper *Western Expositor* reported 358 persons traveled with Ford. Fifty-five married couples, 80 single men, and 168 children departed on May 14 with fifty-eight wagons, five hundred head of cattle (a good portion were oxen), sixty horses, and twenty-eight mules. Wagons were 10' to 12' long farm wagons. Several blacksmiths and five carpenters including Alfred traveled in the Oregon-bound caravan. Conestoga wagons, an eastern favorite, were too heavy to cross the Rocky Mountains. Outfitters in Independence converted farm wagons into covered wagons known as prairie schooners. A bonnet or cover made of five to seven arched wooden bows was constructed over each wagon and covered with sailcloth or linen. Linen was waterproofed with beeswax or linseed oil. Wagon beds or wagon boxes were waterproofed for river crossings. Each wagon carried a barrel of fresh water and items needed for repairs: jacks, spare axles, spare tongues, extra yokes, wheel parts, and a bucket of lubrication for the wheels.

A typical family carried cooking utensils, bedding, clothing, furniture, knives, axes, and guns. Most families ignored sensible advice of outfitters to take only necessities in their wagons and instead held on to family treasures. In years ahead, the trail became littered with discarded items; rocking chairs, mirrors, washstands, trunks, mattresses, and clothing were a few discarded items littering the trail. Men hoarded firearms; for women, it was clothing. Guns became the source of many shooting accidents on the trail. Food included 150 lbs. of flour, 20 lbs. of cornmeal, 50 lbs. of bacon, coffee, sugar, dried fruit, salt, rice, and beans.

Two or more teams (pair) of animals pulled each wagon. Horses did not have the strength to pull wagons over the Rocky Mountains. Oxen were the most popular draft animals used for the journey. They fed on grass found along the trail and were obedient but were the slowest of the draft animals, occasionally suffering from sore feet. When hot and dry, oxen were known to stampede toward water. Mules were faster, stubborn and temperamental, prone to bite their handlers, and easily spooked by thunder and lightning. Grass and the bark of cottonwood trees growing along the shores of western rivers, especially the Platte, was part of a mule's diet. Mules could tolerate alkaline water that would kill oxen.

Oregon settlers were not accepted by everyone. Saint Louis's *Missouri Republican* published an article late in May calling the people heading to Oregon ignorant and poor, asking locals not to support emigrants: "Settling Oregon will provide no advantages to the city of St Louis." Banter such as this was of little or no interest to the emigrants.

The first day of travel ended in Westport, a mere nine miles from the starting point. Days of heavy rain had turned the trail into a sea of mud. Teams of animals struggled in dragging fully loaded wagons through a path of waterlogged ruts. Wagons at the end of the line found the trail wagon axle deep with mud. Heavy loads caused several wagon axles to break. At the end of each day, the lead wagon would transfer to the rear of the line in a rotation system, giving everyone an opportunity to lead the train. On May 15, the caravan covered eighteen miles, stopping at Lone Elm near a Methodist Mission established in 1830. The mission taught English and agriculture to Shawnee Indians who had been removed from their homelands in Ohio. Two days later, the caravan arrived at a split in the trail. Ford took the northwest route toward Oregon. The other trail lead southwest to Santa Fe.

Violent rains continued to drench the travelers for another four days. Heavy downpours blocked evidence of the trail, causing long delays until the way ahead came clearly into view. The prairie suddenly turned into a vast lake. Waters covered shoe tops; in some places, it was knee deep. Wagon bonnets provided little protection from pelting, driving rain. Bedding and clothing became soaked and remained wet, despite all efforts to protect contents from the weather.

Clyman's wagon broke an axle. Everything had to be unloaded to complete repairs. Alfred worked replacing the axle, not completing the job for two days. The next several days produced more rain than sunshine. A bright morning sky would suddenly darken. Strong winds with sharp, stabbing lightning bolts arrived from the western horizon accompanied by rolling thunder sounding like battlefield cannons. Hail the size of marbles pelted the travelers. Small creeks easily crossed in normal times became rushing torrents of water.

The Wakarusa River, at the tributary of the Kansas River, was the first major flooded river to cross, presenting a serious challenge for the emigrants. Riverbanks leading to the water were dangerously steep. Several men joined Alfred in tying ropes to the rear of a wagon. Slowly, each of the fifty-eight wagons was lowered to the edge of the water. Ropes were removed and fastened to a wagon's front. Alfred and others swam the ropes across the river to the far shore where drovers with fresh mules and horses pulled oxen and wagons across the river. This system worked until oxen lost their footing, unable to touch the riverbed. Twenty wagons had crossed when rising water halted crossing. Remaining travelers waited until waters receded and oxen found sure footing to resume their river crossing. Overnight saw less rain, but the Wakarusa continued to rise another six to seven feet.

The next morning, Ford announced he wanted to establish rules governing the wagon train. The following day, a group of men including Clyman met to establish rules approved by, though not always observed, by all participants. The river's level dropped during the morning meeting, allowing remaining wagons to join those who had previously completed the crossing. In the evening, a dry hill was selected as a stopping place for the night. Next to the river, the land was lush and green, providing plenty of grass for animals but lacked wood for campfires. Fortunately, many wagons had limited supplies of firewood for cooking the evening meal.

A welcome clear night and dry morning put everyone in a good mood. Several ladies left the campsite to gather wild strawberries discovered in a nearby field. One lady constructed an oven to bake bread. Younger men took guns to hunt game; others went looking for animals that had wandered away from the campsite. Later in the day, a drover with a string of pack mules passed Alfred, hauling supplies for Fort Laramie.

Rain, mud, and high water delayed progress; on good days, the wagon train would only travel seven to eight miles. Mornings often brought an early fog, followed by more rain. Ford's group continued to struggle westward, reaching a ridge above the next major river crossing, the Kansas River. A thick and constant rain plagued the caravan, accompanied by great quantities of lightning and thunder. Ox yokes, saddles, spare wood, and other items were requisitioned at night to use as a bed to elevate travelers above the wet prairie. Attempts to sleep were impossible; at times, Alfred thought he was sleeping in a lake. The trip from Independence had been long and tedious. Spirits were low, especially among families with young children. Travelers were beginning to become depressed and discouraged but realized they needed to continue their migration. Returning East was not an option. Most emigrants had sold everything they owned for their move to Oregon.

Papins ferry was the best option for crossing the Kansas River. Unfortunately, the ferry had been destroyed by flooding. Alfred and fellow carpenters had no choice. They altered wagons to float them across the river. Crossing began on May 30, completed when the last of the livestock had crossed on June 4. Floodwaters and rain had taken its toll on the integrity of Ford's wagon train. It was no longer intact; a forward section cleared the river crossing before Alfred arrived on the south shore. Another section arrived when he completed his crossing.

New problems surfaced on the morning of June 1. The caravan was deep in Kaw (Kansas) Indian territory. Kaws were thought to be too lazy to work and too cowardly to travel to buffalo territory, where they would encounter enemy tribes. Kaws were root diggers known for stealing and warring with other tribes. Clyman awoke to discover that the wagon train's livestock was widely scattered. His horse and a friend's mule were among the missing animals, a value of $200. Walking to Oregon was not an option. An immediate search for the animals produced no results. Alfred joined Clyman in a posse seeking stolen horses and mules. Clyman pointed to trail signs left by Indians: broken tree branches where animals had been tied, bent grass where they had rested, and hoofprints in mud near water. Four days of searching produced no animals. The posse was forced to return to camp empty handed.

The next morning, Clyman took his posse to visit the head of the Kaws, Fool Chief, an old, wrinkled, and dirty-looking man. He told the chief he wanted nothing from the Kaws other than water for travelers to drink, wood for cooking, and grass for animals. He demanded that Kaws return his missing horses and mules, threatening to bring soldiers from Fort Leavenworth if the Kaws did not stop hassling and stealing from emigrants. Fool Chief promised to return Clyman's animals if they could be located.

The posse resumed its search; coming on a dirt lodge, they found several drunken young braves standing knee deep in water. Clyman demanded that the braves return his stolen horses. Heated words were exchanged. An Indian lunged at Clyman with a knife drawn. Alfred and his companions immediately charged, knocking drunken braves off their feet. Kaw braves found themselves surrounded by Clyman's posse, who knocked them off their feet and forced them to wallow in the muddy floor of the lodge. With nothing gained, the posse departed, leaving the braves to their own devices.

On June 9, two horses and two mules were discovered missing from Ford's company. Ford armed ten men, joined Clyman's posse, and went after the animals. They came on two Kaws who claimed they had taken the animals from the member of an enemy tribe. The Kaws demanded a "finder's fee" for their efforts in recovering the stolen animals. A small payment was made to recover the animals. Indians were warned that soldiers would be coming from Fort Leavenworth with a company of dragoons to stop and punish horse thieves.

Rain, mud, fog, hail, and flooded rivers continued to plague the emigrants for the next two weeks, greatly delaying crossing Red and Black Vermillion Rivers and their tributaries. On June 22, Alderman—an Oregon employee of the Hudson's Bay Company—and two other men returning West from an eastern trip came into camp, returning Clyman's horses and mules stolen on June 1. Their news from the East was grim. The Missouri River landing at Independence was blocked by a sandbar. Piers and docks at Westport Landing were gone. Crops and orchards had vanished. Houses, barns, fences, and animal carcasses were seen floating down the Missouri and Kansas Rivers and other flooded rivers.

A junction in the trail was reached near where the Big Blue River joined the Little Blue. It was the union of the Saint Joseph and Independence trails. The combined trail proceeded in a northwestern direction parallel to the Little Blue until a well-traveled overland route took the travelers to the Platte River. Burr Oak Creek was crossed on June 24. Ford learned that Gen. Cornelius Gilliam had crossed Burr Oak Creek on June 20.

On June 27, Alfred saw a group of twenty men and a Catholic priest led by Andrew Sublette across the river. The men were traveling to the mountains, hoping the climate would improve their poor health. This was the first record of travelers journeying West on the Oregon Trail seeking better health. Unfortunately, three men died before leaving Kansas, a fourth died before reaching the Platte River in Nebraska.

Caravan of Emigrants for California
(Crossing the Great American Desert in Nebraska)

Fort Laramie

Chapter 7

Sandhills and Sagebrush

Land began to change. Limestone outcroppings appeared alongside the trail. Recent rains washed soil from the sides of creeks, exposing fossilized shells from sea creatures who had once lived in the area. Rich dark earth was replaced with sandy soil. Firewood disappeared from the trail, creating a problem. Dried buffalo dung known as "buffalo chips" was the only fuel for campfires. Three bushels of chips were required to cook a meal. Collecting of chips was relegated to women and children, not a popular task.

Early stops along one of the tributaries of the Kansas River permitted Alfred time to try his hand fishing, one of his favorite sports. He was successful, returning to camp with several nice-sized catfish to share with others for dinner. The trail turned north, leaving the Little Blue River. Ford's caravan was entering Sandhills Country. Seventeen miles ahead lay the Platte River, a distant 320 miles northwest of Independence, Missouri. The river was a 3-mile-wide shallow ribbon of muddy water extending to the western horizon, centered in a valley 12 miles wide. *Platte* was a French name meaning "shallow." Water scooped from the river was full of mud. Holes dug next to the river would fill with fresh, clear water. Stretching in each direction from the river were miles and miles of sand hill, grass-stabilized sand dunes covering 20,000 square miles of the American Great Plains. The hills ranged in height from 100 feet in the east to 500 feet in the west. Eastern sand hills saw an annual rain fall of 24 inches; the western section would see only 16 inches of rain. Shrubs and trees were not in existence. Recent seasonal rains created a blanket of bright green grass sprinkled with yellow wildflowers. Wild ducks enjoyed water in small shallow ponds. Ponds were short lived. They would soon disappear from the prairie, evaporating in hot, searing sun.

The caravan needed fresh meat. Tracks pointed to large numbers of buffalo in the area. Alfred, as a youngster, had learned how to hunt. He was an excellent shot who could fire a gun and hit a target while rapidly advancing on horseback. Clyman selected Alfred to join a group of men to hunt buffalo. Clyman led his hunters on tracks, leading several miles away from the wagon train. Approaching a small hill, Alfred and his companions dismounted from their horses, slowly climbing to its crest. Spread below was a wide valley containing hundreds of buffalo. Fortunately, the men were downwind from animals, unaware of nearby hunters.

Clyman motioned for Alfred to retreat down the hill and mount his horse. A signal was given to start. Alfred raced over the hill's crest at full gallop, charging toward several cows. Reins controlling his horse were in his left hand, a Hawken rifle in his right. Alerted, buffalo began to stampede away from Alfred and his riders. Despite the speed of the buffalo, Alfred's horse gained on a big bull taller and larger than his horse. He closed the gap with his prey. Dropping the reins, urging his horse with his boots, he strategically rested his rifle on his left arm, carefully firing at a spot below the animal's shoulder. The great animal continued to charge ahead. Alfred thought he had missed his target when, suddenly, the buffalo's front knees buckled, its head dropped, and the animal collapsed onto the soft earth. Alfred had to act quickly to keep from colliding with his downed prey.

"We brought sixteen horses to pack meat back to camp. In about one hour we killed between thirty and forty buffalo, some weighing from twelve to fourteen hundred pounds. Unfortunately, we had more meat than we could take away, so we selected the choice parts, as the rump, ribs, fleece, marrowbones, tongue and liver, loaded horses leaving the remainder to wolves, coyotes and vultures following buffalo herds," Alfred explained. "I continued to ride shooting four buffalo who fell not more than twenty yards apart."

Clyman, impressed with Alfred, regularly called on Davenport to join hunting expeditions to supply meat for the wagon train. Great excitement greeted the hunters on their return to camp, for fresh meat had not been available in the past several weeks. Cooking and drying fires were soon ablaze. Buffalo hides were stretched on drying racks as part of the curing process. Inside the camp's circle of wagons, a celebratory atmosphere prevailed. Not long after supper, "fiddlers brought out their instruments." Music and singing filled the air. The next day, it was discovered that meat that had not dried overnight had spoiled. Alfred was saddened by the loss of meat, a "terrible waste of a great resource."

Hunting stops provided additional benefits for travelers. Clothes were washed in the river. Oxen, mules, and horses were shod, wagon wheels greased. Women had time to mend clothes and bake pies. A light shower late one afternoon left the air moist and still. The overlanders, as emigrants were called, immediately were besieged by swarms of mosquitoes, which pestered them for the rest of the day until a light breeze disbursed the biting insects sometime after midnight. A common occurrence, late in the afternoon, the sky suddenly became filled with dark clouds. Lightning flashed, and thunder roared; animals became edgy, but no rain appeared. Old-timers said lightning produced prairie fires, a serious threat to man and beast. If fire developed on the prairie, the only safe place was to drive the caravan into the middle of the Platte River.

One night during Alfred's guard duty, he was alerted to disturbance among the cattle; a calf began to bawl and cry. He grabbed his rifle and raced to the sound of the distressed animal. As he approached a panicked calf, a dark shape began sulking away. Taking careful aim, he shot the intruder, who gave a yelp of pain before becoming quiet. Another guard arrived, took a shot, and killed a second wolf. Both wolves were gray in color. Trappers called gray wolves prairie wolves. The attacked calf could stand and walk. She would live to see another day.

Gilliam's attempt to establish martial law was not enforceable. Conflicts arose in the ranks; members of his party refused to follow his often harsh dictatorial orders. On July 15, General Gilliam called together his colony and resigned as its leader. New leadership was divided among previously appointed divisional captains. Internal squabbling had slowed Gillian's wagon train.

Late on July 16, Ford passed Gilliam. Gilliam started early the next day with plans to pass Ford and regain the lead. Three days later, representatives of both wagon trains met, agreeing to travel near each other. They were entering Sioux Indian territory, a dangerously aggressive and warlike tribe. The combined wagon train stretched two miles, an easy prey for rogue Indians. Ford instituted daily wagon rotation. Each morning the previous day's lead wagon would take its place at the end of the line, permitting everyone to move up and have a spot in the lead. The train stopped for an hour at noon dinner. Alfred noted, "A little before sunset we camped. The wagons were drawn into a circle by our captain, guards were posted outside the circle, supper was prepared. Minor repairs and wagon maintenance was performed to keep wagons road worthy."

"On the Platte, we found antelope by the thousands," but only a few hunters had Alfred's skill to harvest these wary and quick animals. One day while Alfred was hunting, he ascended to the top of a high hill. Before him, as far as the eye could see, "the prairie was covered with thousands of buffalo. Wolves were sneaking around the perimeter hoping to catch an animal that might stray from the herd. It was a noble sight to see so many monsters of the prairie in such an immense body." Wind was blowing into the herd, alerting the buffalo of human presence, causing them to quickly race from the scene, not giving hunters a chance to mount a major kill.

Alfred and others left camp at first light to seek buffalo. They found a herd and hunted, returning to camp late in the day. During the hunt, four men became separated from the main group. They were nowhere to be seen when Alfred and the other hunters returned to the wagon train. Arrival at camp minus four men created much anxiety among hunters' spouses and families. They feared the worst. Were they trampled to death or captured by renegade Indians? Would the men ever return, or would their families have to go alone to Oregon? Three days later, four exhausted, bedraggled, hungry men wandered into camp, much to the relief of their families and the rest of the camp.

Alfred's wagon train came to the junction of the North and South Platte Rivers. They followed the South Platte, crossing it with little difficulty at a known shallow ford where they climbed a steep, rutted hill to a plateau and a trail taking them to the North Platte River. The land had no timber. Buffalo grass was everywhere, covering rolling hills; ridges were dry and full of limestone. On the plateau, Alfred passed a colony of prairie dogs, a species of ground squirrels living in a "city" of hundreds of acres. They appeared to be protected by rattlesnakes that lived with the rodents, chasing away visitors. The overlanders' wagons came to a steep hill named Windlass Hill. The base of the hill contained a large green oasis, Ash Hollow, where the caravan stopped for a day's rest among trees, grass, fresh water, wild fruit, and wildflowers.

In the winter of 1835, a great battle between Sioux and Pawnee Indians was waged near Ash Hollow, caused by a dispute for control of the prairie. Pawnee lost sixty warriors, the Sioux forty-five. After hostilities ended, Pawnee—the underdogs—departed, moving 400 miles east. Ash Hollow and surrounding lands became Sioux territory. Indians were not overhostile to emigrants in 1844. Travelers along the Platte to Fort Laramie were a curious phenomenon to Sioux chieftains. Young braves would, on occasion, sneak into camp at night, hoping to steal items from wagons. Posted guards kept intrusions at a minimum. The Sioux wanted to trade; acquiring liquor was a top request.

Alfred, scouting ahead on horseback, took note of the distant shore of the North Platte River. Appearing on the horizon were a series of tall sandstone structures identified by Clyman as buttes. The first two were called Courthouse and Jail Rocks. Each rose over 250 feet above the flat prairie. A third was called Chimney Rock, a singular spire rising singularly from a conical base to a height of over 300 feet from the valley floor. The spire named by the Sioux translated as elk penis. Indian agent Joshua Pitcher called it Chimney Rock, feeling the Indian name might offend Anglo-American people from the East. The trail from Chimney Rock led to Scotts Bluff, a collection of five bluffs, an 800-foot extension of the Rocky Mountains located on the south bank of the North Platte River. The trail along the river ended at a large rock formation referred to as badlands by mountain men. Wagons detoured around Scotts Bluff over Robidoux Pass and the Wildcat Hills before returning to the North Platte. Alfred was given his first view of the Rocky Mountains when they reached the summit's pass, where the travelers found an abundance of dry wood, water, and grass.

Coyotes shadowed wagons following the Platte Rivers. Weighing fifteen to forty pounds, these members of the wolf family fed on animal meat, hunted in packs, and communicated through a mournful long howl accompanied by short yelps. Coyote howls echoed over campsites at sunset and at sunrise, constantly sending chills through travelers. Often seen, they kept a distance from wagons, wary of campfires and camp guards' guns, though young, injured, or old cattle were fair game. Indians knew a coyote as a medicine wolf (*wa-chunka-monet*). They thought a coyote was a messenger sent by the Great Spirit to announce a coming event affecting the welfare of their children; thus, they were sacred and never harmed.

On August 1, Ford arrived at Fort Laramie at the junction of the Laramie and North Platte Rivers. Established by fur traders William

Sublette and Robert Campbell in May of 1834, John Jacob Astor's American Fur Company acquired the fort in 1836. The United States Army acquired the fort in 1849, calling it Fort Laramie. Kansas and Nebraska, in 1844, were Indian territories. They became open to settlement in 1854. Military and fur trading posts were the only locations on the Oregon Trail where travelers could acquire supplies.

Emigrants in 1844 looked forward to Fort Laramie, the first permanent trading post since leaving Independence, Missouri. They had traveled 650 miles, one-third of the way to Oregon, taking seventy-eight days. The fort provided rest from the rigors of daily travel. Its blacksmith replaced shoes on horses, mules, and oxen hooves and repaired iron wagon wheel rims. Weaker animals were traded for stronger stock. Supplies were available for purchase. Many emigrants had depleted their stores of flour, sugar, and other items before arriving at the fort. Clyman felt prices for supplies at the fort were outrageous. Sugar was $1.50 per cup; flour was $1.00 per cup or $40.00 per barrel. The arrival brought about an evening celebration lasting most of the night. Large quantities of liquor were consumed, especially by Indians, who continued to screech, fight, carouse, and yell well into the next day.

Brule Sioux Indians were camped outside the fort, living in conical-shaped tepees. A subtribe of the Teton Lakota, *Brule* is a French translation for "burnt thighs," referring to a historic Indian escape from a prairie fire. The name *Sioux* is derived from a term used by French Canadian trappers. It is a corruption of the French word *sued* meaning "drunken." *Lakota*, the name Indians called themselves, translated as "cutthroat." Alfred described the Indians: "Fine looking fellows, Iron Shell, Bull Tail and other chiefs who visited our camp. We all sat down, Indians asking us to smoke stone pipes, a sign of friendship, peace and a desire to trade."

Lakota chiefs called white men "long knives," an Indian name for French trappers. They welcomed road travelers (wagons) with their white buffalo (oxen). Indian chiefs wanted to trade for blankets and firewater (liquor). One Indian spoke of the Great Spirit who provided their people with lodging, animals, the forest, mountains, and the waters. He complained, "Long knives take and use things given by great spirits to Indian people but do not pay for them. They trade with us but will not give us firewater." Bull Tail, the elder chief, did not agree with the younger chief, exclaiming that the white man's tobacco was a good exchange for use of his people's land; firewater was bad. Long discussions between travelers' men and Indians took place. Tobacco was given to the Indians. When finishing smoking their pipes, Indian chiefs returned to their village.

Lakota tradition has the Sioux nation emerging from the earth in the Black Hills, where they learned the way of the pipe from the White Buffalo Calf Woman. The White Buffalo Calf Woman teaches seven sacred Lakota ceremonies: sweat lodge, a purification ceremony; vision-seeking ceremony, a rite of passage from boyhood to manhood; sun dance, led by a shaman at the summer solstice for cultural unity; *hunka*, when an older man takes a younger man as a son; Buffalo Sing, a puberty ceremony for girls; spirit-keeping ceremony, specific prayers and songs to keep a deceased spirit in place for a year until the spirit is released to the heavens; and throwing a ball, a puberty ceremony for boys.

Lakota Sioux evolved from a hunter-gatherer existence along the rivers of the Great Plains to a warrior horsepower after acquiring horses from Shoshone tribes. Horse culture allowed nomadic buffalo hunters to control hundreds of square miles of the northern plains. They called themselves buffalo people. Trading fur pelts and buffalo hides was a major part of their livelihood by the 1840s. Private property did not exist in Indian culture; there were no territorial boundaries for Indians in contrast to Anglo-American values of land ownership. Sioux government was by consensus. Leadership was hereditary; daily activities were traditional. Wealth was created to be given away. It was measured in horses; everything owned was shared. A white buffalo calf pipe was the Sioux Indians' most sacred symbol, allowing chiefs to communicate prayers, needs, and gratitude to supernatural beings.

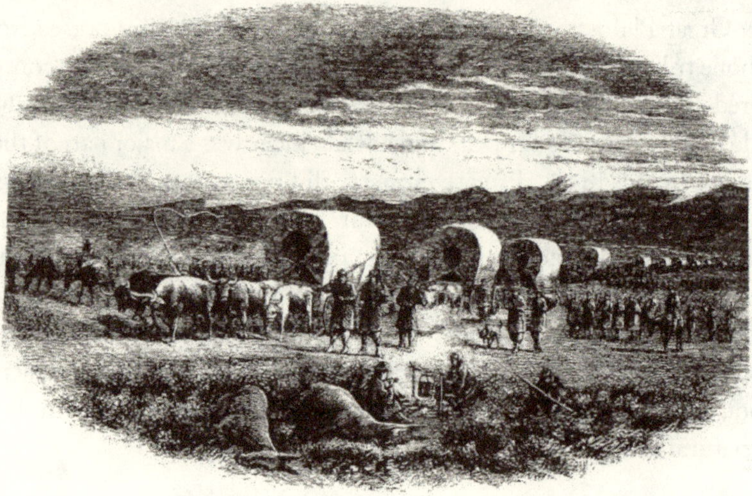

Chapter 8

Platte, Sweetwater, and the Snake

Clyman was anxious to resume the journey, seeing little reason for a long stop at Fort Laramie. Floods in Missouri and Kansas put the travelers a month behind schedule, causing emigrants to face high temperatures with little rain while following the Platte, a sign that summer was at its peak. Days would become shorter, nights cooler. More Indians would be encountered when men from tribes living in the mountains left their villages to ride east for seasonal hunts of buffalo, antelope, and other game necessary for survival in the upcoming winter. He was concerned emigrant wagon trains could be trapped in the Rocky Mountains by early winter storms.

One family traveling with Capt. William Shaw seemed to suffer one misfortune after another. Their problems were self-induced. Henry Sager was unsettled and unpredictable. He lacked the ability to focus on details for a productive life. His children had no discipline nor parental control. Originally from Virginia, Sager moved his young family three times. He started in Ohio and moved to Indiana and Missouri. Traveling with his pregnant wife, Naomi, a reluctant traveler, he joined Gilliam's Independent Colony on its journey to Oregon in the spring of 1844. Naomi bore a daughter not long after beginning her trip West. It was their seventh child. Sager suffered serious problems at the outset of his journey, not able to handle nor control oxen pulling his wagon. William Shaw taught Sager the basics, but the man was not able to master control of his oxen to keep his animals from stampeding. Crossing the South Platte River, Sager lost control of his team, causing his wagon to tip on its side, seriously injuring his wife, who had not recovered from childbirth; tearing off daughter Catherine's dress; and badly scraping Henry's face.

Sager's children were wild and accident prone. Most parents would have disciplined their children, preventing many near disasters. Two girls wandered off and became lost. Luckily, they stumbled into the path of the wagon train, allowing searchers to find the girls. Another time, an older girl walked away from camp at night, taking a stroll to see moonlight. She narrowly avoided being shot by a camp guard when she made her unannounced return. One boy threw gunpowder into a campfire, searing off his facial hair. Catherine's reckless playing on a wagon tongue while the wagon was underway, bumping along a rough path near the North Platte River, resulted in a fall when her dress caught on an ax handle. A wheel rolled over a leg, breaking it. Her father set the broken bone and secured her leg in a splint. Catherine's remaining journey was a painful experience.

Shortly after leaving Fort Laramie, Henry Sager became ill with camp fever (typhus). His condition worsened; he passed away and was buried alongside the Green River in western Wyoming. Naomi, his wife, already ill, became delirious after Henry's death. She passed away near the falls of the Snake River in Idaho. A Dutch doctor who had cared for Catherine drove the Sager wagon and children to Washington. Captain Shaw promised to care for the orphaned children. He delivered them to Dr. Marcus and Narcissa Whitman at their Walla Walla, Washington, mission. The Whitmans became legal guardians of the Sager children, bringing discipline and order to their unstructured lives.

The Oregon trail's route followed a parched, semiarid landscape—masses of rocks, stubby pine, and cedar trees bordering the North Platte River named Black Hills by early trappers. Alfred wrote he was "running through the Great American Desert. We had entered a vast American High Plain lacking timber and water. The land was unsuitable for agriculture." Ford's caravan stopped at nights next to small rivers or streams flowing into the Platte. Vigilance continued, wagons were circled, and guards rotated every two hours. Nocturnal Indian sounds were ever present—continuous rustling of bushes, two owls chatting with each other, clicking of buffalo bones imitating the teeth of wolves, all sounds identified by Clyman as Indian chatter. No one slept well.

Good distances were covered each day, though the pace began to slow because oxen and cattle were tiring, losing their level of energy due to heat, daily work levels, and climbing mountains. Most streams contained fresh water and grass. Elk, mountain sheep, small game, and *tatanka*, the Indian name for buffalo, were often seen grazing or watering at these oases. One stream, Boxwood Creek, contained thickets of currents and chokecherries. Clyman showed Alfred trail signs of grizzly bears in the thickets, but no grizzlies were seen.

Gilliam crossed the North Platte on August 12. Next came Ford, both headed toward a popular landmark, Red Butte. They camped north of the butte, locating the only spring, alarmingly discovering that its water was brackish. Mules could tolerate alkaline water, not oxen. Alkaline water was toxic to cattle, attested by skeletons of dead cattle discovered at water holes. Buffalo chips, sage, and thorn wood fueled evening fires. In the morning, a two-plus-hour climb of nearby hills provided Alfred with a distant view of the Rocky Mountains' spectacular Wind River Mountain Range.

Red Butte was a significant landmark for Indians. It was the western boundary of the Lakota Sioux's sphere of influence and the eastern boundary of Shoshone Indian power. Shoshones were the most skilled hunters and gatherers of the Plains Indians, respected for their preeminence as horsemen. Salmon fishing on the Snake River occupied their days in late summer. In autumn before snow closed mountain passes, Shoshones moved into Green and Sweetwater River valleys to hunt buffalo, elk, antelope, and other game. Spring and summer found Shoshones gathering berries, seeds, and roots to supplement their diet. Emigrants called Shoshones "Snake Indians" due to their primary location on the Snake River. They traded dried and smoked salmon with emigrants in exchange for fishhooks, gunpowder, ammunition, and horses.

The Sweetwater River led the travelers to the South Pass. Alfred counted nine river crossings before reaching the pass 130 miles west of Red Butte. Clyman stopped at a large rock above the Prairie known to travelers as Independence Rock. Clyman told Alfred that the rock reminded him of a beached whale. Fur trappers gathering on the rock to celebrate Independence Day on July 4, 1830, named the rock. It was a mandatory stop for travelers who wished to carve their name and date of travel for all posterity. Martin Van Buren, eighth president of the United States; Henry Clay, a congressman from Kentucky; and John Charles Fremont, explorer and Civil War general were a few of the more than five thousand names chiseled into the rock. James Clyman left his name on a previous visit. We don't know if Alfred Davenport posted his name.

More landmarks were passed, including Devil's Gate, where the Sweetwater passed through a 370 ft. high 1,500 ft. long and narrow canyon known as Split Rock. The chasm, high along a ridge of Rattlesnake Mountain, looked like a giant ax separated the mountain into two sections. Alfred followed Clyman slowly up the eastern slope of the Rocky Mountains to South Pass, the halfway point between Missouri and Oregon. The frontiersman explained they had reached the continental divide. Rivers on the east slope of the mountain flowed into the Atlantic Ocean; rivers on the west flowed into the Pacific Ocean. The path through the mountains was a gradual climb 19 miles wide at its peak. Alfred noted, "The road was good with no rocks or obstructions. The Wind River Mountains were 30 miles to our right and snowcapped Eutaw [Utah] Mountains were 90 miles on our left."

Days were becoming chilly, enhanced by cold winds sweeping down from mountains. Ice covered the surface of water buckets in the morning. Sagebrush, the only vegetation, spread like a gray-green blanket across an endless prairie. Morning found sage tinted with a white frost. Clyman's company remained in camp on August 23, with Joseph Barnett, a single traveler, being too ill to proceed. Shaw and Morrison companies arrived the next day, wishing Barnett the best. Black Harris, who had been traveling with Shaw, remained behind, entertaining travelers with tales of his visits to the area between 1825 and 1836. Perkins and Scott companies, the rear company of the wagon train, arrived at Clyman's camp on August 25. Several ladies helped comfort Mr. Barnett, who passed away from typhoid fever. Clyman had him buried next to the trail. After a brief ceremony, Clyman's group began their travel down the west slope of South Pass toward the Big Sandy and Green Rivers.

Death was an accepted risk endured by 1,475 emigrants traveling to Oregon in 1844. One out of every ten emigrants who departed from Missouri died before reaching Oregon City. Before 1845, no deaths were caused by Indians. Disease and accidents took their toll. Typhus was spread by ticks, fleas, and lice. Cholera came from fecal contaminated water, scurvy from diet deficiency, Rocky Mountain fever from ticks. These diseases and food poisoning were the most serious health problems faced by travelers. Most deaths from disease occurred in the territory east of Fort Laramie. Poor preparation for the journey and a lack of safety failures fueled accidents. Stampeding uncontrolled draft animals or charging buffalo were frequent source of serious injury and death. Emigrants lacked experience handling firearms. Accidental discharging of weapons resulted in death, or serious injury occurred in camp or on a hunt. Crossing flooded or swift rivers presented additional dangers to wagon drivers. When caught in swift currents, overturned or swamped wagons resulted in losses of belongings and supplies, drownings, and death.

Shortages of food and water plagued the emigrants in several locations along the trail. West of South Pass, there were no large herds of buffalo. On the Platte where buffalo were plentiful, hunters brought fresh meat to be divided among all travelers. Rules changed when buffalo became scarce. Any meat harvested by a hunter would be for his benefit, not necessarily shared with others.

Downhill trails on the west side of the South Pass contained loose, sandy soil generating tremendous amounts of dust by wagons. Those at the end of the line incurred a level of dust that was beyond tolerable. Behind the last wagon, extra mules, horses, and cattle were driven by single men. They were forced to endure great clouds of dust. Alfred took his turn herding animals but was not one to complain. Herding duty was expected; he was not a complainer.

Clyman, Alfred, and their company spent two hard long days covering 25 and 30 miles to Blacks Fork. They caught up with travelers who had passed them when they were stopped with Barnett. Alfred's journal described the trail after leaving Red Butte. "An immense plain of sand with nothing growing but wild sage, worm-wood and the accursed prickly pear. Sage and buffalo chips were our only fuel. Water was very scarce. We were without water for two days, which caused animals to become very weak, many cattle died." The trail was littered with the carcasses of oxen and abandoned wagons and furniture, grim reminders of difficulties and hardships crossing desert and mountains in 1844. Water was located at the Big Sandy River crossing, but lateness of the season meant snow runoff from the mountains had greatly diminished the size of Big Sandy. The trail from the Big Sandy crossing to the Green River was without water. New challenges caused travelers to disband large groups and travel in small parties. Small groups generated less dust and located better grazing opportunities for animals. Clyman, familiar with the trail, told Alfred they would travel during the coolness of night, avoiding the hot, burning sun during the day.

Adequate supplies of water and grass were found along the Green River. Crossing the Green was slow due to delays caused by long lines of wagons waiting to use a ferry. Established by mountain men in 1843, it was known as the Green River Mormon Ferry. Alfred and Clyman decided to omit a long wait, fording the Green at another location. Alfred's caravan followed the Blacks Fork, coming to Jim Bridger's trading post, where they met the caravan of E. E. Parrish, part of Gilliam's original colony. Bridger's fort, managed by Antoine Robidoux, offered mules, horses, and other items for sale to travelers. The Ford company's men traded items for moccasins and leather clothing, tired and thin mules and horses for fresh mounts. While the men were trading, women washed bedding in the clear waters of the Blacks Fork. The route to the fort was 46 miles longer than Sublette Cutoff, but it was the only opportunity to acquire supplies and fresh animals between Fort Laramie and Fort Hall.

Alfred described in letters sent home "forts encountered from Ft. Laramie to the Columbia River." They were made of mud bricks about 18 inches long by 10 or 12 inches wide and 4 to 6 inches thick, dried in the sun. The bricks stood the weather well as it seldom rained in the country between Fort Laramie and Fort Walla Walla. The forts provided good protection from Indian attacks because a 16-foot tower stood at each corner with loopholes [placements for guns]. Dwellings were inside fort walls, roofs covered with bricks. Most forts were trading posts owned by the Hudson's Bay Company, profitable commercial centers for their owners.

On September 1, travel resumed with an evening stop on the banks of Muddy Creek. Ford followed the creek to its source, arriving on September 3. The way had been rough, hilly, and extremely slow with steep ravines to traverse. Grass for animals was almost depleted. Adjoining hills were bare and rocky, supporting few patches of sagebrush scrub.

The next morning, Clyman and three other men decided to leave the wagon train, taking a string of packhorses; they headed to Fort Hall. Alfred remained with Ford's caravan, which had joined Gilliam's group. Nights were cold and clear; thick ice was found each morning on water buckets. Ford followed a valley to Soda Springs. Along the way, Shoshone Indians approached Alfred's wagon, seeking to trade. They offered dried antelope meat and smoked salmon, wanting blankets and gunpowder. Ford ended travels early afternoon upon reaching Soda Springs. He wanted time to enjoy the springs' carbonated mineral waters.

The next morning, travelers were again heading toward Fort Hall, where they arrived on September 13 in a greatly diminished train of fifteen wagons. The Snake River valley had plenty of grass and water and an opportunity for rest and make repairs after recent rigorous travel before beginning another tough, arduous journey to Fort Boise. Constant repairs for wagons created time-consuming delays. Hot, dry roads caused wooden wagon wheels to shrink. Wedges had to be inserted between a wooden wheel and its iron rim to keep the rim from falling off. A temporary fix was to place the wheel in a stream when not traveling at night so the wood in the wheel would swell, tightening it to the metal rim. Wagon parts were becoming scarce. Many travelers had depleted spare parts they brought from Missouri when they arrived at the Snake River. A broken axle and no spare parts meant a wagon could travel no further. Emigrants sought parts from abandoned and broken wagons found along the trail. When parts could not be found, borrowed, purchased, or made, an unfortunate traveler abandoned his wagon and rode with other travelers.

Alfred suddenly was seized with a great urgency to get over the Blue Mountains of Oregon before winter storms expected to begin in about a month. Concerned that wagon travel was too slow and he would be caught in the mountains unprepared for the oncoming winter, Davenport felt it was time to travel on his own. "When we came to the Snake River, I left the wagons with three young men to walk down here [Oregon City], as wagons were slow and short of provisions, all who could leave did the same."

Chapter 9

Oregon, 1844

Early in the morning of September 14, Alfred and three friends departed on foot from Fort Hall for Fort Boise, 260 miles closer to Oregon. They had been kept awake most of the night, attacked by pesky mosquitoes and gnats living in marshy lands surrounding the fort. The men passed Bannock-Shoshone Indian villages located on the shores of Bannock Creek. Indian squaws, half-naked children, and many dogs were present. Squaws carried bundles of cottonwood sticks on their backs, following trails from the creek to their settlements. Mules and horses fed on cottonwood bark, replacing corn and oats. Indian villages were home to many dogs, mixed breeds of all sizes and shapes. They were known to interbreed with prairie wolves (coyotes). Dogs pulled loaded travois during tribal migrations. Dogmeat was part of Sioux, Nez Perce, and other Indian diets. Explorers in the Lewis and Clark Expedition and fur traders claimed that dogmeat tasted like pork.

The four travelers continued south and west, following a well-worn trail along the top of basalt rocks 200 feet above the Snake River. Their first stop was at the American Falls, where the river plunged 50 ft., roaring as it dropped over cascades to a lower level. An emigrant campsite north of the falls was reached at dusk where the four ended their day. Night came quickly on their campsite. Soon after the sun dropped behind tall mountains west of the river valley, a chill in the air descended on their camp. Stars filled the vast space of the heavens with a brilliance the travelers had not seen since they left the Platte River.

Morning saw another hot, dry day. The last rain felt by the emigrants was over six weeks ago near Fort Laramie. The trail continued along a high plateau running parallel to the Snake. Sparce sagebrush grew alongside the barren path. Every step created a cloud of fine particles of dust and sand. Wind racing down from mountaintops met thermals rising from heated earth, creating whirlwinds of dust. Dust was everywhere, covering men's clothes, getting into their hair and eyes. Alfred needed water and could hear the Snake River racing over cataracts and through deep gorges but could not safely climb down steep cliffs lining the river's canyon walls to reach the river.

Noon found the four dusty, hot, tired travelers stopped at the edge of a small mostly dry creek, drinking stagnant water from shallow holes, the only available to meet their needs. They stopped for the night at a tributary of the Snake, the Raft River, a less challenging river to cross in the dry season. Near the river, the trail split. Travelers called it the Parting of the Ways. The Oregon Trail continued west; the California Trail headed south. The barren, dry plain continued to face Alfred and his friends as they followed the river for several days, reaching a point overlooking its winding through a wide valley. Leading to the river, the men faced a steep incline before crossing two islands located between the river's south and north shores.

Northern Shoshone Indians camping at the crossing wanted to trade, offering fresh salmon and cakes filled with berries in exchange for gunpowder, knives, or clothes. They were a friendly but sorry-looking lot, mostly naked, wearing a brief loincloth made of rabbit fur. They lived in flimsy three-sided grass-covered willow huts. Their diet seemed meager—fish; insects, mostly crickets and grasshoppers; berries; and roots. Game was gone in the area. Alfred traded fishhooks for fresh salmon.

Several wagons were preparing to ford the Snake. Alfred and his friends assisted emigrants lowering wagons down to the rivers to the water's edge with ropes tied to the rear of each wagon. Slowly, an empty wagon was lowered to the river. Women and children carried the contents of the wagons down the slope, loading wagons before making the crossing. Passage to the north shore was completed without incidence. Alfred noted that the water was very cold, swiftly running though less than a foot deep. Alfred crossed two islands. Later, floods created a third island, thus the name Three Island Crossing.

After the river, the trail turned left, rambling through a

rattlesnake-infested sagebrush desert, skirting the foothills of the Salmon River Mountains. It was the most challenging part of Alfred Davenport's trip West. "We walked about two hundred miles when we discovered our little stock of provisions bought from the wagons and acquired from Indians was about used up. It took us three more days to reach Ft Boise. Those days were the hardest I ever experienced in my life, as we nearly starved." In the end, the four travelers—weak, exhausted, craving food, throats dry and parched—arrived at the fort, where they feasted on dried salmon and fresh milk, which Alfred described as "the sweetest meal I ever ate."

A trading post was established by John Reid in 1813 at the mouth of the Boise River where it joined the Snake, part of John Jacob Astor's fur trading empire. In 1834, Thomas McKay built a small fort on the site for the Hudson's Bay Company. It was managed in 1844 by French Canadian Francois Payette, who staffed the fort with Owyhee (Hawaiian or Sandwich Island) employees. *La riviere Boise* or "wooded river" was located in a cottonwood, tree-lined valley in the high desert east of today's Oregon border, part of the Columbia Plateau, flowing into the Columbia River and the Pacific Ocean. The plateau was bounded by the Rocky Mountains and Snake River on the east and the Cascade Mountains on the west. Nez Perce (French for "pierced nose") Indians lived near the fort. The Lewis and Clark Expedition encountered the tribe in 1805, who fed the explorers buffalo, smoked salmon, and bread made from camas roots. Henry and Eliza Spalding established a mission in the area for the Nez Perce in 1836, converting several tribe members to Christianity. Emigrants appreciated the help and advice from Spalding's converts, learning Indians would not help on the Sabbath (Sunday).

Alfred spoke with Payette, seeking the best route and landmarks that would guide him over the Blue Mountains. Several different routes were currently followed by emigrants. He filled his knapsack with supplies from the fort, "to last to Dr. Whitman's Mission distant two hundred miles on the west side of the Blue Mountains." Two of his companions decided to wait for wagons, complaining they were too tired to continue walking. Alfred and Doty (N. R. Doughery or Dotey) resumed their westward journey, crossing the Snake River at a ford south of the fort. They followed the trail, passing over more barren, sagebrush-filled plain, to the Malheur River, where they camped for the night. Malheur, or river of misfortune, was named by French Canadian trappers because of an incident early in the nineteenth century. Trappers cached beaver pelts along the river. Upon return, they discovered their pelts had been stolen by Indians.

The Oregon Trail west of the Snake River crossing was rough and challenging. Diaries of James Clyman and E. E. Parrish described this section as the most difficult part of their western journey. Dry, dusty, and steep, it traversed mountains of granite and slate, barren and sparsely sprinkled with sagebrush. It crossed the Burnt River at a location containing blackened, scarred rocks and burnt timber along its shores. The route had been especially difficult for oxen, stressed by days of little grass and dusty trail conditions. It was not uncommon to find the remains of cattle who had collapsed while struggling to pull their burdens through such hostile, uninhabitable country.

Plateau Indians were friendly toward white men in the early 1800s, especially French Canadian fur traders. The 1840s brought Indian hostility due to the flood of emigrants consuming limited amounts of firewood, depleting grazing grasslands, and taking game, all without Indian permission. Lower Columbia River Indians included Cayuse (people of the rye grass), Umatilla, and Walla Walla. In autumn, these Indians migrated from mountains and plains to river valleys. Cayuse and Umatilla owned large herds of horses, often two hundred to three hundred horses per man, up to two thousand horses for a family. They were especially adept at stealing horses from rival tribes and emigrants. Large herds of horses were part of Indian commerce, enabling tribes to travel over large areas of the plateau for forage. The Burnt River Canyon was part of their extended territory.

Clyman wrote that certain groups of Plateau Indians detested strangers in their territory, demonstrating their hostility by starting grass fires to destroy forage for emigrant animals in an attempt to drive visitors from their lands. Alfred and Doty found the Burnt River valley smoke filled. Smoke was an irritant, but they charged ahead, suffering through several smoke-filled days. The men crossed the Powder River, whose name described the river's shores covered with sand and dirt with the consistency of powder. It flowed through a grass-filled valley bordered on the west by the Blue Mountains.

Fifteen miles ahead, they found themselves in a 20-mile-wide green oasis, the Grande Round Valley. Water from the mountains created a lush landscape full of vegetation with plenty of game—bear, deer, and elk. The valley was a bowl surrounded by Blue Mountains. Two-hundred-foot-tall lodgepole pines, firs, and other species of evergreen trees covered the mountain slopes. Several groups of Nez Perce Indians riding on Appaloosa (spotted) horses approached the two men, who were beginning their climb up the mountain trail. They asked to be hired as guides to take them across the mountains. The trail was well marked, so the two men declined their services. Alfred reported, "Part of the way near the top of the mountain was covered with snow. Cattle could not get any grass," and many starved or were "lost by eating a species of laurel that looked very fine and green" but was poisonous. The men rested at the mountain summit before proceeding down the mountain, following the headwaters of the Umatilla River to a split in the trail that would take them to Dr. Marcus and Narcissa Whitman's mission.

Marcus Whitman, a doctor and missionary, and his wife, Narcissa, established a Christian mission in 1836. It was located 25 miles east of the Hudson's Bay Company's Fort Walla Walla called Waiilatpu (the place of rye grass). A few Indian men assisted Whitman with the building of his house; most of the tribe's men were off hunting buffalo. Cayuse women, as was their custom, built lodges near the mission. The mission brought Christianity, farming, and Dr. Whitman's medical knowledge to the Indians. Indians suffered from a variety of illness, frequently suffering from an inflammation of the lungs. Tribal medicine was practiced by a medicine man or shaman, a spiritual leader who treated illnesses that were thought to be created by evil spirits. According to Indian custom, if a tribal chief died while under the care of a medicine man, the medicine man must give his life to avenge the chief's death. When Cayuse chief Umtippe became ill, Dr. Whitman cured him. Cultural differences, over time, caused the Cayuse and the Whitmans to drift apart. By the year 1844, Whitman's efforts had been redirected from helping Indians assist emigrants. In 1847, an epidemic of measles broke out among the Cayuse, decimating about half the tribe. Tribal leaders blamed the Whitmans. They murdered Marcus, Narcissa, and eleven others on November 29, 1847, blaming them for the death of over two hundred Cayuse Indians. Fifty-two women and children were taken hostage. The Hudson's Bay Company paid the Cayuse Indians ransom demands, freeing forty-nine living hostages on December 29. The company never received reimbursement for the ransom payments.

Alfred and Doty arrived at the Whitmans' early in October. The Whitman compound contained several buildings: a mission house, an emigrant house, flour mills, a blacksmith, a sawmill, and a corral for horses. Agricultural fields were surrounded by irrigation ditches and apple and peach orchards. The sight of gardens raising peas, potatoes, turnips, other vegetables, and grain crops reminded Alfred of his Circleville, Ohio, home. He consulted with Doty. They decided to stay and rest at the Whitman mission.

Each day saw the arrival of a steady stream of emigrants. Many were sick; often, they had depleted their provisions. Early snows in the Blue Mountains were causing extreme travel difficulties. Housing space at the mission became tight as were food supplies. Beef was replaced with horsemeat. The two men decided to cut short their stay at the mission, loaded their knapsacks, and began the 25-mile trip to Fort Walla Walla. The original fort was built by the North West Company as a trading post in 1818 named Fort Nez Perce. The Hudson's Bay Company acquired the fort in 1821. In 1841, it was destroyed by fire. A rebuilt structure constructed of adobe bricks came to be known as old Fort Walla Walla. The site of the fort was dramatic. Tall barren mountains faced it along northern and eastern Columbia River shores.

The fort was isolated on a sandy point of land jutting into the wide Columbia River. Constant swirling winds blew fine sand into the eyes and nose of travelers visiting the fort. Most departed after a brief visit. The trail west followed the south shore of the Columbia.

> We got along very well on the Columbia until we were beset upon by about twenty Indians. We had only one gun, so we could not give then a good fight. They surrounded us, and a scuffle commenced. Three or four got a hold of Dotey who was wearing his knapsack and was not able to do much. I attempted to get to him, threw off my Knapsack, preparing for a fight. They surrounded me drawing their bows. One tried to take my gun, but being stronger, I threw him head over heels. After a great deal of trouble, we succeeded in getting away from them. In the scuffle my knapsack disappeared, the Indians stole it, taking it across the Columbia. I lost my blanket, coat, shirts, extra shoes, food and other items. We thought we were through with hostile Indians after we finished crossing the Blue Mountains, but we were mistaken. The worst lived along the Columbia. Several Indian Villages

lay ahead, and no whites were in sight. We were compelled to endure the Indians. More appeared indicating they would give us another tussle. I turned and sighted my gun on one of them. Had he taken another step further, I would have shot him, but luckily he retreated.

Alfred learned later that most emigrant groups traveling along the Columbia River between Fort Walla Walla and the Dalles were robbed by young Indian braves. Walla Walla and Umatilla Indians were river people. They intermarried with other bands, hunting together and fighting common Southern enemies, the Shoshones and Bannocks. Missionaries considered them dirty Indians who largely rejected Christianity. Many women and men were scantily dressed, wearing only a flimsy leather or bark loincloth. Winter camps along river valleys explained why large numbers were encountered by Doty and Davenport as they journeyed westward toward Oregon City.

Three rivers needed to be crossed: Umatilla, John Day, and Deschutes. Umatilla, draining the Blue Mountains, is an Indian name translated as "laughing waters." John Day was named for a fur trapper. Day and fellow trapper Ramsay Crooks were robbed and stripped naked at the mouth of the river during the winter of 1811–1812. In their naked condition, they traveled 80 miles to a village of friendly Umatilla Indians who clothed and gave them food. Deschutes, or river of falls, drains most of the eastern Cascade Mountains. It is widely known for trout, not salmon.

Their journey took the two men through four Indian villages between the Umatilla and John Day Rivers. Across the river on the north shore of the Columbia, they observed three additional Indian villages inhabited by Yakama Indians. Wintering tribes were housed in semisubterranean lodges built of logs and sealed with sod to protect inhabitants from winter's cold and seasonal rains with accompanying strong winds blowing upstream from the Pacific Ocean. Dugout canoes, an integral part of the river people's existence, were seen near the Yakama's villages. The John Day River ford was easy and shallow despite recent heavy rains. The land through which they were passing was rocky and volcanic, void of trees.

Alfred and Doty assisted emigrant wagons fighting deep, swift, and dangerous waters when the trail crossed the Deschutes River. Indian problems failed to cease. The red men continued to pester and hassle travelers, so Alfred and Doty stayed with the wagons until they reached the Dalles. *Dalle* from the French word for "sluice or rapids" describes the narrowing of the Columbia as it races through a half-mile long channel 300 feet wide dropping 50 feet in 2 miles. Smaller Indian tribes lived near the Dalles, the Niculuita Indians living in cedar lodges. Strange customs were practiced by the Niculuita. Newborn babies' heads were bound in cloth, causing their foreheads to become flat. Adult members of the tribe painted their faces red and yellow.

The Methodist Church constructed a mission north of the Dalles, a stopping point for Alfred. Views from the mission provided a good look at snowcapped mountains. Mount Hood, 11,250 feet high, rose south of the river. Mount Saint Helens, 8,366 feet high, was seen north of the river. Downstream next to the Dalles, the wagon trail ended. Travelers needed rafts, canoes, or bateaux to travel downriver. Overland travel was not an option in 1844, for there were no wagon trails. Mountains facing the river were impenetrable. Rental of a bateau from the Hudson's Bay Company was beyond the financial reach of most emigrants. Purchasing a raft made by Indians was also expensive. Emigrants were forced to construct their own rafts. Indians, willing to work for tobacco, helped emigrants harvest pine trees. Logs were cut into 20-foot lengths, lashed together to make a raft. Wagon wheels were removed. Wagon boxes were secured to the raft's deck. Wheels and undercarriage were secured on top of the wagon box; contents were tied on top of the wheels.

Strong winds blowing upstream were a problem, slowing or halting progress downriver. Rowing or sailing was needed to continue. Few had skills needed to guide and propel rafts downriver. Thirty-five miles after leaving the Dalles was another challenge as rafts arrived at the final non-navigable stretch of the Columbia before Fort Vancouver. The river was full of rocks, waterfalls, and whirlpools as it broke through the cascade mountains range. This passage on the water was not possible. A 3-mile portage was required to get the next negotiable water, creating more challenges for emigrants. Alfred decided to purchase space on a bateau for his final 41-mile passage to Fort Vancouver.

The Hudson's Bay Company came to the Columbia River basin in 1821. They built Fort Vancouver on the north side of the Columbia River in 1825. It was located 115 miles east of the river's mouth, 6 miles east of the Columbia's confluence of the Willamette River. The company did not desire locations near coastal Indians. Thirty years of trade before 1821 destroyed much of the culture of coastal tribes, creating an environment where Indians were known for begging, theft, treachery, and murder.

Fort Vancouver was the headquarters of the Hudson's Bay Company's Columbia (River) Department. The company supervised thirty-four outposts, twenty-four ports, six ships, and six hundred employees according to reports published in 1843. They were self-sufficient, producing agricultural products on the company's two-thousand-acre farm, creating and storing a year's surplus from each annual production. The fort exported salmon, lumber, furs, hides, and agricultural products to the Sandwich Islands and Asian and European countries. The fort, a large fortress containing forty buildings, provided all services enjoyed by a small- to medium-sized town. Houses for workers were built outside the fort walls. Astor's American Fur Company, recognizing an excellent work ethic of native Hawaiians, Kanakas, employed eleven in Fort Astor by 1811. Their presence and influence grew to four hundred Hawaiians, employed by the Hudson's Bay Company in 1844.

The company's chief business manager was called a factor, in today's parlance a general manager. Dr. John McLaughlin held the post from 1822 until 1845. He was respected for instituting conservation practices. He insisted on trapping in a manner that would not deplete animal populations, allowing for the creation of steady supply of furs. He ran the company like a military camp, acting wisely and sternly in dealing with Columbia River Indians. McLaughlin's efforts created stability in the areas where the Hudson's Bay Company had a monopoly.

Fort Vancouver was the last stop for emigrants on the Oregon Trail who had arrived overland from Missouri. Massive groups of emigrants arriving at the fort, after 1843, were destitute after the long and dangerous journey from Missouri. Most had expended their resources. McLaughlin met these problems, extending credit, overriding the objection of his superiors. Loans of food and merchandise were given to emigrants with no interest costs. They promised to repay the fort when they could after they became established in Oregon. Sadly, over $60,000 in loans were never repaid. McLaughlin is known today as the father of Oregon.

Alfred sought employment at the Hudson's Bay Company. He needed to pay for his passage from the Dalles and needed employment for the six or so months he planned to stay in Oregon. The company needed skilled carpenters. Rapidly growing Oregon City had only five carpenters in November 1844. Years 1843 and 1844 saw a surge of newcomers entering the Willamette Valley. The Organic Laws of Oregon permitted married couples to acquire 640 acres of valley land at no costs. Unmarried settlers could acquire 320 acres. The Hudson's Bay Company served as a de facto government until the number of American settlers exceeded the British population. Year 1843 saw the establishment of a temporary legislature and executive committee created by Americans to serve as the government until territorial issues could be decided by Washington.

Alfred wrote home in April of 1845, giving his impressions of his first four months in Oregon City.

> This a fine country for farmers, as grass keeps green during the whole winter allowing cattle to become very fat. The winter weather is warm and mild, but it rains every day. Wheat is the main crop yielding 20 to 30 bushels per acre. Corn does not grow well. Potatoes and all kinds of vegetables thrive. There is an abundance of timber, red and white fir, yellow pine, and cedar. Fir trees grow straight and tall reaching 300 to 400 feet above ground. The landscape contains numerous hills or small mountains with an ample supply of water from creeks and rivers running through broad stretches of prairie creating land suitable for farming. Brigs and schooners can easily navigate the twenty-five miles trip on the Willamette from Oregon City to the Columbia River. A 22 ft. falls on the Willamette blocks the river at this place. Indians are often seen spearing salmon at the falls.

He spoke about the local economy. "Carpenters earn $60.00 per month, laboring hands $1.50 per day. Rail splitters earn $1.00 for each 100 rails they produce. Wheat costs $1.00 per bushel, potatoes 75 cents a bushel. Beef costs $6 to $7 for 100 pounds, pork is more expensive $10 to $12 per 100 pounds. There is plenty of work for everyone, but no cash" and no banks. Wheat and other agricultural products were legal tender. The Hudson's Bay Company and other merchants kept tallies for customers requiring balances to be settled regularly. Farmers settled balances using crops; laborers used hours working for their earnings. Promissory notes and bills of exchange were used for cash and discounted based on the risk to the holder.

Alfred ended his letter, stating, "I shall leave here in July or August for the Sandwich islands about an 18-day sail from the mouth of the Columbia and thence to California. I hope to make it home in 1847. I am sending this with a party returning to the states by the land route."

Chapter 10

Sandwich Islands and the Hudson's Bay Company

Polynesians came to Hawaii before recorded history. They arrived in sailing canoes, settling in the islands. British captain Cook, the first *haole* (foreigner), arrived at the island of Kauai, anchoring off Waimea in 1778. He named the islands Sandwich Islands for Lord Sandwich, first lord of the British Admiralty. Development of America's northwest fur trade brought ships to the islands after 1786. European countries discovered that the islands were an important port of call between Asia and America, where they could acquire fresh water, meat, vegetables, salt, and firewood. Islanders acquired iron, grapevines, almond trees, vegetables, garden seeds, and firearms. Iron was in such a short supply; natives would trade a whole pig for a few moderate-sized nails.

King Kamehameha I began a dynasty in 1795 that reigned over Hawaii until 1874. He united the islands in 1810. Trade with *haole* was by barter before 1820. By 1822, over 140 whaling ships were stopping at Hawaii each year. New Englanders from Ladd and Company formed a business partnership with the kingdom of Hawaii in 1833, leasing land to produce sugar and coffee. Sugar mills were built on Kauai, Oahu, and Maui. Ladd and Company grew faster than the capital available to finance its growth, causing it to fail in 1844. By 1840, the native politico-economic system could not handle problems facing the system due to the impact of foreign interests. King Kamehameha III attempted to keep land the property of Hawaiians. His new constitution provided one-third of the land for to the king, one-third to the chiefs, and one-third to the people. Land ownership was new to the people, resulting in less than 1 percent of the land claimed by native people. American ships, missionaries, and businessmen dominated foreign interests in Hawaii in the 1840s, often forming partnerships with the kingdom.

The Hudson's Bay Company was the largest of three British commercial houses operating in Honolulu in 1845. Midsummer found Alfred Davenport leaving Oregon on a Hudson's Bay Company ship carrying merchandise from Fort Vancouver to the company's agency in Honolulu, Hawaii, a 2,600-mile trip to the islands located in the northern Pacific Ocean. He spent the previous six months using his carpentry skills, working for the company, and found employment as a ship's carpenter on a trip to Honolulu. Carpenters were needed on oceangoing ships. Their status was higher than a seaman but lower than a ship's officer. Carpenters were often not expected to man a watch, so they could spend daytime plying their trade. Dining was in the crew's galley, sleeping in crew quarters. When a ship's captain called for "all hands," carpenters dropped what they were doing and performed preassigned duties with the rest of the crew. These included deck duty and watches, especially during bad weather, and a climb of the ship's rigging to retrieve or set sails.

The Hudson's Bay Company owned three brigs to transport freight to Honolulu. Their brigs were speedy, highly maneuverable sailing ships, each with two square-rigged masts. They were rated about 320 tones. They brought smoked salmon, wheat, flour, lumber, and furs to the islands, returning with sugar, coffee, indigo, cotton, yams, cabinet lumber, and items brought from China. Chinese mandarins, the ruling class, had a great appetite for furs from America, especially sea otter, which was used for trimming robes and vests. Sea otter fur was extremely soft, containing over one million hairs for each square inch of fur. Alfred continued worked at the company agency in Honolulu until spring of 1846, when he signed aboard a company ship heading to the company's San Francisco, California, location.

Trading in a typical Hudson's Bay Company post

Part II

California, 1846–1847

Chapter 11

Arrival in California

Companionway steps seemed to shift under the feet of sleepy Alfred. He pulled himself up to the aft deck of the ship to find the sky pitch black. This morning would be his final graveyard watch. He approached the helmsman, who nodded for him to take the wheel so he could enjoy a quick smoke. A moderate breeze over the stern billowed the sails, pushing the brig toward California, causing the wheel to have a firm but steady touch. The helm gave Alfred a feeling of strength and power as he guided the ship through an endless ocean. The helmsman spoke after resuming his duties. "California's coastal mountain range will be seen before the current watch ends at eight in the morning." Davenport signed on as the ship's carpenter. Few repairs were needed on this journey, allowing Alfred free time to enjoy himself and learn about sailing a brig. Spring winds were fresh and favorable, making the voyage from Hawaii comfortable.

A weak, dim light appeared in the east. Colors of pink and orange suddenly filled the sky before a fiery sun climbed above the distant ocean's edge. Daylight brought a new sight, mountains on the horizon. A brief conversation with the helmsman confirmed that the ship would be in Yerba Buena before noon. Yerba Buena, the name of an herb found on the site by Spanish Catholic missionaries, was changed to San Francisco during the war with Mexico.

Running before the wind, the ship approached a three-mile-long, one-mile-wide strait cutting through California's coastal mountains. It was called Puerto de San Francisco (mouth of the San Francisco Bay). Strong winds pushed the ship through outgoing tide and whirlpools. She stopped, dropping anchor several yards offshore, facing the embarcadero (pier). Alfred joined several men manning one of the ship's longboats, rowing officers and crew to shore. He immediately began to explore the area. A series of paths led to the top of hills, where he passed a few whitewashed buildings constructed with adobe bricks. The bricks were similar to those he saw in forts on his journey to Oregon. Adobe bricks were new to him, for they were not used in construction in the East. Bricks found in the East were kiln-fired clay. Adobe bricks were made of clay, sand, and animal dung placed in the sun to dry.

A climb to the top of the tallest hill rendered a soul-stirring view overlooking the strait dividing the coastal mountains. The western horizon was dominated by a vast and endless Pacific Ocean. Coastal mountains to the north and south were covered with carpets of green trees and lush vegetation. San Francisco Bay filled the eastern horizon. Warm, moist air mixing with gentle breezes added to the comfort of the day. On all sides of his path, fields of waving grass were sprinkled with wildflowers. Few houses were to be seen. Standing as lone sentinels on the windswept peninsula was a Spanish mission and a fort. Alfred walked to the ruins of the Presidio, an abandoned military fort, noting its strategic location at the mouth of San Francisco Bay. A path south along the crest of a hill wandered down to Mission Dolores. A sign at the mission pointing to a dirt path leading downhill had the word *mercado* (market). The embarcadero was an easy walk from the market, where he caught a boat returning to his ship.

Trading houses were the primary businesses of San Francisco run by English and American merchants. Major imports were sugar, coffee, tea, molasses, and other items that many brought for Hawaii. Exports were furs, hides, and tallow, the latter from Mexican ranchers known as Californios. A Californio was a Spanish-speaking native born in California before 1848. Their ancestors were from Spain, most likely from the province of Catalonia. Catalonian and other Spanish priests settled California in 1769, establishing twenty-one missions in a line from San Diego in the south to Sonoma in the north. Mexico gained independence from Spain on August 24, 1821. The Mexican government secularized California's missions in 1834, expelling priests. Between 1784 and 1846, the Spanish and Mexican government issued over five hundred land grants for large tracts of land or rancheros (ranches). Prominent Californios purchased land and were awarded land grants by the government. The average ranchero contained over 89,000 acres of land. One recipient was Gen. Mariano G. Vallejo of Sonoma, who acquired over 175,000 acres of land.

Cattle raising was the primary ranchero business. Native Americans worked on ranches herding cattle and performing limited agricultural activities. They were technically free but, in practice, bound to the ranchero at the wishes of its owner. Compensation to natives was food, meager clothing, and primitive shelter but no pay. American emigrants felt California natives were worse off than slaves in the United States. Californios valued leisure time, enjoying horse racing; bull and bear fights; music; performing the fandango, a Spanish dance; fiestas; and rodeos. Men wore heavily decorated sombreros and brightly colored wool shawls called serapes. Women, especially the young, were attractive, good natured, and smart. They were known for coquettish glances and flirtation. Californios were friendly people following established customs of extending hospitality to all travelers. They lived in the grand style of Spanish noblemen called hidalgos and thought all who were not landowners should support their class. Californios paid no taxes, only a meager tithe to the church to support its efforts. Government revenue came from duties collected at customhouses.

The viceroy of Spain established Las California Province in 1804. In 1845, Gov. Pio Pico moved the capital from Monterey in Alta (Upper) California to Los Angeles (the city of angels). Monterey continued to have a customhouse and a presidio where Gen. Jose Castro headed the military. The office of United States consul Thomas O. Larkin was in Monterey. Two important Alta California towns were San Francisco, a trading center, and Sonoma. Gen. Mariano Vallejo was appointed military commander of the north in 1835 and moved the Presidio from San Francisco to Sonoma, where he maintained his residence.

Nueva Helvetia (New Switzerland) had become an important northern location by the time Alfred arrived. In 1839, John A. Sutter—a Swiss emigrant—applied to Gov. Juan Bautista Alvarado for permission to settle in California. He was told he must live on the land for one year and become a naturalized Mexican citizen. Sutter completed his emigration requirements and moved into his fortified settlement in June of 1841. A naturalized Mexican citizen, he was awarded a grant of 48,827 acres of land by Governor Alvarado. The governor hoped Sutter's settlement would be a frontier outpost for keeping track of Americans, British, and Indians. New Helvetia, known as Sutter's Fort or Sutter's, was located on the Sacramento River at the confluence of the American River. Two important trails ended at Sutter's. One led north to Oregon. The second led east to Missouri.

Davenport was comforted when he saw Hudson's Bay Company's large warehouse on the waterfront but concerned when he learned it had been closed two months before his arrival. The building was sold later in the year to American merchants. Alfred was confident his employment record at Hudson's Bay Company would assist him in finding work.

A major ongoing construction project was a new customhouse. It would open late in 1846, built with materials taken from the closed presidio. Supplies of lumber seemed not to be plentiful. Shops and businesses found in Fort Vancouver were absent. All food, agricultural product, and supplies were brought into the village from nearby rancheros. One gristmill, the first in California completed in 1840, served the community. Alfred began searching for work and a place to rent a room and get meals, for there were no hotels in the area. He was told to check at Ridley's, who could tell him who was taking in boarders.

Bob Ridley owned a liquor bar and billiards saloon. It was headquarters for all strangers in town—Americans, British, Californians, and Indians—and soon became well known to Davenport. On the wall of the barroom was a local map from Vioget's survey of 1845, listing the name and locations of all locals and land grants. Ridley and his barkeeper, John Henry Brown, were the purveyors of all news—good, bad, true, and not so true. There were no newspapers in May 1846. Ridley helped Alfred find a room and where to seek work. Brown was the daily source of all news, giving newcomers updates of current political developments and the developing strife between the United States and Mexico.

Col. John Charles Fremont was instructed by President Polk in late spring of 1845 to conduct a topographical survey of the Sierra Mountains of California and locate routes to the Pacific Ocean. Fremont's father-in law, Senator Benton from Missouri, promoted the trip to the president. Both Benton and Polk maintained a keen interest in expanding the Western United States border to the Pacific Ocean; they wanted San Francisco Bay for America. Fremont was quietly told to keep Washington aware of foreign, especially British, activities and intentions in California.

Fremont's 1845 expedition was his third western topographical survey for the army. Fremont, upon reaching the eastern slopes of the Sierra Mountains, split his army into two groups. Theodore Talbot and Ned Kern, a cartographer, took the main force with Joseph Walker, an experienced guide, heading south. Walker would lead them across California's southern point mountains. The expedition planned to regroup at a small lake known as Tulare Lake.

Fremont, with his fifteen best men, headed into the Sierra Mountains. Several in Fremont's party were well-known mountain men, scouts, and friends of John Charles including Kit Carson; Alex Godey, a Creole Frenchman from Saint Louis admired by the ladies for his good looks and respected as a brilliant tracker and fighter; and James Sagundai, a Delaware Indian chief who was Fremont's personal bodyguard. Fremont followed the Salmon Trout River (Truckee) into the mountains. The men were fortunate to clear Sierra's mountain passes before the winter's heavy snows closed the routes. Fremont continued taking astronomical observations and noted flora changes from pine trees to oak trees as they descended from the mountains into the Sacramento Valley, arriving at Sutter's Fort on December 10. John Bidwell was commander of the fort; Sutter was absent. A year earlier, when Fremont was on his second western mapping expedition, Sutter gave him a warm welcome and provided all the supplies Fremont requested. Bidwell was different. He appeared aloof and standoffish, reluctant to fill Fremont's requests, saying the fort was short of supplies. Fremont felt Bidwell's attitude was because his loyalties were with Mexico.

Fremont's party acquired horses and cattle, heading south on December 14, planning to connect with the rest of the expedition. Rancheros encountered on the trip treated Americans with a lack of warmth and friendliness they had shown Fremont when he visited in 1844. An air of mistrust and aloofness was felt by Fremont's men, surveying and measuring travel routes. The explorers reached the San Joaquin Valley, where they followed the San Joaquin River toward its source. Numerous sign of Indians traveling with large herds of horses were evident at the Mariposa River. Indians in this area of California were described as horse thieves. Spanish missionaries taught them to farm and the ways of the white men, including equestrian skills. Year 1834's secularization of California missions left Christian Indians without mentors. Tribes retreated to isolated areas of the Sierra Mountains, returning to wild and uncivilized ways; their principal diet consisted of horsemeat from animals stolen from California rancheros.

After a couple of brief skirmishes with Indians, Fremont's sixteen men headed into to the mountains, where deep snow caused travel to be slow and difficult. Indians ceased to be a problem. Fremont's exploration party found Tulare Lake but did not locate Talbot and Kern's larger group. On New Year's Eve 1845, they decided to return to Sutter's to see if anyone had knowledge of the rest of the expedition. They later learned Talbot had been camped on a lake 80–90 miles south of their intended meeting point. Sutter, in residence, was friendly, providing Fremont with passports and lending his schooner *Sacramento* to transport the group to San Francisco, where the explorer visited U.S. vice-consul William Alexander Leidesdorff and made plans for a trip to Monterey.

Talbot and Walker found supplies running low. The men struggled to reach Sutter's on foot, for their horses and pack animals were worn out, unable to carry the weight of a rider. Game had been difficult to find; weaker animals were sacrificed to feed near-starving men. Walker found an old friend at Sutter's, mountain man William O. "Le Gros" Fallon, who informed Talbot that Fremont was headed toward Monterey. He was camped near Pueblo de San Jose, south of San Francisco. Walker, Talbot, Fallon, Kit Carson, Dick Owen, and the rest of the company set out for the coast mountains, locating Fremont at a vacant ranch named Laguna owned by William Fisher, a retired Boston sea captain.

Fremont continued to Monterey, where the United States consul introduced him to former Mexican governor Juan Bautista Alvarado and General Castro. The latter permitted Fremont to spend the winter if he stayed in the San Joaquin Valley. Fremont stayed in camp until February 25, when he left the valley to continue his mapping. He traveled west to Santa Cruz and south to the western point of Monterey Bay. March 1, 1846 found the expedition camped at Hartnell's ranch, 25 miles from Monterey.

Relations between the United States and Mexico began to disintegrate. On December 29, 1845, President Polk admitted Texas to the United States. The Mexican government rejected the acquisition. Officials in Mexico City ordered the halt of Anglo-American immigration from Oregon and Missouri into California. A state of war broke out between the United States and Mexico, officially ratified by Congress on May 13, 1846.

Year 1846 began with over two thousand American emigrants living in northern California. Alfred discovered they were a cross section of all types with varying interests, skills, and backgrounds. Many were families wanting a new start as farmers where large tracts of land could be acquired at little or no cost. Some emigrants heading to Oregon heard of free California land and diverted from the Oregon Trail to California.

Mountain men and explorers, like James Clyman, wanted to settle, wishing to leave the rigors of mountain life, overland travel, and an increasing hostility of Plains Indians toward travelers. Trappers were discovering that supplies of game were harder to locate, recognizing an end was coming to their trapping livelihood.

American emigrants who made the difficult long overland journey to California presented a rough appearance to Californios. Most had spent their life savings to travel West. They arrived without wealth, bringing few belongings. Clothes were plain, having been crafted from homespun cloth. Trappers, hunters, and mountain men harvested wild animals and dried their skins, which they stitched into clothes. Men living on the western frontier paid little attention to personal grooming. Their hair was long, unkept, and uncut. Beards were not trimmed, often stained by tobacco juice. Sharply dressed Californios maintained a feeling of superiority over humble American frontiersmen and farmers. Emigrant women were bright and engaging but lacked the elegance, voluptuous traits, and beautiful clothes of California ranchero women.

Alfred quickly picked up on the contrasts and friction between the two groups. Alfred and his friends were brought up following American ethics of hard work. They did not understand or respect the easygoing lifestyle of Californios, who appeared to avoid hard work, lacked motivation, and would not take risks. Emigrants and other newcomers thought they were lazy.

Gen. Jose Castro began demanding that emigrants provide passports to Mexican government officials. Alfred and most emigrants did not need passports when they departed from Missouri or Oregon. They entered California without knowing about a passport requirement.

On June 7, ten days after Alfred's arrival in San Francisco, news came to the Americans that would forever change Alfred Davenport's life.

Chapter 12

The Surprise

Mexican lieutenant Jose Chavez found Fremont at Hartnell's ranch. He produced a letter from General Castro demanding that Fremont immediately leave California. Chavez was obnoxious and arrogant. Fremont was insulted. He told Chavez he was rude, his letter an insult. He would leave California at a time of his own choosing. Chavez, his temper flaring, replied that Castro would punish this group of renegade Americans.

A couple of incidents affected the Fremont expedition. Mexicans were known to scam Americans. An unsuspecting emigrant would purchase a horse. A few days later, a man claiming to be the original owner, not the seller, would show up demanding his horse, claiming it had been stolen. One ranchero, Don Sebastian Peralta, tried this game with a member of the mapping expedition. Peralta's claim was answered in an unexpected manner. He found himself staring down the barrel of a pistol. Angry and humiliated, Peralta hastily departed from Fremont's camp without his claimed horse.

Separately, an uncle of Castro entertained a few men from the Fremont party. Liquor was plentiful; the party lasted many hours. One of Fremont's men aggressively described the host's voluptuous and flirtatious daughter. Comments of this nature were considered rude in Mexican society. The party broke up; the host felt insulted by his American visitors.

Early in 1846, distrust and dislike between Americans and Mexicans started to smolder like a small brush fire. General Castro took a hard line toward Americans. Castro realized Fremont's topographical engineers were skilled hunters and marksmen. He assumed they were dragoons (mounted soldiers skilled in the use of rifle on horseback or on foot) from the U.S. Army illegally mapping his country.

Fremont left Hartnell's, moving to Hawk's Peak in the Galvin mountains. The location had abundant water, grass for horses, and a mountaintop view overlooking the surrounding country. One surveyor cut down a small tree. He attached an American flag, hoisting it to the top of the hill at the camp. Fremont's camp overlooked Pueblo San Juan, headquarters of Castro's army and the San Juan Bautista Mission.

On March 8, General Castro circulated an impassioned plea to local landowners requesting they assemble at his headquarters to "confront the U.S. Army's band of robbers commanded by Colonel J. C. Fremont." His pleading called for help to "lance this ulcer that would destroy Mexican liberty and independence." Fremont was able to monitor Castro's recruiting efforts at the pueblo and mission. Using a spyglass, he counted the number of men arriving at Castro's fort. The colonel reacted by fortifying Hawk's Peak, constructing multiple battle locations, employing cross fire for ambush to decimate any attacking foe.

Fremont's small contingent of sixty were prepared to take on Castro's force of three hundred. Castro thought a superior number of troops provided a strategic advantage. He ordered his men to mount horses and charge Hawk's Peak. His troops were armed with lances and a few old muskets. They began a charge up the mountain. Halfway up the mountain, Castro's citizen soldiers soon realized they were riding into an ambush. Their lances would be facing Americans armed with Hawken rifles, prized for accuracy at long distances. Rancheros and farmers soon realized they were significantly outgunned. They were not willing to risk losing a comfortable life and beautiful senoras to evict a few Americans from Hawk's Peak. They turned around, retreated, and fled toward Monterey, scattering in the mountains and hills away from General Castro.

Three quiet days later, Fremont—not wanting to create an incident—departed for the San Joaquin Valley. He took his time traveling about six miles each day, continuing to map the valley, the river, and its tributaries. His planned route would exit California by way of Sutter's Fort, the Sacramento Valley, and Oregon. Castro, acting like a proud rooster, strutted around Alta California, boasting he had driven the U.S. Army from Mexican territory.

News reaching Alfred was not good. General Castro was headed to San Francisco to enforce his April 30 proclamation demanding that all foreigners must leave California. Captured American men would be transported to jail in Mexico City. Alfred learned the news at Ridley's. He needed to quickly find protection and safety.

Three friends gathered with Alfred to explore options. They agreed to meet at night on the waterfront two hours after sunset. The embarcadero was empty when four men assembled at half past ten. Several small boats used by sailors to reach ships moored offshore were tied to the pier. One was selected by the men to take them the northern coast. Each man carried a knapsack with clothing and a small amount of hardtack. Alfred had a rifle, a pistol, and a large hunting knife. His companions carried similar arms. Six hours of darkness remained before a missing boat would be discovered. Quietly, they pushed back from the pier, manned oars, and began rowing across the turbulent waters of the strait (today's Golden Gate), heading toward distant coastal mountains.

Alfred had memorized a map of local waters. He recognized Alcatraz Island, kept close to the west shore of Angel Island. He needed to avoid the harbor at Sausalito and wanted to get beyond Mission San Rafael before leaving the boat. The night was clear. A small sliver of moon appearing late in the journey was often obscured by clouds. Winds blew inland from the west. A slight chop blew spray into the travelers' faces until they cleared the strait. The men made good progress. Their efforts prevailed despite challenges of rowing through moving tides and surface winds. Past San Pedro Point, entering San Pablo Bay, they slowed. Tiredness and fatigue began to take hold, and light was coming to the eastern sky; the men had been on the water for almost seven hours.

Alfred consulted with his partners; they decided it was time to travel on land. He guided the boat into a marshy shore filled with thick patches of reeds. Dark clouds of mosquitoes swarmed to greet the boat. The pests attacked every part of one's body not covered with clothes, flying into eyes and ears, slowing progress. The four men pushed the boat through reeds, some as tall as fifteen feet, thick enough to turn back a horse. Alfred knew reeds would hide the stolen boat. The men abandoned the boat when there was not enough water under the hull for it to continue to float. Land adjacent to the marsh contained animal trails leading inland. The selected trail merged into a well-traveled Indian path. They were hungry, meager supplies of food brought on the voyage had been consumed, no game was seen, and they continued heading north.

A few hours after sunrise, Alfred came on a Digger Indian village. Mexicans thought Diggers were cowardly, lacking intelligence. Their diet consisted of dug roots, gathered acorns, grasshoppers, and an occasional fish. Housing was in huts built partially underground. Wood bins near their huts stored acorns, the staple of their diets. No men were to be seen, only women naked except for a thin loincloth drooping from the waist. A totally naked young Indian was seen fast asleep on top of one of the acorn bins. Alfred made signs to the women, telling them his men were friendly and hungry. An older squaw produced two baskets. One basket contained a loaf made of pulverized acorns and berries. The other was filled with water. Both baskets, made of tightly woven grass, were beautifully crafted. Alfred was amazed that the basket containing water did not leak. The acorn loaf was very tasty and filling.

Sign language and a limited amount of Spanish told the men the route they were heading would take them to Sonoma, home of General Vallejo's presidio. Another route less traveled led north away from the Mexican fort. The men decided to follow the path north through cross-coastal mountains with plans to proceed east toward Knights Landing on the Sacramento River, where they hoped to find American settlements.

MAP
SHOWING THE
SALT WATER
TIDE LANDS.
Scale:
10 Miles to 1 inch.
NAPA
SONOMA
SOLANO
MARIN
CONTRA COSTA
ALAMEDA
SAN MATEO
PACIFIC OCEAN
BAY OF SAN PABLO
SAN FRANCISCO BAY
SUISUN BAY
SAN FRANCISCO
GOLDEN GATE
HALF MOON BAY
R.7 W.
R.6 W.
R.5 W.
R.3 W.
R.2 W.
R.1 W.
T.6 N
T.4 N
T.2 N.
T.1 S.
T.2 S.
T.3 S.
MT. DIABLO MERIDIAN
SONOMA
NAPA
PETATUMA
LAKEVILLE
SUISUN CITY
CORDELIA
BLACK POINT
MARTINEZ
Pacheco
Clayton
San Pablo
La Fayette
Alamo
Danville
SAN RAFAEL
PT. BONITA
PT. LOBOS
OAKLAND
BROOKLYN
ALAMEDA
SAN LEANDRO
SAN LORENZO
MT. EDEN
ALVARADO
SAN PEDRO
MILLBREA
SAN MATEO
HALF MOON BAY
BELMONT
REDWOOD CITY
MOUNTAIN VIEW

Chapter 13

Osos

Fremont completed mapping lower and upper Sacramento River valleys and the eastern routes around Mount Shasta along the way, leading to Oregon. May 8 found them at Oregon's Upper Klamath Lake. Scouts learned that U.S. Marine lieutenant Archibald Gillespie, a courier from Washington, was headed to camp with dispatches for Fremont. Fremont, Kit Carson, four Delaware Indians, and several other men left the main camp to meet Gillespie, finding him in late afternoon.

Gillespie's pouch contained letters from Fremont's wife, Jessie, and her father, Senator Benton. Gillespie provided verbal instructions from Secretary of State Buchanan, for Washington would not risk written documents falling into wrong hands if Gillespie was stopped by Mexicans or unfriendly Indians. Instructions were new orders for Fremont. His mapping tour and expedition would end. He was to remain in California, keeping Washington appraised of British activities and any "foreign schemes" in California. He was expected to use his power as the only U.S. Army officer in California to stop any schemes. War with Mexico was inevitable. Polk wanted California. Benton's letter reinforced that the Pacific Ocean would become our country's western border.

Late in the afternoon, the small group established a camp near Klamath Lake with plans to return to the main body of men the following day. The men went to sleep. Carson was awakened by a thump. A callout was answered by a companion's groan. Carson shouted, "Indians!" The thump was an ax wielded by an Indian splitting the head of a Fremont companion, Basil Lajeunesse. Fremont's men swiftly reacted, pouring gunfire into dimly lit attacking shapes, killing the leader of the war party, an Indian chief. The leaderless attackers retreated, melting into the darkness surrounding the American's camp. Three of Fremont's men were murdered including one of his Delaware Indian scouts. The next day, joining the rest of the expedition, the combined force set out to locate and punish the murderers. Sighting the Indian's village, Fremont's men acted quickly. Huts were burned, food supplies destroyed. Fourteen Indians who stayed to resist the Americans were eliminated.

The expedition began their return to California. Fremont's Delaware Indians remained behind, wanting to revenge their companion's death. When they caught up with Fremont, two bloody scalps were tied to their saddles. The next day, his caravan came to a clearing in a deep forest where a lone Indian prepared an ambush. Carson in the lead saw the Indian and pointed his gun. It misfired. Fremont took a shot, missing his mark. He surged his horse forward, jumping on the attacker, causing the Indian's arrow to fly wide off its target, missing Carson. A few steps behind Fremont, his faithful bodyguard, Sagundai, raced into the fray, burying his war club in the Indian's head. Sagundai took the warrior's scalp, posting it in a tree as a warning not to attack Americans. Fremont examined the attacker's arrow. The arrow point was metal covered with poison. The metal was forged in England, acquired from trading posts located on the Columbia River Plateau and Oregon.

Sixty miles north of New Helvetia, Fremont chose Three Buttes, now Sutter Buttes, for his next camp. He arrived on May 31. The buttes, a 6-mile-long isolated mountain range rising 2,100 ft. above the Sacramento River valley, contained ample sources of grass and water. The location was a natural fortress for protecting nearby American settlements. Crops raised in the 400-mile-long Sacramento Valley were wheat and wild oats, currently ready for harvest. Settlers came to Fremont with fears of imminent Indian attacks. Word was spreading that Castro planned to arm Indians, attack all foreigners, and burn crops, houses, and barns. Settlers remaining in California would be maimed and killed.

Fremont promised to protect settlers. Troubled by losses in Oregon, he assembled a company of men to solve the Indian problem. A small army crossed to the west bank of the Sacramento River. The army followed the river south, coming on a large Indian rancheria (village). The village men were preparing for war, covering their faces with black war paint. Many were dancing ceremonial war dances.

Fremont's troops began their retribution for past Indian attacks. They shot every Indian male old enough to wield a bow. Huts were torched, stored and drying food destroyed. Women and children scattered to woods, wherever they could hide. Raiders destroyed the first rancheria, moved onto the next, and continued until not a single Indian settlement remained on the west side of the Sacramento River.

Fremont, aware of pending hostilities, needed to build an arsenal of military supplies. He sent Lieutenant Gillespie to San Francisco Bay, where the USS *Portsmouth* was anchored. The ship's commander, Montgomery, loaded a boat with guns and ammunition, dispatching it to Fremont's camp.

Early in June, Gen. Jose Castro sent Lt. Francisco Arce to Vallejo's home in Sonoma to collect 170 horses to be relocated at Santa Clara for his army. Arce gathered the horses, taking the herd to the Sacramento River, crossing at Knights Landing. Young Arce liked to talk. He bragged that Castro would use the horses to drive Americans out of California. William Knight, owner of the ferry, immediately left for Fremont's camp, reporting Arce's announcement.

Ezekiel "Zeke" Merritt and three friends were visiting Fremont when Knight arrived with his disturbing news. No tougher group of mountain men could be seen in the area. Zeke, a trapper, wore tattered, greasy buckskins. His beard was tobacco stained and shaggy. His graying hair was unkempt and long. A love of whiskey and stuttering speech fueled a quarrelsome personality, but when asked to perform a task, he followed instructions without question. Zeke, his three followers, and ten volunteers decided to put Castro in his place.

Fremont coached Zeke on tactics needed to intercept Arce and take his horses but refused to go with Merritt's group. Zeke's men rode hard and fast, arriving near Arce's camp late at night. Early the next morning, Zeke surprised the Mexicans, disarming Arce's men before they could fire a shot. Zeke showed mercy toward Arce's men, permitting each to keep a horse. The remaining horses were taken to Fremont.

Zeke was excited to follow up his successes against rancheros. He developed a plan to attack General Vallejo's presidio at Sonoma before Castro could use it as a base to attack settlers. Fremont felt an attack was beyond his scope of orders from Washington and would not send his men with Merritt; however, he appointed Merritt a lieutenant, commander of a band of men who called themselves Bears (*Osos*) and discussed tactics for the capture of Sonoma. The Bears departed later in the day. Bear or *oso* was a name for grizzly bears found in California.

Merritt and twenty men crossed Sacramento Valley to Cache Creek, where they were joined by several men. One was William Todd, nephew of Mrs. Abraham Lincoln. The group crossed Berryessa Valley, entering Pope Valley, stopping at the home of Elias Bennett, who slaughtered a young steer to feed Merritt's hungry men. Zeke continued toward his destination, riding into the upper Napa Valley. He stopped for a rest at Dr. Bale's located between today's Calistoga and Saint Helena, where four men joined him, making the group total thirty-three. One of the newcomers was Alfred Davenport.

Chapter 14

The Californian Republic

Alfred and his companions were exhausted and hungry. They found themselves in a valley where travel was less challenging. They hoped to locate an emigrant settlement where they could rest and obtain food. The first sign of civilization was a discovery of a large gristmill owned by Dr. Edward Turner Bale. They stopped at the mill. Dr. Bale offered to feed the hungry men and permitted them to sleep in his stable.

Their rest was cut short when a large group of men were heard outside the stable. Alfred, always alert, awoke his companions and grabbed his rifle, racing to see if the visitors were friends or the hated Mexican Army. Much to his relief, Alfred discovered Americans led by Zeke Merritt and William Ide.

Merritt shared his experiences, telling Alfred about capturing horses destined to be used against Americans and the advice he received from Fremont. He described Mexican soldiers as slow and lazy, not born fighters who easily retreated when fighting got tough. Zeke explained that his men were headed to Sonoma, where General Vallejo resided in a lightly defended presidio. Americans planned to seize the garrison, depose Vallejo, and establish a new country free from Mexican rule. He asked Alfred and his companions to join his men. Alfred Davenport eagerly joined Merritt.

Zeke was pleased to have four newcomers in his army. He noted that Alfred was tall and strong, and like Merritt, he was leading his men. Zeke asked him how he came West. Alfred replied, "Overland to Oregon in

1844 with James Clyman and Nat Ford." Clyman was a friend of Merritt's. The two men recently hunted grizzly bears.

Zeke asked Davenport if he knew how to use his rifle. He answered, "I provided buffalo and antelope for the '44 trip. Clyman said I was a good marksman."

The *Osos* were tired, complaining they needed to rest, wanting to spend the night at Bale's gristmill. Zeke said they could not stop. Long Bob Semple, a six-foot eight-inch Kentucky dentist, spoke sharply, emphasizing the *Osos* must attack Sonoma before they were discovered. Zeke, Alfred, and Semple decided to lead the *Osos* on their climb out of the Napa Valley. Rugged Mayacamas Mountains needed to be crossed to reach Sonoma Valley. Animal trails were followed until they disappeared. Travel became more challenging. Thick clumps of briars, oaks, and pine trees and fatigue slowed the progress of the men and their horses.

Early on June 14, they cleared the mountains, reaching the valley. The *Osos* continued south to Sonoma, arriving at its wide plaza a little before sunrise. Local citizens remained asleep. Merritt divided the men into groups. Alfred and one group would take the barracks with its store of armaments. A second would remain in the square, controlling townspeople.

Zeke and Semple went to Gen. Mariano Guadalupe Vallejo's La Casa Grande, a spacious, two-story adobe house facing the square. They pounded on the door, demanding to see the general. After a delay, he appeared clad in full military dress. Merritt placed Vallejo under arrest. Soon two local men arrived at La Casa. One was Salvador Vallejo, brother of Gen. Mariano Vallejo. The second was a Frenchman, Victor Purdon, Mariano's secretary. The two were immediately arrested by Merritt and Semple.

Negotiations began between the Mexicans and Americans. It was hot and warm in the house; Vallejo offered his captors wine and brandy from his cellar, causing negotiations to slow to a crawl. Hours passed, and the men staying in the square became impatient. They selected John Grigsby as their leader, sending him inside La Casa to see what was delaying negotiations. Mariano Vallejo asked for his brother-in-law Jacob Leese, an American, to join the negotiations to help with language translation. Delays continued, and Grigsby failed to return and report to the square.

The Bears held another election, selecting William Ide as their leader. Ide, from Massachusetts, was a schoolteacher with a historian's knowledge of the United States Constitution. Ide entered Vallejo's La Casa, finding

Merritt and Grigsby sleeping after enjoying the bounty of Vallejo's wine cellar. Semple and Jacob Leese were struggling with terms of the articles of capitulation. Ide and Semple decided to take their captives outside, where both men spoke to the Bears and Sonoma residents.

The Bears announced the creation of a new California republic. Retention of property and full rights would be granted to all Mexicans who would join the movement. The new republic would be based on the structure of the United States government. When General Vallejo learned about Fremont's discussion and approval of Merritt's expedition, he felt the U.S. government was behind Merritt. Vallejo thought an alliance with the Americans would be good for Alta California. He turned over keys to the fort's barracks, surrendering over 250 muskets, 100 pounds of powder, and 9 brass cannons.

At eleven thirty, about six hours after arriving in Sonoma, Merritt, Semple, and Grigsby departed with prisoners: Salvador Vallejo, Gen. Don Mariano Vallejo, Victor Purdon, and Jacob Leese, who was serving as Sonoma's alcaide (mayor). The prisoners were to be held at Sutter's Fort on the Sacramento River.

Merritt arrived at Sutter's on June 16, finding Fremont in charge. John A. Sutter was not pleased to see his Mexican friend a captive of Americans. Fremont had strong words for Sutter. He must support the uprising. The fort was now under the command of Fremont's appointee, Ned Kern. Sutter could leave and join Mexicans in the south or stay and report to Fremont. He would be responsible for the prisoners and would be severely punished if his prisoners escaped. Sutter was not long in making up his mind. His philosophy in a tough situation was always "Do what was best for John A. Sutter." He agreed to stay. Later, Commander Montgomery asked Sutter to serve the United States, acting as Kern's adjutant. The new appointment carried the title of lieutenant in the dragoons.

The Bears did not want to be considered a band of marauders by Mexicans. Ide's declaration of a "republic of California" with its written constitution was designed to legitimize the takeover of Sonoma. The men wanted a flag to tell the story of their movement. Peter Storm, a Norwegian emigrant living in Calistoga and an *Oso*, designed the flag. Materials for the flag were provided by Nancy Kelsey, Mrs. John Sears, and Mrs. Benjamin Dewell, who sewed together the materials. William Todd inked the words "California Republic" using pokeberry juice in place of ink. Todd drew a star and a grizzly bear on the flag. A few of Todd's companions and some Mexicans thought the bear looked more like a pig. They laughed at the image. The flag was raised above the square at Sonoma shortly after sunrise on June 15.

On the same day, Fremont received requested military supplies from Commander Montgomery. Early the next afternoon, Lt. John S. Missroon from the USS *Portsmouth* came to Sonoma, where he assured Mrs. Vallejo and Alcalde (town administrator) Jose S. Berryessa they were safe under occupation by the *Osos*. Ide's men would respect the citizens of Sonoma and their property.

The Sonoma barracks became the headquarters for Alfred and the twenty-four remaining Bears. Alfred inventoried the Bears' military supplies. Gunpowder was in short supply. They could not survive an attack by General Castro without more powder. He discussed the shortage with Lt. Henry Ford, commander of the *Osos*. Ford decided to send Todd and another Bear to Bodega to locate gunpowder. The same day, he sent Thomas Cowie and George Fowler north to the Fitch Rancho (near today's Healdsburg) to acquire gunpowder from the rancho manager, Moses Carson, Kit's brother.

Two days passed; nothing was heard from the two groups. Ford sent five of his best men north to Fitch to locate Cowie and Fowler. Carson told them that Cowie and Fowler never reached the rancho. Carson immediately supplied gunpowder to Ford's men to take to Sonoma. On the return trip, a small group of Californios attacked the Bear Flaggers, who fought hard driving off the men. One of the attackers, the notorious "four-fingered" Garcia, was captured and taken to Sonoma. Garcia admitted he helped kill Cowie and Fowler. He reported that the Mexicans were led by Mexican Army captain Juan Padilla. Before Cowie and Fowler were shot, they were tied to trees and stoned, their flesh was cut, and the men were mutilated. Five Californians drew weapons shooting Cowie and Fowler. Padilla and his comrades departed for Rancho Olompali after the incident.

Ford's reaction was immediate: he would take the war to Padilla at Olompali. He selected Davenport and a total of eighteen men to ride west. The riders discovered multiple horse tracks leading toward San Rafael near the mouth of the Petaluma River. The tracks were fresh, pointing to an adobe house with a nearby corral of horses. Ford's small army approached the house. He was facing De la Torre and fifty of his men. The Americans dismounted. Ford strategically placed his troops in the woods, using the cover of trees to disguise the size of his force and the location of his men.

Tension grew; soldiers streamed out of the adobe's front door, walking behind the house to their mounts. A Mexican soldier was expected to fight on horseback. Fighting on foot was not honorable for a Mexican cavalry trooper. Ford instructed Davenport and his troops to wait until Mexicans soldiers came into rifle range. Mounted soldiers began their charge. Alfred and his associates held their fire, waiting for a firing advantage. Orders were given; Americans hit their enemy with a barrage of fire. Mexicans continued to charge. Holding in place, Alfred and the Bears reloaded their rifles, continuing firing, killing several, wounding many charging Mexicans. (Later, graves of eight Mexican soldiers were found at Olompali.)

De la Torre soon discovered that lances and muskets with limited firing range were no match for Ford's long rifles. He regrouped, gathered his soldiers, and raced away from the battle toward Mission San Rafael. Todd, held by De la Torre, took advantage of the chaos of battle to escape, finding security with the *Osos* troops. Americans walked away unscathed. The *Osos* returned to Sonoma on June 24.

Fremont, with his army of mountain men, rode into Sonoma the next day. It was time to protect Americans and halt Mexican troop activities. Alfred met and liked John Charles Fremont. He decided to join Fremont's new regiment.

Fremont's troops left Sonoma early on June 26, racing toward Mission San Rafael to engage De la Torre. They arrived to discover their adversary gone, fled south with his army. Carson, Delaware Indians, and other scouts began looking for clues pointing to the possible routes the Mexicans had taken. During their search, they noticed a small boat containing three Mexicans landing near San Rafael. Angry about the murder of Cowie and Fowler, Americans shot and killed the occupants when they attempted to come ashore. The deaths were a mistake; the men were friends of the *Osos*. One was the father of Jose Berryessa, Sonoma's alcalde. The other two were his nephews. Fremont was blamed for the deaths as commander, though it was never determined who ordered the shooting.

A local Indian was captured by Fremont's scouts the same day. The Indian produced a "secret" message. De la Torre was planning to attack Sonoma. Fremont reversed course, racing to return to protect the town. Ide received a similar message of an impending Sonoma attack. He ordered his men to prepare for a fight. *Osos* were strategically placed in defensive positions, cannons readied, soldiers alerted and poised to fire on enemy movements. Carson headed the American troops returning to Sonoma.

He immediately saw the *Osos* army's fight preparations, shouted out, and identified himself, narrowly averting a disastrous reception.

Fremont spoke to Ide. The men realized that the "impending" attack on Sonoma was a ruse. It was designed to delay Fremont while De la Torre escaped to San Francisco. Fremont planned a quick return West. Alfred was back in a saddle, racing with Fremont overland to Sausalito, where Americans encountered no enemy soldiers. Fremont borrowed a launch from the *Moscow*, a merchant ship, to carry his men across the strait to San Francisco. His troops raced to the fort overlooking the entrance to the bay. The fort was deserted. Cannons strategically placed to fire on invaders were discovered and spiked. Americans rested long enough to enjoy the view from the fort, which Fremont named the Golden Gate. Alfred and the troops seized all military supplies and returned to Sonoma. Long Bob Semple and a few men returned to San Francisco with instructions to capture the captain of the port and take him to Sutter's for imprisonment. The captain was Robert T. Ridley.

Sonoma's July 4 was a grand party. Alfred would long remember the Independence Day celebration. Vast quantities of food and liquor were consumed; cannons and guns were fired. Young and old, Californios and Americans celebrated together. Music, fandango dancing, and revelry lasted until the wee hours of the fifth.

Fremont, with Ide's approval, took command of the settler's army, forming a battalion of mounted riflemen. The military unit was composed of members of Fremont's original expedition, leaders of the Bear Flag Revolt, and recently arrived emigrants. Alfred was excited to join the California Battalion. He was a typical recruit—tall, sunburned, bearded, and wearing a broad hat, blue flannel shirt, buckskin trousers, and moccasins. He carried a large sheathed hunting knife, a brace (pair) of pistols, and his trusty Hawken rifle.

Fremont addressed his new battalion. Their goal was to subdue Gen. Jose Castro. The men would be trained in military tactics and learn military discipline. They were told they must act honorably, especially toward women, and obey their officers. The battalion headquarters was Sutter's Fort, now commanded by Ned Kern. Fremont renamed Sutter's "Fort Sacramento."

U.S. Pacific Squadron's commodore Sloat learned of the United States war with Mexico late in May. Concerned that British admiral Sir George Seymour would want Monterey for the British, Sloat arrived at Monterey on the second of July. On July 7, he demanded surrender of the town, hoisting the American flag. Two days later, a navy officer, J. W. Revere, arrived at Sonoma with American flags for Sonoma and Sutter's Fort, formally ending a twenty-five-day-old Bear Flag republic.

The Conquest of California, June 1846–January 1847

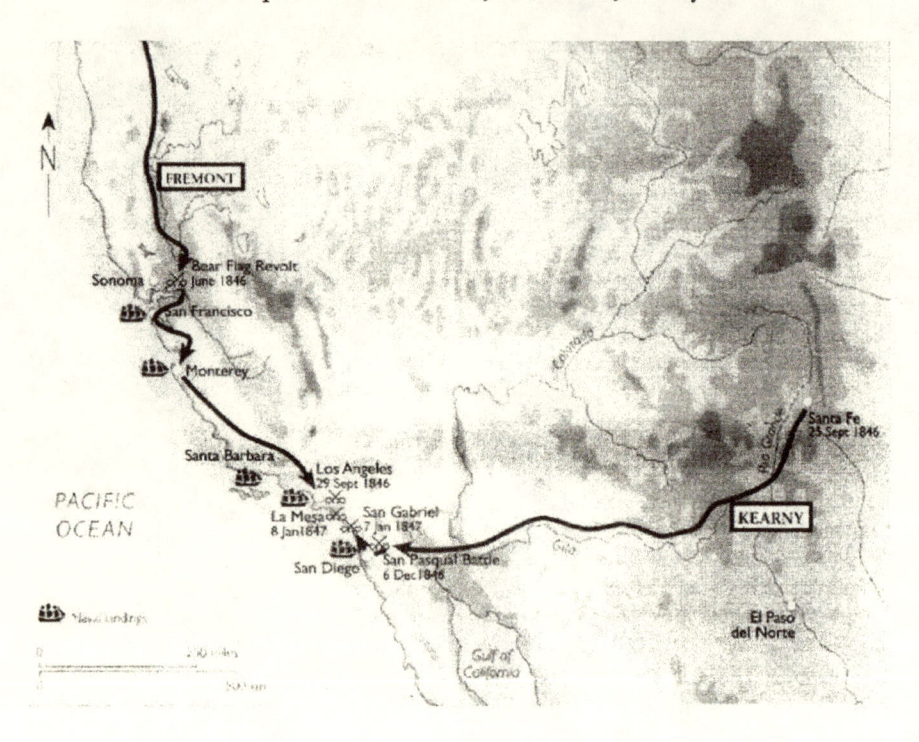

Chapter 15

The California Battalion

A ribbon of a path appeared to shift and bounce on the horizon, warmed by hot thermals of air playing tricks on one's eyes. Alfred's column slowed their pace; massive amounts of dust floated up from a narrow dirt road, obscuring signs of the way ahead. Davenport was located near the head of a column of 160 men slowly snaking south from Sacramento to California's San Joaquin River.

John Charles Fremont, flanked by five Delaware Indian bodyguards, headed mounted troops of the California Battalion. The men were in a race to support U.S. Navy's commodore John Sloat in Monterey, where he recently defied Mexican authorities, raising the United States flag over government buildings. California's dry summer provided scant fodder for horses. Pools of brackish water for men and animals were all that was available in riverbeds dried by a hot sun. There had been no rain for weeks; none was in sight. The landscape was parched, dry, and hot. Green grass yellowed and turned brown, leaving no fodder for animals. Experienced as explorers, frontiersmen, and emigrants, the riders found the journey similar to past western summers.

The scene changed when the caravan reached the Merced River at its confluence with the San Joaquin. Merced was fed by melting snow and ice cascading down from high Sierra Mountains. Clear, cold water created acres of lush green grass, attracting herds of hungry and thirsty elk, wild horses, and an occasional grizzly bear. The river junction was an oasis for tired riders and their mounts.

Alfred joined a group selected by Fremont to provide fresh meat for the battalion's hungry troops. Success created a welcome a feast. The men rested and relaxed before starting on a new trail on the western side of the San Joaquin River. A ford was found crossing the San Joaquin upriver from the Merced. Fremont crossed using a rubber raft that he made available to men who did not know how to swim. Alfred, with other experienced swimmers, took the battalion's horses to the west bank.

The trail led west toward the Pacific Ocean, crossing a saddle in the coastal mountain range, before descending into the pueblo of San Juan. Battalion troops arrived on San Juan on July 17. Locals favorable to Americans advised Fremont about General Castro hiding a cache of arms before heading south. Alfred and several men were dispatched to find and recover Castro's weapons. Eight cannons were discovered buried in a wheat field. Six miles away at the Mission San Juan Bautista, two hundred arms and nine kegs of powder were recovered and presented to Fremont. Americans raised the flag over the mission before leaving for Monterey.

A proud, rough-looking battalion made a magnificent entrance into the town of Monterey. Locals and British and American sailors looked with awe and amazement as mounted soldiers exited a cloud of dust, stopping at the town square. Their rugged appearance added to the mystique of the group. Each man was prepared for war, carrying a rifle, two pistols, and a long knife. Some members of the battalion were so sunburned that they looked darker than Indians. Missing were broadcloth uniforms and jackets adorned with brass buttons and medallions worn by army dragoons. One could not determine if a man was an officer or a volunteer soldier. The battalion soldiers camped on a hill overlooking the town of Monterey and its harbor. Fremont and Gillespie visited Sloat on his flagship *Savannah*.

Sloat asked Fremont to show him a copy of his orders taking arms against Mexicans; he was shocked when Fremont told him he had none. Sloat said he raised the flag in Monterey and other locations thinking written orders had come to Fremont from Washington. Fremont explained his instructions were oral provided by Washington's courier, Gillespie. Without written orders, Sloat refused to take further actions against General Castro. Concerned he had made a grave error taking over Monterey, Sloat made plans to leave California and rejoin the fleet. He turned his command over to Commodore Robert Stockton, who recently arrived aboard the USS *Congress*.

Stockton was pleased to learn that northern California was under the control of Fremont and the Americans. Both men felt they needed to seize the rest of California from Mexico. Stockton gave legitimacy to Fremont's troops. He conferred the rank of major on Fremont, appointing him commander of the California Battalion of Horse Marines, a navy unit headed by an army officer. Their goal was to corner Gen. Jose Castro and Gov. Pio Pico, forcing them to surrender to United States forces. The leaders crafted war plans. Stockton sailed on the *Congress* with 350 men to San Pedro, near the Pueblo de Los Angeles, the location of the governor and the general. Fremont would sail on the *Cyane* with 160 men, capture San Diego, and ride north to join Stockton. The combined show of force should force Californios to surrender.

Alfred enjoyed three days sailing to San Diego. Winds were fresh and brisk, seas choppy and rough, bringing back recent memories of enjoyable voyages to and from the Sandwich Islands. He welcomed relief from days in a saddle, climbing rough mountain passes and traversing dust-filled roads. Some of the mountain men on board the *Cyane* did not share Alfred's love of the sea. Kit Carson found sea travel very difficult. The rolling of the ship as she plunged through ocean swells found Carson on the lee rail spewing the contents of his stomach into the deep blue sea, a malady that possessed other mountain men on their first ocean voyage.

San Diego was a gem. The days were warm, dry, and comfortable. Irrigation provided an abundance of fruits and vegetables and a bumper crop of flowers. Leading citizens welcomed Americans and a change in government; they felt ignored and neglected by Mexico City. A week was needed for Fremont to gather horses and supplies for his ride north to join Stockton. He departed on August 8, leaving a garrison of 50 men at San Diego commanded by Major Gillespie.

Alfred's trip north out of San Diego was a mixture of arid brush-filled desert land interspaced with small valleys containing wells or springs and a network of irrigation systems supporting agriculture. Olive trees and grapes were the principal crops. He had little time to enjoy the country bounty, for Fremont's army was racing to join Stockton's troops near Los Angeles. Stopping might encourage skirmishes from unfriendly Californios.

Californio spies informed General Castro and Governor Pico of the sizable force facing their 250-man army. They were not prepared to fight nor to surrender to the Americans. Castro and Pico dispersed their troops, sending them home. Castro escaped, traveling at night, heading east and south to the safety of Sonora, Mexico. Pico was sequestered at a relative's ranch before being smuggled into Baja California.

Alfred described the "capture" of Los Angeles as a spectacular event. Stockton and Fremont led a long procession of troops into the town. Immediately behind the two men was a brass band. Next marched sailors and marines dressed in their best parade uniforms. They were followed by the mounted California Battalion. Four ox carts each holding a deck of guns primed and ready for action were behind the battalion, trailed by wagons carrying ammunition and supplies. Ship's officers rode at the rear of the procession. The parade headed to the government house. "Hail Columbia" was played by the band; the Stars and Stripes were sent up a flagpole. Stockton and his troops camped within the walls surrounding the government buildings. Fremont camped beside a river. Alfred was surprised to see the capital of California taken by Americans without a shot being fired. Stockton issued a proclamation placing Californians under martial law. His instructions outlined citizens' responsibilities to the United States.

He delivered a letter of instructions to Fremont, who had recently received an appointment to the rank of lieutenant colonel in the U.S. Army. Fremont was to command all military forces in California, now a territory of the United States. The territory would be divided into three military districts. Lieutenant Gillespie was placed in charge of the south in Los Angeles, Commodore Stockton was in charge of the middle in Monterey, and Lieutenant Colonel Fremont would head the northern district at Fort Sacramento. They would meet in San Francisco late in October to formally appoint Fremont as governor of California. This was the law of the land. Stockton drafted a letter to President Polk describing these events and sent it with Kit Carson to Washington, asking the letter to be delivered within sixty days no later than October 24.

Stockton gave new orders to Fremont. He was to go north to add recruits for the California Battalion. Alfred joined 35 men returning to Fort Sacramento, finding the trip pleasant and enjoyable. He traveled along the coast, stopping at Santa Barbara to enjoy its beautiful location at the foot of coastal mountains. In Santa Barbara, they acquired fresh horses and more cattle for the balance of their journey to Sacramento.

Traveling through Salinas Valley, the men stumbled into a thicket filled with grizzly bears. Disturbed bears became excited, immediately charging their intruders. Quick-acting William Knight wielded his double-barreled shotgun, saving himself and others from being mauled by a dangerous grizzly. Travel was delayed while Alfred and his companions harvested twelve bears.

Fremont and his men arrived at Fort Sacramento late in September but did not stay long. A message from Stockton in San Francisco brought bad news from the south. Los Angeles Californios revolted, attacking the small garrison with 400 men led by Jose Maria Flores. Gillespie was forced to surrender on September 29. He retreated to San Pedro, where he boarded the U.S. ship *Vandalia* for a return north. Stockton needed the California Battalion to retake Los Angeles.

Alfred and 170 men departed from San Francisco for San Pedro aboard the merchant ship *Sterling*. Stockton led the way south with his flagship *Congress*. Capt. William Mervin, stationed at Monterey, was sent ahead on the *Savannah* with 400 marines and sailors to land at San Pedro to assist Gillespie. Mervin wasted no time confronting the Californios. Moving inland, he immediately attacked Flores's army without first obtaining horses or artillery. In the ensuing battle, four of his men were killed; several suffered wounds. Californios had a decided advantage using mounted men and a cannon, a tough lesson for Mervin. He realized the weakness of his position, retreated to San Pedro, boarded the *Savannah*, and returned to Monterey.

The *Sterling* began to lag behind the *Congress*, which quickly sailed out of sight. The sky darkened; the ship plowed into a fogbank where light and fluky wind slowed the ship to a crawl. A day later, the fog lifted, finding the *Sterling* alone on the sea. The next day, the *Vandalia* appeared. Both ships exchanged messages. Fremont learned that Gillespie and his troops remained in the south. News from Mervin caused Fremont to realize he could not expect to find horses or food for his army, with Californios controlling Los Angeles and its surrounding territory. His only course of action was to return to Monterey and acquire horses and cattle. The battalion would need to travel overland to retake Los Angeles.

Chapter 16

Fremont Takes the Battalion South

The California Battalion created by John Charles Fremont was officially authorized by U.S. Navy's commodore Robert F. Stockton, commander of the Pacific Squadron, on July 23, 1846. Stockton promoted Fremont to a (brevet) army rank of lieutenant colonel. The battalion became part of the navy, not the army. Fremont appointed all officers. He was the founder, leader, and source of all authority for the battalion. Its ranks were filled with American citizen volunteers.

A messenger reached Stockton late in September stating that Gen. Jose Maria Flores, under orders from Gen. Jose Castro and Gov. Pio Pico, staged a revolt in Los Angeles with about 300 men, attacking the American garrison of 40 men commanded by Lt. Archibald Gillespie. Gillespie was forced to capitulate on September 30, retreating to San Pedro, where he boarded the American merchant ship *Vandalia* and returned north.

Stockton ordered Fremont go south to retake lost cities and towns. Fremont immediately began increasing the size of his battalion, needing 425 men to meet his new challenges. The selection of troops was wide and varied. Retired frontiersmen, emigrants, Indians, and adventurers—men from varying backgrounds—were signed on for the coming expedition. Ned Kern sent from Fort Sacramento 10 Walla Walla Indians, valuable as scouts and spies. Alex Godey brought recently arrived settlers from Sonoma. One colorful recruit was Capt. Buford K. "Hell Roaring" Thompson, a known gambler with a questionable provenance in military matters and anxious "to get Mexicans." Thirty-five men with nefarious backgrounds elected to join Thompson.

Fremont needed a staging area to prepare for his campaign. He chose Mission San Juan Batista to assemble his army. Organizing and training recruits to follow military rules and discipline was his greatest challenge. Military discipline and following orders were new to the men. Alfred was given an important role in training recruits. He worked to teach the use of a rifle when riding on a charging horse. All men were schooled on the necessity of following orders given by a company commander. Training days were long and, at times, frustrating. Rules of military discipline slowly evolved; progress could be seen at the end of a month. Alfred felt his trainees were prepared for a journey south.

Food and transportation for a mounted battalion was a challenge. Fremont sent soldiers to the countryside to acquire animals for his expedition. Two thousand horses and five hundred head of cattle were required to meet his army's needs. A dozen cattle had to be slaughtered each day to feed his troops. Fremont issued warrants, a promise to pay, for animals taken for the army. Several soldiers failed to provide payment warrants for seized animals. Local rancheros felt resentment and hostility toward Americans when livestock was taken without a promised warrant.

Californios' militant guerillas were becoming a problem. Motivated by military successes in the south, Mexican guerillas became active near Monterey. Thomas O. Larkin, U.S. consul to the former Mexico governor in Alta California, moved his family to San Francisco after news of revolts in southern California reached Monterey. He learned that his daughter, who remained in Monterey, was seriously ill. Larkin felt that he must visit her. On the night of November 15, he stopped at a rancho owned by American sympathizer Jose Joaquin Gomez. Late in the evening, Manuel Castro—a cousin of Gen. Jose Castro—learned that Larkin was at the ranch. He rode to the rancho and captured the consul, taking him to Santa Barbara. Eventually, he was imprisoned in Los Angeles. Larkin was released when the war was over. His daughter died while he was in captivity.

Fremont began his move south. He soon realized he needed more horses. Capt. Charles Burruss was sent to collect additional mounts. He was joined by Hell Roaring and his men. The men were gathering horses in Salinas Valley on Rancho Natividad when Joseph Foster, James Hayes, and 2 Walla Walla Indians scouting ahead of the main group in a thinly wooded area found themselves surrounded by Californios led by Castro. Shots were fired. Foster, Hayes, and the Indians took cover and returned fire, hitting enemy soldiers with well-placed shots. The Californios retreated.

Thompson impulsively insisted on charging the retreating Californios. He took a small force of his troops, raced ahead of his other companions, and began firing at a retreating enemy. The Californios' retreat was a feint. Mounted lancers quickly regrouped, turned, and charged the Americans. Thompson and his troops were caught with empty rifles with no time to reload. Without firepower, they were forced to flee. The day was saved by two Indians and several sharpshooter mountain men who attacked charging lancers, killing 10, wounding a significant unknown number. Burruss, Hayes, and two other Americans were killed; 5 were wounded. Castro gathered his battered guerillas, fleeing to a distant, unknown location south of Monterey.

Chapter 17

San Juan Bautista to Santa Barbara

Fremont was anxious to begin the journey south. He conferred with Commodore Stockton, discussing strategies. Californios intended to move all livestock inland, denying the American Army access to beef and horses when landing by sea. They realized the U.S. Navy would control the California seacoast. Fremont must travel inland, bringing supplies, horses, and beef needed for the campaign against Californios. The Mexican strategy, control of the interior, would be their bargaining point when peace arrived.

The rainy season began with a vengeance late in November, making an inland trip south challenging. Fremont decided not to follow the coastal routes where many locations provided Californios opportunities to ambush Americans. He would take a more difficult route from San Juan Bautista to Santa Barbara. Departure was scheduled on November 28.

A large mounted army was cumbersome and prone to delays. Inexperienced "green recruits" with little sense of organization and demands of dragging heavy artillery over rough, mud-filled, rugged terrain made progress slow. Security was an ongoing concern for the battalion. Fremont answered this challenge by establishing forward and rear guards. Each group was composed of eight to ten marksmen and scouts strategically placed ahead and behind at the main body of his battalion, creating warning and defense lines in the event of an attack. Alfred was a member of the front guard.

The first night's stop was eight miles south of the San Juan Bautista

Mission on the banks of the San Benito River. Fremont was joined by Edwin Bryant from Fort Sacramento, who brought a detachment of emigrants and friendly Indians. Steady rain, heavy at times, hampered progress. Struggling through mud-exhausted horses, many of the weakest had to be abandoned. New challenges occurred the next morning. Gabilan mountain passes were filled with fallen rocks, boulders, and downed trees. The way ahead needed to be cleared for passage. New paths were cut to replace washouts. Cannons laboriously pulled up to the summit were rigged with ropes to be lowered to the next level of the trail. A few cannons broke from their handlers, dropping into steep, brush-filled gullies. While the slow climb over the mountain proceeded, Alfred was dispatched with other scouts to visit nearby gullies, looking for signs of guerilla activities. Their efforts revealed a deserted campsite used by Californios who fled south after the Battle of Natividad.

The Salinas River valley was reached at noon on December 7; riders continued south, following the west shore of the river for three days, when they found a grove of oak trees with ample forage for their animals. They were four miles below Mission San Miguel owned by Englishman William Reed. Beef from the troop's diet was replaced by mutton from the mission's large number of sheep, for the battalion's beef supply was nearly depleted.

Travel was resumed after two days of heavy rain. Soldiers were ordered to walk, allowing exhausted horses a rest. Men complained of sore, blistered feet, a common complaint on the day's twelve-hour march. Battalion advance guards captured an Indian scout named Santa Maria near Rancho Paso de Robles. Don Jose de Jesus Pico of San Luis Obispo, cousin of Gov. Pio Pico and the military commander of the central coast, sent the Indian to spy on the Americans. Documents found on the spy were destined for Governor Pico.

That evening, Mr. Stanly—a friend and traveling companion of Bryant—died after a long fight with typhoid fever. He was buried the next morning. Immediately after the burial, the spy Santa Maria was executed by a firing squad in full view of the battalion and members of the Indian's rancheria.

The battalion struggled south along the Salinas River; weather continued to be cold and rainy. Normally dry streambeds became raging torrents of water. Crossing shallow rivers flooded by seasonal rains was slow and difficult for horses, riders, and men towing artillery. At four in the afternoon, the column was startled by gunfire coming from the advance guard. The main body troops rushed ahead, preparing for an ambush. They found that Alfred and his guards had disturbed a large sloth of grizzly bears gathering acorns from oak trees. Old bears pushed cubs up into trees to shake down nuts, a sweet and favorite food of grizzlies. Guards harvested older bears before sunset, adding to the battalion's meager meat supplies. Heavy rain and downpours prevented fires from being lit that evening. Wet and tired men were exhausted, unable to sleep in the rain; they broke camp early the next day. Weather improved midmorning, allowing a noon stop for dinner. Fires were lit to prepare meals for hungry men.

The San Luis Obispo Mission was reached after dark on December 14. Fremont divided the battalion into three groups to approach the mission, anticipating problems that were nonexistent. The battalion arrived unopposed. Housing was found in the church and in houses on mission grounds. The mission and its buildings were surrounded by high walls. Inside the walls were lush orchards growing orange, lemon, olive, and fig trees. Rain resumed; the men used the church and adjoining housing to stay dry. Alfred explored the grounds, enjoying fresh fruit, especially oranges. He purchased frijoles, a welcome change from a diet of beef. Ed Bryant noted in his journal that the weather-beaten, rough-looking men of the battalion adhered to Fremont's rules, respecting the rights and property of the enemy population.

Jose de Jesus Pico's taking up arms violated his parole. An attempt to escape from Fremont's men failed when Pico jumped out of a window of a ranch house at Rancho Los Osos, a few miles west of the mission. Pico was placed in irons and returned to San Luis Obispo for a court-martial led by Fremont. He was charged with breaking parole, participating in the attack at Natividad, and forcing Californians to join the insurgents. He was scheduled to be executed by firing squad at noon on December 17.

The hour of execution neared. Troops were in place at the plaza. A group of weeping women and their children were off to one side, guarded by Fremont's troops. Capt. Dick Owens entered Fremont's chambers with a woman dressed in black accompanied by her children. She was the beautiful wife of Pico, Senora Javaela Villavicencio. She and her children fell to their knees, crying and pleading for the life of Pico. She stated that Pico did not know he committed a crime. He was simply defending his country and was ashamed that he remained behind while the others rode off to war. Fremont listened to her story; moved by her plea, he took pity on the distraught lady, telling her to go home. He brought Don Jose de

Jesus Pico forward to tell him he was saved by his wife; he was a free man. Pico immediately joined the battalion as a loyal servant where he served faithfully until Fremont's campaign was completed and the war was over. Other captives were given freedom the same day. Freeing Pico and other Californio leaders later proved to be a great benefit to Fremont.

Cold air, frost on the ground, and a clear sky welcomed the travelers on the morning of December 18. The battalion followed a creek toward today's town of Avila and a nearby beach on the rugged coast of the Pacific Ocean before turning inland. Peaks of distant mountains were covered with snow. Their route came to a wide valley at Los Berros Creek, part of the 38,000-acre Rancho Nipomo of William Goodwin Dana, where the battalion camped for the night. Dana's large casa frequently welcomed guests traveling between San Luis Obispo and Santa Barbara. He was friendly to the Americans, inviting the battalion commander to join him for dinner. Dana ordered enough beef killed to feed the battalion's hungry men. He advised Fremont to head inland to Foxen's ranch and avoid Gaviota Pass, a narrow opening between the coastal mountains and the sea where ambush risks were high. Californios hid at the top of the pass, releasing boulders to fall on and crush unsuspecting soldiers traveling through. Foxen would offer a guide to cross the San Marcos Pass over Santa Ynez Mountains to Santa Barbara.

Camp was broken, and the men proceeded up a valley crossing the Santa Maria River. Exhausted, worn-out horses were again a problem. Over one hundred gave out during the day. Weak stock in poor condition were traced to their acquisition at Mission San Juan Bautista, another Californio ploy to harm the battalion. Alfred's advance guard arrived at Foxen's on December 20. The battalion was strung out, with stragglers falling miles behind the advance guard. Foxen urged Fremont to allow him to guide troops over the San Marcos Pass. On December 21, a foot march was ordered. Weary men, exhausted horses, and stragglers were rounded up by the rear guard, goaded to catch the main body of the battalion. Fremont chose a camp near a deserted rancho on small stream 4 miles from the Santa Ynez Mission, halting after dark at ten o'clock. The day's trip covered 15 miles. Alfred's advance guard surprised two Indians who revealed a hidden location with 25 fresh horses. A quick search brought the battalion new stock. Fremont permitted his men to rest on December 23 in preparation for the next day's climb over San Marco Pass.

December 24 began a 2,250 climb over the mountain leading to Santa

Barbara. The climb was backbreaking, slow, and exhausting. The so-called trail was a narrow, rock-strewn, abandoned mission path not suitable for horses and artillery. Men and animals struggled the entire day to reach the summit, dodging boulders, rocks, and fallen trees. Camp was established for the night. When a break in the clouds developed, Alfred could see the Santa Barbara plain and the Pacific Ocean and spires of the mission church 10 or more miles in the distance.

A storm with gale force winds and driving rain struck the mountain at noon on Christmas Day. Winds were hurricane strength. Torrents of rain reduced visibility; progress came to a slow crawl. Descending became impossible due to a deluge of water washing down the mountain trail. Military discipline was lost; only horse guards and artillery continued to function as a unit. Horses were driven ahead of their riders, stumbling and tripping over loose rocks, stones, gravel, and downed trees. Some panicked, breaking away from their handlers, blindly racing ahead, only to fall to their deaths, leaping over cliffs into canyons far below the trail. Foaming torrents of water charging down the mountain halted all progress; walking became impossible. Men abandoned weapons, supplies, and personal belongings to huddle behind large boulders or trees for protection from surging water. Everyone acted alone to save himself. Night was well underway before the advance guard reached a plateau at the base of the mountain. Fires could not be started nor tents pitched; sleep was impossible.

Rain stopped at two in the morning the day after Christmas. Fires were started before dawn to allow men to begin drying their clothes. Search parties were sent up the mountain after daylight to find survivors, live horses, weapons, supplies, and baggage. It was estimated that 150 horses perished during the Christmas Day storm. Alfred spent the day drying his clothes and bedroll and cleaning and oiling his rifle and pistols.

William Streeter and three senior Santa Barbara officials visited the camp on December 27. Fremont was told many residents were gone from Santa Barbara. Those remaining pleaded for the town not to be destroyed. They would show no hostility and would swear allegiance to the Americans. Fremont reluctantly agreed to the request. He visited the town with Streeter, selecting a billeting site for the battalion a half mile outside the town. His men were instructed not to leave camp without his permission. On December 28, Fremont took residency at the Saint Charles Hotel, raising the American flag on the public square.

George Nidever, a Santa Barbara resident, was employed by Fremont to search houses for illicit arms. Soldiers were instructed to burn a house if its residents objected to a search.

Senora Bernarda Ruiz de Rodriguez, a prominent citizen, asked for an audience with Fremont. She pleaded for an end to the war in California. They discussed the future of California. She told Fremont what Californios desired. Californios wanted to keep their land, and people who rebelled needed be allowed to return to their lives and property if they swore allegiance to the United States. Peace terms should call for release of all prisoners, equal rights for Californios, respect of Californios' property rights, and the allowing of Mexican citizens who so desired to return to Mexico. The Californios would respect their American bosses and welcome the United States government to California. These terms became the basis for the Treaty of Guadalupe Hidalgo. The battalion prepared to resume its journey south after a week's rest in Santa Barbara.

Chapter 18

Kearny Arrives in California

Kit Carson was in Taos, New Mexico, on October 6, briefly stopping to visit his wife, after a twenty-six-day, eight-hundred-mile trip from Los Angeles. He was traveling under orders from Commodore Stockton, carrying dispatches to Washington describing military successes—Lieutenant Colonel Fremont's conquering Mexicans and Stockton's establishment of a civil government in the California territory.

United States military governor of New Mexico Gen. Stephen Watts Kearny had been in Santa Fe since August. He was headed to Los Angeles under orders from President Polk to take California and establish a civil government. Kearny learned that Carson was in Taos. He met Carson, ordering him not to proceed to Washington but to guide his army to Los Angeles. Carson, who carried a temporary rank of lieutenant in the army, reluctantly turned Stockton's dispatches over to Tom "Broken Hand" Fitzpatrick for delivery to Washington when Kearny threatened him with a court-martial if he did not follow his orders. Carson provided Kearny details of Stockton's successes in California. Hearing the news, Kearny decided to cut the size of his army's western expedition from three hundred to one hundred men, leaving two hundred men to handle local Navajo Indian problems.

Kearny was commissioned during the War of 1812. In 1836, he was stationed at Fort Leavenworth, where he was promoted to colonel as commander of the First Dragoon Regiment (later redesignated the First U.S. Cavalry). The regiment's principal responsibility was protecting peace on the American frontier. Outbreak of the Mexican-American War took Kearny to Santa Fe. His responsibilities included establishing a joint civil-military New Mexico government and executing duties of the commander of the United States Army west. He was given a (brevet) rank of brigadier general by Secretary of War William L. Marcy. Kearny was a fastidious, no-nonsense, and disciplined officer. Like his contemporaries, he saw U.S. Army dragoons as vastly superior to any mounted troops Mexico could field. He was anticipating success in California. It would be a boost to his career.

Carson, leading the cavalry, departed for California on October 7, 1846. On November 23 at the junction of the Gila and Colorado Rivers, one of Kearny's officers, Lieutenant Emory, intercepted a lone Californio militia rider with dispatches from Gen. Andres Pico for Gen. Jose Castro located in Sonora, Mexico. The dispatches detailed a new California revolt, with Californios recapturing Los Angeles along with several coastal communities. This news was a shock to Kearny. Carson was relieved to learn that U.S. losses were from guerrilla activities, not from the enemy's army.

Kearny crossed the Colorado River, reaching Warner's Ranch on the California border on December 2. He was low on supplies; men were exhausted, their mules worn out. Edward Stiles, a neutral Englishman, agreed to take a letter to Commodore Stockton in San Diego. Kearny's letter requested supplies and updated news of the current political situation in California. He did not mention the sorry condition of his men and animals, nor did he relate the size of his army. Cold, wet, without winter clothes, and suffering in a December rain, the Army of the West camped at Edward Stokes's ranchero at Santa Ysabel. Officers were cooked a large meal of mutton and tortillas to be served with wine. Serving was delayed when near-starving enlisted men stole and gobbled up food prepared for officers.

Stockton's answer to Kearny's plea was to send Capt. Archibald Gillespie, who located Kearny on December 5 between Santa Maria and Santa Ysabel, not far from San Diego. He brought thirty-nine marines with supplies for Kearny's dragoons. Gillespie's scouts reported that Californios' mounted militia was camped at the Indian village of San Pasqual located between Kearny and San Diego, led by Gen. Andres Pico. Kearny and his aide, Capt. Abraham Johnson, saw an opportunity for an early morning charge by his dragoons to drive off the Californios' militia. Kearny looked at the attack as an opportunity to capture much-needed horses, for most of his dragoons were riding mules.

A late-night scouting trip failed to provide details about the strength of the Californios' army. Kearny's scouts were not clandestine. Their survey carelessly alerted the Mexicans to the presence of American troops. Kearny realized he had lost the advantage of surprise. He ordered his army to advance at midnight to face Pico's army nine miles away. Kearny was unable to keep his troops in a single cohesive unit. Instead, his forces became strung out as they advanced the nine miles toward their enemy.

Captain Johnson, leading the column of dragoons, was anxious to begin battle. Kearny gave Johnson an order to "trot" his column. Johnson heard it as an order to "charge," racing toward Pico's men. He left the protection of his army's cannons located at the end of the long line. A wide gap was created between Johnson and Kearny's main force. Johnson's ammunition was damp and wet, causing dragoon guns to fail when fired. Americans, unable to use their rifles, found themselves in range of militia muskets. Johnson was killed by a shot to his head; other officers were killed. Dragoons were at a serious disadvantage. Mules weakened by their cross-country jaunt faced Californios with fresh, battle-trained horses. Sabers were a poor choice to fight against lancers. The fight became a disaster for the Americans. Eighteen Americans lost their lives. Gillespie, Kearny, and sixteen others were wounded by lances; some would later die of their wounds. Most dragoons suffered from a lance piercing. Kearny, wounded, was forced to turn his command over to Capt. Henry Turner. Seeing a battle success, Pico withdrew his men to surrounding hills to survey the battle scene and plan his next moves. General Pico claimed a victory for his Californios. Kearny argued he won because Californios departed from the field of battle.

American soldiers buried their dead in a mass grave after dark. The next morning, Kearny resumed his march toward San Diego. Their path was shadowed by Pico's troops. The dragoons approached a hill where hidden Californios began firing. Americans returned fire and charged a fortified hill, dislodging the enemy, killing five. No American lives were lost. Pico's remaining militia retrieved their dead comrades, departing in great haste.

Kearny soon learned he was isolated, surrounded, and watched by Californios who were adding new men to their army each hour. Californios would soon outnumber Americans by a ratio of over two to one. All paths off Kearny's hill leading to San Diego were covered by Pico's militia. Food supplies were almost gone, mules needed to be slaughtered to feed the army, and grass on the hill for animals was nonexistent. The only water was found in mud-filled holes dug by his troops. Kearny, seeing the situation deteriorating, waited until after dark to send Alex Godey to get help from Stockton. The next night, Kearny—not knowing if Godey made it through the lines to San Diego—sent Carson, Beale, and an Indian scout to Stockton.

Stockton was surprised when Carson appeared. He was very upset with Kearny when he learned how he used Carson, forcing him to return to California instead of taking messages to the president in Washington. Kearny's interception of Carson created a major rift between Stockton and Kearny.

On December 10, Kearny decided he would need to leave his fortified hill (later known as Mule Hill) and fight his way to San Diego. He ordered all documents burned, not wanting them to fall into Californios' hands. He planned a dawn departure. Shortly after midnight, guards heard men approaching; 90 marines and 120 sailors armed for battle appeared, bringing the U.S. strength to over 300 men. The American display of military strength was too much for Andres Pico. Sunrise revealed that Pico's militia had melted into the countryside. Mule Hill is currently the site of San Diego Zoo's Safari Park.

Kearny's battle plans failed on several accounts. He began battle not knowing the size of enemy force. He ignored the condition of his men and failed to consider that wet powder would render the dragoon's rifles useless. Mules were no match against well-trained, healthy military horses. Kearny lacked control over subordinate officers, rendering his battle plan useless.

Stockton was anxious to retake Los Angeles. He departed from San Diego on December 28 with Kearny and a force of over 600 men, including six pieces of artillery. Kearny's contribution was 57 men. Kearny felt he should command the expedition, but Stockton—with a significantly larger number of troops, local knowledge of Los Angeles, and six cannons—prevailed as commander. Neither man outranked the other.

American scouts located Jose Maria Flores's troops on January 7, manning a bluff overlooking the San Gabriel River. Kearny wanted to soften the Californios' position with artillery fire. Stockton disagreed. The American troops formed a square and crossed the river early the next afternoon. Stockton brought up artillery, decimating Flores's cannons as they fired on Americans. A 300-man Californio militia was turned back by Americans, skillfully directing well-placed firepower from Stockton's cannons. The Californios' appetite for battle lasted one and a half hours before they departed. American losses were one man killed in action.

The U.S. troop resumed their march toward Los Angeles on January 9 through country filled with enemy soldiers. Californios' militia could be seen at the front and on their flanks of their column. Occasional spotty, unfriendly fire at passing Americans was returned with a vengeance. Flores waited until the Americans reached the plains of Mesa before he began battle. He initiated the fight with artillery, soon silenced by Stockton's six cannons. Skirmishes, advances, and charges by lancers were quickly turned back. The battle lasted two hours.

Large numbers of militia, seeing their plight, left the field, returning to the safety of their ranchos and families. Americans suffered three dead, fourteen wounded in two days of fighting. The enemy suffered a great many more casualties, yet the numbers were not known, for their dead and wounded were quickly removed from the battlefield and not reported. Los Angeles surrendered to Stockton and Kearny on January 10, 1847. Stockton immediately ordered the construction of a fort for protection of U.S. troops should hostilities resume at a future date.

Fremont resumed his march, leaving Santa Barbara on January 3. Alfred was rested and ready to fight after his holiday in a seaside town. He enjoyed being on the road, for the day was warm and springlike with no rain in sight. The battalion traveled, following the sea, at times riding on hard sand, with horses getting into the surf of belly height. The *Julia*, a U.S. Navy brig with eighteen guns, followed Fremont offshore, providing available cannon power, marines, and weapons if required to assist the battalion. The way to San Buenaventura Mission was quiet.

Alfred saw signs of Californios on a hill near the mission, a sizable enemy force, the first encountered since Fremont departed from San Juan Bautista. Fremont immediately called his men to arms. Cannons were rolled into position and began firing. Shortly, the Californios departed. The battalion secured the hill for the night.

On January 5, advance guard troops captured Jose de Arnaz at his home. He was taken to Fremont's headquarters. Lieutenant Colonel Fremont threatened to execute Arnaz if he would not deliver the mission's owner to the Americans. Arnaz replied that the owner was gone, joining the militia. The next day, Arnaz was taken home. He provided horses and cattle for the battalion and was released.

Fremont moved inland along the Santa Clara River. Sixty to seventy Californios continuously shadowed Fremont's troops but carefully stayed out of range of American rifles. Fremont made camp at a rancho owned by Carlos Carrillo, who was away, fighting with Flores. Alfred and the men feasted on Carrillo's plentiful hoard of food. On June 9, Capt. George Hamlyn rode into camp with messages from Stockton, telling him he and Kearny were on their way to Los Angeles. The battalion continued to follow El Camino Real toward Mission San Fernando.

Shortly before noon on January 11, Alfred entered the Pass of San Bernardo, anticipating armed resistance. The pass was empty. It was clear to Fremont that California rancheros wished to end hostilities. Camp was established at Mission San Fernando, the home of Gen. Andres Pico, commander of all Californio troops. Andres was camped with his troops a few miles away. Fremont sent a message with Don Pio de Jesus Pico to Gen. Andres Pico to discuss capitulation. The next morning, Fremont and Don Pio de Jesus Pico went to the camp of Gen. Andres Pico, where the details of a treaty of capitulation were settled. It had been suggested that Fremont's handling of Don Pio de Jesus Pico and his document of capitulation coupled with the overwhelming strength of the U.S. forces led Californios to seek peace with Americans.

On January 13, in an abode owned by Tomas Feliz near Cahuenga Pass, Gen. Andres Pico—cousin of Don Pio de Jesus Pico—signed a treaty of capitulation with Lt. Col. John Charles Fremont. The war in California ended. The Treaty of Guadalupe Hidalgo signed on February 2, 1848 formally completed the peace process, ending the war between Mexico and the United States.

Chapter 19

Alfred Leaves the Battalion

Alfred rode through heavy rain to the plaza of the Pueblo de Los Angeles, capital of Alta California, arriving on January 14, 1847. The pueblo was located on a rolling plain near the San Gabriel River twenty-five miles from the sea. As a provincial capital, there was not much to see, lacking the charm and beauty of eastern towns and state capitals in the United States. Its few streets were laid out in irregular patterns, showing a lack of planning. Houses were constructed of adobe-clay bricks containing one room with a clay floor. Inside were a table, a chair, and a bed. The roof was a composition of mud and straw covered with bituminous tar. Houses lacked glass windows. They had no lawns nor shade trees. The church, government house, and homes of a few important people had tile roofs. The residence of the church's priest was vacated when missions were closed and priests expelled. It was used as a school for a time. After the revolution of 1845, it was used as a jail. The government house was taken over by Commodore Stockton. He used it as a barracks for the military.

Alfred found that Los Angeles was much warmer in January in contrast to what he experienced in the Midwest. Tropical plants, fruit trees, and an abundance of vineyards thrived in the area. Food staples were plain: corn, beans, chili peppers, and beef. Breakfast was coffee and tortillas. Dinner was served at eleven in the morning. Stewed beef, frijoles, tortillas, and a local wine were the extent of a menu. Supper was the same menu. Alfred thought the locals, a population of about 1,500 people, were cordial but hesitant to make friends with Americans. Women were well mannered and polite. They had dark eyes and regular features but were not beautiful.

Stockton and Kearny both felt Fremont's terms of the capitulation were too lenient, especially for Andres Pico and Jose Maria Flores, leaders of the militia armies. Fremont sent William H. "Owl" Russell to military headquarters in Los Angeles with signed treaty documents. Kearny would not accept the documents, saying he was not the officer in charge, turning the documents over to Stockton, who signed them.

The battalion settled in camp after the letters of capitulation were signed, awaiting orders. Commodore Stockton, as commander in chief of all U.S. forces in California, appointed John Charles Fremont governor of California on January 16, following his intentions stated in a letter to Fremont on August 24, 1846. Kearny stated he would accept Fremont's appointment by Stockton, but he began a process that would result in Fremont's remaining in office for only fifty days.

While Governor Fremont tackled issues demanded by territorial leadership, Kearny challenged Stockton over the leadership of civil and military government in California. Stockton showed Kearny orders from the navy war department, issued before Kearny received his orders. Stockton threatened to contact the war department and have the president remove Kearny from California. Stockton told Kearny that California had been conquered long before Kearny had set a foot on California soil.

Fremont was loyal to Stockton. He could only answer to one superior officer. He felt Kearny and Stockton should work out their differences. Meanwhile, he would be responsible only to Stockton. This decision placed Fremont in a difficult position. He commanded a group of volunteers, the California Battalion, under navy commodore Robert F. Stockton, who appointed him governor, yet he remained a lieutenant colonel in the army and answerable to any superior-ranking army officer.

Kearny carried a personal dislike for Fremont, whom he considered a flamboyant, popular topographical engineer lacking a military education and career. Kearny instructed his adjutant, Lt. W. H. Emory, to send written instructions to Fremont ordering no changes in the battalion unless approved by Kearny. The effect of this letter was to strip the command of the California Battalion from Fremont. Kearny would henceforth give orders to Fremont as his superior army officer. Fremont wrote to Kearny reminding him that Stockton was the officer in charge of California. He would remain loyal to his commanding officer, Stockton. Kearny's reaction eventually led to charges against Fremont of defiance, lack of discipline, and failure to follow a superior officer's order. Kearny's position was acting under the president's orders; he would establish a military and civil government in California. He set a plan into motion to remove Fremont from the position of territorial governor.

Fremont tackled the challenges of governorship. The new American territory had no revenue. He needed funding to pay warrants issued for acquisition of horses and beef requisitioned by his California Battalion. The battalion had not received pay and were due back wages. Requests made to Kearny to obtain funds were ignored. Fremont was forced to pay some of the outstanding warrants from his own resources.

In late February, Stockton's command of the Pacific Squadron was replaced by Commodore William B. Shubrick. This change ended Fremont's support from the navy. Kearny sent a letter written by Capt. Henry Turner to Fremont from Monterey, where Kearny currently resided. It had five points. The California volunteers were to be mustered into the U.S. Army. Their new commander would be Lt. St. George Cooke, recently arrived in southern California with the Mormon Battalion. Gillespie, current commander of the California Battalion, would return to Washington for reassignment by the Marine Corps. Cooke would appoint an officer to collect all public records in San Diego. The quartermaster and paymaster were to report for duty to Kearny in Monterey. He did not mention that army general Winfield Scott had requested that the California Battalion be mustered into the U.S. Army, nor did he discuss a November 5, 1846, letter from the secretary of the navy to Kearny and Stockton (to be delivered by Shubrick) saying that the president wished civil and military command of California be vested in Brigadier General Kearny. Turner's letter was addressed to Lieutenant Colonel Fremont, commander of California Battalion. He demanded that Fremont meet in person and bring all records of the government to Kearny's office in Monterey. He signed the letter with "S. W. Kearny, Brig. Gen., Governor of California."

Fremont's reaction was swift. Four days and 420 miles later, Fremont presented himself to Kearny. Fremont expected to meet Kearny alone, but Kearny had other ideas, inviting Colonel Mason to join the meeting. Kearny asked Fremont if he agreed with the letter sent by Turner. He and Mason spent two days grilling Fremont.

Kearny's strength was his adeptness at political maneuvering. He had surrounded himself with officers who had spent decades in a military career. Most, like Kearny, were critical and contemptible of any officer who quickly had risen to senior officer status and had not attended a military academy. Among Kearny's allies were Commodore Shubrick; Captain Cooke; Col. Richard Mason, a fifty-year-old officer of the dragoons; and Lt. William Emery, a career officer who carried an intense dislike for Fremont. Shubrick, the new commander of the Pacific Squadron, held in great esteem traditional values of rank. He immediately sided with Kearny in the Fremont controversy.

Fremont lost his prime supporters, Gillespie and Stockton, who had been reassigned and were no longer in California. Navy and marine presence in the territory had been replaced by a recently arrived Mormon Battalion. Kearny would not negotiate with Fremont. Fremont had no options. He asked to resign his commission from the army. Kearny was not through with Fremont. He would not allow him to resign. His grand plan was to get Fremont back in the United States, strip him of his rank, and take him to Washington to be court-martialed. He ordered Fremont to return to Los Angeles, gather the California Battalion, and return to Monterey.

On April 15, 1847, Mason was in Los Angeles. He ordered Fremont and his battalion to meet him at Mission San Gabriel. Mason told the battalion that Fremont had been revived as their commander. The news did not set well with the men. They claimed a right to be discharged. Mason was offended by their attitude, discharging all of them at once. Kearny's answer to the resignations was to prohibit Fremont's California Battalion of volunteers from receiving pay for their service in California's war with Mexico. Topographical engineers and their supplies were to report to Kearny in Monterey. All other supplies and horses were to be turned over to Fremont for forwarding to the First Dragoons. Alfred and the other volunteers were told they no longer served the United States military.

Chapter 20

Alfred Returns East, 1847

Alfred returned north from Los Angeles with Fremont, nineteen topographical engineers, and several of his loyal volunteers to prepare for a return East to the United States. They camped on the Salinas River near Monterey. Kearny prohibited Fremont from remaining with his followers, insisting Fremont must stay alone in Monterey. He declined Fremont's request to travel to San Francisco to collect his scientific instruments and botanical and geological specimens from his third expedition. All requests Fremont made to the brigadier general were answered with a simple and firm reply, "no." Word was sent that Kearny would leave Monterey on May 31. He would lead an eastern expedition with sixty soldiers. Fremont was to follow Kearny with a second group of men.

The Salinas Valley was beautiful in the spring with sweeping green meadows and rapidly running rivers. The valley was alive with white, pink, and yellow spring wildflowers. Grazing elk were ever present. Grizzly bears fished for salmon along banks of rivers. Alfred would miss this country when he returned home to orderly farms covering flat Midwestern farmland.

Both groups crossed the Diablo Mountain Range at Pacheco Pass, which led them into the San Joaquin Valley. East of the valley rose imposing granite peaks of the Sierra Mountains covered with snow deposited by an extremely harsh winter. Water thundering over normally dry precipices created spectacular waterfalls at the end of boxed canyons facing the valley. Warm, cloudless June days melted snow at a rapid rate. Large volumes of water rushing down from mountains raced into normally placid rivers, leading to the valley's main waterway, the San Joaquin River. Excess volumes of water overflowed riverbanks, creating lakes that travelers needed to cross to reach Fort Sacramento.

Kearny and then Fremont came to the first lake. Alfred and several volunteers immediately began to construct bullboats, an Indian-designed craft used by fur trappers to carry pelts downriver to markets. Small trees, often willows, were cut, bent into an oval shape, tied together, stacked, and covered with animal hides to create a wooden tub, a waterworthy vessel. A bullboat held one man and a small amount of goods. It handled easily in placid waters but could be a challenge to its operator in choppy waters or rapidly running currents. No incidents nor problems were reported from Fremont's company with their bullboats.

Kearny's army had a different story to report. Inexperience and lack of familiarity in handling the boats plagued the army. Several incidents of capsized boats were reported among army officers. Major Swords and Colonel Cook swamped their boats, losing all their belongings except the clothes they were wearing. Another army boat swamped, losing spare horseshoes and nails Kearny needed for his eastern trip.

Sutter gave Kearny a royal welcome when he arrived at Fort Sacramento. He planned a special dinner for the army officers, ignoring the presence of Lieutenant Colonel Fremont and his associates. Alfred assisted Fremont in gathering horses for Walla Walla Indians camped near the fort. The chief threatened trouble if not paid by the United States for services his tribe provided to the California Battalion. Horses served as payments to the Indians.

Kearny's troops departed from Sutter's on the June 16, led by Le Gros Fallon, with Fremont following in a second group. Fremont suggested that Kearny should follow a shorter route around the Great Salt Lake to reach South Pass and the Sweetwater River. Kearny refused to consider this option, insisting on taking a longer route through Fort Hall. Alfred was happy to be leaving Sacramento Valley, rainy and wet with hordes of mosquitoes that were particularly bothersome. He was anxious to begin the long journey to reach eastern civilization after a four-year absence.

Fremont's caravan crossed foothills until they reached the Bear River. A steep trail led into mountains and Johnson's Ranch, the last outpost of civilization before the high Sierra Mountains. The route beyond Johnson's was challenging and treacherous, ascending over difficult-to-traverse mountain passes. The path was narrow, winding over ice-covered rocks. One misstep, and a traveler could fall hundreds of feet to a canyon floor hundreds of feet below the trail. Heavy snow, fifteen feet deep, accumulated during the prior winter faced Alfred and the army, slowing the pace of travel. It took three hard days of riding and extremely skilled horsemanship to reach the mountain summit. Nine miles below the summit (Donner Summit) on the eastern slope of the Sierra Nevada was Lake Truckee (Lake Donner). Fremont's men descended to a lake where they experienced a horror unreal and unimaginable to Alfred or any of the men traveling in the two groups.

Eighty-seven emigrants in the Donner-Reed party departed for California from Missouri in May of 1846. Advice received at Fort Bridger encouraged the emigrants to travel using the Hastings Cutoff, which would save a considerable number of miles in their western journey. They were told a new trial was mostly level; grass, water, and wood were plentiful except for one forty-mile stretch. Digger (Paiute) Indians would not be a problem. The party rested at Bridger for four days, making repairs and purchasing supplies before starting on the shorter new route to California. The Hastings route was not as described. It was rough, crooked, and unproven with narrow canyons through which the men had to hack and dig their way in instead of traveling on the well-used route from Fort Hall. Paths needed to be cut across the Wasatch Mountains. Wagons had to be floated downriver. The party skirted the south shore of the Great Salt Lake, traveling west through desert landscape, crossing a pass at Ruby Mountain to the south fork of the Humboldt River, which flowed into the main river. Their caravan became stretched out during the passage along the river.

Occupants were exhausted, hungry, and unable to keep up with the pace set by their leaders. Broken wagons carrying supplies for repairs were abandoned. Indians, present but not seen, communicated to one another by use of signal fires atop tall rock outcrops bordering the river. Paiute Indians used night stops to attack the Donner-Reed party. Oxen and cattle were shot with bows and arrows. One hundred animals were lost, creating severe food shortage. The desert between the Humboldt Sink and the Truckee River took six days to cross. Normally, it was traversed in three.

A much-delayed caravan reached Truckee Lake and River late in October. They were two months behind schedule for a safe crossing of the Sierra Nevada before snow blocked passes to the Sacramento Valley. Fierce early winter storms began plugging mountain passes in October. Emigrants were forced to establish camps on the Truckee in early November. Rough cabins with flat roofs or tarps covering lean-to structures became homes. Wood and water were abundant in the area, but little game was to be found. Food was almost gone. Faced with drastic decisions for survival, emigrants killed their remaining few head of cattle, their oxen, and finally their prized horses. When those supplies were exhausted, family dogs were sacrificed. Later, in desperation, oxskin rugs, harnesses, saddles, anything made of leather became part of a soup. Late in December, the unspeakable happened. Flesh from deceased members of the traveling party was cut from limbs and boiled in a stew.

Fremont and Kearny rode into the camps on July 22. They found caldrons filled with boiled body parts. Near the main cabins, mutilated bodies were discovered with tongues, hearts, livers, and limbs missing. Broken bones, skulls with tops sawed off, and skeletons picked clean by man or wildlife were encountered. Fremont ordered his men to dig a large pit for the internment of bodies and body parts. All remaining cabins and lean-tos were ordered torched. Fremont and Kearny's groups finished the Donner camp cleanup and resumed their journey east.

The Truckee River valley, Great Basin, and Humboldt River lay ahead. All was new territory for Alfred. The Great Basin is a desert landscape stretching from the Sierra Nevada to the Rocky Mountains. The first forty miles of the Great Basin was a hot, treeless desert stretching from the Truckee River to the Humboldt Sink, a dry lake bed absorbing water flowing from the Humboldt River. There was no trail, simply signs of travel left by emigrant wagons from previous years. Fallon and Fremont knew the way. The going was tough; horses sank into hot, dusty sand. Alfred thought the fine particles of sand were worse than what he had encountered on the Oregon Trail. Stops were made when dictated by Kearny. The two armies followed the Humboldt, a ribbon of water snaking through mountains for three hundred miles in a northeast direction across today's northern Nevada.

The river did not impress Alfred. It was narrower than the Erie Canal in most locations and half as deep. The country was rocky and barren except for plentiful greasewood and wild sage. An occasional mountain sheep could be seen on rocky outcrops high above the river. Lack of Indian presence was noted by Alfred. Puffs of smoke would appear at irregular times from signal fires Indians lit on top of distant ledges above the riverbed, announcing the presence of American travelers. Indians realized their bows and arrows were no match for armed American dragoons and left the soldiers alone. Two Delaware Indian scouts rode at the head of Fremont's column with Indian scalps tied to their saddles, warning Indians to stay away.

Alfred was comfortable on the trails. He studied weather patterns, identified edible plants, and avoided rattlesnakes, listening to advice and warnings provided by Fremont. He assisted in the selection of campsites and provided forage and water for animals. Placement of bushes, groves of trees, and rock formations were critical for defense against raiding Indians. Three guards were posted in two-hour shifts whenever the caravan stopped. Fires were out at eight at night; men rose at four in the morning. Men slept close to one another, each man sleeping behind a packsaddle that provided protection from Indian arrows. Arms were easy to reach so they quickly would blow apart any unwelcome intruders. A stop was made midday, allowing animals to rest, graze, and obtain water. During this stop, men enjoyed their major meal of the day. Whenever an opportunity presented itself, Alfred gathered a few men, leaving the caravan to bring back fresh elk, antelope, or other game, for the Fremont group carried few supplies of food.

Davenport was pleased when he reached the junction of the Raft and Snake Rivers. It was familiar country over which he had traveled in 1844, yet he found many changes. The route was scarred with ruts left by wheels of hundreds of wagons traveling to Oregon and California since he last passed this way. Broken wagons, wagon parts, and pieces of abandoned furniture were viewed along the trail. Bones of dead draft animals were visible. Sadly, the caravan passed an increasing number of graves and grave markers of deceased emigrants, a subtle reminder of disappointments faced by men, women, and children who never fulfilled dreams of a new life in the West. An estimated 4 percent death rate faced emigrants who used the trail for western emigration, mostly from disease and accidents. Less than 1 percent of reported deaths were the results of Indian attacks.

Big Sandy River was a stop where Kearny and Fremont had an opportunity to discuss California trail conditions with westbound emigrants. Kearny, cold and aloof, suggested that emigrants could visit him at his camp and receive trail updates. No visits to Kearny were reported. Fremont went directly to emigrant camps, counselling them on the dangers of a late passage over the Sierra Mountains, describing the horrific disaster faced by the Donner party. He urged all emigrants to hurry and cross the Sierras as quickly as possible to avoid dangers of being trapped by early winter storms.

Fort Laramie was full of westbound emigrants. A larger number of Indians than seen in 1844 camped outside the fort walls. Indians approached the Fremont caravan, wanting to trade, begging for whiskey. Alfred was happy the stop at the fort was short.

Beyond the fort, Kearny headed along the Platte River past familiar landmarks—Scotts Bluff, Chimney Rock, Courthouse Rock, and Ash Hollow—pushing hard toward Missouri. He passed a considerable number of emigrant wagon trains heading West. Peeking from inside white canvas-topped wagons were children fascinated with viewing long lines of army troops and frontiersmen marching east. Their mother held the reins of the family's draft animals while their father marched alongside the beasts with a long prod, encouraging his animal to keep up with the wagon train's pace. Days were hot and dusty on the trail.

The remnants of thousands of buffalo killed for sport, not consumed for meat, concerned Alfred. He passed miles of this carnage. Pawnee Indians, always a pest, planned to steal Fremont's spare horses after the eastbound travelers left the Platte River. Aggressive braves raced at Fremont's men. Alfred reported that a few well-placed shots halted this behavior. Fremont asked Kearny to take a direct route toward Westport, Kansas. Kearny refused, insisting on the longer way through Fort Leavenworth.

Two white block towers on a bluff high above the Missouri River came into sight on August 22, signaling arrival at Fort Leavenworth, located 1,905 from Fort Sacramento. Kearny immediately summoned Lieutenant Colonel Fremont in front of the fort commander who relieved Fremont from his command, ordering him to proceed to Washington to be court-martialed. All property owned by the government was to be turned over to the army. Fremont's men were not paid for their services. Kearny departed, taking the steamboat *Amelia* in a hurry to get to Washington, DC, and take his case against Fremont to President Polk.

Alfred traveled with Fremont to the Kansas Landing (Westport). John Charles Fremont's wife, Jessie, learning of his return, arrived early at Westport to join her husband for his trip to Saint Louis. Townspeople on the route downriver gathered to cheer Fremont at each stop made by the riverboat. Davenport said goodbye to the Fremont when they docked in

Saint Louis on August 28. John Charles asked Alfred to write letting him know if he would be interested in a future trip West.

A military court in Washington found Fremont guilty of insubordination, expelling him from the military. The decision was controversial, causing political dissention in the U.S. capitol. President Polk, recognizing Fremont's contributions to the development of the West and his role in securing California for the United States, released Fremont from arrest, reinstating his military rank on March 15, 1848. Fremont had enough of the military. He elected to remain a civilian.

Part III

Gold Rush, 1849–1861

Chapter 21

Alfred Joins the '49ers

In the middle of planting season in 1848, Alfred received word that Fremont would be starting his fourth expedition in the fall. Alfred planned to join Fremont in Saint Louis. He would leave Ohio after helping his brother Charles finish farmwork.

Alfred looked forward to seeing Kit Carson, Alex Godey, and Colonel Fremont, for these men taught him to be a frontiersman. Kit Carson, the best of the mountain men, taught him wilderness survival skills. He learned to identify and harvest edible plants when game was not available. Alex, whom Fremont admired as much as Carson, shared knowledge of the habits of wolves, bears, and other predator animals; he learned to differentiate between coyote and wolf sounds, important when traveling alone or with small groups. The men taught Alfred about Indians, recognizing Indian chatter when red men imitated birds and animals. Importantly, he was taught Indian tactics of an ambush, when he should fight, when to flee, and when to bluff and negotiate. By autumn, Alfred finished spending a year on family farms in Ohio. He was excited to be heading West to join Fremont for a new expedition.

Fremont's father-in-law, Missouri's senator Benton, foresaw the western expansion of the nation's railroads and persuaded local businessmen to fund a Fremont expedition to look for possible southern railroad routes to California. Fremont started his expedition upon departure from Bent's Fort. Investors paid for supplies, but there was no funding for wages. Explorers were promised a share of profits earned from a new western rail route. Fremont departed from Saint Louis on October 4 with twenty seasoned explorers and several greenhorns, hoping to discover a winter route over the Sierras between Walker Pass and Mono Lake. Weather delays kept Alfred from completing his Ohio work until the early October. He arrived in Saint Louis, learning he had missed Fremont by a few days. Heartbroken, he sadly returned home, hoping that he could join Fremont on a future expedition, promising to keep in touch with the explorer.

By year end, stories of tremendous gold discoveries in California were filling eastern newspapers. Alfred missed the excitement of the trail and all aspects of living in California. Men he knew were leaving farms, closing shops, selling businesses, leaving medical practices, wives, and children to go to California, where they hoped to find fame and make a fortune in newly discovered gold fields. Great romantic visions of the West were written by James Fenimore Cooper, Washington Irving, Edwin Bryant, Joseph E. Ware, and other authors. Discovery of gold ignited flames of desire for gold and western adventures. Fremont's early exploration routes and maps were copied, printed, and widely distributed to the American public. The country suffered an economic depression after the Mexican War. Thousands of army veterans were unemployed. Gold was an answer to these woes. A quest for gold reached hysterical levels in some quarters. The end of March 1849 saw men from small towns and cities all over the Midwest, forming companies traveling to California for gold.

Dr. Charles E. Boyle—a Columbus, Ohio, physician—joined the Columbus and California Industrial Association, departing in April, as did Amos Piatt Josselyn with ten men from Zanesville, Ohio. Alfred spent the winter of 1849 formulating plans for a spring return to California. He would travel by steamboat to Missouri, by horseback from Independence to Sacramento. His trip East in 1847 from Sacramento to Fort Leavenworth had taken seventy-two days. His goal was to better that record when returning to California.

Alfred first encountered gold seekers in Cincinnati. Steamboats were crowded beyond capacity. A long wait for passage was almost certain. Alfred's answer was to volunteer as a wood handler on the route from Cincinnati to Saint Louis, gaining him instant passage. Upon arrival in Saint Louis, he discovered crowds of people waiting for boats to take them to one of the many departures points up in Missouri. Another wooding job provided a quick way for Alfred to reach Westport.

Davenport's arrival in Westport, Missouri, was a shock. No longer a quiet trailhead town catering to travelers on the Santa Fe and Oregon Trails, the town was bursting with thousands of strangers on their way to California. Supplies needed for an overland trip were twice the cost he would have paid in the East. Hotel rooms were nonexistent. Men were sleeping in hallways, on floors of public rooms, on porches, or wherever they could find a space to drop. California-bound travelers were different from those he met in 1844, when rural farm families emigrated from the East, Middle West, and South, looking for better life and an opportunity to start anew in Oregon. Year 1849 travelers were mostly men from cities and towns. Many lacked the rudimentary skills and knowledge needed to live off the land; most did not know the difference between a cow and an ox. A strange mixture blended in Westport's streets, creating a carnival-like atmosphere.

Yankees, Southerners, Mexicans from Santa Fe, French Creole gamblers from New Orleans, a few Europeans, and Indians were trading and negotiating with vendors, hurrying to complete preparations and begin their journey to find gold. Men could be seen dressed for the trail, wearing all types of clothing from formal frock coats and top hats to wools shirts with homespun pants, wide-brimmed Mexican-style hats, or homemade mountain man attire. Every profession seemed to be represented—businessmen, doctors, preachers, lawyers, unskilled laborers—all hoping to strike it rich. Every day over five hundred wagons departed from Westport for California, their places filled by steamboats full of new arrivals. It had been estimated that 22,500 gold seekers arrived in California from Missouri in 1849.

New arrivals brought health concerns. Cholera descended on Missouri in epidemic proportions. It was prevalent in Saint Louis, on overcrowded steamboats, in Independence and Westport, and other departure points along the Missouri River. A few gold seekers became discouraged, suffered poor health, and returned East. A significant number died before reaching the West Coast. The greatest mortality was from cholera. Estimates suggested that over 2,000 died of the disease while on the trail. Most cholera deaths occurred before reaching the mountains west of Fort Laramie. Death from other diseases, drownings, and accidents, especially accidental discharge of firearms, took their toll. The deceased were buried in shallow graves along the trail, only to be dug up by wolves who feasted on flesh, leaving bones to bleach in the hot prairie sun. Death from Indian encounters was not a major factor.

Alfred avoided crowded Westport, camping on his own outside town. He selected two horses and a mule for the trail. Horses were easy to train, not so the mule. His mule was a stubborn young animal. Despite a tough training regimen, the mule kicked, bit, and attempted to strike its trainer with its front feet. Alfred's strength, determination, and stern hand soon won out. After three days, his mule was tame enough to accept a halter and backpack and be ready for the trail.

Alfred quickly gathered supplies for the long trip West. He carried dried and smoked food, an India rubber rain slicker, small water casks for desert country, extra and horseshoes, all necessary for the trail. Armament included a pair of Aston-Johnson percussion pistols, a 9.25-inch bowie sheath knife with a cross guard, and his trusty Hawken rifle. The rifle was a flintlock converted to a percussion load, firing a .50-caliber ball with an effective range of 400 yards. The best time to be on the trail was early in the morning when the sky first became light. Sight and sounds of the start of a fresh new day were an energizing tonic for Alfred.

April was wet, but flooding was not comparable with the challenges endured in 1844. The California-Oregon Trail was well marked by evidence of its use. A thirty-day period before Alfred's arrival saw fourteen days with varying amounts of rain. Hundreds of wagons ahead of Alfred scored the prairie with deep ruts carved into wet turf. Traveling by horseback had advantages. Alfred avoided muddy wagon tracks, bypassing slow oxen teams struggling in mud slowly plodding to reach hilltops. His third day found him climbing to the ridge of a moderate hill where he paused to get his bearings. Ahead was an incredible sight. Miles and miles of white canvas-topped wagons stretched West as far as he could see.

Western migration in 1849 began in early spring. An extremely cold winter slowed the growth of prairie grass needed to feed draft animals. Lack of fodder led to delays in western departure while scores of emigrants poured into Missouri, gathering at embarkation points. The result was unforeseen crowds putting pressure on an already thin natural resources when gold seekers hit the trail. If one started West too early, inadequate or shortages of grass growing along the trail stressed animals, causing many to die. Travelers starting late or delayed along the trail risked mountain passes closed by early winter storms, creating problems like those faced by the Donners in California in 1846.

Forty-niners were often organized companies like Ford or Gilliam in 1844. Unlike the earlier trips, if a wagon broke an axle, it would be abandoned, for stopping to make repairs would slow the progress in the race to reach California.

The Kansas River was always a difficult challenge to cross. French Canadian Papin brothers continued to operate their ferry on the river. Today the location is known as Topeka. Alfred came on long lines of wagons waiting to cross the river; some would need days to make a river crossing. Alfred left the trail, riding several miles upstream, crossing the river at a ford near Uniontown.

Pawnee Indians' hassling of emigrants in 1844 was not a problem. Continuous wars with the Sioux weakened their resolve to fight; more importantly, it was estimated that the tribe lost over 1,200 members to cholera epidemics. The tribe lost many to starvation during the exceptionally cold winter of 1848–49. A few young braves insistent on proving themselves to their companions attempted to steal horses, but most Indians approaching emigrants were simply begging for whiskey.

Fort Kearny, Grand Island—Nebraska's army post and way station erected as a stopping point on the California-Oregon Trail for emigrants— was crowded with travelers. Alfred noticed argonauts lightening loads, getting rid of excess food, heavy equipment, and tools they had purchased for California's gold fields. Heavily weighted wagons significantly slowed travel time. Vendors in Independence recommended a maximum weight of 2,500 pounds of freight per wagon. A maximum of 1,800 pounds was suggested at Fort Kearny. Davenport chose not to stop. The fort brought back memories of rude treatment that Fremont and his followers received from the army when stopping at the fort on their trip East in 1847.

Prairie sounds were constantly changing. Late one morning, a low rumble was heard along the trail. It was a familiar sound. Alfred asked a fellow traveler to take his extra horse and mule and follow him toward the noise, excited about what lay ahead. A full gallop brought him to a rise in the prairie where he dismounted and slowly crept to a crest of a hill. Beyond the hill, he saw hundreds of buffalo. Wind was blowing in his face; his scent had not been noticed by the animals. The herd was in rifle range. Slowly and quietly, Alfred carefully aimed at a buffalo and fired, dropping a large bull to the prairie. He was thrilled to have returned to a buffalo hunt. Fresh, tasty buffalo was a welcome addition to one's diet.

Alfred spent the balance of the day beside a campfire, preparing and drying meat to carry on his journey, sharing his harvest with other travelers. Nightly stops gave Alfred an opportunity to meet many gold seekers.

He heard universal complaints about dust, heat, and mosquitoes. Most travelers were friendly, offering to share their food with a lone traveler, which he augmented with fresh meat whenever possible. The Platte River section of the Oregon Trail was littered with buffalo bones, skulls, horns, and an ever-growing number of heavy items discarded by gold seekers. Beds, rocking chairs, dressers, and blanket chests were tossed by people wanting to lighten their loads before reaching the Rocky Mountains.

Prairie storms were nothing new for a seasoned traveler. Weather changed with little warning. Dark clouds rolling in from the west turned day into night, bringing gale force winds and sharp bolts of lightning accompanied by loud thunderclaps. Hail and blinding rain stopped everyone. Canvas tops were ripped off wagons; tents were collapsed and blown away. During one storm, two hundred head of panicked cattle, mules, and oxen stampeded from a loosely constructed corral. It took their owners two days to find and return most of their scattered animals.

Alfred had no reason to visit Fort Laramie. Travelers who stopped at the fort complained about its lack of supplies and high prices for few available items. He left behind the fort, following the North Platte River. One hundred fifty miles north of Fort Laramie, the Mormons established a ferry on the North Platte in 1847. Alfred arrived at the landing to see a long line of four hundred wagons waiting to take the ferry; more wagons were added to the queue every hour. The ferry could carry fifty wagons per day. The river, over 200 yards wide due to spring rains and melted mountain snow, was cold, running at a rapid pace. He crossed the North Platte using a new ferry not generally known to travelers.

Some '49ers not wanting to pay a toll attempted to cross the river on their own, resulting in the river claiming their lives. Drowning became a daily experience. Hundreds of animals were lost. The 50-mile trail from the North Platte to the Sweetwater—arid and dry and full of sagebrush, pools of alkaline water, and rattlesnakes—was filled with carcasses of oxen and cattle. Experienced travelers fed pork fat to cattle poisoned by alkaline-tainted water, which saved some animals. Unfortunately, many traveling in 1849 did not have a clue of how to care for cattle in such a harsh environment. Alfred's animals suffered from a lack of decent grass. He carried a limited amount of palatable water and dried grass needed for these conditions. He would not push them, often walking to ease their burden.

One hundred miles of the Sweetwater River provided an abundance of good water and lush grass. Beyond the river, Alfred climbed to the South

Pass, where he found tepees manned by fur traders and their Indian wives, headed by Louis Vasquez, part owner of Fort Bridger. Traders were selling buffalo robes, deerskin clothing, horses, and mules. They offered advice and guidance about three popular routes to California. One route was the Sublette Cutoff to Fort Hall. The second was a route to Fort Hall by way of Fort Bridger. The third was through Fort Bridger to the Great Salt Lake and West. Alfred chose to leave the original trail at Little Sandy River, where he would take the Sublette Cutoff to the Green River and Fort Hall. The cutoff, a 45-mile trek across the Green River Desert bypassed Fort Bridger, saving three days of travel.

He began late one afternoon, wishing to benefit from the coolness of night travel, stopping several times to feed, water, and rest his animals with supplies brought for the desert crossing. Sandy, ash-filled soil covered by six inches of dust made progress slow. Trail markers were not needed. One emigrant complained, "The stench of dead and decaying draft animals would take one all of the way to the Green River."

Sublette Cutoff abruptly ended at the Green River, with a long steep descent dropping to the water. Horses and draft animals, scenting water on their approach to the river, frequently became uncontrollable. Suffering from the effects of a hostile dry desert, they galloped down a steep incline to reach water, much to the detriment of riders or wagons they were pulling. With great difficulty, Alfred reined in his horse, controlled his animals, and brought them safely to river. Emigrants called the cutoff Journado, Spanish for "a day's journey without water." The Journado was busy; many '49ers took the cutoff. Alfred noted that large companies originally containing dozens of wagons had broken into small groups of four or five wagons. Estimates suggested that one-third of the California-bound emigrants in 1849 selected the cutoff.

Fort Hall, on the Snake River, was an easy trip after departing from Soda Springs (or Beer Springs). Alfred learned that many travelers, no matter the urgency to reach California, could not resist enjoying bubbly water from hot springs. The springs were located between the Green and Snake Rivers. Alfred stopped at Fort Hall to have his animals reshod. The fort was an important stopping place for travelers. Salmon, trout, fresh vegetables, and fruit from the fort's garden were available for purchase. Mormons maintained a large herd of cattle brought from Salt Lake City, offering cattle, meat, milk, butter, and cheese for sale.

Sixty miles south of Fort Hall at the Raft River, the path to California

Trail turned southwest. The river cut through a flat, dusty plain. Grass alongside the river was exceedingly thin due to overgrazing by '49ers' animals. Alfred passed wagons full of gold seekers. He carried enough food supplies to meet his needs and enough fodder to keep his animals from starving. Fishing in the Raft River provided 4-inch-long freshwater crawfish, which emigrants called "bush fish." Forced to find other sources of meat, '49ers dined on rabbits, rattlesnakes, marmots, prairie dogs, and ravens.

Cassia Creek joined the Raft River near the junction of Hudspeth's bypass and the California Trail. High snowcapped mountains rose south of the valley. West of the trail, white granite rock formations could be seen, later known as the City of Rocks. Highlighting the formation were individual rocks soaring skyward, reminiscent of Gothic church steeples. Near the steeples, the California Trail was joined by a trail from Salt Lake City. The location was 90 miles north of the Humboldt River. The river was renamed by Fremont in 1848 to honor German geographer Baron Alexander von Humboldt. It carried enough water to support grass for emigrants and their animals. Wagon trains spent three long weeks along the Humboldt. Alfred's trip was much quicker. The river was discovered by Hudson's Bay Company fur trapper Peter Skene Ogden in 1828. He named it Mary's River after his Indian wife. Gold seekers, despondent and tired of traveling, called it the "Humbug River."

Along the Humboldt lived Digger Indians, a name given to Paiute by emigrants. Paiute women spent summers gathering roots and seeds to store for survival during winter months when game was hard to locate. Indian women had not been able to gather seeds during in 1849 because '49er traffic decimated most of the vegetation along the river. Indians needed to find new sources of food for the upcoming winter. Paiute men enjoyed adding mule and ox meat to their diet. They were not afraid of the white man's weapons. An Indian could fire several arrows into an enemy in the time from when a gunshot was fired until reloading was complete. Digger men increased raids, seeking animals, targeting solo or small groups of travelers. During daylight, travelers were ambushed while passing groves of willow trees. Smaller parties faced Indian ambushes after dark. Alfred, aware of Indian threats, planned arrival at emigrant camps late in the day. He instructed travelers on the methods of protection from Indian attacks. Camp perimeters were established, animals corralled and secured, and guards posted. Success was noted, for no animal losses to Indians occurred at camps he visited.

Beyond the Humboldt Sink, Alfred recrossed his 1847 route through the Great Basin. The pathway was littered with broken wagons, discarded contents, and the remains of many draft animals, flesh rotting, bones bleaching in the sun. Crossing the desert was unpleasant and difficult. The river north from Truckee Lake (renamed Donner Lake) had to be crossed twenty-seven times before one turned away to begin climbing to reach the mountain summit. Treacherous narrow *S* curves, narrow ledges, and twenty-six broken, abandoned wagons were passed before Alfred reached the pass. The way down from the mountain pass seemed agonizingly long, for Alfred knew he soon would be in the Sacramento River valley.

Before reaching the valley, he entered a forest of stately tall pine trees following a stream, the upper reaches of the Bear River. Suddenly, sounds of the forest stopped. His horse slowed; its ears pointed up in an alert mode. The canopy above the trail was dark, with a limited amount of light filtering down to the trail. An unusual amount of brush grew on each side of the trail 60 yards ahead. Alfred halted; the location was perfect for an ambush. A tree-covered mountain rose on the right side of the trail; a sharp drop to a stream and another mountain was on the left. There was no alternative route, only the trail ahead.

He checked his pistols, making sure they were loaded and ready for use. He loosely held the horse rein in his left hand while securing his rifle ready to fire. His right hand was on the gun's trigger. Bushes on the right side of the trail began to quiver. Alfred brought his rifle to a shooting position. Out of the brush popped a large grizzly bear, followed by two cubs. The bruin paused, looking at her intruder; waited for her charges to cross the trail; and followed them into the stream, which they quickly scampered across before disappearing into the forest bordering the stream. Alfred enjoyed grizzly meat but was intent on reaching Sacramento with its ample food supplies. He saw no need to stop and hunt. Later in the day, he rode into Johnson's Ranch, the first outpost on the Bear River west of the Sierra Mountains.

California Gold Mining

Chapter 22

Sacramento

John A. Sutter smelled the sweet perfume of success. Sutter arrived in California in 1839. In 1841, after becoming a naturalized Mexican citizen, he received a land grant from Mexican governor Alvarado for 48,827 acres of land located at the confluence of the Sacramento and American Rivers. He immediately constructed a fort, naming it New Helvetia after his home country, Switzerland. The fort was strategically located for emigrants arriving from the East and travelers arriving from Oregon and the North.

Sutter's, in 1848, had become a center of commerce. It contained a flour mill, bakery, distillery, blacksmith, and carpenter shops. A 10-acre vegetable garden grew beneath fruit trees. Large herds of cattle and horses were raised near the fort. An embarcadero had been constructed on the Sacramento River to accommodate cargo ships from San Francisco. Tied to his pier was a twenty-ton sloop named *Amelia*. Mexicans and Hawaiians (Kanakas) were employed at the fort along with 350 California Nisenan and Miwok Indians.

Sutter continually sought new business opportunities. Emigrants arriving in California had a large appetite for rough-cut timber. In autumn 1847, he hired James Marshall to construct a sawmill on the south fork of the American River 50 miles east of his fort to supply lumber for his store. Early morning on January 24, 1848, Marshall was inspecting the millrace bringing water to his mill when he noticed a gold glint from a rock in the stream. Upon close inspection, he discovered several pieces of gold mixed with red dirt. Most pieces were small, the size of a head of a pin. Using a tin plate, Marshall washed more dirt until he obtained an ounce of gold.

The next day, he discovered more gold. Still not sure if it was real gold or pyrites (fool's gold), he decided to take three ounces to Sutter's to be analyzed. Sutter and Marshall tested the minerals and proved the find was indeed gold. News of the discovery spread slowly, for many doubted the news. On May 12, Sam Brennan, who ran Sutter's store, returned to San Francisco with bags of gold, announcing "the find" located on the American River. By the end of May, gold hysteria was raging in California.

San Francisco's newspaper the *Californian* was forced to suspend publication on May 29 because the printshop was empty. Employees fled; all sought gold in the Sierras. Sailing ship crews landing in San Francisco deserted their ships, leaving no one to unload cargo or man their ships. The harbor was soon filled with dozens of abandoned sailing vessels. New finds were announced weekly along the 200-mile-long stretch of western Sierra Nevada between Yuba River in the north and Mariposa in the south.

California's gold news was slow to be acted on in the East. The *New York Herald* first reported the discovery of gold in California on August 19. President Polk confirmed the discoveries on December 5. Reports from San Francisco stated that half the able-bodied men in San Francisco had gone to the mines, resulting in labor shortages. Stores and offices closed; businesses were shut.

Sutter was hit especially hard, losing his large force of laborers. His mills, forges, and tannery closed, lacking workers. Crops at his compound were untended and died. Sutter seemed unable to capitalize on changes to his business brought by the gold rush. He attempted to bring merchant partners into his business, but those efforts failed. Creditors began pursuing him. He lacked funds to repay large amounts of borrowed money. Before 1849 ended, he was forced to sell his fort. Alden Bayley purchased it for a mere $7,000.

Most of the early miners in the gold fields found success due to their small numbers. Overland emigration in 1848 was low. Four hundred emigrants were reported coming to the Sacramento Valley from Missouri. These numbers changed rapidly. The SS *California* sailed to San Francisco from New York, arriving on February 28, 1849, with the first load of '49ers. By the end of 1849, 697 ships brought over forty-one thousand gold seekers to California. Only seven hundred women were counted in this group.

Forty-two thousand came overland; seven thousand arrived from Mexico and Latin America.

Alfred rode out of Johnson's Ranch early in the day. It was his last stop in the mountains on the California Trail. He crossed several minor Sierra ridges before entering the Sacramento River valley. The trail was well marked due to numerous signs left by large numbers of people who had preceded him to Sacramento. He was traveling in the middle of the dry season. Foliage for his animals was gone near the trail, causing detours to find grass. Dust on the trail was as bad as any he encountered since leaving the Rocky Mountains.

Davenport was startled by the sight of Sacramento when he approached the settlement. No longer was it a sleepy frontier post. It had become a sprawling town with more people than Westport, Missouri. It was the strangest town he had ever seen. Buildings were small, constructed of four tree trunks pounded into the ground, creating a square or rectangle. Posts were connected by overhead sticks fastened to a ridgepole. A roof and sides were made of canvas. He found less than a dozen wood buildings that he doubted could survive a severe windstorm. Floors were nothing more than packed dirt. Stacked shipping boxes with their lids off contained merchandise available for sale. Packing boxes littered shops, making a business crowded, disorganized, and chaotic. Streets were filled with abandoned goods, empty shipping containers, rotting and moldy food, and garbage. Taverns, bars, and large gambling halls were overflowing with crowds of dirty, disheveled miners.

A quick check revealed that prices were as outrageous as the look of the stores, over ten times the rate Alfred paid in the East. A metal pan to use for washing dirt to recover gold cost $8.00 ($246.00 in 2017 dollars), a shovel cost $36.00 ($1,000.00), and cheap boots $6.00 a pair. Point-of-sale counters where business was transacted were primitive, constructed of planks of wood stretched between two packing crates. Proprietors used overturned empty barrels as chairs. Each counter had a scale used to weigh gold and gold dust. Currency was not seen. Transactions were paid with gold dust at a rate of $16.00 per ounce. Food was very expensive. Pork and flour sold by the barrel at a cost of $125.00. Cheese was $1.50 per pound, potatoes $1.25 a pound, rice $8.00 per pound. Eggs, brought from the valley, cost $1.00 each soon to cost $3.00. Alfred was advised by merchants to purchase what he needed in Sacramento for prices were much higher at mining towns. Needing a stopping place for the night, he began a search for a rooming house, finding only gambling saloons.

A walk to the riverfront led him to strange-looking structures. Stretching for a mile along the edge of the Sacramento River was a collection of all types of watercraft permanently tied to the river's edge. Boats varied from small skiffs, rowboats, and barges to large merchant sailing ships, all abandoned by their crews who had departed, racing to find gold in the Mother Lode. Enterprising businessmen took over the watercraft constructing stores, saloons, and rooming houses on decks and inside abandoned and wrecked vessels. Some of the "improvements" appeared to be well-built wood structures, yet due to a shortage of wood and a race to compete for newly found gold, stick and canvas structures were prevalent. Alfred inquired about a room to let for the night. None were available; he was told he could sleep on a rooming house floor for a fee of fifty cents. If he needed a blanket, he would have to pay an additional fifty cents.

The journey from Johnson's Ranch had taken two days. Alfred was hungry for a good meal. He located a boardinghouse serving dinner. A meal of boiled beef, bread, butter, and a glass of milk cost $5.00. He decided to dine from his own stores, spending fifteen cents ($4.25 today) for a cup of hot coffee. Shopkeepers, barmen, and barbers were friendly, helpful, full of advice, and offering a myriad of comments, instructions, and opinions about all sorts of topics.

Alfred questioned locals about the most promising areas to prospect for gold. He was told to try the northern Sierras, 90 miles north of Sacramento on the Feather River or 50 miles east on the south branch of the American River. Alfred felt no need to remain in Sacramento. He purchased food and a few supplies, riding into the Sierras near the location where some of the first gold was discovered. North of Sutter's on the American River, he came on a camp of men at Coloma, a transient town, where Marshall first found gold. Alfred stopped for the night. Excitement and expectations of the men in Coloma were at a remarkable fever pitch. They expected to be rich beyond their dreams and return home with their new wealth by Christmas. In the morning, Alfred continued along the American River, following its south branch toward the gold fields. He needed to find work, for his supply of money was dwindling, and California had become frightfully expensive.

Chapter 23

Hangtown

On July 4, 1848, John Bidwell—a former employee of Sutter's—made a strike on the middle fork of the Feather River, located about seventy-five miles north of Sacramento. The strike provided Bidwell with enough gold to build and furnish a three-story mansion and to provide an additional $100,000 ($2.5 million in today's dollars) for savings. The same summer, on a creek joining the south fork of the American River, a claim owned by a Capt. Charles Weber produced $17,000 worth of gold in one week ($2.5 million today). Nearby, another creek produced an abundance of gold mined from its ancient gravel bed, which Weber named Dry Diggings, later called Old Dry Diggings because other locations in the mother lode were known as Dry Diggings. Dry digging was a location where miners collected buckets of soil and gravel to take to a source of running water where the soil was washed. Washing removed gravel and dirt, leaving gold (if the miner was lucky).

Year 1848 saw little crime in the gold fields. People went about their businesses and lives, not troubling their neighbors. This soon changed. An influx of emigrants in 1849 brought men from different cultures and backgrounds, creating formidable challenges to the gold country. Thousands of men crowded into the foothills of the Sierra Nevada. Food and materials were in great demand and short supply, resulting in steep price increases. Mixed nationalities, different ethnic groups, and new and strange customs were sources of friction in gold fields.

Not all miners were honorable. Early in 1849, three men—known robbers—were apprehended in Old Dry Diggings and taken before a group of local citizens. California, a U.S. territory, had no local laws of governance nor law enforcement officers and jails. Citizens, acting as judge and jury, were presented with ample evidence of criminal activities of the three. The men were found guilty of all charges. A large group of townsfolk gathered at the scene. The "jury" asked bystanders for advice. Answers came quick and to the point. "Hang 'em." A giant white oak tree in the center of the town was chosen for the execution. Late in the day, three bodies were seen swinging from the tree, telling all who passed by that crime would not be tolerated in Old Dry Diggings. This was the first hanging in the gold country but not the last. Throughout the mother lode, word of the hangings spread; soon Old Dry Diggings was called "Hangtown."

Alfred continued along the river. He had been advised by merchants to stop in Hangtown, one of the best places to seek work in the area. It was a typical mining town built along one long street of a hollow next to a stream appropriately named Hangtown Creek. Steep hills bordered each side of the creek. Hills were clear-cut of trees and honeycombed with holes dug by miners. Significant amounts of gold had been recovered from the sites. Residue from mining remained abandoned along the stream, destroying a once beautiful area.

Gold strikes in Hangtown were extremely successful and continued to be profitable despite hundreds of miners who arrived in 1849. The town, like Sacramento, was full of tented businesses and few wooden buildings. Banks, barbershops, every type of business located in Sacramento could be found in Hangtown. Merchants sold all types of items—mining equipment and tools, clothing, weapons, food, and liquor. Luxury items including tins of sardines, preserved meats and vegetables, bottles of brandy and champagne were all sold at extraordinarily high prices. Boardinghouses served meals. A single place setting could be purchased for $5. The town's largest tents housed gambling establishments. Streets, dusty and rutted, were filled with discarded and broken items. Mines were located everywhere—in front of one house, in a privy, even in the floor of a local doctor's house.

Alfred spent Sunday seeking employment. One mining company was looking for a carpenter. Their claim was located about four miles out of town. The claim had good prospects. Pay was $12 to $20 a day. Alfred accepted the company's offer, working every day except Sunday. He sold his two horses, raising enough money to live on until he was again at work. He kept his mule to carry belongings and supplies.

Argonauts or gold seekers arriving in California in 1849 frequently organized as a company with a set of bylaws, stating duties of elected officers and directors. Penalties for noncompliance to company rules were listed. A separate section dealt with financial matters including the sharing of profits and losses. Companies ranged in size from a handful to over one hundred members. Shares in a company could be purchased for as little as $50 to over $2,000.

Gold in streams, creeks, and hills around Hangtown seemed to be found wherever one looked. Easy to find gold was discovered in 1848. By late summer 1849, most gold was recovered from gravel located on top of a bedrock. This type of gold recovery was called placer mining. *Placer* is a Spanish word alluding to a glacial deposit of sand and gravel. Panning was the simplest way to find gold. Gravel, containing gold, was scooped into a shallow pan, water added, and the pan swirled. Sand and gravel washed out; heavier gold remained in the bottom of the pan. Gold panning was slow, taking an experienced miner twelve working hours to wash fifty pans of gold.

A faster mining technique used a rocker. Miners removed gravel from a streambed, dumped it into a box with attached cradles, added water, and rocked the box, separating gold from sand and gravel. Gold was caught in riffles on the floor of the box; gravel and small rocks exited the lower end of the box. Sand was then removed and panned to capture small particles of gold and gold dust not remaining in riffles. Long Tom was a rocker with a ten- to twenty-foot trough needing three men to operate. It required a continuous source of running water supplied by ditches diverting water from a stream or creek. A sluice box was a very long extension of a Long Tom.

Alfred discovered that the trail to the mining camp was at best primitive. He climbed hills and crossed ravines, taking several hours to reach his destination, arriving just before the sun set. He was fortunate to find a space to sleep in a miner's cabin. The cabin, roughly built, was constructed with logs, stuffed with mud to keep out rain. The roof was made of pine boughs heaped on top of canvas. It had no windows. A primitive stone fireplace was located at one end of the cabin.

After a breakfast of coffee, beans, and salt pork, Alfred began work constructing a sluice box. Alfred selected a large pine tree that he harvested for his project. Wood was cut into lengths needed to construct a box, taken to the creek, and assembled. Building and maintaining wooden boxes, digging waterways, and searching for new sources to mine gold occupied Alfred until the first part of October. Sunday was an eagerly anticipated break away from six strenuous, backbreaking twelve-hour days.

Early Sunday morning, Hangtown's narrow street began to fill with men clamoring for a break from mining and an opportunity to purchase supplies for the upcoming week. Many diversions in Hangtown tempted miners to part with the past week's earnings. Gambling and drinking were favorite activities. Most of all, the men enjoyed sharing stories with fellow miners, comparing their gold findings for the past week. Others, missing the companionship of a lady, elected to visit one of the town's brothels.

Air in the narrow valley became stagnant, filled with dust from the trampling of dry streets, mixing the scent of horse and mule manure, tobacco smoke, and spent tobacco juice. Miners rarely took time to heat water for a bath while working the mines. Shaving was a bore; haircuts were infrequent, only enjoyed when finances permitted. Clothing rarely changed. Flannel shirts, heavy cloth pants filled with holes, shoes with toes flapping in the breeze, and a large Mexican sombrero was a miner's uniform.

Outside gambling halls, barkers climbed on empty shipping boxes, exclaiming how easily one could double his earnings playing twenty-one or other card games. Inside a gambling house, a miner was welcomed to a plush ostentatiously furnished "palace." Large mirrors, chandeliers, and oil paintings exuded a feeling of wealth and luxury, all created from the losses of luckless minors. Gamblers made more money on Sunday than the total income from the prior six days. Merchants filled their pockets on Sundays, for miners had money to spend. Gold bought luxury items, French wines, champagne, an expensive rifle, or a pair of matching pistols.

Jewish peddlers, speaking in broken English and Yiddish, gathered alongside the street in a small group, offering great deals and reduced prices for bright flannel shirts, shoes, jewelry knives, and pistols. A few miners attended the only church in Hangtown run by a Methodist minister. It was a small church, yet most Sundays, it was filled.

More and more '49ers came to Hangtown in the summer and autumn of 1849. Irish from New York and Boston, farmers from the Midwest, teachers, businessmen, lawyers, doctors, clergy, Northerners and Southerners, and people from every background came for gold. Riches eluded many. Backbreaking mining forced men not used to hard labor to seek less strenuous work. They could be found driving cattle or mules, cooking, working as store clerks, or doing other menial work, for they did not have the physical strength for mining. Alfred was tough and strong, well adapted for the rigors of mining.

Europeans came from England, France, and Germany. Men from Peru, Chile, and Mexico were the largest groups from south of the border. Wealthy Chinese from San Francisco brought shiploads of countrymen to work in the mines, paying $2 to $3 a day, much to the displeasure of locals. English convicts, escaped from Australia, boarded ships and found their way to California's gold fields.

Alfred needed Sunday to purchase a few essential items before returning to the claim. A wheelbarrow would replace buckets used to carry gravel to the claim's sluice box. Wheelbarrows and wagons were manufactured by a man named J. M. Studebaker, who, after the gold rush, moved his business to Indiana, where his descendants began manufacturing automobiles in 1902.

Most Sundays, Alfred stopped at a butcher shop owned by Philip Armour to purchase meat for camp. Armour made $8,000 in Hangtown. He returned East, where he started the Armour Meatpacking Company in Chicago. In the grocery store owned by Mark Hopkins, Alfred purchased flour, beans, coffee, and vegetables. Hopkins would move his business to Sacramento, where he met merchants Leland Stanford and Collis Huntington and banker Charles Crocker. The four established the Central Pacific Railroad, which owned and built the western end of the first transcontinental railroad. Midafternoon found miners hurrying to finish Sunday activities, soon scattering in all directions to return to mining claims.

One Sunday in 1849, a miner appeared at the El Dorado Hotel with a bag of gold. He asked for the most expensive item on the menu, for he had been living on canned beans for weeks. The hotel's chef replied, "We have three expensive items on our menu: eggs, because they must be carefully brought over rough roads from the coast; bacon, because it comes by ship from the Eastern United States; and fresh oysters, harvested from San Francisco Bay, brought on ice to our hotel."

"Scramble the eggs with oysters and toss in a bunch of bacon," replied the hungry miner. From that day forward, "Hangtown fry" has been a favorite menu item in the gold country.

Year 1850 found the temperance league and local churches beginning a movement to change the name of Hangtown. By 1854, the town was the center of commerce for the mother lode. It was California's third largest city behind San Francisco and Sacramento. Hangtown's name was changed when it was incorporated as Placerville in the same year. Year 1857 saw the county seat of El Dorado County transferred from Coloma to Placerville.

Gold mining had its share of excitement and disappointments. One day early in September, Alfred and his companions discovered $280 in gold from a placer where water had been recently diverted, exposing the river's gravel bed. The next day the placer yielded gold worth $390. Three weeks later, the gold was gone; no more was to be found. A seemingly rich source had played out. The men would need to move on, find another promising claim, and begin the recovery process, building boxes and diverting water. Their biggest challenge was competition. Nearby locations were filled with claims worked by the mass of humanity coming into the mother lode. Alfred would need to go deeper into the mountains, farther away from Hangtown and his source of supplies.

Chapter 24

San Francisco, Autumn 1849

California's seasonal rains began on October 8. Water levels in mountain streams became too high for Alfred and the men to work, causing the entire mining operation to halt. On a day when he saw a break in the clouds, Alfred headed into the mountains for game. With all gold production closed, the camp needed to return to land for a food source. He avoided trails frequented by miners, slowly climbing into high Sierra wilderness where deer had recently been seen.

Walking along the top of a mountain ridge, he heard a loud sound like a cannon shot coming from below. Mountaineering senses alerted, he carefully looked for signs of danger, moving toward the source of the sound. It did not take him long to discover a disaster in the making. Several miles above his camp, a large claim with a wooden dam was the source. Heavy rains flooding mountain streams emptied into the dam's collection basin and exceeded the holding strength of the dam. The noise was the structure's collapse, causing stored water to race through a newly created opening.

A gigantic wave was headed to his camp several miles downstream. Surging water soared ahead, uprooting trees, toppling boulders, destroying any man-made structure in its path. Alfred raced to warn his companions but could not outrun speeding water. He arrived minutes after a giant wave swept through his claim. Most of the mining operation was washed away, including the structures he had laboriously put together for the past several months. The camp cabin built on a hillside was flooded but still standing.

Alfred was concerned about the welfare of his companions. He learned that most were safe. They were in Hangtown. Two men who remained in camp would never again be seen.

Alfred realized winter rains would keep creek waters high. No more gold would be recovered until next year's dry season. His best option was to head to San Francisco, where he hoped to see his old friend and mentor John Charles Fremont and find employment. Fremont, before departing from Fort Sacramento in 1847, completed the purchase of 44,378 acres of a Mariposa land grant from Juan Bautista Alvarado, a former governor of Las Californias.

Traveling from camp to Hangtown was tough. Parts of the trail were knee deep in mud; some parts had been washed out, requiring detours. Rain made walking slippery and difficult. The route from Hangtown to Sacramento showed no improvement. Alfred received good news when he arrived in Sacramento—the steamboat *McKim* began sailing from Sacramento to San Francisco on October 26. She sailed every Wednesday and Friday. Cabin passage cost $30, deck was $20, and best of all, the trip took only seventeen hours. In 1846, the trip took two to three days.

New challenges faced Sacramento after Alfred left for San Francisco. The city filled with thousands of miners unable to work. Merchants extended credit to known customers whose claims flooded out, promising to repay the debt in the spring. Living conditions deteriorated. Miners were forced to endure mud, bad food, and undesirable sleeping places. Many developed poor health.

On January 10, 1850, the American and Sacramento Rivers crested, flooding the entire town. The City Hotel and other low-lying establishments were completely submerged, their contents destroyed. Merchants, places of business, rooming houses, gambling houses, and saloons all housed in tents were swept away by the flood's angry current. Boxes and barrels with supplies, food, and clothing stored in town and on the embarcadero were flooded, never to be seen again. Horses, mules, and cattle struggled to find dry land above the flooded rivers. Animals who failed in their struggle to reach safety perished. Their bloated carcasses were seen floating in the floodwaters ravishing the town.

Town residents used every available boat to assist stranded people but not without a cost. Boatmen charged $5 to $8 a person for transport to dry land. Boat rental was $15 per hour. A boat for sale, if one could be found, cost $1,000.

The *McKim* slowed as she approached San Francisco. Heavy fog typical of San Francisco was beginning to break up, revealing hundreds of abandoned ships, brigs, and barks in the cove at San Francisco, a sight shocking to Alfred. Hills near the cove had been leveled, dirt and sand used as a filler around ships beached, scuttled, and abandoned. Ship hulls were converted into a variety of businesses. Warehouses, boardinghouses, saloons, gambling houses, and other places of business sprouted on the top of old ships, filling demands for commercial space. During early gold rush years, over one hundred abandoned ships became the foundation of the city's business district. Lumber and laborers were hard to find, resulting in the use of tents for commercial businesses and lodging throughout the city. Two wharves, Broadway and Central, were extended past San Francisco's shallow cove into the bay to reach deeper water needed to accommodate the influx of ships bringing '49ers. It was estimated that more than 1,000 newcomers arrived by ship each week, including 250 women. Of the 41,000 gold seekers who came by sea to San Francisco in 1849, 25,000 remained at year-end; the rest headed to the mother lode (the Veta Madre).

Alfred sloshed up the muddy Clay Street, looking for Ridley's Billiard Room and Saloon, where he started his 1846 journey. J. H. Brown bought the bar from Ridley in September 1846, turning it into the Portsmouth House Hotel. Alfred found the building. It currently housed a store owned by two men from Baltimore, Johnson and Austin. The proprietors updated Alfred on recent events in San Francisco. They told him where Fremont was living.

Alfred was told to stay at a new boardinghouse, the Saint Francis Hotel. It was constructed of prefabricated wooden cottages bound together, stacked three floors high, much more pleasant than mud-floored, insect-filled, rat-infested boardinghouses located in tents throughout the city. Gambling was not permitted at the Saint Francis. A bathhouse and barbershops were located near the hotel. Storekeepers offered a warning. Avoid stopping at saloons on the waterfront. Unscrupulous ship officers would befriend an unsuspecting miner enjoying a beer and secretly lace his beer with opium. When he came to his senses, he would find himself at sea, forced into a ship's crew, having succumbed to the ancient practice of shanghaiing.

Unruly growth of population from less than 500 people in 1847 to over 25,000 in 1849 resulted in weak government, corrupt politicians, gambling, prostitution, and criminal activities for San Francisco. A gang of 60 thugs—all young men, reported to have emigrated from New York City slums—were located on Kearny Street. They were referred to as the Hounds, calling themselves Regulators. They disliked all people of Spanish or Mexican heritage and extorted money from businessmen for "protection." On Sundays and at night, they roamed the streets, creating fear in well-meaning citizens.

A group of 230 infuriated men banded together as policemen to arrest the Hounds and take them to justice. Twenty were apprehended and imprisoned on the USS *Warren*. A trial found the men guilty. They were sentenced to ten years in prison, hard labor, and large fines. Most punishments were not enforced, for there were no prisons in San Francisco. The *Warren* was running out of space to house criminals. A few Hounds who escaped capture fled to the mines. Discovered by miners whom they had assaulted in San Francisco, they were caught and immediately hanged.

Another group, the Sydney Ducks from Sydney, Great Britain's penal colony in Australia, were ex-convicts and criminals. Ducks operated gambling houses, boardinghouses, and brothels. Miners, sailors, and the uninformed were beaten and robbed when visiting a section of San Francisco controlled by Ducks known as the Barbary Coast. Ducks were blamed for setting six San Francisco fires from 1849 to 1851. Fires created diversions for criminals to rob empty businesses and homes whose owners were off premises, fighting fires to save the town from destruction. A citizen's vigilance committee was created in 1851 to administer justice to Ducks. Ninety-one Ducks were arrested, 4 were hanged by angry mobs, 14 were deported, and the remaining fled. After the purge, incidents of fires dropped in San Francisco.

Alfred needed to find work. Board was $3 a day; lodging was $30 a month. Emigrants and gold seekers of every class were looking for a way to pay for the necessities of life. People took whatever type of job they could find. Doctors and dentists from back East became barbers or shoeblacks; lawyers and clerks took jobs as waiters. Merchants became laborers; laborers became merchants. Emigrants ran rooming houses, gambling halls, and saloons. Speculation in real estate, foodstuffs, lumber, and dry goods was rampant. Disorder prevailed in all businesses.

The weekly influx of newcomers put pressure on all sectors of the economy. Hundreds of new shanties and tents were needed for housing. Fleas, lice, and insects plagued boardinghouses. Merchandise sold rapidly, quickly replaced by new items from arriving ships. Rain and mud made streets almost impassable, especially for mules and oxen that became swallowed up in quagmires of mud. Brushwood, tree limbs, discarded boxes, and barrels were thrown on streets to provide a temporary road surface until the next heavy storm destroyed these efforts.

San Francisco Post Office opened in 1849. Men lined up in pelting rainstorms, spending miserable nights to be first in line when windows opened, wanting to avoid long hours waiting in line for mail service. Wealthy people paid others to take their places in line. Some men joined a line forming at night with the intent to sell their place when the windows opened the next day. News at the postal window was distressing when a clerk announced, "There is no mail for you." Those who received mail were excited and ecstatic to hear from home.

Alfred posted a letter to his sister Harriet in Ohio, telling her about his adventures in California's gold fields. He was happy to be out of the mines. A haircut and shave made him feel normal. Clothing merchants offered decent shoes, a white shirt, and a new black suit. He inquired at several locations to see if a carpenter was needed. The results suggested that there were many unemployed carpenters in San Francisco. It was time to visit Fremont to see if he had any employment leads.

Fremont's Rancho Las Mariposas was rich with gold deposits. Mining on his Mariposas grant brought the Fremonts back to San Francisco in 1849; Jessie and her daughter came by ship through Panama. John Charles arrived by land from Monterey. Jessie suffered from a fever contracted in Panama. Winds and fog of San Francisco bothered her breathing, causing Fremont to move to the Monterey, where he established his headquarters. Jessie's health rapidly improved in Monterey's drier, warmer climate. John Charles took regular trips over the 140-mile route from Monterey to Rancho Las Mariposas. On his return, he carried hundred-pound bags of gold mined by his Sonoran workers, packed in buckskin bags, which he stored in his Monterey home.

Fremont needed to spend time in San Francisco. In autumn, he returned to San Francisco, bought a small prefabricated Chinese-made house, erecting it on land he owned. Living in the city gave him an opportunity to learn about California, its problems, and its politics. He was able to meet a variety of people, friends or acquaintances from previous stays in the territory. He frequently brought them to his home for French wines and a home-cooked meal prepared by his houseman and cook. It was during Fremont's return to San Francisco that Alfred met and dined with

John Charles at his house. Alfred related his disappointment in missing Fremont's last expedition. The men exchanged news and stories about the gold country. Fremont was helpful, directing Alfred to a company needing skilled carpenters.

In Monterey during September 1849, a constitutional convention created documents needed to establish California as a state. Documents were approved by the United States Congress, signed by Pres. Millard Fillmore. A year later, September 9, 1850, California became the thirty-first state. In December 1849, the California legislature elected Fremont and William M. Gwin as senators. The positions became effective when California joined the Union. Fremont departed from Monterey on New Year's night in 1850 for Washington by way of Panama to lobby for the acceptance of California as a new state.

Smoke bothered a lightly sleeping Alfred on the morning of December 24, 1849. It was more intense and acidic than the usual source from morning cooking fires. A curious Alfred rose, dressed, and headed outside. Alfred was startled and shocked. Several streets away an entire block of buildings facing Portsmouth Square was consumed by flames. A call for help brought hundreds of men to fight the conflagration. There were no fire engines or ladders available to aid in fighting fires. Wet blankets were placed on rooftops of nearby buildings to keep hot ash from burning through a roof. Alfred joined a team using battering rams to level buildings in the fire's path, creating a firebreak, an open space to stop the path of flames.

Many businesses were constructed of thin canvas-covered boards. They were quickly consumed by the fire and turned to ash. Blowing up buildings in front of the leading edge of a fire was the quickest way to clear a space or create a firebreak to slow or stop rapidly advancing flames. Restaurants and saloons gave away bottles of wine before their place of business was blown up. Sacks of gold were taken to the fireproof customhouse for safekeeping. Brigades of men lined up, throwing buckets of water and mud on structures threatened by flames.

By the end of the day, the first of six devastating fires suffered by San Francisco between December 1849 and May 1851 was stopped. A fire had been set at Dennison's Exchange, a saloon and gambling house located next to the Palace Hotel and the Bella Union, two large gambling establishments. Tom Bartell, proprietor of Dennison's, refused to serve whiskey to an out-of-luck laborer. It was the custom to provide a glass for one down on his luck, asking the person not to call again anytime soon. Bartell, short tempered, ignored the custom. He reacted to the laborer by grabbing a club, beating the man. The laborer swore he would get even with Bartell. Dennison's Exchange, Parker House, and Bella Union were obliterated in a $1 million fire started by the upset man.

Fremont and his family evacuated their house as the fire raced toward them, but fortunately, the fire was stopped, saving the house. In June the next year, Fremont's luck ran out, losing their house and belongings to a second major San Francisco fire. March of 1850 found many of the gambling establishments, boardinghouses, and stores destroyed by earlier fires reopen for business. New buildings were constructed of wood; canvas structures were gone from central San Francisco.

One draw of gambling houses was prostitutes. Saloon owners offered free rooms to a prostitute for a percentage of the $300–$500 earned in a night's work. Irene McCready, the first madam in San Francisco, opened her own bordello in a parlor house. It was not located in a gambling saloon. She was known for her elite clients—successful miners, senators, judges, a California governor, and the city's leading citizens. Her parlor house became an elite social club. San Francisco, with its "get rich and leave" attitude, lacked laws and moral foundations found in eastern cities. Its rapid population growth led to an "anything goes" cultural environment. Prostitutes were the city's fashion stars. The madam of a house was a businesswoman. She collected payment from the house's clients, managed social affairs, and paid bribes but was not a prostitute in her own house.

Early in 1850, a series of fire companies were created; Alfred volunteered his services at one of the companies. When not at a fire company, he would spend an evening visiting one of the city's newly opened theater companies. He was sorry to see the loss of the Jenny Lind Theater, which had been located on the second floor of the Parker House. The theater was known for its Shakespeare productions.

San Francisco's restaurant scene grew, with many restaurants serving large numbers of rooming house tenants. Tadich Grill offered coffee and fresh charcoaled fish on the Long Wharf, Boudin Bakery was credited with creating San Francisco's famous sourdough bread. Chinese restaurants identified by a triangular yellow flag displayed at the restaurants' entrance became popular. French restaurants and their wine cellars were always in demand.

New to the city were bookstores, enjoying brisk sales. The *Alta California* changed from a weekly to a daily newspaper. Newspapers served many interests. One was a French newspaper, *Le Californien*.

January 1850 was a busy month. Construction to replace burned structures and new housing for the continuous stream of newcomers gave Alfred all the work he could handle. He had one concern, when to head back to Hangtown. In the middle of January, San Francisco was rocked by an earthquake. Alfred never became used to a sudden trembling of the earth. He made plans for a return to gold mining.

Chapter 25

Gold Fields, 1850

May 1850 ended winter rains in the gold fields. Miners, discovering high water would prevent them from working claims until late June or early July, found themselves in Sacramento. Provisions in Sacramento had become plentiful in contrast to the shortages of 1849. Prices had eased but remained higher than charges for similar items purchased in San Francisco. There was no danger of starving in 1850.

Sacramento's tented businesses destroyed by January's floodwaters were being replaced. Strong, substantially built hotels, boardinghouses, and merchant stores built of bricks and wood were under construction. Houses painted white with green trim looked like they belonged in New England. Streets wide and straight and located parallel to the river were given numbers. Cross streets were identified by a letter. Carpenters were in demand, giving Alfred an opportunity to work until waters subsided, and he could return to the claim he had been working.

A large part of the city was devoted to gambling. Gamblers were entertained by musicians and served fine wines and imported liquors. Diners found tables covered with cloth, fine china, and crystal wineglasses. Stores offered an unending supply of goods for sale. Sam Brennan's Sacramento store could provide a new outfit of clothing for $100. Boots were an additional $40.

Sacramento city commissioners met early in January 1850 to arrange for the construction of a levee to keep floodwaters out of the city. A temporary embankment prevented the city from a new flood in the spring. Levee construction completed in October protected the city until floodwater breached it in December 1852.

As a result of mines being closed, men were idle and unemployed. Crime became a problem in the gold country. Alfred was a victim. He entrusted his mule to a friend for safekeeping during his absence. The mule was stolen. Alfred discovered the animal for sale at a livery in Sacramento. The livery owner refuted Alfred's claim of ownership. Alfred met with a citizen's committee to show he was the rightful owner. The mule had a torn right ear when purchased in Missouri. Alfred pointed to the ear, verifying his ownership. His animal was returned.

A bright June morning found Alfred and his trusty mule returning to Hangtown. He was passed by a variety of coaches, ranging from a simple rectangular box with four boards secured across its top, pulled by two teams of mules, to elegant horse-drawn, brightly painted stagecoaches. The final leg back to the mining camp was slow. The trail, normally a steep climb, was strewn with rocks and the remains of trees washed down the mountainside during heavy rains. Stops to clear a path were frequent and necessary. The path was a thin ribbon overlooking a deep gorge. He wondered what remained of his camp, which he had not seen since autumn. Nearing camp, he realized that water levels in the creek remained too high for reconstructing a dam, flues, and a Long Tom lost by flooding. He was encouraged to find men sawing trees and cutting lumber, ready for installation when water receded. He would join his associates preparing for lower water.

Alfred listened intently to stories describing sufferings endured in the winter by those who remained after the flood. Men living in tents fared the worst. Beds on hard ground frequently flooded. Tent inhabitants found it difficult to stay warm and dry; many became ill, and several died. Poor diets and poorer hygiene led to massive sickness. Friends in camp were excited to hear about San Francisco and receive Alfred's copies of newspapers. Lack of news was one of the most persistent complaints from miners. The *New York Herald* and the *Alta California* brought by Alfred made a man's day. Especially welcome was news about the East, politics, and what was happening in other parts of the gold country.

Davenport listened to the latest complaints. Masses of newcomers were arriving at gold fields. It was becoming impossible to locate unclaimed land when an existing claim paid out. An estimated 75,000 newcomers came to California in 1850 (including 3,700 women).

Sundays continued to be a miner's favorite day of the week. Washing and mending clothes, baking bread for the upcoming week, and repairing mining equipment were activities for those who remained in camp and did not journey to nearby mining towns for supplies. Some took the time to keep a diary or write letters for those at home. Sunday was a day for visitors at the claim. Most were newcomers looking for a place to stake a claim; others were gamblers. Gamblers could be found in every location. They sought the smallest mining location or settlements to set up monte tables or play twenty-one. They brought liquor and occasionally were accompanied by female companions to entertain men. Men would rather spend $5 on a game of monte rather than get a haircut, bathe, and shave for the same money.

Gold was mined wherever it was found. One man in a small mining town was digging and pulling weeds from a piece of ground where he planned to build a house. He noticed that the root of a weed sparkled in the sun. Close exanimation revealed that the sparkle was gold dust. A further look in the ground around where he found the plant produced more gold dust. Instead of a house, he had a gold strike.

A funeral was held for a miner who passed away. He was to be buried a couple of hundred yards beyond his claim. A preacher was called for the burial. This preacher liked to talk. A man standing in the rear of a crowd of mourners began fiddling the dirt with the toe of his shoe while waiting for a long-winded preacher to finish the service. He struck something with his shoe. It was a nugget of gold. The discovery stopped the service. It turned out to be a rich find; the deceased was interred at another location.

A great realization came to many miners working the mother lode. A year of gold mining often found men without riches, not what they had hoped for or expected when leaving eastern states. Some were substantially poorer. Life in the mines was hard, often spending sixteen-hour days in waist-high icy-cold water, only to have their worksite destroyed by unexpected floods. They missed family and the comfortable surroundings of home. Wives sent letters begging husbands to return home. A few discouraged men would join a group in early summer, heading home over the California-Oregon Trail to Saint Louis and points East.

Others would stay at placers in the summer and fall. If their luck did not change, they would spend their earnings on boat passage East by way of Panama. Ship captains in late 1850 began noticing more departures than arrivals at San Francisco. A lone miner could not leave his claim for a long period. During an absence of several days, a stranger might attempt to take over a man's claim.

Express companies assisted miners in communicating with the outside world. Alexander Todd had been noted as one of the first people to deliver mail to miners from mail distribution centers in San Francisco, Sacramento, Stockton, and Marysville. He charged $1.00 for delivering a letter, $2.50 for mailing a letter. Mail delivery became a growth business.

His express companies delivered merchandise and carried gold to banks in San Francisco. Todd packed gold dust in boxes, placing boxes in an empty barrel that had been used to carry butter. Gold-filled barrels were too heavy to carry. He would roll a barrel up a plank to a deck of a steamboat at a distribution center. Steamboats landed at the Central Wharf in San Francisco, where Todd delivered the contents to banks for safekeeping.

The growth of inexpensive and reliable U.S. mail delivery eliminated the need for many express companies. Most merged or were out of business by 1856. One well-known express company survivor was created by two men from Syracuse, New York, Henry Wells and William Fargo. Wells Fargo acquired many smaller companies in the early 1850s. They expanded throughout the gold country, establishing express stations at dozens of locations. This enabled them to land to a contract from the U.S. Postal Service to provide mail and package deliveries to the mining community.

Alfred turned in most nights shortly after sunset, a custom for the men at his claim. The claim was productive but not outstanding. The past month had been hot; the was soil dry. The ground of the camp was covered with decades worth of fallen pine needles, providing a springing feel and crunchy sound when walked on. Two miners were enjoying a nightcap at a small campfire when a puff of air arrived from across the main creek. Sparks were blown from the fire into the air, landing on dry pine needles. The miners grabbed buckets, racing to the creek, bringing water to extinguish the blaze. Their efforts were too little too late. Shouts for help brought Alfred and other miners to the scene. Despite heroic efforts, the men could not gain control of the fire. It quickly approached a camp cabin containing bedding, clothing, food supplies, and personal belongings. Alfred and his associates watched in horror as their belongings were turned into ashes.

The fire continued, climbing a mountain behind the camp, growing in strength and speed as it spread until it reached a large rock ledge and faltered due to lack of fresh fuel. Meanwhile, burning timbers filled the campsite with thick smoke. Alfred's group retreated to the creek to find clear fresh air. The next day, the men were off to Hangtown to replace items lost in the fire.

Rain began early in 1850 on September 8. Within a few days, Alfred realized the wet season had begun. The summer's mining season had been short, a little longer than sixty days. He made plans for his return to San Francisco, wanting to find work ahead of other carpenters who would be coming from the gold fields when their diggings were shut by rain. The quickest route was by steamboat from Sacramento.

Magnificent steamboats brought from the East after sailing around Cape Horn provided a comfortable means of travel from Sacramento to San Francisco. His early departure was fortunate. Sacramento suffered a cholera outbreak first noted on October 20. Cholera was quick in its arrival, killing over 1,000 people including 17 doctors. People fled from the city. Population numbers in Sacramento reported at the end of the first week of November suggested a decline of 20 percent from pre-epidemic levels. Two hundred fifty cases were reported in San Francisco; fortunately, the epidemic was over by Christmas.

Alfred found prices in San Francisco cheaper than when he left in the spring. Enormous sales and profits in 1849 brought greater supplies to California in 1850, more than the market could bear. This led to a fall in prices in 1850, extending into early 1851 for wholesalers, sellers of merchandise, and the real estate market. Many merchants became bankrupt. A financial panic ensued. Values of goods dropped daily. Shipments arrived at the Central Wharf, with sea captains discovering they were worth less than their cost. To get rid of merchandise, items needed to be sold as quickly as possible at whatever the market brought. This led to the development of large auction businesses. Sea captains hired auctioneers to quickly dispose of cargo before prices suffered another drop.

One menu item remained in short supply. Eggs selling for $1 each in 1849 rose to $3 in 1851, about $84 each in today's prices. There were few farms in the valley producing enough eggs for protein-hungry miners. Twenty-eight miles west of the Golden Gate, on barren, rocky, cold-wind-swept Farallon Islands, was the largest seabird rookery in the United States with plenty of eggs from a seabird, the common murre. Bigger than chicken eggs, they were difficult to gather and found on high rocky cliffs in extremely dangerous locations for eggs to be harvested. Poachers prevailed, providing fresh eggs for the mother lode. Early poachers arriving at the Farallons smashed existing eggs to ensure only fresh eggs would be available for their return visit. During the early 1850s, nearly a half million eggs were shipped each year to the gold country. The population of forty hundred thousand murres dropped to six thousand before the federal government declared commercial egging off limits in the Farallon Islands.

The unusual became the usual in San Francisco. One hundred forty-seven tons of ice from Boston, packed in sawdust, arrived at the wharf, selling for eighty cents a pound. Rats escaping from sailing ships had become a San Francisco problem. A shipload of cats arrived from Mexico; each cat sold for $8 to $12 as an answer to a growing rat menace. Shipowners, especially those sailing back East by way of South America, needed freight for their return voyage. Their answer was to fill a ship hold with guano (bird dung), which they sold in the East as fertilizer, reaping a handsome profit.

The new year, 1851, brought fewer emigrants to San Francisco; most were foreigners, many from China. Men and women arrived from France and Germany. A ship arrived from France in June with attractive young ladies. Saloon proprietors paid them a handsome wage of up to $7 a night to dance a waltz with a patron. After a dance, a girl would march her partner to a bar, where he would buy "drinks." During the dance, the couple would not speak, for a girl was instructed not to become familiar with her dance partner.

The city of San Francisco was forever changing. Entertainments abounded including New York and European theater, opera, concerts, circus, and other amusements. Elegant shops offered gold jewelry, watches, and diamond stickpins. Chinese curiosities, bronzes, ornaments, and shawls became popular items for travelers returning East. Alfred occasionally dined at one of the city's finer restaurants. One restaurant, found in the grandest hotel in the city, was located near the intersection of Clay and Montgomery Streets. In prior times, the building housing the hotel was a nine-hundred-ton, three-mast whaling ship that evolved into a San Francisco storehouse. After the fire of 1851, it became a luxury hotel. (During an excavation for the Mark Twain Plaza complex in 1978, six intact bottles of champagne were discovered in the remnants of its charred hull.)

Alfred visited newly opened markets. Purveyors offered fresh fruits, vegetables, fish, wild fowl, meat, and game—abundances created by gold.

Gone were the 1849 days of semistarvation where potatoes were a rarity. Reading a daily newspaper was one of his favorite activities. The city was a busy place; activities seemed better organized than during his previous visit.

Davenport made a critical decision during his San Francisco stay. It was time for him to leave his mining company and begin prospecting on his own. He wanted to own a dig. He never would become wealthy working for someone else. Alfred knew the risks, working for days with barely enough return to pay his expenses; but if he got lucky, he could have wealth beyond his wildest dreams. He would take his chances and return to Sacramento in the early spring. Before he departed, he met with his old friend Colonel Fremont, where he discussed his plans to strike out on his own. Fremont suggested that Alfred should consider southern mines, but Alfred felt northern mines offered the best opportunities.

Chapter 26

Northern Mines, 1851–1852

Changes in San Francisco during the fall of 1850 were impressive. Alfred noted a diversity of new restaurants. Dining American-style was unchanged. It continued to be a quick experience, with diners not engaging in conversation. Meals were diverse; food was high quality and well prepared but served and consumed in silence.

Foreigners brought new ideas of dining to their San Francisco communities. Frenchmen treated dinner as an event. Restaurants were decorated in the style of a Parisian café. Elaborately prepared food was served by elegantly dressed ladies while ample amounts of wine and conversation flowed. There was no hurry to complete a French meal, food was excellent and diverse, and every participant treated his meal as an event. German meals were hardy and not complete without beer and much conversation. Chinese ate using chopsticks; food was unlike anything Alfred was served at home. Dining at one of San Francisco's many restaurants and attending theater were Davenport's favorite leisure-time activities.

Cultural diversions on Sunday offered a special type of entertainment enjoyed by miners. After Sunday's church services at Mission Delores, crowds adjourned to a nearby arena to watch a bull and bear fight. The arena, a small enclosed circle, was called "the pit." Spectators, including women and children, watched activities from a raised platform surrounding the pit. A space between spectators and the pit allowed men on horseback to patrol the area, shooting any escaping bear or bull. Sunday's event began with cockfights and dogfights, generating interest and excitement leading to the main event. An eight-hundred-pound grizzly bear was chained to a post, faced by a Spanish fighting bull. Swiping, biting, and charging ensued; in most cases, the bear was the victor. Social pressure initiated by the *Daily Alta California* led to an 1852 ordinance from city council suppressing gambling and animal fights on Sunday. Enforcement of the ordinance was delayed until 1864.

Men crowded into saloons day and night. Patrons entering a bar would be directed to tables filled with soup, cold meats, cheese, and fish served at no charge. It was expected that men would buy a drink after enjoying free vittles. Bartenders created drinks to attract new clients. A favorite was a champagne cocktail created by adding bitters to a glass of champagne.

A bar patron's dress revealed his background. Englishmen were recognized by their shooting coats, New Englanders wore black dress coats with black pants, and men from New York, Charleston, and Paris supported the latest Paris fashions. Miners wore red or blue flannel shirts, wide-brimmed hats, and rough-looking pants.

San Francisco's development permitted Davenport an opportunity to supervise the construction of a variety of buildings new to the city. The latest answer to dreaded fires was an iron-framed building covered in corrugated metal painted brown. Alfred thought they were ugly. It turned out that iron-framed buildings contained enough combustible material, causing them to burn when located in the path of a roaring fire.

Like Sacramento, Alfred discovered small wooden cottages imported from New England looking like they belonged in a Maine fishing village. The Chinese offered premade houses shipped in pieces, assembled on-site, a quick answer to housing shortages. Fremont purchased a premade house after a fire destroyed his house in June of 1851. It was so small that he found himself sleeping in a carriage located next to his house.

In the autumn of 1850, six thousand square feet of extension was added to the Central Wharf, extending it into the bay at a cost of one million dollars. Funds were raised through sales of stock in a joint-stock company. Tolls were collected from wharf users. The wharf, known as "the pier," was a minicity featuring lately arrived merchandise sold in the pier's shops and stores.

Suddenly, spring of 1851 arrived; Alfred was anxious to return to the Sierra Mountains to try his luck at gold fields north of Sacramento. He planned to look for a claim on one of the northern branches of the American

River. Departure was from the pier. Alfred's tickets for Sacramento had previously cost $20 for deck passage. Competition by a large numbers of steamboat companies brought the fare down to $1. Fares did not remain low for long. Shipowners met and set rates of $5 from San Francisco to Sacramento and $8 from San Francisco to Stockton or Marysville.

Alfred boarded a steamboat, noting that the deck was carrying more foreign passengers than Americans. Huddling in one corner were Spaniards, recognized by wide sombreros and a blanket over one shoulder. Chinese crowded into another location wearing conical woven reed hats with a blue or purple silk shirt. Chinese did not carry suitcases; they suspended bundles of belongings and supplies from the ends of a bamboo pole balanced on the back of one's neck. Massive numbers of emigrants were arriving daily from all over the world, seeking riches from the mother lode.

Alfred was pleased to find more improvements in Sacramento after a six-month absence. The entire town had a new look. Wood buildings were fresh and clean. Stores offered an abundance of merchandise and mining equipment. Food was plentiful. New hotels and gambling establishments filled formerly empty spaces. Volunteer guards patrolled streets at night to deter organized bands of thieves. Merchandise was stored outside due to a lack of interior storage spaces. Streets, though organized into a grid, were still unpaved and unchanged, constructed from compacted red clay, creating red dust in dry season and a sea of mud during rainy season. Like San Francisco, abandoned ships were permanently moored to the city's levee used as storeships and houses.

Both cities had one problem in common. Abandoned ships were home to a large population of rats. Rats departed nests under a cover of darkness, attacking stored merchandise and food. It became a problem for local governments. Cats, rat-hunting dogs, and recurring floods helped control the rodent problem in Sacramento.

Roads leading from Sacramento were filled with long lines of wagons bringing merchandise, newly arrived miners, and men returning to claims, camps, and remote mining towns. Stagecoach companies raced along roads, hustling to bring express packages and mail from Sacramento to Hangtown, Auburn, Nevada City, and scores of other mining communities. Alfred stopped at a livery to retrieve his mule. He loaded equipment and supplies, heading north, following the American River, passing Rocklin and Secret Ravine, potential mining locations mentioned by his old friend from Bear Flag days, Jerome Davis. Near Spanish Bar, Alfred chose to follow the Middle Fork of the American River with hopes of locating a site for establishing a claim.

A narrow, steep rocky path threaded along the river, barely wide enough for Alfred and his mule. The river churned over rocks through narrow passages bordered by two-thousand-foot-high canyon walls. Steep mountains were covered with thick groves of pine trees clinging to their sides. Each bend of the river contained a gravel bar filled with miners digging for gold. Miners worked claims whose sizes measured from a ten-foot square to a forty-foot square. Claim sizes were proscribed by local miners' law. Every mining camp had a name. Some were reminiscent of places back East—Boston Bar, Hoosier Bar, and Kennebunk Bar. Others were whimsical—Poverty Bar, Drunkards Bar, Humbug Flats, or Jackass Gulch. Gravel bars along the Middle Fork of the American River were filled with miners. During the gold rush, over 10,000 miners worked the one-hundred-mile-long Middle Fork extending from Lake Tahoe to the river's mouth.

Alfred continued up the Middle Fork, stopping at Murderer's Bar. The bar received its name from miners who came on a camp littered with scalps, bodies, and bones. Miners were surprised to discover that gold had not been taken from the deceased, suggesting that carnage appeared to be caused by an Indian raid. Leader of the discovery called the place "Murderer's Bar," carving the name on the face of an alder tree. He was California explorer Capt. Zeke Merritt, Alfred's acquaintance from the Bear Flag Revolt. Zeke controlled a vacant claim that he offered to Alfred. Terms of the offer required Alfred to pay Zeke one-third of any gold he recovered from the claim, which Alfred accepted.

His first week at the claim produced much excitement. He netted $1,800 in gold after payments to Zeke. This was ten times the amount of his weekly earnings from the year before, confirming that he made a correct decision in choosing to mine on his own. Some claims on the American River were extremely challenging and dangerous because gold was located deep underground next to the bedrock. A shaft had to be dug to reach gold-bearing gravel. Miners using a small pick removed hard-packed clay to reach gravel located at the base of the hole. A partner on the surface operated a windlass to retrieve buckets of gravel he would wash to recover gold. Any disturbance at the camp would be heard by miners working inside a hole, causing them to pop out of the shaft like a coyote popping out of its hole. The holes came to be called "coyote holes," the mining known as "coyote mining."

Expenses were high, supplies had to be carried to remote sites by pack animals, and trails to claims were not suitable for wagons. Alfred spent most Sundays riding his mule to Greenwood, the closest town, for mail and supplies. Greenwood was a thriving community serving several mining camps with fourteen stores and several hotels, restaurants, and gambling halls. A blacksmith was available to shoe his mule and a brewery to quench his thirst. A prominent feature of the town was a large hanging tree, a reminder that lawlessness would not be tolerated in the area.

Murderer's Bar experienced a catastrophe in the fall of 1850 before Alfred's arrival. During the summer, Zeke gathered miners from his bar along with men from Sailor's Claim, Bruckner's Bar, New York Bar, and Vermont Bar to build a giant flume to enhance production efforts. Men toiled under difficult conditions, working in icy-cold water, struggling to remove rocks and boulders, clearing space for the project. Completion was on a Saturday in September after months of hard work. It would be fully operational on Monday morning. Sunday morning found two eager miners working the new fume, a masterpiece in mining construction. Prospects for riches looked excellent; the two men recovered nine pounds of gold that day. In the evening, rain began. The next day, work was impossible due to rising water. Rain continued for a week, water in the river rose, and flooding increased. The fume could not survive raging river currents. It broke away from its foundation, floating downstream, where it was smashed to pieces, crashing into boulders on the river's edge.

Alfred's mining experiences were varied. Looking back at the end of the summer, he realized his work had produced mixed results. Some weeks, his findings were excellent; other weeks, it slowed, not generating enough income to cover expenses. He discovered gold but never got rich. Seasonal rains were lighter than normal, permitting Alfred to work his claim through much of the winter.

Gold mining had become addictive. He always was hoping for a "big discovery." When barely covering costs, he thought he was better off working in mines than working on a farm or as a carpenter. "Tomorrow" might be his lucky day to discover a major vein of gold. Alfred was not like impatient young miners who, when seeing diminishing results from their efforts, would abandon their claim and move on to another prospect. Sometimes abandoned properties proved rich with hard-to-find gold for those who reworked an abandoned site. Alfred stayed with a claim until all signs of gold were gone. Mining had become part of Alfred's life and personality. He enjoyed California, the variety of people, especially visits to San Francisco, a city unlike any other in the country. He thrived on hard work and was able to make the most of life's challenges.

Alfred's camp contained about 250 men. Sun-bleached canvas tents were called home for Americans from various backgrounds. A large number hailed from locations east of the Mississippi River. They had attended school and learned a trade. In the mixture were businessmen, a doctor, several lawyers, farmers, tradesmen, and a couple of preachers. Their stay was temporary; they expected to get rich and return home.

Mining camps established their own laws, electing a sheriff and a judge to enforce the camp rules and regulations. Civil responsibilities were provided on a part-time and as-needed basis. Laws were few and simple, all set by a miner's committee. Camp meetings were held on Sunday afternoon. A chairman was chosen to lead discussions about administrative matters, establishing or amending rules and regulations. Votes on critical matters were taken. Results were recorded by a secretary; committee actions became law of the camp. A copy of new or revised rules and laws was maintained in the county recorder's office. When a chairman adjourned camp meetings, formalities of the meeting ceased. Legislators moved to an establishment where a round of cocktails were provided to all constituents.

A committee of miners investigated and ruled on all disputes. Most arguments were about claim sizes and locations. A jury of 12 men were selected for more serious crimes. Stealing called for a jury trial. Thief of miner's tools was punished by whipping. Stealing gold was another matter. A first offender might receive a serious whipping and banishment from camp, only if outright theft was not proven or the accused was well liked and had no prior problems with the law. Mining laws provided no second chances. A miner who previously appeared before a court for stealing gold or was suspected of murder was hanged, usually performed within an hour after conviction. A felon's body would swing on a rope until taken down at sunset as a reminder to all of the cost of crime. Miner's lynch law provided for no appeals nor delays. Fear of punishment proved to be excellent crime deterrent in the gold country.

On July 4, 1851, at Downieville, California, an event occurred, starting a new phase of California mining country history. A day of hard drinking found several men drunk. Joe Cannon and his companions wanted a woman. The men entered the home of a Mexican dance hall girl, Juanita Segovia, demanding sex. She drove the group off, but Cannon, a strong, muscular Scotsman, returned the next morning to finish what he failed the previous night. Juanita wanted nothing to do with Cannon. She hid a large bowie knife in her blouse, stabbing Cannon when he assaulted her; Juanita struck one blow, which proved to be fatal. Word spread about the stabbing. Juanita sought refuge in a gambling house, but an angry group of miners threatened to tear down the establishment if the owner did not release the woman. A trial commenced. A San Francisco lawyer climbed atop a barrel, pleading for her release. The barrel was kicked from under him; he was escorted out of town. Downieville's quickly assembled a jury produced a guilty verdict, ordering death by hanging. A scaffold was built on a bridge over the Yuba River. Juanita had nothing to say, only uttering, "Adios, senores," before becoming the first woman executed for murder during the gold rush.

Miners were diligent workers. They spent hard, painstaking long hours working claims six days a week. Time not spent in the quest of gold was infrequent, except on two occasions, Christmas and July 4. Christmas celebrations began after work on Christmas Eve with a grand celebration hosted by camp leaders. A large tent was decorated with bright red calico fabric. Discarded wine bottles were used as bases for dozens of candles. Jugs of brandy and bottles of champagne provided all the refreshment a miner might desire. Fried oysters, fresh beef, fried salmon, minced pie, potatoes, onions, and brandied fruit were on the dinner menu. Toasting and speeches abounded as alcohol flowed. Men began to sing, a fiddle was played, some began to dance. Revelry became drunkenness; a few sobered up late night after being thrown in the river.

July 4 celebrations started with a meeting called by camp leaders. It was held under a large pine tree under an American flag. One camp leader was selected to read a version of the Declaration of Independence. Cheering, shouting, and firing of guns highlighted talks given by political party leaders, both Democrats and Whigs. Much alcohol was consumed; little mining was accomplished during the day.

Year 1852 saw changes in the mining country. Two conditions persisted. Much of the easy-to-find gold found in placer mines was depleted. Winter had been warmer than most years, rain lighter than normal; snowpack was small in the Sierras. Midsummer found many creeks and streams flowing into the Middle Fork dry. Lack of water shut down placer mining. Gravel could not be washed, halting gold recovery.

A late August visit to Greenwood revealed Alfred's concerns about the future of gold on the American River. Green Valley creeks were dry. Cabins in the valley's hillsides were vacant, their occupants gone. The town of Greenwood was almost empty. Alfred was still finding enough gold to cover expenses, but it took more work and longer hours to maintain his level of income. He would remain on the Middle Fork for another month and return to San Francisco. He planned to find carpentry work and return to gold mining in the spring of 1853. Alfred was interested in learning about a new method to extract and recover gold, hydraulic mining. He planned to meet with Senator Fremont to learn about this process.

Chapter 27

Northern Mother Lode in 1853

Winter's torrential rains and blinding snowstorms kept miners from working claims; they needed activities to fill their days. Washing and mending clothes, sharpening knives, oiling guns, repairing tools, and reading a very limited selection of camp books and old newspapers helped keep men busy; but when out of the mines, men were bored and restless. Alfred stayed at Murderer's Bar for the winter. He joined fellow miners playing backgammon, euchre, or other card games. Drinking and games of chance at saloons were of no great interest to Alfred, for many a miner lost his shirt on a rainy day. Hunting made no sense during rain or snowstorms. Sunday trips to Greenwood Valley became a highlight of the week.

Year 1853's summer season had just begun when miners began to arrive at Murderer's Bar from Hangtown and other locations, complaining their claims were "worked out." A "lucky" day, they complained, was finding $3 to $5 worth of gold dust. They heard that the Middle Fork (of the American River) still had good diggings.

Food at Murderer's Bar was served in a large tent. Near the tent's entrance, a table was stocked with cheap liquor, cigars, and chewing tobacco. Meals were a social event. A horn sounded, announcing meals. Its blast was heard at breakfast, at the opening of the liquor tent one hour before noon's dinner, and at opening one hour before evening supper. Alfred did not care for a rigid dining schedule. If he was working a gold strike, stopping for a meal at an appointed time was not on his agenda.

Changes in the gold country concerned Alfred. Population exploded with thousands of newcomers. New towns brought new amenities and fresh problems. Roads suitable for coaches replaced foot trails. Placer claims were crowded and less productive. Davenport was not getting rich in 1853. Only a very few lucky miners boasted riches.

Businesses serving miners, owners of boardinghouses and hotels, made more money than most miners. Two storekeepers, Cromwell from Michigan and Moss from Missouri, did a brisk with miners from Murderer's Bar. Careful purchasing and stocking of stores gave them excellent profits. Profits could turn quickly, subject to changes beyond a merchant's control. An oversupply or cheaper prices from competitors could drop prices below a merchant's cost. If miners were unable to find gold, they vanished, causing businesses to shut for lack of customers. It appeared that merchants in mining communities seemed to take on more risks than miners. They had plenty of opportunities to lose money through poor business decisions or through conditions out of their control, such as disastrous fires or floods.

One profitable venture near Murderer's Bar intrigued Alfred. A ferry crossing the American River's Middle Fork connected a road from Georgetown to Kelly's Bar, Giant's Gap, Humbug Bar, and other mining camps located along the North Fork of the American River. The ferry was reported to have generated $60,000 in collected tolls during a recent twelve-month period. Davenport needed to find a better way to make money. He wanted to remain in gold fields. New techniques were being developed for difficult-to-recover gold, though these systems required large capital expenditures. The next winter provided an opportunity for Alfred to study and learn about alternatives to placer mining.

Alfred caught an evening boat from Sacramento in early October. He chose to travel cabin class to avoid standing in the rain while crossing the bay. He would use the trip to plan his winter work in San Francisco. One part of his daily routine would change. Meals served at Murderer's Bar were horrible, consisting of the same food day after day: boiled salted ham, beans, potatoes, and onions. He was looking forward to restaurants with diverse menus. Fresh meat, fish, vegetables and fruit, sweets, and beverages were served in San Francisco's many eating establishments. He longed to buy books, read current newspapers, and visit the theater.

Alfred landed in San Francisco with a smile on his face. He felt comfortable in the city, enjoying all aspects of its diversities with new opportunities and its ever-changing looks and atmosphere. The rough side of the city—drinking, gambling, and prostitution—did not bother Alfred; he realized they were the cost of rapid growth caused by the quest for gold. He would miss every aspect of his San Francisco experience if he returned to his small-town roots.

Men in San Francisco had a cavalier attitude about money. A man would spend more than he earned and had little fear of the future, knowing he could always find work and make a living. If he got into a financial bind, a request for aid from an acquaintance would be made, knowing he would repay his debts. It was not unusual for a man to climb out of poverty, only to sink again into its abyss. Wages were high, just like business profits, the cost of money, and the level of intelligence. Luxuries found in most American cities were commonplace in San Francisco. Wealth and status were newly created, unlike American societies of "old money" in the East.

An omnibus located on Mission Street, one block south of Market, took Alfred and seventeen passengers in an oversize horse-drawn coach to Mission Dolores for ten cents. It stopped near a familiar boardinghouse. Market Street was under construction; walking was impossible. Large steam shovels known as paddy shovels, so called because they replaced Irish "paddy" laborers, were removing sixty-foot sand dunes filling low, wet locations along the street. Sand and mud not used in street construction was taken to the waterfront, filling marsh and mudflats at the city's water edge.

Many new faces were now in the city. Large numbers of emigrants hailed from Europe, especially from France. They lived in their own community or "town" within San Francisco. French people dominated several trades: cooks, wine importers, hairdressers, professional gamblers, and bootblacks. Several important street intersections had rows of chairs where patrons with muddy shoes had them cleaned and polished by a Frenchman for twenty-five cents. About half the population from France were women, responsible for establishing leading fashion styles during the early 1850s. French people were well liked because of their polite manners and the ease with which they would engage in conversation. They were admired for their role in developing arts in San Francisco. Architecture, design, theater, opera, plays, and vaudeville were led by French-speaking people. In 1851, Frenchmen established a benevolent society. It became the country's first mutual insurance company.

Chinese immigrants were not liked in San Francisco nor in the gold fields. Ten thousand men and seven women landed in California from

China by the beginning of May 1852. Prejudice against Chinese was high. They were referred to as "celestials." America was a refuge for all nationalities, but American miners considered Chinese miners as a subhuman group stealing gold for their mandarin rulers in China. A Chinese miner or "coolie" was reputed to have been paid slave wages of $4 to $5 a month. Chinese purchased nothing from American merchants for consumption in gold fields. Equipment, clothing, and food were brought from their homeland.

Prevailing attitudes led to the development of an isolated Chinese community in San Francisco. Stores in Chinatown displayed items from China: dried fish, dried ducks, hams, tea and spices, copper pots and pans, paper fans and clothing, everything one in their community wanted or needed. Members of the Chinese community built theaters and temples. They were great gamblers; betting was a favorite pastime. Gambling games were played with small copper coins having a square hole in the center. When money was gone, watches, rings, and anything of value were waged.

Despite narrow-minded attitudes toward the Chinese, Americans were curious and intrigued by them. Men returning to eastern cities frequently stopped in Chinatown to bring shawls, wood boxes, vases, and other curiosities back to their friends and loved ones at home. Chinese laundries were thought to steal jobs from capable American men and women. Chinese, from their own perspective, felt white men were lazy. It was said, "A Chinaman will work day and night if the moon is shining and if work is profitable." Chinese landlords in San Francisco rented rooms from white property owners, charging tenants twice the rate. A Chinese landlord squeezed more men into a living space than Americans would tolerate, all to enhance profits. California governor Bigler, under pressure from miners, introduced legislation to limit Chinese immigration. The legislature failed to act on the proposal; the issue died. Chinese were good citizens. They paid foreign mining taxes to California and kept to themselves.

Exchanges, as gambling halls were called, remained the social center of life in the fall of 1853. Staggering sums were spent on new halls, creating extravagantly decorated establishments to attract new clients. All types of liquors were served. Green-felt-covered tables headed by card dealers were piled high with bags of gold dust. Music played by string instruments added to an establishment's excitement and noise. Vices, follies, and the art of living in ways shunned in the East were accepted by all in San Francisco despite the emergence of three new Christian churches in the city. Prostitutes employed at exchanges, available for all, were noted for entertaining the most prominent men in town. In time, madams developed elite private clubs known as parlor houses, earning the prostitute a privileged place in San Francisco's society.

Good news reached Alfred when he began his job search. A construction company he knew was looking for a supervisor. He was offered the position, which he happily accepted, agreeing to stay with the company for six months.

Fremont finished his fifth expedition in March of 1854. Sierra mountain passes were blocked with deep snows. He was forced to travel south, crossing mountains near Walker Pass. Fremont did not return to San Francisco until April 16. Alfred, upon hearing that John Charles had returned, arranged a meeting with his old friend. He shared his recent experiences and observations of northern mines, discussing what he had learned about hydraulic mining. Fremont explained that placer mining was no longer profitable in California's southern mines. He told Davenport that large profits could be made mining quartz-bearing gold. High capital costs were required to equip and run quartz mining companies.

Chapter 28

Nevada City, 1854–1855

Early May was beautiful in the mother lode. The countryside was a green blanket filled with wildflowers. Alfred traveled aboard a popular steamboat, *New World*, to Marysville, bound for northern mining communities. Marysville, his first stop, was a major transportation hub with steamboat service on the Sacramento River to San Francisco. By 1854, gold rush tents in Marysville had been replaced with brick and wooden buildings. The city had mills, factories, schools, churches, and two daily newspapers. A large Chinese population lived in the city. They constructed a temple to the deity Bok Kai. Chinese New Year was celebrated each year with a festival and parade.

Alfred traveled by Concord coach from Marysville through Grass Valley to Nevada City, a prosperous mining town facing snow-covered peaks of the Sierra Mountains. Nevada County was the largest gold-producing county in California during 1850–1851. Coach service connecting Nevada City, Marysville, Auburn, and other major northern mining communities was well established by 1854.

Concord coaches, the Rolls-Royce of stagecoaches of mid-nineteenth-century America, were the pride of Concord, New Hampshire. Each coach was carefully built with a light, strong body riding on leather braces designed to absorb jolts encountered on nineteenth-century roads. Made for speed, they were designed to remain upright while making fast, tight turns. Two twenty-five-year-old New England men, James Birch and Frank Stevens, introduced Concords to California. Birch consolidated dozens of independent stage companies into the state's largest stage company, naming it the California Stage Company. He achieved success by establishing fixed routes and realistic time schedules with set rates for people and freight. Sadly, Birch perished when returning to Massachusetts while on board the SS *Central America*. The steamship sunk on September 12, 1857, in a hurricane off the coast of North Carolina. Eight million dollars in gold coins ($292 million) with gold valued at $1,000 per troy ounce and 425 people were lost. The monetary loss contributed to a nationwide financial panic and depression.

Alfred's mission was to locate Edward Matteson, who pioneered developing hydraulic mining techniques in 1853 at a location near Nevada City. He hoped to work for Matteson, learning how to design, build, and manage hydraulic systems. Matteson's plan called for impounding water at locations high above a mining site. When released to lower levels, water was fed into hoses fitted with iron nozzles called monitors. Fast-moving, high-pressure water from monitors blasted hillsides, removing plants, trees, boulders, and soil to expose gold-bearing gravel. Loose gravel was forced into large sluice boxes, where gold was separated from sand and gravel. The process was highly effective though extremely damaging to the landscape.

Hydraulic mining escalated the destruction of the countryside begun by placer mining. It brought unforeseen havoc no one could have imagined. Sediment, rocks, minerals, dirt, and gravel residue from mining known as tailings washed into creeks and river systems. Crystal-clear mountain streams, once filled with trout and other fish, became yellow and clouded. Heaps of tailings filled mountain waterways. A canyon in Bear Valley forever lost its original wild and beautiful presence. Heavy winter rains washed tons of sediment from mountain streams and rivers into the Sacramento River valley, covering valuable farmland used for pasture and growing of grains and vegetables, destroying fruit and nut orchards. Streams and riverbeds in the valley filled with sediment, causing water to reach new heights during spring runoff. Locations not prone to flooding before the gold rush were inundated by floodwaters. New channels were created in the Sacramento River. Towns became vulnerable to seasonal floods. River navigation was disrupted. Sediment from Feather and Yuma River systems blocked steamboat approaches to Marysville. Environmental damage was unimaginable.

Malakoff Diggins on Humbug Creek became an artificial canyon seven thousand feet long, three thousand feet wide, and three hundred feet deep as a result of hydraulic mining. Sediment began filing San Francisco Bay. Hydraulic mining continued to devastate the western Sierras until farmers prevailed in a lawsuit against miners, ending large-scale hydraulic mining in 1884. Additional environmental damage was caused by mercury used to recover small particles of gold remaining in sand after passing through a sluice box. Gold was recovered from the sand with a process using mercury. Ten to 20 percent of mercury used for processing was lost in sediment.

Nevada City, reported Alfred, was a typical mining town splattered with a mixture of log cabins, white frame houses, and dirty canvas structures located on a hilltop alongside Deer Creek. At one time, it had been surrounded by beautiful tall pine trees. The trees were gone; their ugly stumps scarred the hills surrounding the town. Its creek filled with heaps of white tailings, residue from extracting gold.

The city was home to large numbers of European miners. Emigrants from France were the largest group. They were patrons of Hotel de Paris, which Alfred was told served the best meal in the mining country. He was not disappointed. Supper's menu began with soup, followed by filet de boeuf, cabbage, green peas, onions, and a good cup of coffee. It ended with a glass of cognac.

The restaurant had no lodging; Alfred stayed in a boardinghouse. The "house" consisted of one large room filled with cots stacked in three layers. Each sleeping space was about six feet long, two to three feet high. He got his choice occupying a top cot. Alfred made no comment about boardinghouse noise. Snoring was significant, for nocturnal sounds were heard blocks away from the house. Next door was an exchange where gamblers separated gold from miners. Liquor was cheap; exchanges were full seven days a week. Theater in the city presented a version of Shakespeare's *Richard III*. Shakespeare plays were favorites of men working in the gold country. Alfred frequently attended the theater when opportunities abounded. He enjoyed the Nevada City version of *King Dick*.

Hydraulic mining was not the only new type of corporate mining replacing traditional placer mining in 1854. Hard rock mining, as underground mining was known, was evolving as the premier technique to recover gold in the mother lode. Both hydraulic mining and hard rock mining were capital intensive, requiring large amounts of money for equipment and personnel for a successful operation. This led to the development of mining companies. Grass Valley, located four miles from

Nevada City, became the center of underground mining in the northern mines. Alfred needed to learn how gold was recovered from quartz before returning to San Francisco.

Miners sunk shafts in the earth to reach gold-bearing quartz. Holes in shaft walls, drilled by hand, were filled with black powder charges and ignited to break up rock formations. Miners carried baskets and containers filled with rocks to the surface to be crushed by stamping mills into a consistency of sand. Residue was washed, mercury added to extract gold. Empire Mine and Gold Star Mine were two of the most successful hard rock mining operations in Grass Valley.

Mining companies initially lacked skilled miners. Searches brought men from Cornwall, England. Cornish miners knew how to timber a mine, blast a rock formation, and follow a vein of gold-producing quartz. Cornish emigrants left their mark on the mother lode. Cornish Christmas, Saint Piyan's Day, was named for the patron saint of miners. Well-loved meat and vegetable pastry pockets (pasties) became popular. A miner earned $5 per day.

Alfred's stay in Grass Valley was not all work. Attending the Alta Theater, he enjoyed the Swan of Erin, Kate Hayes, a famous European opera singer. There were other entertainment venues. Grass Valley was home to an internationally famous actress, Lola Montez, known for touring Europe as the Countess Landsfeld. Visiting Bavaria, she infatuated King Ludwig, becoming his mistress. A seductive spider dance, shedding clothes to get rid of a pesky spider, was a delight to men who traveled from distant mining camps to see her risqué dance. Her show brought howls of pleasure from miners, who serenaded her with showers of gold nuggets.

Alfred's return to San Francisco was filled with awe and curiosity as he viewed changes made during his short absence. Reclaimed swampland from Mission Bay was now farmed by Chinese, who grew produce for sale in several city market locations and available at the city's better eating establishments. San Francisco cuisine was becoming famous. Top hotels and restaurants were reported to serve food comparable to meals found in New York and Paris. Marin County supplied game and venison; butter and cheese came from Point Reyes.

Mission Delores, a delightful rural setting, offered a chance to escape from the city's hectic crowded life. Horse racing tracks, saloons, and exchanges were popular places to visit on Sundays. Christian Russ, a successful businessman, opened his family garden to visitors. The garden, known for its topiary designs, held a large canvas circus tent where music could be heard and acrobatic acts performed; puppet shows and magicians were regular entertainment. Russ enjoyed ethnic holidays. He supported Germans, French, Irish, and Americans, helping celebrate national holidays.

Some things amazed Alfred: one was the plank road running from the waterfront toward the mission. The road itself was not a curiosity; the fact that it was continually sinking into the ground puzzled Alfred. Part of the road crossed a former swamp. Contractors filled the swamp with sand when the road was constructed to provide a level road surface. Despite the filler, the road continued to sink. Decades later, it was learned that peat was the road base located below sand filler. Peat rested on top of subterranean lakes thought to be forty feet deep. Weight of sand, wooden road planks, and heavy wagons caused peat to settle, necessitating continual filling. Eventually, the road was ten feet below its original surface level.

Chapter 29

Southern Mines, 1856–1857

A slight rocking motion awakened Alfred from a deep sleep. He was traveling by steamboat from San Francisco to Stockton, the first stop for his destination, Columbia, where he had signed on as a construction supervisor in an ambitious aqueduct project. Stockton was the end of the line for steamboat passengers heading to the southern mines. Sharp horn blasts announced the arrival of California Steamboat Company's *Surprise* as the vessel coasted into its berth.

Crowded around the wharf were a collection of rigs waiting to meet the boat's six o'clock arrival. Drivers of wagons, carts, carriages, and stagecoaches shouted destinations and fares for transport to one of many mining towns. Alfred chose Sonora for the day's run. He secured a place on top of a shiny new Concord coach, pulled by three pairs of eastern American-bred horses, the best-looking horseflesh he had seen in months. Nine men traveled in the coach interior. Each traveler was armed; robberies were becoming more prevalent in the gold fields, especially in southern mining areas. Traveling inside a coach was no picnic; men were squashed together. All used tobacco, a smoke, or a chew, the residue of the latter spat at targets outside the coach, frequently falling short of a coach window. Luggage was carried in the coach boot, most notably bedrolls because, often, they were home to a colony of fleas.

Alfred's coach followed a trail next to the San Joaquin River, winding along a flat piece of ground where a Concord could make ten miles per hour. On this day, travel was considerably slower because of heavy traffic using the route. Wagoner's hauling freight and mule pack trains set the paces of travel. The worst part of the trip occurred while passing a marsh filled with bull rushes, where hordes of mosquitoes made their home. Scores attacked every living thing passing through their community. Traveling ahead of the coach, a pack train was targeted by airborne pests, providing limited relief for Alfred and his companions next in line.

Travel came to a standstill while crossing a shallow ford at the Stanislaus River. A mile past the river, the coach stopped at a roadhouse for dinner. A typical traveler's meal was served—boiled beef and potatoes, stewed beans, and a dessert of dried apples swimming in molasses. Alfred was one of the first to finish dining. He exited the roadhouse to find a surprise: his elegant coach was missing. It had been replaced by a sturdy covered wagon pulled by six mules for the next leg of the journey, across rugged mountains. The road, a former Indian trail, was winding and narrow with an abundance of ruts, holes, and rocks. On more than one occasion, the driver stopped, ordering passengers out of the wagon, while he slowly crept down a dangerously steep incline. Day was turning into night when Sonora came into sight.

Sonora, Queen of the Southern Mines, was built in a sheltered valley between two creeks, Sonora and Woods. It was the winter home of the Mi-Wuk Indians until white men arrived, forcing Indians to relocate farther into the Sierra Mountains. The 1848 discovery of gold prompted men from the Mexican Sonora to immigrate to California, settling at a camp near Jamestown. Bad feelings due to the recently completed war with Mexico sparked conflicts between Americans and Mexicans. Americans forced Mexican miners to relocate to Woods Creek, thinking the area had poor prospects for gold production. The Americans were wrong; the site turned out to be full of gold.

Unlike American miners, Mexicans brought their wives and families. Naming their mining camp Sonora, it became a center for all things Mexican—bullfights, fandango dance halls, saloons, and gambling (monte). Emigrants from Latin American countries, Europe, and China arrived with wives and girlfriends. French brought wine; Germans produced lager beer. Mining in Sonora was different from placer mining in the north. Gold was produced from "pocket mines." Highly concentrated gold deposits were found in quartz. Found in underground pockets, rocks were brought to the surface, where gold was broken loose from quartz.

The development of mining prompted a need for government.

Early in 1850, Sonoma became the county seat of Tuolumne County. A July 1850 incident at a mining site referred to as Greens Flat Diggings murders polarized Americans against Mexicans. Local customs followed by Mexicans was to burn instead of burying the dead. Two bodies that Mexicans claimed had been dead for days were burning when American miners happened on the scene. Suspected of foul play, the Mexicans were seized and taken to a hill near Sonora, where a mob had gathered. Angry mobsters selected a judge and jury with intentions of trying and hanging the Mexicans. Four American law officials arrived, three judges and a sheriff. The law officers broke up the mob before an execution occurred. A proper trial was scheduled in Sonoma.

On arraignment day, two thousand fully armed men from a broad spectrum of nationalities wielding shotguns, rifles, pistols, knives, and lances arrived at the courthouse, all in a high state of tension. During the trial, a guard dropped his gun, causing it to accidently discharge. Men inside the courthouse drew weapons. Shots were fired, knives were brandished, and men stampeded to get out of the courthouse. Two days later, a new trial was held, finding no evidence of foul play. Mexicans were acquitted and released, and war was averted; however, relations between American and Mexican communities had turned sour. A suspicious fire destroyed most of the town in June 1852. Builders immediately rebuilt destroyed wood buildings with structures constructed of brick and iron. A well-prepared fire department was able to extinguish more suspicious fires in 1853 and 1854.

The next morning, Alfred proceeded to Columbia, four miles north, for his new posting. Columbia was the third largest city in California in 1853. It placed second in a vote to move the state capital from San Jose, losing to Sacramento. Called the "gem of the southern mines," the city boasted a diverse population of twenty-five thousand when Alfred arrived. The town's water sources from rivers and creeks were seasonal, without a supply during some dry summers. In 1851, the Tuolumne Water Company was established to bring water to the town. The mining community was not happy, complaining that a $4 per day usage rate was excessive. Miners formed a competitive company that they named Columbia and Stanislaus River Water Company to bring water sixty miles from the south branch of the river using ditches, flumes, and aqueducts. Construction would not be completed until 1858.

Alfred was hired as a construction supervisor for $18.00 per day.

A wage for construction supervisor in the East was $3.00 a day. Living expenses in Columbia remained high. The cheapest accommodation in a rooming house cost $30.00 per month. In the East, a family could rent an entire house for $10.00 a month. Food was expensive, for little was produced locally. Flour cost $5.00 per pound, stores in the East charged 75¢ a pound. Beef stew cost $1.25; if you wanted the stew to include potatoes, cabbage, or squash, you paid 50¢ extra per item, bringing the cost of stew to $2.75 per serving. If you were dining at a well-known hotel restaurant in New York City, a porterhouse steak with vegetables cost 50¢.

Alfred went to work, examining the sixty-mile-long construction site. Flumes were needed to bring water from the river to a series of aqueducts, with wood trestles carrying it around mountains and over streams and ravines. Each supervisor would be responsible for completing a section of the aqueduct.

Columbia's July 4 celebration was a big event. The town's population swelled, attracting partygoers from surrounding towns and mining camps. Independence Day celebrations began with a parade. Throngs of spectators crowded the sides of Main Street. American flags were brilliantly displayed on buildings lining the parade route. Statues of American eagles were displayed outside saloons, causing the parade to slow, permitting parade participants to stop and salute an American eagle wherever displayed. The parade was led by schoolchildren accompanied by their mothers and teachers. Hundreds followed—merchants carrying posters advertising their businesses; miners carrying a pick and shovel; members of fraternal organizations supporting red, white, and blue banners; volunteer firemen; the sheriff and political leaders; anyone who wanted to walk in a parade. Participants not wishing to walk rode on scruffy horses that barely could walk, stubborn mules, and flea-bitten donkeys.

The long, seemingly endless parade found its way to the town's bullring much too small to hold the crowd. A self-appointed speaker stepped up to a platform, reciting the Declaration of Independence. Other patriots spoke about Pilgrims; Plymouth Rock, which an Irishman called an American Blarney Stone; and the evils of long-departed King George of England. Speeches were halted with an announcement of the start of the day's bullfight. The bull had no interest in fighting, attempting to escape from his tormenting matador, losing when a red-flag-bearing sword was plunged into its neck. A few spectators dined well that day. Celebrating lasted through the day and well past midnight. Much gunpowder was expended as revelers discharged their weapons into the air. Saloons and exchanges reaped great profits on Independence Day.

August 27, 1857, was never forgotten. A Chinese miner was cooking dinner when hot grease from his fire ignited the canvas wall of his house. Flames rapidly spread, destroying the house. Local firemen struggled to contain the fire but soon ran out of water. A dozen square blocks were destroyed, including buildings constructed to be fireproof. One shopkeeper saved his place of business using two barrels of vinegar stored on his roof to extinguish flames. Five men died when a storehouse filled with black powder exploded. New construction codes were issued after the fire. Brick buildings must have double walls. Storage of black powder was prohibited in the town. Every merchant was required to keep three barrels filled with water on the premise along with three buckets. Chinese were banned from living within city limits.

Chapter 30

1858: A Request from Fremont

Near the end of 1857, construction on the Columbia and Stanislaus aqueduct project was complete. It cost investors one million dollars. The company's revenues had begun to slide; fewer deposits of gold were being discovered. The company could not cover its debts, causing it to file for bankruptcy. It was sold to the Tuolumne Water Company for $150,000.

The number of placer miners and the hours spent seeking gold in California from 1848 through 1858 were beyond belief. Reports of immense wealth gained from discovering gold was well documented by early discoveries in the mother lode. In 1848, competition was low, and the field of prospectors was small but rapidly growing. After a slow start, word of gold discoveries in California spread around the world. People raced to California to get rich. Wherever gold was found on a river flat or sandbar or in a stream or creek, hundreds of '49ers flocked like a plague of locusts, staking out small claims. Mining camps and towns sprouted along the two-hundred-mile mother lode on the west side of the Sierra Mountains at a hard-to-believe rate. Gold changed the face of California. Emigrants from around the world left their mark, forming a culture unlike other states.

By the middle of 1854, a new reality faced Alfred and the men in gold fields. Placer gold production was drastically slowing, especially in southern locations. In 1856, gold discoveries were smaller, and the metal was more difficult to recover. Costs of living had not declined; miners had to work harder and spend longer hours to make a living. Mining towns began to shrink as miners, not finding wealth, were unable to earn a living.

They began to leave California. Only well-financed big companies using expensive heavy mining equipment continued to achieve stellar results, mining deep veins of gold-filled quartz.

Alfred ended his supervisory work on the aqueduct. He decided to leave early in 1858, returning to his family and friends in Ohio. His brother George owned a prosperous lumber company in Circleville, Ohio. Sister Harriet was married to John Smith Wilkes, owner of warehouses handling freight on the Ohio and Erie Canal and newly established railroads. Family would help Alfred find employment. Travel plans included a steamboat to Panama City, Panama; a trek across the Isthmus; and a boat from Charges, Panama to New Orleans. Another steamboat would carry him to Cincinnati, where it was an easy trip to family in Circleville. He left San Francisco without wealth from gold but was filled with thirteen years of rich experiences learned during the explosive beginning and early growth of the thirty-first state. Before leaving, Alfred visited John C. Fremont and an old friend from the Bear Flag Revolt and California Battalion days, Jerome C. Davis.

Circleville had changed. Commerce on canals was moving to railroads; fortunately, major rail lines served Circleville. The town's circle had been squared by 1856. Most industries were related to agriculture; the city was the largest producer of broomcorn in the country and a large producer of canned vegetables. Alfred enjoyed seeing his sisters, his brothers, and their families but quickly found that he missed life in California.

Late in the year, Davenport received a letter from John Charles Fremont requesting that he return to Mariposa. Fremont needed him in Bear Valley.

Benton Dam, Merced River

Murderer's Bar

Chapter 31

Mariposas

James Buchanan defeated John Charles Fremont in the 1856 election for president of the United States. A disappointed Fremont returned to Mariposa in the spring of 1857. Jessie, visiting France, remained in Paris with her children. Late in the year, word reached the Fremont's that Jessie's father, Senator Benton, was seriously ill at his home in Washington, DC. Both immediately returned to the capital to be at his side.

Problems continued to plague Fremont's California estate, necessitating a return to the Mariposa grant in February 1858. Claim jumpers, squatters, and a group who called themselves the Merced Mining Company used Fremont's absence to take control of twenty-nine of the estate's gold-bearing quartz properties, including Josephine and Pine Tree Mines. Disputes concerning the validity of the original Mexican land grant boundaries were ongoing for several years. The boundary argument found its way to the United States Supreme Court. During an 1855 session, Chief Justice Taney confirmed Fremont's legal title to 44,386 acres of land. Despite his federal patent, Fremont continued to deal with prospectors who were digging up his fields, destroying trees and grasslands on which he paid $16,000 a year in property taxes on land that the Supreme Court confirmed belonged to Fremont.

The Merced Mining Company refused to follow the court's directions. Unsavory men and criminals from the Hornitos League joined together, threatening violence against Fremont if he did not give up his interest in Josephine, Pine Tree, and other mines. Trouble began at the Black Drift

Tunnel of Pine Tree Mine. Charles left Jessie at their home in Bear Valley, traveling 3 miles to the tunnel as soon as he learned about the threats. He found that his workers were armed with an ample number of guns, black powder, and a cannon but lacked significant supplies of food and water. They were arming themselves to take on criminals, even though they were greatly outnumbered.

Fremont began the construction of a fortification, a breastwork located on top of the mine's entrance. The tunnel entrance was several hundred feet below the peak of a mountain. Its opening was 1,600 feet above the Merced River. Fremont and his miners were quickly surrounded by 50 to 60 angry drunken men, demanding he vacate the property. A Hornitos representative threatened to starve out Fremont. Anyone who attempted to leave for help would be shot. Fremont cautioned his men. He wanted a peaceful solution to the standoff. Shooting, he warned, could get out of hand; many men would be killed.

Jessie, at the family home in Bear Valley, received a visit from another group of wild and drunken outlaws, demanding the family, guests, and servants get out, or they would burn them out. She was concerned, for there was no way to escape and find help. All roads and paths out of the area were guarded by the Hornitos League men. Cleverly, Jessie negotiated a twenty-four-hour delay to allow her to get ready for the move. She was smarter and stronger-willed than her captors had anticipated. Late in the day, she crafted a plan.

A seventeen-year-old English houseguest, Douglas Fox, was an accomplished equestrian. Fox had recently spent days riding and exploring mountains and valleys in and around Bear Valley and the Merced River. He knew of a hidden path over a mountain summit leading to Fremont-friendly Coulterville. Hidden by the cover of brush, trees, and tall grass, he crossed the mountains, riding at night, to Coulterville. Local militia took the news of the revolt quickly to Stockton, where a telegram was sent to California's governor describing Fremont's plight. The governor acted quickly. Soon Hornitos outlaws and Merced Mining Company men were facing 500 well-armed government troops. They saw no reason for the hundred men in their group to continue their struggle. The "war" was over; not a shot was fired. Future land complaints, which were frequent and expensive for Fremont, were argued in court.

Alfred was excited to receive Fremont's letter. He immediately settled his affairs and departed for Mariposa. Fremont was planning major developments on his estate. The colonel wanted Davenport for a construction project. His Benton Mills located on the Merced River, processing quartz from Pine Tree and Josephine Mines, were powered by steam. Quartz-bearing gold was processed by crushing ore to allow the separation of gold from quartz before sending it to an amalgamator to recover gold. Steam generation consumed large amounts of wood. Nearby hills had been stripped of timber; wood had to be brought long distances to power stamping machines. An increase in mine production and more stamping machines were needed for the business to remain profitable. Fremont planned to build a dam on the Merced River using waterpower to run his mills. It was the first power dam built in California. The colonel recruited Davenport for his company to supervise the building of the dam called Benton Dam, named after Jessie's father.

The dam was 120 feet long, 30 feet high, crossing the river upstream of Benton Mills. Posts were sunk into the riverbed at 4-foot intervals. Large planks of wood were attached to the upstream side of the posts. Three rock walls stacked on one another, capped with large boulders, provided downstream support for the dam. Alfred organized work teams, each providing a vital part of the dam's construction. The first group sank tall posts in a line crossing the river. A second crew began attaching planks to the upstream side of the posts. A third team erected a three-tier rock wall on the dam's downstream side. Another crew constructed a large flume to carry water to a giant wheel running Benton Mills stamping machines.

Labor was a problem. Chinese workmen, living in a village of 1,800 Chinese inhabitants near the town of Mariposa, were hired to construct a 4½-mile-long railroad to bring ore from Pine Tree and Josephine Mines to the stamping mills. More workers were needed. Alfred found a labor source. Miners who were "plumb strapped" were hired. They had run out of money for supplies and provisions and would take any type of work. Recruiting from this group filled labor needs for construction of the dam and other mining projects.

Fremont demanded that his workers maintain order in their personal lives. His rules were strict, forbidding the consumption of alcoholic beverages or carrying weapons into his mines. Men living in his company town were mostly single. He saw the need for good meals. A baker was brought from Vienna, and an Italian chef was employed at his restaurant to cook for miners. Fresh vegetables were grown for the kitchen. Despite adequate housing, healthy food, and a fair wage, some unhappy miners remarked that Bear Valley was reminiscent of an ancient feudal domain.

A heat wave descended on Bear Valley in June 1859. Jessie Fremont, in a letter to Francis Preston Blair on July 9, explained, "Daytime temperatures hovered between 104- and 107-degrees Fahrenheit," retreating only to the high nineties by midnight. Life was unbearable during the day; one could not sleep at night. John Charles's work would not permit him to move to the coast to enjoy a better climate with soothing ocean breezes. He wanted to help his family escape the oppressive summer heat. His answer was to choose a location on top of Mount Bullion to build a family summer camp. Jessie reported that Mr. Fremont asked "Mr. Davenport, whom he had known since '46–'47, to construct a camp." It was to be built at an elevation of 4,000 feet, compared with his valley's home elevation of 850 feet. The camp was in a grove of oak trees with a natural spring producing 55°F water on the hottest days. "We installed a great tent with floorboards, two feet off the ground." Planks were brought up by mules from the valley floor. "The canvas roof was 12 feet high, suspended between four oak trees. The side of the tent nearest the bed head was fastened down" to the floor. Mattresses were brought up and laid on piles of fragrant heather. "Oak trees are so close together the sun did not penetrate our enclosure. We have the most delightful open-air dining room with a view that cannot be matched in the Alps." Yosemite was 30 miles east. "Every morning we get produce from our garden & dairy supplies of meat, milk [and mail] from below." Mr. Davenport named the retreat "Camp Jessie."

Six weeks after the completion of Camp Jessie, a startling event changed summer plans. The colonel, as Fremont was known, left camp every morning for the mines and his office, returning late when the heat of the day had passed. He never left his family alone, insisting one of his trusted servants, Isaac or Burke, remain with them. A young Indian chief and two of his warriors from a "restless and fighting tribe" arrived at Jessie's camp. The chief, who would not talk to a woman, carried on a spirited conversation with Isaac. He spoke of conflicts with white miners who had taken their land. He explained that disgruntled Indians were banding together to take back what they had lost. The chief demanded Mrs. Fremont must leave the mountain. Colonel Fremont and others, upon hearing about Isaac's encounter, felt it wise for his family to leave and not return to the camp.

Heat in Bear Valley remained stifling. The colonel decided to move

Jessie and the children to San Francisco. He purchased 12 acres of land named Black Point, jutting into San Francisco Bay, not far from the Golden Gate across from Alcatraz Island. This became the Fremont home from August 1859 until June 1861, when they moved to Saint Louis at the beginning of the Civil War. Fremont commuted to Bear Valley, where he kept a room at the hotel Oso House.

One hundred fifty thousand Native Americans lived in California before the discovery of gold. Their philosophy was one of universal ownership. Everything found in their world—the earth, sky, water, trees, plants, and animals—was for tribal use and pleasure. They subsisted on gathered nuts, herbs, fishing, and hunting. Their views sharply contrasted to non-native ideas of private ownership. Bear Valley was historically home to a considerable number of grizzly bears, which thrived on the nuts in the valley's trees. Bears were gone from the valley by 1858, depriving Indians of a source of food. Chinook salmon and steelhead trout were hunted in pools on the Merced and other rivers until barriers erected by miners stopped fish migration. Salmon runs on rivers emptying into the Joaquin River basin were the largest runs on the Pacific Coast before the gold rush. Conflicts between Indians and miners grew as Indians lost homes and hunting grounds to miners and settlers.

Pressure from miners caused Peter Burnett, California's governor, to enact anti-Indian legislation in 1850. "The Act for the Government and Protection of Indians" was created to solve the Indian problem. Indians, by decree, were removed from traditional lands. Children and adults could be indentured to whites. "Vagrant" Indians who could not produce bail or bond could be "hired out" to the highest bidder at a public auction. The state would assist militias protecting mining settlements from hostile Indians by paying for bullets supplied to them. A bounty of $10 to $25 was to be paid for a renegade Indian scalp, head, hand, or body. Burnett's legislation resulted in the mass murder of indigenous peoples. Many who escaped death and capture died of disease and starvation.

The 1850 legislation provoked Ahwahnechee Indians to attack miners in Merced and Yosemite Valleys. Fighting slowed in March 1851, when a treaty was signed with six tribes at Camp Fremont in Mariposa County. A 200-man militia, the Mariposa Battalion, fought three campaigns in April–May 1851 against Miwok and Yokuts tribes who would not sign a treaty with white men. Miwok were captured at Lake Tenaya in May. They were forced to reside on a reservation near Fresno; later, it was moved to Mono Lake. California spent $1.5 million between 1850 and 1860 to "solve" the Indian problem. By the mid-1860's, 34,000 Native Americans remained alive in California.

During a meeting with Fremont in September 1859, Davenport was given new opportunities and challenges. Fremont wanted him to take over management of the Pine Tree Mine, known as the mother lode of California's quartz mines. It was one of the largest quartz mines in the state with a quartz vein producing uniform amounts of gold, making it easy to work. The vein was 30 feet thick. Pine Tree was located near the end of Mount Bullion along the Merced River.

The mine was a successful enterprise. A major improvement was a 4.5-mile gravity railroad descending from the mine's entrance, traversing numerous *S* curves ending at Benton Mills. Operators riding on ore cars applied brakes to control the speed on the railroad. Mules were used to pull empty cars up steep grades for their return to the mine's entrance. Several tunnels were needed for miners to reach the mine's gold-bearing quartz vein. The men drilled 3-foot-deep holes into rock walls using a bit slammed by a sledgehammer. Black powder charges were placed in the hole. A fuse was lit, and miners raced away from the blasting area. Miners returned after explosions with picks, axes, shovels, and crowbars and gathered rock for railcars heading to stampers.

Alfred's challenges as a mine manager were substantial. Mines on the estate were generating healthy revenues from gold, though profitability was a concern. Production numbers recorded for Pine Tree and Josephine Mines were combined, counted as unit of production from Benton Mills. The monthly revenue reported in 1860 was $39,500, growing to $53,500 in 1861. Tonnage increased from 12,154 tons a month in 1860 to 21,576 tons in 1861. Profits dropped from $9.34 a ton in 1860 to $8.05 in 1861. What was the reason? Increased tonnage required additional manpower both underground and on the surface. Additional railroads, stamping mills, trails, wagon roads, workshops, and warehouses were required. Benton Mills ran sixty-four stampers at its peak.

Two factors concerning mining operations were not under Davenport's control. Assayers' examination of the amalgamation process in 1864, after Fremont had sold the estate, noted that particles of gold from Pine Tree's quartz mines were extremely fine, resulting in gold recovery of only 30 percent. An assay of tailings confirmed 70 percent was lost through processing at Benton Mills.

Another factor weighing on Davenport was Fremont's tremendous monthly debt payments. Banks who lent him money to equip his Las Mariposas Estate mines were owed $2.25 million. Monthly interest was 2½ percent or 30 percent a year. This came to $56,250 per month, payable in gold. Alfred and Fremont discussed reducing wages as a means of solving some of profitably issues. Davenport recommended reducing labor costs. Fremobt, in a June 2 letter from Black Point to Bear Valley's manager Hopper, stated, "In regard to the men whose wages we consider reducing at the mines, and Mr. Davenport's action in regard to them, I think it will be as much as possible to let it stand until I get back." On June 5, Fremont wrote to Hopper, asking him to "have a friendly conversation with Ketton and Davenport about the pay of the men and let it rest until I get back." Throughout the year, financial issues continued to plague Fremont despite healthy revenues from his mines and rents paid from leasing land and mining properties.

Alfred joined a fraternal organization, a popular social center for hundreds of single men working and living in gold towns. The Independent Order of Odd Fellows (IOOF) had 60 lodges in the California by 1856 and 266 by 1898. Lodge no.39 was in Mariposa. Lodge no. 110, Oso Lodge, was in Bear Valley. Other lodges could be found in nearby Hornitos and Coulterville. Alfred joined Mariposas' IOOF. It became the core of his social life. He strongly believed in its motto. "Visit the sick, relieve the distressed, bury the dead, and educate the orphan." Alfred's IOOF affiliation became an important part of the rest of his life.

Mariposas' lodge planned a grand ball on April 26, 1859, celebrating their new hall and club and the fortieth anniversary of IOOF in the United States. John C. Hopper was the grand marshal of the ball. Most managers of Fremont's Las Mariposas Estate were members of the organization. The ball featured a procession led by a brass band, several orators, a benediction, and a very ample and excellent dinner. Entertainment was music provided by the Mariposa Quadrille Band. Mrs. Fremont and her children were the honored guests. A Virginia reel was danced after dinner. Some families brought their children. One room of the hall was used to care for members' children including a dozen babies. A couple of unmarried pranksters entered the baby room during dinner, swapping cloaks and wraps of the youngsters, moving them to different beds, causing confusion, concerns, and finally a laugh from everyone, including the children's mothers. The party lasted until midnight; some diehards continued to party until dawn.

January 1861 found Fremont and his lawyers in Europe, attempting to sell shares in his Las Mariposas Estate to reduce its debt burdens. Europeans smelled the scent of war in the United States and were reluctant to make financial commitments to Fremont. The beginning of hostilities at Fort Sumter, South Carolina, brought Fremont back to the States and an end to pursuing financial remedies for his California mines.

President Lincoln needed to replace experienced army officers who had left the U.S. Army to join the ranks of the Confederacy. He appointed John Charles Fremont major general in charge of the U.S. Army's Department of the West on July 3, 1861. Headquarters were in Saint Louis, Missouri. The department oversaw all lands west of the Mississippi River to the borders of California and Oregon. Illinois, western Kentucky, and New Mexico Territory were added on August 15, 1861. Fremont met his family in New York, taking them to Saint Louis, where he assumed command on July 25. He sent a letter to Alfred, providing an opportunity for dramatic changes in Davenport's life.

Campaigns in Missouri

Part IV

Civil War

Chapter 32

Missouri, 1861

Jessie was happy to be returning to Saint Louis, a city of 160,000, home of her late father, Missouri's powerful senator Thomas Hart Benton. Travel from San Francisco had been hurried and tiring for her and the children. They sailed on the steamer *Sonora* to Panama and crossed its Isthmus by railroad, taking a second steamer to New York City, where Major General Fremont joined his family for the trip to Saint Louis. Union supporters were pleased that national hero Fremont was selected by President Lincoln and advisers Atty. Gen. Edward Bates and Post-Master-General Montgomery Blair to command the Western Department. Blair was the son of Saint Louis's powerful U.S. senator Francis Blair, a longtime friend of Jessie's father.

The United States did not have a large standing army when the Civil War began. Many army officers were Southerners, resulting in their joining the Confederacy. Enlisted men in the Union army signed on for a three-month enlistment, returning home when their time was completed. The War Department issued orders in May 1861 redefining the composition of companies and regiments. It took six months to complete this task. Army companies contained about 100 men. The company leader was an elected officer with the rank of captain. This role was frequently awarded to men who filled a company with recruits. A regiment was made up of ten companies, led by a colonel appointed by a state governor and approved by President Lincoln. Politics and business success determined what rank an officer might have in a regiment or company, not his military knowledge or experience. Corruption and incompetence were a big problem for the U.S. Army in 1861.

The Fremont family's rail journey from New York was tense, filled with anxiety. Union army's disaster at Bull Run had everyone on edge. No one knew where the rebels would strike next or if they had moved to take control of border states. The major general's arrival at Saint Louis was an unexpected eye-opener. Shores of the Mississippi River were strangely quiet. Steamboats were empty along the Mississippi River wharf. Machine shops and foundries were deserted; businesses and stores were closed. A Confederate flag was flying in front of several buildings in the business district; one was the local recruiting office for Confederate soldiers. Unemployed workers roamed streets at night.

The southern counties of Missouri, a border and slave-owning state, favored the South. A larger number of the state's residents and most of Missouri's northern counties supported the Union. Jefferson City, located west of Saint Louis, was the state capital. Gov. Claiborne Jackson, his lieutenant governor, and many state legislators were pro-South as were the state capital's leading newspapers. Union army troops clashed with secessionists outside Saint Louis's Fort Jackson on May 10. The governor appointed Sterling Price as major general in charge of the Missouri State Guard on May 11.

Price met with Gen. William S. Harney, commander of Union forces, the next day to sign a truce; Missouri would remain neutral. Meanwhile, in secret, Jackson was communicating with Confederate president, Jefferson Davis, promising the Missouri State Guard would cooperate with the Confederate army in a march on Saint Louis with its armory's rich trove of weapons, its strategic position on the Mississippi River, and its railroad center. Governor Jackson and Price met with Union general Nathaniel Lyon and Col. Frank Blair Jr., a U.S. congressman, at the Planter's House Hotel in Saint Louis to discuss stopping open conflict in the state. The meeting was halted when Lyon refused to limit his military activities, stating any federal limitation would mean war. Missouri held a state convention in July 1861 with a vote against secession. Governor Jackson fled to Arkansas, leaving the governor's post vacant until after the war.

General Lyon and his army arrived in Jefferson City on June 14, occupying the capital without a shot being fired, reaching the town of Springfield in southwestern Missouri on July 13 with 7,500 volunteer troops. He was dangerously overextended, 120 miles beyond the nearest supplies at Rolla with its railhead and union military camp. Union general Benjamin Prentiss near Cairo, Illinois, wrote to Fremont in late July, stating 12,000 well-armed Confederates were within 50 miles of his location, which was seriously undermanned. President Lincoln needed to keep control of the confluence of the Ohio and Mississippi Rivers to maintain its line on the Ohio River and gain control of the Mississippi. Fremont recognized the strategic importance of Cairo, sending men and supplies to Prentiss, telling Lyon to leave Springfield and fall back to the army's base in Rolla. Lyon's second-in-command, General Schofield, urged his superior to start toward Rolla.

Fremont issued a second order for Lyon to retreat to Rolla, but General Lyon had his own agenda. Taking 5,400 troops, he attacked Confederates at dawn on August 10 at Wilson's Creek near Springfield. Colonel Sigel was first to see action, hitting the army's flank. Lyon's troops surged ahead, driving back the center of the line, taking the high ground known as Bloody Hill. Sigel's forces were counterattacked by troops from Louisiana, whose gray uniforms were mistaken for Union troops from Iowa. By the time the uniform error was discovered, Confederate troops had overrun Sigel's position, causing him to retreat, giving Southern troops a battlefield advantage. Lyon's advance was stopped by artillery fire. Both sides contested the hill for several hours.

Lyon, who had received two wounds earlier that morning, led a charge at the enemy line. He was shot in the heart. Maj. Samuel Sturgis took command of the Union army. Realizing he was outnumbered by 12,000 Confederates, he withdrew to Springfield. Lyon was the first Union general to be killed in battle. Union press made Lyon a fallen hero, turning the blame for the general's death and losses at Wilson's Creek on Fremont.

Challenges facing Fremont were staggering. He suffered from acute shortages of officers, men, arms, and supplies. Little help came from Washington. Commanding general of the army, Winfield Scott directed all states to send men, arms, and supplies for the defense of the nation's capital putting pressure on Fremont's limited resources. Rebels controlled pockets around Missouri, which Fremont needed to neutralize.

Fremont's letter to Alfred Davenport was brief and to the point. Fremont needed experienced and reliable officers in his newly formed Missouri cavalry. Alfred's experiences in the California Battalion in 1846 and his work at Mariposas placed him high on a list of recruits for his war effort in Missouri. Davenport would be commissioned a captain in

Fremont's Body Guard, assist in the training of cavalry officers, and serve as a scout for the army. The Body Guard's commander was Maj. Charles Zagonyi, a Hungarian trained in European cavalry tactics. Alfred resigned from his position at the Pine Tree Mine, hurrying East to join Major General Fremont in Saint Louis.

Fremont felt that a strong cavalry was critical to the success of any army. His cavalry later became recognized as the best in the Union army in 1861. The cavalry, popularly known as the Body Guard, was designed to lead troops into battle using European cavalry tactics and fighting methods. Capt. Alfred Davenport was soon spending long hours training recruits to be an effective fighting force. The process, in normal training times, could take years. Training was necessarily condensed into a few weeks of intensive work. He taught his men riding skill and the use of a rifle, pistols, and a saber while riding at a full gallop. Day after day, he worked on basics until each student became an accomplished rider and fighter.

Zagonyi trained men to follow Napoleonic tactical skills. Speedy battlefield assaults by cavalry soldiers shocked enemy infantry troops with an intent to shut down an infantry charge and create chaos in their ranks. Enemy infantry troops hit with fast-charging mounted troops faced firepower of up to seventeen-gun shots before an infantryman could reload his weapon. Weapons were Colt's New Model Revolving rifle, carrying five or six rounds depending on its caliber, using a rotating cylinder like a pair of six-shot Colt pistols. The speed and firepower of men on horseback quickly demoralized men fighting on foot. Effectively deployed cavalry tactics frequently caused enemy troops to break and flee from their battle line. Zagonyi explained, "Cavalry is necessary for reconnoitering the enemy. Small incursions day and night will cover our [Union] movements so the enemy will not know our strength or disposition. Cavalry is to find where to fight a battle and how to finish it." The first cavalry company was sworn in on August 12. Zagonyi had four companies by September 19.

Fremont spent August implementing his plan. He began to fortify Saint Louis and improved rail transport to expedite troop transport and supplies by creating one central rail (union) station instead of multiple ones. He organized military river service, constructing thirty-eight mortar boats and eight steam tugs to move mortar boats. Steamboat sides were covered in iron plates for conversion to gunboats. Veteran river captain Thomas Maxwell was asked to organize three companies of Marine Corps troops to staff all boats. Fremont enlisted the service of his old friend Edward M. Kern to head an intelligence-gathering unit. A unit of mounted men called Jessie Scouts wore Confederate uniforms, spending days in rebel territory. They identified themselves by wearing a white scarf in a particular manner or used a conversation code that would identify them from real Confederates. They mapped bridges, highways, and fortifications in Kentucky and western Tennessee, taking note of troop strengths and movements. Sensitive information was wrapped in tin foil and carried in the cheek like a plug of tobacco.

Saint Louis army headquarters was moved to the elegant J. B. Brant house, a large mansion with many rooms, permitting all military administration under one roof. Critics complained about the cost of renting an opulent building by the army. They also complained about lack of access to Fremont and his staff. Contracts were awarded as Fremont saw fit, often upsetting local political customs and relationships. Col. Frank Blair Jr. and his allies lost control of lucrative army contracts for beef, mules, horses, hay, and grain. Fremont had his own sources for supplies. Blair Jr. asked Fremont for an appointment as a major general in the Missouri militia. Fremont turned him down.

Confederates and their allies, the Missouri State Guard, stepped up guerilla activities around the state after their success at Wilson's Creek. Bridges were torched, trains were wrecked, pro-Union farmers began leaving the state. Fremont's answer to the chaos and threats of secession was to declare martial law for all Missouri. On August 30, he issued a controversial proclamation:

> All persons who shall be taken with arms in their hands within these lines shall be tried by court-martial and, if found guilty, will be shot. The property, real and personal, of all persons in the State of Missouri who shall take up arms against the United States, and who shall be directly proven to have taken active part with their enemies in the field, is declared to be confiscated to the public use; and their slaves, if any they have same, are hereby declared free.

Fremont did not consult any authorities in Missouri or Washington before issuing his edict. He wanted to punish Missouri citizens who rebelled against the Union. The Emancipation Proclamation made him a hero in New England and parts of the Midwest. It helped give the U.S. Army recruiting an upswing. Lincoln felt the proclamation was not appropriate. Any emancipation of slaves might cause border states and neutrals to consider leaving the Union. He reversed the proclamation on September 11.

Fremont and Col. Frank Blair Jr., brother of Montgomery Blair, each wanted to dominate Union interests in Missouri. Blair family members were slaveholders. Frank Blair. Jr had the president's ear. He disliked Fremont's proclamation and was continually critical of Fremont's military activities, blaming him for Lyon's death, calling him incompetent. Fremont felt Blair was a drunk and often out of order. He had Colonel Blair arrested on September 18 for insubordination.

September opened with relative calm in the eastern part of Fremont's military territory. Fremont appointed Brig. Gen. Ulysses S. Grant as commander of southeastern Missouri and southern Illinois late in August. Grant, with troops provided by Fremont, took Paducah, Kentucky, across the Ohio River from Cairo, Illinois, gaining control of the mouth of the Tennessee River, strengthening Union positions along Ohio and Mississippi Rivers.

Lexington, Missouri, located on the Missouri River not far from the Kansas border, was a business and agricultural center of over 4,000 residents and an important control point on the river. Many Lexington residents were pro-South; slaves were 31 percent of the population. Col. James Mulligan with the Chicago Irish Brigade arrived to command a 3,500-man army group on September 9 with orders to protect Union interests. He established headquarters in the Masonic College, which he began to fortify.

Missouri State Guard's Confederate General Price, fresh from his success at Wilson's Creek, arrived on September 11 with 15,000 troops, planning to seize Lexington. Skirmishes began the next morning. Fremont replied, ordering three generals to come to the aid of Mulligan. Gen. John Pope replied that he would have 4,000 soldiers, cavalry, and 4 artillery pieces in Lexington in four days. Sturgis was ordered to take 2,500 men and artillery to Lexington; Brigadier General Davis from Jefferson City was to provide five more regiments. Sturgis learned Price's forces outnumbered his and Mulligan's troops. Price controlled the Missouri River. With this news, he halted his advance. Pope never made it to Lexington during the battle.

Overnight on September 19, Price's men soaked bales of hemp in the river. In the morning, the rebels formed a line of wet bales and began rolling them toward the Union fortification. Much of the battle was an artillery duel; however, soaked hemp bales provided Price's men immunity from red-hot federal shells. Mulligan, out of water and hopelessly outnumbered, could not stop the rebel advance. Mulligan surrendered his 3,500-man garrison to Price at two o'clock that afternoon.

Frank Blair Jr. was released from arrest. He immediately filed suit against Fremont, charging him with rash acts, the death of Lyon, and Mulligan's surrender. Blair became obsessed with a need to remove Fremont from Missouri. He was reported to have been responsible for a letter a Northern newspaper, the *National Intelligencer,* asking, "Why 60,000 well-equipped elite Union soldiers could not drive half-naked ill-armed rebels out of Missouri?"

The Blair-Fremont quarrel divided the Union supporters in Missouri into two factions; the fight disabled the war effort. Lincoln was fed up with the mess in Missouri. He sent Secretary of War Simon Cameron to Saint Louis. Cameron was authorized to relieve Fremont if warranted. Blair continued his attacks and outbursts against Fremont, urging Fremont's own generals to undermine him. Generals Pope and David Hunter and Adj. Gen. Lorenzo Thomas met with Cameron in Saint Louis, reporting that Fremont was guilty of reckless expenditure and excessive issuance of commissions and surrounded himself with too many foreigners with whom it was difficult to communicate. Foreigners, men like Zagonyi, knowing what worked in European wars, were key advisors to Fremont. West Point–trained officers disliked Fremont's handling of orders, reporting his approach was erratic and irregular, breaking traditions historically followed by U.S. military teachings. General Thomas, a close friend of Blair, voiced a well-known dislike of Fremont. He was one of the first generals voicing disappointment in President Lincoln's decision to appoint Fremont commander of the Department of the West. He described Fremont as brash and outspoken and unskilled in military protocol. Thomas overlooked Fremont's success as a pathfinder and his ability and skills using unorthodox methods to solve challenging and fluid problems. Fremont could never escape West Point men's dislike of an army general who had received a presidential appointment and was not a career soldier.

Fremont knew it was time for him to demonstrate battlefield leadership. The Union was on the losing end of many battles fought to date. Army generals had failed to blunt the rebellion. A victory was needed for the Union to gain creditability in Missouri. His Guard left Saint Louis on September 26, traveling to Jefferson City, where they were joined by Fremont. Their objective was to defeat and drive General Price from Missouri. Supplies and material for the mission were limited, and equipment was in poor condition. Fremont, from his frontier days, knew how to live off the land. He instructed the Guard to take what they needed from the countryside. Loyal citizens were to be paid with government bills; secessionists' property was to be confiscated. Pope was asked to join the October campaign. He refused, saying there was not enough transport to carry his army 100 yards. Pope complained, a battle with his troops in their current condition would cost him half his men.

Fremont's army reached Warsaw on the Osage River at noon on October 18. All bridges had been burned and destroyed by Price's retreating Confederates. Using frontier ingenuity, Fremont turned his troops into carpenters and builders constructing a pontoon bridge. His army was across the river by evening three days later. Davenport's skills in managing construction projects were invaluable to Fremont at Warsaw. Wood, from pulled down log houses and barns, was used to build bridge sections on the north side of the river. Trees cut from virgin forests supplied wood on the river's south side. Members of the Guard, using teams of horses, brought large logs to the river's edge. Union army volunteers, from German settlements in Missouri, cut logs and planks for pontoons.

Tools for construction were gathered from locals. One secessionist shopkeeper "didn't care to sell materials to Union troops." He paid a price. Angry unionists ransacked his store, destroying kegs, barrels, and merchandise. Only a few augers, two sledgehammers, and six chisels remained after mobsters finished with the rebel sympathizer. Spikes were needed for construction. Blacksmith fires were seized; men hammered out spikes using iron taken from cellars, barns, and stores, wherever it could be located. A night sky lit by fires and a full moon allowed construction to be continued in darkness. The scene was far from quiet—men shouting, hammers slamming, and an occasional cheer when a completed pontoon was successfully put in place on the swiftly running Osage River.

The Guard's 150-man elite cavalry left the army's main body, traveling ahead, arriving at Yost's Station, where Davenport and fellow scouts reported that 300 to 400 rebels occupied Springfield. The Guard moved on, departing in early evening. The night was cold and dark; the Guard had no overcoats to protect them from intermittent rain. Near Springfield, just before dawn, scouts found Price and his army of 2,000 men. Fremont received word of the situation from Major Zagonyi. He advised not to attack Springfield and wait until Price "leaves town which he will do when he hears of my approach." Zagonyi left the Bolivar Road north of Springfield, crossing to the Mount Vernon Road to locate the Guard south of known rebel locations. He advised the Guard, "Never become defensive, go in and make the enemy defend himself. You were selected to fight and kill the enemy, not to march in a parade."

Zagonyi raced out a grove of trees toward an open field with a lane running along its center. Hiding on each side of the field back from the lane were enemy troops planning to establish a crossfire situation. The major opened a heavy fence gate, drawing enemy fire, proceeding to lead the Guard in a sweeping charge. His men yelled, "Fremont and the Union!" His troops entered the field, unleashing an unbelievable amount of firepower at the enemy.

Forty-seven men in the first company of the Guard faced 500 or 600 men. Noise of the attack, fast-moving riders, and rapid-firing guns quickly panicked rebel infantry, who left their positions, racing for the shelter of nearby woods. Slower men faced the wrath of the Guard's sabers. Price's volunteer country boys were no match for Fremont's well-trained, superiorly armed calvary. Rebel's feeble resistance lasted a few minutes before Price's men abandoned their positions. They were seen fleeing in every direction to get away from the battle. Loss for the Guard was 15 men killed. Twenty-six were reported wounded; some wounds were not reported. Forty horses were killed in the engagement; more than sixty animals suffered wounds that did not put them out of action. One guard had three horses shot from under him. Eighty-three rebel bodies were recovered. Davenport was in the second company of the charge. His experience as a sharpshooter caused several enemy troops to topple in place.

A victorious Zagonyi returned to Springfield, raising the flag over the courthouse. He released Union prisoners from the local jail and, later in the day, returned to join Fremont, placing a Union-friendly home guard in command until army troops arrived the next morning. Celebrations of the Guard's victory were held across the North. Liberal newspapers were full of praise for Fremont and his Guard, comparing Zagonyi's charge to the Charge of the Light Brigade in the Crimean War. Springfield's success was a tonic for Union troops, especially those in Missouri. Fremont had plans to pursue Confederates until they were driven out of Missouri. His army generated spirit and momentum needed for success.

Celebrations soured when word arrived from Washington that Fremont was to be relieved of his command and replaced when Major General Hunter arrived on November 2. Happiness in the ranks of the Body Guard turned to hatred and despair. Army general George McClellan dismissed everyone in the Guard. The unit was mustered out on November 28 without pay, quarters, or rations. Alfred left Missouri, returning to Circleville, Ohio, and his family. Fremont had the only success in Missouri during 1861. Hunter pulled back Union troops to the safety of Rolla and Sedalia. Momentum earned by Fremont was lost to benefit the enemy.

Fremont's Body Guard Led by Major Zagonyi
Springfield, Missouri

Chapter 33

The Mountain Department, Western Virginia

Davenport, at home in Circleville, was contacted by Maj. Gen. John C. Fremont and ordered to report to the general's headquarters in Wheeling as an aide-de-camp with duties as a special messenger. He would carry dispatches from Major General Fremont to Mountain Department's field generals. President Lincoln faced a storm in Congress from Fremont's staunch allies when the president dismissed him from Missouri. Fremont's backers, especially the eastern press, demanded he should be given a command. Lincoln, bowing to pressure, appointed Fremont to head his newly created Mountain Department effective March 29, 1862. Fremont's experience in fighting enemy guerrillas in Missouri would be an asset in western Virginia, where guerrilla activity was becoming a growing problem. He was tough on guerrillas in Missouri. A captured guerrilla would be given a military trial before being shot or hanged.

Fremont replaced Gen. William S. Rosecrans, whose star had faded in Washington. Fremont's headquarters was in Wheeling. The Mountain Department's western Virginia territory, known as the Kanawha Division, was based in Charleston, (West) Virginia, under the command of Brig. Gen. Jacob D. Cox.

Early on April 15 in a cold, driving rain, Alfred—with dispatches in hand—left Wheeling for General Cox's headquarters in Charleston. He traveled light, carrying meager food supplies, a few biscuits and slices of ham. Following a turnpike south along the Ohio River, he realized

Confederate guerillas operating in the area had no taste for foul weather, for he was alone on the road. Dressed in the attire of a local farmer, wearing a wide-brimmed hat covering his head and face, a long great coat covered a pair of navy Colt pistols and his sheathed Colt Revolving rifle acquired from Fremont. He reached Parkersburg's Union army post at ten in the evening.

The next morning, learning that guerrillas were active along roads south of Parkersburg, Davenport took a ferry across the Ohio River to safer Ohio territory. A trail on the north side of the river led southwest to Gallipolis, where he arrived at dusk. In the morning, Alfred recrossed Ohio near its junction with the Kanawha River and proceeded to follow a trail along the river to Charleston. General Cox had pacified the area, but a solitary rider risked being stopped by Confederate loyalists, secessionists, and guerillas. Alfred needed to be extremely vigilant. He detoured around settlements, forded streams, and cut through wooded areas avoiding all contact with locals. Fremont's dispatches were delivered to General Cox's at eleven in the evening. Return messages were given to Alfred early the next morning. He arrived in Gallipolis at seven in the evening. The next day, he rode to Belpre, Ohio, and crossed the Ohio River by ferry to Parkersburg, where he found a steamboat leaving for Wheeling and Major General Fremont's headquarters.

Fremont gave Davenport new dispatches on April 22 to take to Brig. Gen. Robert C. Schenck in Moorefield, Virginia. Davenport boarded the Baltimore and Ohio (B&O) Railroad to New Creek (now Keyser). The route from New Creek to Moorfield was a hard long trek by horseback to Schenck's camp near an army supply station. Rising hours before the first light, he left New Creek station, making the forty-mile journey to General Schenck's headquarters by six thirty in the evening.

No sign or evidence of guerrilla activity had been reported on his route. This meant fewer detours and delays were needed, but Alfred, always wary, was continually on the alert for an unexpected guerilla attack. He avoided hamlets and villages, finding it necessary to detour around settlements and farmsteads, where he had no way to discern the politics of local inhabitants. His route was difficult and challenging. Narrow switchback mountain trails over Patterson Mountain were muddy and slippery; rocks and boulders frequently blocked the way, causing unexpected detours and delays. Parts of the road that Alfred felt were ready made for an ambush were avoided. Davenport remembered mountaineering skills of traveling incognito from western experiences in the 1840s. Cautious and alert, he safely navigated through terrain where safe passage was questionable. His greatest challenge was to ford the south branch of the Potomac River swollen by spring rains and filled with treacherous currents, a task not for the faint of heart. Dismounting, he carefully and slowly led his horse into the swirling waters, proceeding to cross the river without incident.

Western Virginia counties contained pockets of secessionists who encouraged guerrilla activities. Confederate raiding parties conducted by rebel cavalry troops were considered guerrillas by Fremont. They lived off the land harassing and stealing from pro-Union citizens, collaborating with Southern partisans, and creating a multitude of problems for Union forces. The Confederate government sanctioned covert military operations using civilians as a cover to enhance sabotage against the Union. Targets were federal property and disruption of military activities. Confederates were operating in all counties of western Virginia. Their leaders, men too old to be drafted, performed targeted military operations while refraining from overt thievery or vandalism. A Southern partisan, known as a bushwhacker was a name given to a rogue guerrilla who robbed and murdered at will without a government sanction. Bushwhackers frequently were destitute, starving, homeless men; some were simply filled with anger. Often illiterate, they were the most dangerous guerrillas for a messenger to encounter.

The Baltimore and Ohio Railroad line extended from Parkersburg and Wheeling in the northwestern Virginia east to Harpers Ferry, where it crossed the Potomac River into Maryland, ending in Baltimore, Maryland. It was a major artery carrying men, material, and food supplies from the Midwest to Washington. Controlled by the Union army, the railroad was a frequent target of Confederate raiders and guerrilla attacks. Bridges were burned, supply depots seized, and tracks, telegraph lines, and equipment targeted and destroyed. The army found they needed to establish a series of fortifications along the B&O Railroad route to protect rail travel. Four thousand eight hundred men were required for the task. Locomotives were armor plated; railroad engineers and crew were armed. When requested Alfred used this important rail artery to deliver dispatches as Fremont's aid-de-camp.

Railroads, turnpikes, and roads were not the only routes susceptible to guerrilla attacks. The Union was forced to build a series of gunboats to patrol eleven western Virginia counties facing the Ohio River after rebels disabled Union River boats *Ben Franklin* and *Captain Jack* based at Parkersburg.

Fremont's appointment was part of a broad reorganization of the United States Army by President Lincoln. Disenchanted with the results of the general-in-chief of the army, George B. McClellan, the president relieved McClellan of his responsibilities in northern Virginia and the valley, leaving himself as successor commander in chief. He would direct the strategic and tactical operations in wartime theaters assisted by his secretary of war, Edwin M. Stanton. Each was a lawyer; neither had formal military training. The men worked together starting in the spring of 1862; both had different temperaments. Lincoln did not display the skills of planning and administration of Stanton, causing disagreements between the two, yet Stanton respected the president as master even when he disagreed on issues. Lincoln was cool and levelheaded, Stanton outspoken and impulsive. Both men were devoted to the preservation of the Union.

Fremont's Mountain Department encompassed western Virginia, eastern Kentucky, and parts of Tennessee. Headquarters was in the McLure Hotel in Wheeling. The hotel, built in a circular shape, opened its doors in 1852. The first floor's open lobby had feed and watering troughs for horse and mules, hitching posts for carriages, and strategically placed spittoons. Registration and offices were on the second floor, so patrons could avoid an often muddy lobby. Fremont brought staff members from Missouri including Germans, Frenchmen, and Hungarians. He appointed Col. Charles Zagonyi as commander of his cavalry. Alfred renewed his friendship with Zagonyi upon arrival at Fremont's headquarters, looking forward to serving with Zagonyi if given an opportunity.

Fremont wisely devoted his time to military matters. Civil policy issues and relations between Union and Southern factions were given to Francis H. Pierpont, the provisional governor of the new state of West Virginia, and Judge Advocate R. R. Corwine. President Lincoln planned for Fremont to cross mountains in western Virginia into East Tennessee, seize the railroad at Knoxville, and rescue Union sympathizers in the area. Lincoln's orders for Fremont included instructions to march into the Shenandoah Valley and take the Virginia and Tennessee Railroad. It ran west from Lynchburg, through a gap in the Blue Ridge Mountains near Big Lick (today's Roanoke), traversing a wide valley to Bristol on the Virginia-Tennessee border.

The commander in chief lacked an understanding of complexities and challenges facing troops in western Virginia. The army must cross a hundred miles of mountain wilderness in southwestern Virginia and East Tennessee, where the only roads were unimproved dirt paths. Troops would have no supply depots. Men would have to carry all supplies and weapons; forage found along the route would not supply enough sustenance to maintain an army's horses and mules. Dangerous and difficult travel through enemy territory would expose troops to constant guerrilla harassment and skirmishes from the Confederate army.

Major General Fremont, following Lincoln's orders, moved his army's field operations to New Creek on the first of May. New Creek was the chosen marshalling point for Fremont's southern campaign. An important rail center on the B&O Railroad, New Creek was strategically located on a hilltop, providing views of roads leading in several directions. One road faced east to Romney and Winchester. Directly south was the route to Petersburg and Franklin, crossing mountains to Staunton at the upper end of the Shenandoah Valley. A bridge at New Creek crossed the Potomac into Maryland. It joined a route following the river northeast to Cumberland, Maryland, an industrial city served by the B&O Railroad. The city was the western terminus of the Chesapeake and Ohio Canal connecting to Washington, DC. Cumberland was also an important center on the national road that began in Baltimore. It led west through Ohio's capital, Columbus, and Indiana's capital at Indianapolis, ending in Vandalia, Illinois, seventy miles east of Saint Louis.

Davenport was busy the first four days of May, leaving his courier duties, assisting Fremont in his move to New Creek. On May 5, Fremont's army departed from New Creek, heading south through Moorefield to a post at Petersburg. Early on the ninth, Davenport was in the saddle, carrying dispatches for General Rosecrans located in Romney, a thirty-eight-mile trip. He was back in Petersburg on the tenth.

A long and dangerous journey faced Alfred on May 11. He needed to deliver dispatches to the Kanawha Division in Charleston and to Gen. Jacob D. Cox fighting at Princeton, (West) Virginia. He began his journey, retracing the road to New Creek, where he boarded the Baltimore and Ohio railroad to Parkersburg. Steamboat *Ben Franklin* took him to the Kanawha River and upstream to Willow Bank opposite the city of Charleston. Military headquarters were in Willow Bank at the mouth of a stream named Ferry Branch, across the Kanawha River opposite Charleston. After delivering his first batch of dispatches, Alfred took another steamboat upstream on the Kanawha to Malones Landing at the village of Belle located fifteen miles south of Charleston. The landing was a steamboat hub for Union troops and their supplies. It was known as Camp Piatt.

Davenport, on horseback, followed the south shore of the Kanawha to Big Falls, the junction of the Gauley and New Rivers, where they combined to form the Kanawha River. He took the road south to Vandalia (Fayetteville after 1873), fording or crossing several streams: Cabin Creek, Paint Creek, and Big Loop Creek, all overflowing their banks because of heavy spring rains. Vandalia, a beautiful mountain town, was founded by a Revolutionary War farmer, Abraham Vandal. Its location, almost two miles west of the New River gorge, is one of West Virginia's most spectacular natural wonders.

Many area residents were pro-Southern when the war broke out. By winter of 1861–1862, the Union army controlled the Kanawha River valley and much of the trans-Allegheny territory. Union victories caused many secessionists to leave Fayetteville and its surrounding territory. When local men enlisted in the Confederate army, their wives and children left home to live with relatives at other locations. Vacant houses were appropriated for housing of senior Union army officers. Lt. Col. Rutherford B. Hayes (the future U.S. president) occupied one of Fayetteville's empty houses.

On November 18, 1861, Union troops under Col. E. P. Scammon were ordered to occupy Vandalia and construct fortifications for 1,500 men. By the end of December, three forts housed men of Ohio's volunteer regiments—the Twenty-Sixth, the Thirtieth, and the Twenty-Third, led by Lt. Col. Rutherford B. Hayes—plus a cavalry troop from Pennsylvania. Army reports from Hayes stated that bushwhackers were not active in the Kanawha Valley along the turnpike from Vandalia to Princeton because of a large presence of Union troops and his army's efforts at pacification of locals.

Leaving Vandalia, Alfred passed through Raleigh County Courthouse, now Beckley, which billeted a significant number of Union soldiers. He arrived at General Cox's headquarters outside Princeton Courthouse on November 16, to find a battle underway. Cox was up against Confederates led by Brig. Gen. Humphry Marshall, a West Point graduate, head of all Confederate armies in southwestern Virginia and eastern Kentucky. Marshall was accompanied by Gen. Henry Heth. Cox had been attempting to reach Dublin, Virginia, to destroy an important center of the Virginia and

Tennessee Railroad. Both Rutherford Hayes and Sgt. William McKinley (a future president) were serving under Cox's command at the time.

Cox's men advanced as far as Pearisburg when Marshall and his eastern Kentucky army arrived, driving Cox back to Princeton. A skirmish pushed Cox's men out of Princeton. Confederates established a position south of town on Pigeon Ridge, overlooking the town. On May 17, fresh troops from the Thirty-Seventh Regiment of Ohio Volunteers nosily marched back past Pigeon Ridge with plans to retake Princeton. Lying in wait was the Fifty-First Virginia Infantry, secluded and hidden, waiting to ambush the Ohioans. (Where were Union scouts?) Taken by surprise, the Thirty-Seventh had 23 soldiers killed, 50 wounded, and 14 taken prisoner. The ambush ended the day's battle. Neither side pursued the enemy. Cox retreated twenty miles to the security of his camp atop Flat Top Mountain, ending his thrust toward Dublin. Alfred carried Cox's report back to Fremont.

Alfred's travels permitted him to witness the impact of war and suffering of local populations in western Virginia. He learned many homesteads were isolated, long distances from villages and towns. People lived on farms along mountain creeks and hollows or on ridges far from any neighbors. Forests had been cleared, timber used to build a homestead and barns and enclosures for farm animals. People raised corn, wheat, and vegetables. Corn was consumed for food, animal forage, and making whiskey. Apple trees provided fruit for the kitchen and hard cider. Hunting provided extra protein for a mountaineer family. Twice a year, inhabitants from the most remote settings visited town to acquire salt, sugar, gunpowder, and bullets.

Western Virginians were extremely loyal to their family, clan, and state. When the war broke out, men eagerly signed up for ninety-day enlistments in Virginia's Confederate army. Three-month enlistments created manpower shortages for the army, causing enlistments to be extended to a one-year term. Volunteers, early in the war, were often granted leave for planting and harvesting crops. Later in the war, leave was not granted. If they left the army to help their family, they were deserters.

A deserter brought a new type of problem to western Virginia mountains. They lived off the land, robbed, stole, and bushwhacked for survival. Fear of capture by the rebel army caused them to become nomads. Absence of fathers, husbands, or male companions created a great burden for women. As head of a household, women stood between starvation and survival of her children. Normal chores, keeping house, preparing meals, canning and storing food, care of clothing, and helping children with school lessons were suddenly only part of a woman's daily life. Fields needed to be prepared for planting and harvesting crops. Animals needed care. Hay had to be gathered for winter forage. Grain crops harvested for bread. Cows needed milking twice a day. Meat supplies required animal butchering and processing. Older family men past army age helped a younger family's members, though most farms lacked labor needed to complete tasks of successfully running a farm. Some women received no help; they faced the possibility of starvation.

Life was worse for those living in war-torn communities. When a village or community changed sides due to struggles of war, residents suffered the greatest hardships. Limited supplies of stored food, animals, clothing, or any belongings of use were stolen or destroyed by conquering soldiers. Confederates punished towns harboring Northern sympathizers; Union did the same for towns with secessionists. Houses and whole towns were burned; men were beaten, shot, or hanged, women abused and raped. Great fear developed in communities changing sides during the war. Women would hide food, children, and themselves from soldiers, bushwhackers, and strangers. Homesteads were no longer safe havens. No one trusted their neighbors. Families split apart; brothers who were on opposite sides of the war killed each other when their armies met on a battlefield.

Alfred was relieved that extreme suffering and the horrors of war had not reached his Ohio family. He maintained a great loyalty to the army and his country and was proud to be serving under Major General Fremont. He believed the Southern rebellion must be crushed and slavery abolished. He would participate in his small way to help make the Union become whole again, a day he hoped he would live to see. Davenport arrived at Fremont's headquarters in Moorefield on May 27 to learn a new assignment for Fremont was in the works; it would be remembered as Fremont's pursuit of Stonewall Jackson.

Chapter 34

Mountain Department: Early 1862 Shenandoah Valley

The Confederate war situation in March 1862 worsened. Gen. Joseph E. Johnston, commander of Army of Northern Virginia, was aware of Union troops gathering on the eastern shore of the Potomac across from Occoquan and Dumfries, Virginia, south of his location at Manassas. Scouting reports stated that large army recruitment efforts were under way by the federal army. The reports filled Johnston with grave concerns. He ordered all troops east of the Blue Ridge Mountains to fall back to a defensive line of the Rapidan-Rappahannock River, a strong position to defend the Confederate capital fifty miles south of the line.

General Johnston held the central division of his army in Manassas until March 9 to allow massive army stores to be moved. Departure was slow, for wagons struggled in axle-deep muddy roads left by winter rains. Trunks carrying personal items of soldiers were abandoned along railroad lines and burned. One million four hundred thousand pounds of meat stored at the army's commissary plant near Thoroughfare Gap were given to farmers or destroyed. Barrels of whiskey were smashed, pouring their contents on the ground. Heavy ordinance was abandoned. The cavalry was the last to leave, departing on the tenth, destroying all remaining property and firing depots. Union soldiers did not reach Manassas until March 11.

General-in chief of the Union Army of the Potomac, George B. McClellan, arrived at Virginia's peninsula between the York and James

Rivers with 100,000, men planning to take the war to the Confederate capital at Richmond eighty miles west. The Navy Battle of Hampton Roads, or the Battle of Ironclads, was held on March 6–8. Two ironclad ships, the USS *Monitor* and the CSS *Virginia* (*Merrimack*) fought to a draw. The action prevented the CSS *Virginia* from sinking wooden U.S. Navy ships bringing men and supplies to McClellan's army on the peninsula. The U.S. Navy's blockade remained in place, continuing to prevent international trade and military supplies from reaching industrial centers at Norfolk and Richmond.

Thirty-five thousand Union troops under Gen. Irvin McDowell arrived at Fredericksburg, Virginia, awaiting orders from Lincoln. Union major general Ambrose E. Burnside had taken Roanoke Island off the North Carolina coast; securing the coast, he began moving inland. Maj. Gen. Ulysses S. Grant took two important Tennessee forts. Fort Henry was seized on February 6 and Fort Donaldson ten days later where 14,000 Confederate troops were taken prisoner. The South lost control of both Cumberland and Tennessee Rivers. Confederate general Thomas J. "Stonewall" Jackson, with 4,200 troops, was defeated by Gen. Nathaniel Banks's 9,000-man brigade at Kernstown, Virginia, in the lower Shenandoah Valley on March 23. Confederate losses and Johnston's retreat from Manassas without being pressed by Union troops, was greatly criticized by Confederate leaders. President Jefferson Davis decided to change leadership of the Confederate army, appointing Robert E. Lee as commander-in-chief.

Despite Jackson's losses at Kernstown (one-quarter of the participants in the battle), Jackson's actions in the valley kept Lincoln from sending additional troops from General McDowell to General McClellan. A concerned President Lincoln refocused on the valley and the defense of Washington, which the president felt was not secure. Stonewall Jackson slowly retreated up the valley, keeping General Banks occupied. General Blenker's arrival with 10,000 men brought Banks's army strength to 30,000, outnumbering Confederate troops six to one. Banks slowly moved up the valley, reaching New Market on April 19, Harrisonburg on April 26. Jackson was east of Massanutten Mountain at Conrad's Store. West of the valley, Fremont's General R.H. Milroy was moving on the Parkersburg-Stanton Road towards Confederate General Edward "Allegheny" Johnson who was defending a critical approach to Staunton.

General Banks sent reports on April 19–21 to Secretary of War Stanton stating that Jackson had left the valley. On April 30, he wrote, "Jackson was headed to Richmond." Banks was told to establish a defensive line in the lower valley through Strasburg. President Lincoln removed Shields's division from Banks, sending the men to General McDowell for a move on Richmond. Gen. Louis Blenker's division was ordered to leave Winchester and join Fremont in western Virginia.

Thomas R. "Stonewall" Jackson was unique. Tall and soft spoken, he was quiet and secretive, never sharing tactical plans with his generals. His skill as a strategist forced the enemy to fight on his terms. He pushed his troops hard to gain desired objectives. The early hours of May 3 found Jackson's army abandoning the valley, departing east through Browns Gap in the Blue Ridge Mountains. When he arrived at Mechums River Station of the Virginia Central Railroad near Charlottesville. His army boarded a train to return to Staunton. Secrecy was paramount; no one was to know of his presence in Staunton. No one could enter or leave the town. Jackson, with 9,000 troops, left before dawn on May 7, heading northwest to support Johnson and take the fight to Fremont.

On May 8, eighteen miles west of Staunton at the junction of the Warm Springs and Harrisonburg Turnpike, Generals Johnson and Jackson encountered Union army troops. Confederates sought and occupied a high pasture known as Sitlington's Hill one and one-half miles east of McDowell. They looked down on Union camps in a valley called Bull Pasture. General Schenck's brigade arrived from Franklin, joining Milroy to fight Jackson. Union troops stormed the hill but were not able to dislodge stubborn Confederate defenders. Rebels were silhouetted against the sky, making them targets for Union sharpshooters. When holes appeared in the Confederate line, new troops arrived to fill the slot. Every Union frontal or flank attack was repulsed. Fighting lasted for four hours until eight thirty in the evening. Jackson's losses were 461, Schenck's 256.

After dark, Union troops—outnumbered over three to one—pulled back, leaving the village of McDowell to Jackson. The next day, May 9, Schenck realized he did not have the manpower to defeat the Confederate army. He began an organized withdrawal from McDowell to Franklin, fighting in stages, using rugged, mountainous terrain to ambush advancing rebels with hidden artillery, and firing forests on each side of the turnpike to delay and confuse the enemy. Schenck fortified Franklin, awaiting the arrival of Fremont's 15,000 reinforcements.

Jackson realized he would be outnumbered with the arrival of Fremont. He planned a return to the valley to join Ewell and hit Banks, who had established a weak defensive line at Strasburg. Schenck and Milroy were no longer threatening Staunton. Jackson departed from McDowell on the evening of May 14, sending Captain Hotchkiss to block major roads leading from McDowell and Franklin to Harrisonburg by felling trees, destroying bridges and culverts, and rolling boulders in paths over which large guns would be pulled.

Fremont arrived at Franklin on the same day to assist Schenck. Seeing Jackson had departed, Fremont stopped to rest his exhausted troops for the next ten days. Blenker's army took thirty-eight days to catch up with Fremont after leaving Martinsburg. They arrived in a wretched condition, traveling without tents or shelter through the inclement April weather. Many in Blenker's army were ill; clothing and shoes were inadequate. Forage was very limited; horses were starving.

Jackson continued to move his men toward the valley. He met with Ewell on May 18 to discuss strategy fighting Banks. Ewell split his troops. One group would unite with Jackson at Sparta. The rest of his men would continue up the south fork of the Shenandoah to Luray. Brigadier General Ashby's cavalry was to remain in place in front of Banks to prevent him from learning that Jackson had returned to the valley. Jackson left New Market on May 21 and crossed Massanutten Mountain, joining Ewell in the Luray Valley. Jackson now had 17,000 men and forty-eight pieces of artillery. Banks's army had been reduced to less than 7,000 troops. On May 21, Jackson initiated his move against Banks, beginning by storming the 1,000-man Union outpost at Front Royal. Ashby charged ahead, cutting all communication lines between Front Royal and Strasburg.

Results of the day, General Banks lost Front Royal. Nineteen Union men were killed, 63 wounded, and 691 taken prisoner. Banks, in his headquarters at Strasburg, was skeptical of the size of the rebel force until he heard from multiple sources of losses at Front Royal. Weighing his options, he would fight to save Winchester, the key to the valley and the major supply depot for the Union army. Fortunately, the road to Winchester was still open. Banks left at three in the morning on May 24. His army faced numerous Confederate units at Middletown, causing much confusion and a considerable loss of Union supply wagons to the delight of Ashby's cavalry, whose momentum was slowed while his men picked through spoils of war. Confederates were thrilled to capture abandoned supplies. Their clothes were worn and dirty; food supplies, coffee, sugar, and salt were almost depleted. Twenty percent of the men in one Confederate division were barefoot.

Jackson continued the battle fighting Union forces, all night, nipping at Banks's rear guard. Stonewall was anxious to control the heights overlooking western Winchester. By daybreak, his men—despite tough resistance—overwhelmed 2,100 Union defenders on Winchester's heights. This gain eliminated one of Banks's flank positions. Ashby controlled Berryville, roadblocking Banks's other flank, preventing a Union retreat to Harpers Ferry. Banks's only option was to race north to Martinsburg and retreat to Williamsport, where he would cross the Potomac River into Maryland. Banks, during the rout, lost half his army. Three thousand were taken prisoners by Confederates.

Jackson's position in the lower valley brought large risks to his army. He learned that Lincoln was reinforcing valley troops. Lincoln ordered General McDowell to send a brigade to Harpers Ferry and move the balance of his army to the valley, join Fremont, and trap Jackson. Fremont was ordered to abandon plans for an East Tennessee campaign. He was to race to Harrisonburg and cut off Jackson's retreat. The route to Harrisonburg from Franklin was impassable due to Hotchkiss's efforts, rendering the Franklin-Harrisonburg Turnpike unusable. Secretary of War Stanton approved Fremont's request to retreat through Moorefield, taking the road to Strasburg to "attack the enemy whatever you find him."

News of Lincoln's plans caused Jackson to return up the valley. He stopped at Winchester on May 30 to quickly gather scattered army units before traveling to Strasburg the next day. On the same day, Shields—with McDowell's army—was moving into Front Royal, twelve miles from Strasburg. Lincoln expected Fremont to be in Strasburg on May 30, but Fremont was in Wadesville, twenty miles east, planning to be in Strasburg by five thirty the next afternoon. Unfortunately, the next day, Fremont halted several miles west of Strasburg. Shields remained at Front Royal on May 31. He was ordered to link up with Fremont, but orders did not state what day he should move to Strasburg. If he abandoned Front Royal, it would be undefended against Jackson. General Ord's army had not yet arrived from Alexandria to join Shields. Fremont had no idea of the location of the armies of Banks and McDowell.

Stonewall scouts kept the Confederate general appraised of Union locations and strength. Jackson was facing the combined armies of McDowell and Fermont, three times the size of his forces. Banks had another 14,000 across the Potomac, ready to move on retreating Confederates. Jackson briefly occupied Strasburg before racing south toward Harrisonburg, ahead of his two approaching foes.

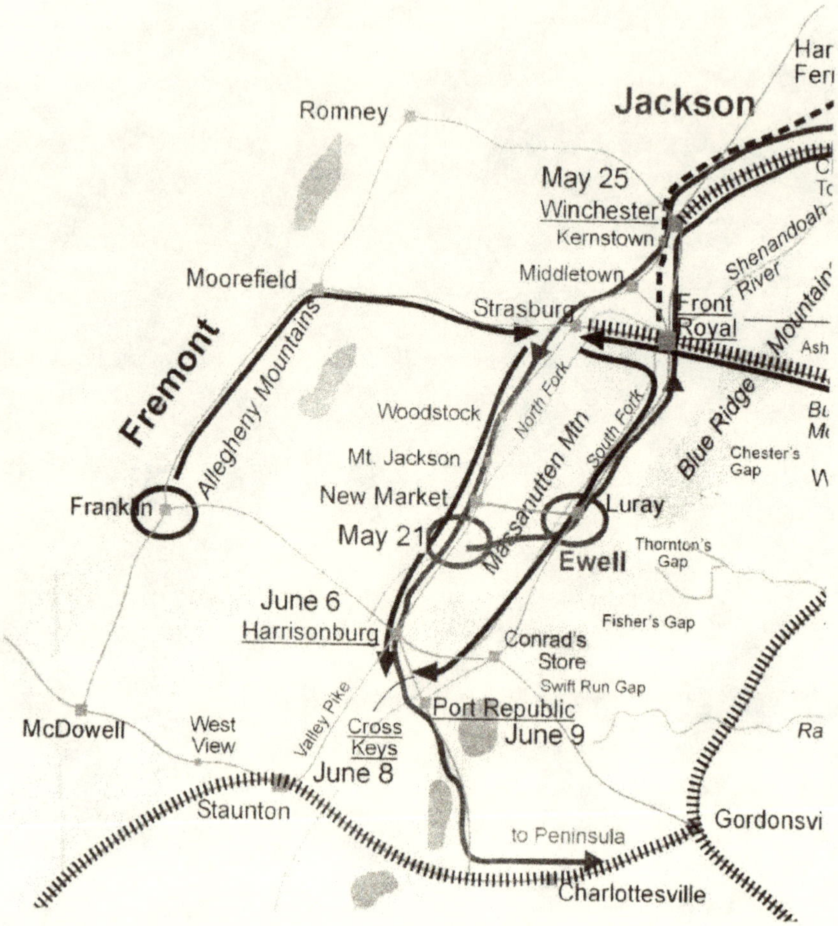
Jackson
Romney
May 25
Winchester
Kernstown
Middletown
Shenandoah River
Moorefield
Strasburg
Front Royal
Blue Ridge Mountains
Fremont
Allegheny Mountains
North Fork
South Fork
Woodstock
Massanutten Mtn
Mt. Jackson
New Market
Chester's Gap
Franklin
May 21
Luray
Ewell
Thornton's Gap
June 6
Harrisonburg
Fisher's Gap
Conrad's Store
Swift Run Gap
Valley Pike
Port Republic
June 9
McDowell
West View
Cross Keys
June 8
Staunton
to Peninsula
Charlottesville

Chapter 35

Shenandoah Valley, May–June 1862

Alfred reconnected with Fremont in Moorefield when he delivered dispatches from General Cox. His return had been horrendous. In addition to avoiding unfriendly partisans, unusually heavy rains filled his route with washouts and mudslides. Winter and spring storms were some of the worst ever recorded. Record rains made travel in western Virginia almost impossible. Alfred's arrival at Moorefield on May 27 coincided with Fremont's departure for Strasburg. Ten miles were traveled that day. The next day, the army reached Fabius on Branch Mountain.

Alfred was appalled at the condition of the men arriving from Brig. Gen. Louis Blenker's division, who had struggled to join Fremont. During a thirty-eight-day march, illnesses and exhaustion broke up military companies, leaving them strung out along mountain roads. Less than six thousand men in Blenker's army were fit for duty. Military discipline had disappeared. Abandoned, disabled, and broken army supply wagons lined Blenker's route. A lack of wearable shoes plagued his army. Fremont, listening to pleas from his medical officer, ordered a day of rest and reorganization. Davenport reported that the army resumed its march the next morning in heavy rains, slowing crossing of the summit between Lost River and Cedar Creek to a crawl. Two roads led from Cedar Creek, one leading to Winchester, the other to Strasburg. Fremont took the Strasburg Road.

Lt. Col. Gustave Paul Cluseret, a French Army officer serving in Fremont's Mountain Department, reached Ewell's pickets outside Strasburg early on June 1. Confederate's Ashby responded to Cluseret with a cavalry attack supported by well-placed artillery. Firing from infantry troops suggested that Fremont faced several regiments. Confederate artillery stopped at noon. Alfred joined the Union cavalry, who pushed ahead, discovering the enemy had withdrawn. He returned to headquarters, giving this report to Major General Fremont.

Reconnaissance discovered Jackson's rear guard two miles south of Strasburg on the Woodstock Road. Union cavalry fired on the enemy; Ohio's Sixtieth and the Eight (West) Virginia formed the head of a reconnoitering column, checking for any advance against Union troops by the Confederates. Fremont became aware that Jackson had slipped through Lincoln's trap, evading two armies. He was moving quickly toward the upper valley.

Alfred continued to bring reports to headquarters despite heavy rain and a hailstorm, creating hazardous travel on Virginia's red clay roads. Beyond Strasburg, Alfred found a macadamized turnpike (a road constructed of graded gravel), the main turnpike of the central Shenandoah Valley. The turnpike was a welcome relief from the muddy paths crossing Virginia's mountains. The next morning, Fremont's calvary continued tangling with Jackson's rear guard. Midmorning, Ashby's forces turned and gave battle. General Bayard, with a cavalry of eight hundred, arrived from Front Royal, joining Colonel Zagonyi's cavalry of six hundred. Fighting lasted for an hour before the rebels turned and fled. The enemy's pattern was for their cavalry to retreat, turn and fight, again retreat while their main army tore up roads, burned bridges, and destroyed culverts. In five hours, the Confederates retreated eighteen miles.

Fighting between armies was often at close quarters; rebel troops frequently were less than one hundred yards in front of Union troops. Colonel Pilsen, chief of Union artillery, had his horse shot from under him, suffering minor wounds. A hot Union pursuit netted recapture of five hundred union prisoners, troops lost during Banks's retreat from the lower valley. Alfred noted that Confederates rapid retreat caused their army a considerable loss of equipment, several hundred small arms, deserted ambulances and wagons. It was estimated that one thousand enemy stragglers fled into nearby woods. Stonewall spent the night of June 2 at Mount Jackson.

On June 3, Alfred continued delivering position reports and estimates of enemy strength to headquarters. Heavy rain and torrential downpours were conditions to which he had become accustomed. Bad weather did not stop Jackson from retreating. A bridge over Stoney Creek at Edinburg, five miles from Woodstock, was damaged but repairable for Fremont's infantry troops and artillery. Zagonyi and Bayard were able to cross the creek at a nearby ford. Swift cavalry action prevented rebel troops from destroying another bridge over Cedar Creek at Mount Jackson.

North Fork of the Shenandoah contained an important bridge torn up and burned by Ashby's men. Union forces facing withering fire from rebel artillery and infantry were unable to halt the destruction of the bridge. Fremont brought up pontoons to assemble for crossing the river. Major Haskell swam his horse across, taking ropes to secure the pontoons to the opposite shore. Heavy rain did not stop engineers who worked through the night completing the pontoon bridge assembly. Cavalry and infantry troops began crossing at dawn until rising water threatened to destroy the temporary bridge. Ropes were cut, allowing the bridge to swing to the north shore, causing a considerable loss of timber and several swamped boats. Troops on the south shore established defensive perimeters, aided by strategically placed artillery on heights above the crossing for a possible enemy attack that never materialized. Early the next morning, waters receded, allowing replacement of the army's pontoon bridge. A day had been lost in the pursuit of Jackson.

Stonewell's army reached Harrisonburg in midday on June 5. He changed his route, electing to take a side road to Port Republic and Browns Gap, where he would be closer to the Virginia Central Railroad. The enemy's path was easy to track. The secondary road was a sea of mud, slowing progress.

Jackson sent Hotchkiss to a post on Massanutten Mountain where Hotchkiss signaled Jackson, reporting General Shields's strung-out position in the Luray Valley. Stonewall previously ordered the burning of bridges over the Shenandoah to slow Shields's progress. Fremont entered Harrisonburg, where he received a letter from McDowell. He had previously asked McDowell for additional troops to join the Mountain Department in Strasburg. McDowell replied in a letter from Front Royal stating he would not take orders from a subordinate, only from the secretary of war or the president. Request denied. An additional request was made to General Banks for cavalry. Banks replied he could not help. His cavalry was in poor shape; they would be a hindrance to Fremont.

Confederate general Ashby established a defensive line two miles south of Fremont on the Port Republic Road. Col. Sir Percy Wyndham, an English cavalry officer serving with Fremont, pursued Ashby with a force of eight hundred. A bitter fight ensued. Ashby was assisted by Ewell's infantry. Wyndham's advance was repulsed; the colonel and sixty-three men were taken prisoner. Fremont responded by sending General Bayard and Colonel Cluseret's cavalry to cut off Ashby's advance on June 6; intense, fierce combat ensued. Union troops poured destructive fire into rebel lines, causing them to weaken. Ashby darted ahead; his horse was shot. Immediately recovering, he continued to lead his troops, charging on foot, until a sharpshooter shot and killed him. Confederates answered Ashby's death with heavy fire, charging Fremont's front and flank, driving them from their positions, creating heavy losses. After dark, Fremont pulled back toward Harrisonburg to regroup.

Ashby's death weighed heavily on Jackson. Ashby's remains were taken to Port Republic, where a military honor guard took the corpse to Waynesboro. A train took the remains to a burial site at the University of Virginia in Charlottesville. Jackson gave his infantry a rest on June 7.

Fremont's army was the size of Jackson's, Shields's somewhat less; but together, they outnumbered Jackson close to two to one. Jackson elected to stop retreating. He was determined to fight while the Northern armies were separated. He made Port Republic his headquarters and supply center. His army was placed in a defensive position on the north side of the South Fork of the Shenandoah River. On June 8, Ewell's was sent ahead of Jackson to the hamlet of Cross Keys at its intersection with Keezletown Road. Ewell established a line along a wooded ridge overlooking cleared fields next to Mill Creek, south of Cross Keys. Jackson's strategy was to fight Fremont, turn, and fight Shields. He would maintain an avenue for his escape from the valley through Browns Gap in the Blue Ridge Mountains.

Pontoon Bridge on the March

Chapter 36

Cross Keys and Port Republic

Fremont sent Colonel Cluseret's brigade on point at five in the morning on June 8. Fremont's regiments were unorthodox by army standards, each regiment formed as a separate army unit containing cavalry, infantry, artillery, supplies, and ambulances. This sequence and organization, appropriate for a group of explorers, was cumbersome and repetitive, causing delays in deployment of a military regiment. Mud-filled roads contributed to the slow deployment of troops, artillery, and wagons. Fremont's last brigade got underway at seven thirty in the morning. In contrast, Stonewall Jackson's cavalry, pickets, artillery, and infantry marched with ammunition and a limited amount of food. His men did not stop or eat until his objectives were met. All of Jackson's supply support was located at the rear of his army.

Captain Davenport joined Cluseret's advance group. A line of enemy was discovered in front of Union Church at about eight thirty. Rebels fired on Union skirmishers and retreated to their right, falling back to Ewell's main defensive line. Davenport hurried to the rear to give Fremont an updated view of the opening battle at Cross Keys. Fremont relied on several special messengers (aides-de-camp) to bring situation reports to headquarters at the rear and to deliver orders (dispatches) to frontline commanders. Early in the morning, Capt. Nicholas Danka, carrying orders from Major General Fremont to General Blenker, was killed by a rebel sharpshooter. Jackson, in contrast to Fremont, used few messengers, preferring to be on-site located at or near his front lines, where he could personally direct and instruct his generals.

Fremont's battle line placed Col. Julius Stahel's brigade (Julius H. Stahel-Szamwald, a Hungarian officer) with five regiments of Blenker's division on the far left. Gen. Henry Bohlen (German born) was next, General Milroy in the center, and General Schenck on the right. Ewell placed his most aggressive general, Trimble, opposite Stahel, followed by Courtney/Latimer and Generals Elzey and Steuart. Both sides used skirmishers (sharpshooters) to lead a brigade's advance, probing enemy lines to discover enemy troop locations, strengths, and weaknesses.

The Battle of Cross Keys began at nine o'clock with an hour of artillery barrages. Milroy received the most fire. Stahel received less artillery fire, permitting him to quickly advance his Eighth New York toward the Confederate line. Stahel decided to move ahead without employing skirmishers. Trimble's Confederates, benefiting from knowledge of terrain and ground cover, planned an ambush. Stahel's line of 500 green troops—primarily German emigrants. The men spoke little English, knowing little about military tactics, proudly advanced their line toward the enemy. Suddenly, less than one hundred feet ahead, Confederate soldiers, hidden by leaves and fallen logs, rose from the earth. Screaming a fearful battle cry, they delivered decimating fire, destroying Stahel's column. Panicked men broke formation, racing toward the rear. Losses were heavy at 223 killed or wounded. Tremble's men charged after the panicked troops until Stahel's heavy artillery broke apart their charge. Confederates were turned back, failing to reach their objective of capturing Union artillery.

Milroy's front was a different story. He advanced to Mill Creek with plans to flank the rebel line. His men crossed the creek, advancing up a ridge above creek, pushing hard against Ewell's men. The battle was fierce. Confederate generals Elzey and Steuart were wounded. Milroy requested more men to turn and destroy Ewell's flank. Instead of receiving support, Fremont ordered him to fall back to form a balanced line. Milroy was so distressed by Fremont's order that he could not face his men. He asked a subordinate to deliver Fremont's instructions.

General Schenck reached Ewell's defenders on the Mill Creek Ridge. Like Milroy, he was enjoying a good level of success. His progress was stopped when Schenck received orders to pull back. Fremont was directing commanders from field headquarters near the intersection of the Keezletown and Port Royal Roads. Learning his front left line had collapsed during Stahel's retreat, Fremont decided to restructure his line. Cluseret was ordered to maintain his forward position in the center of the Union line. Orders sent to Milroy and Schenck to shift troops to rebalance the front line suggested that Fremont was unaware of the success Milroy and Schenck were having against the enemy. Not being on the scene, Fremont was unable to see advances his troops were making against Confederate positions.

Late in the day, a scout appeared at Fremont's headquarters, carrying a dispatch from General Shields, and reported, "Twelve pieces of artillery should be opposite Jackson's train in Port Republic. Two brigades are in Port Republic with two more en route." Certain that the Port Republic bridge was in Union hands, Fremont ordered his men to rest for the remainder of the day. Picket lines were set for the night; preparations were made for a general advance in the morning. During the day, a Union messenger and his documents were captured. Documents revealed the presence of seven Union brigades. Ewell, knowing that he was greatly outnumbered, returned to Port Royal to consult with Jackson. He sent Colonels James Patton and Trimble to spend the night on their front lines a few yards away from the enemy camps to maintain a picket line. Dawn found the enemy gone from Fremont's front.

Shields was ordered by Lincoln to move south into the Luray Valley to link up with Fremont. Shields delayed, remaining in Luray; Confederate deserters reported Confederate general Longstreet was moving toward him with an army of 10,000 men. Shields sent Gen. Erastus Tyler into the valley on June 7. A forward brigade of Shields's army led by Col. S. S. Carroll was a day ahead of Tyler. Carroll commanded four infantry brigades and a 150-man cavalry along with Battery No. 1 of the First Ohio Light Artillery. Twenty-two-year-old captain Miles W. Keogh, who had served as a papal guard in Rome, led the final six miles to Port Republic, arriving at six in the morning, one mile below the village, as the battle started at Cross Keys.

The village of Port Republic is located at the confluence of the North and South Rivers where it forms the south branch of the Shenandoah River. Crossing the North River was a covered bridge. The river was flooding due to recent rains. North of the bridge was a rolling countryside, where Jackson's infantry and artillery were camped. Jackson maintained his headquarters in Madison Hall, southwest of town, a quick ride from the bridge. The morning was a quiet Sunday. Residents and army troops were preparing for Sunday church services. No one suspected the arrival of Colonel Carroll and his men.

Carroll learned from scouts that Port Republic was lightly defended by cavalry. He began his battle plan, placing two of his four pieces of artillery in a position to cover the entrances of the covered bridge. Additionally, two were placed opposite the middle of the village on a high piece of ground, Yost Hill. Artillery fire opened the action, followed by a charge from his cavalry as they forded the South River. Confederates were initially shocked when artillery landed in their midst. Alerted to Carroll's surprise attack, they quickly returned fire. Jackson, seeing the attack unfold, saddled his horse and raced through town across the bridge as it was shelled by Union artillery. He escaped to the safety of his army on the north shore of the North River.

Men in the village threw up barriers; artillery was brought into battle. Great confusion descended on a quiet Southern community thrust into war by Carroll's attack. Union men took the bridge that Carroll had been instructed by Shields not to burn. A burned bridge might have kept Jackson's army from escaping. He would have been trapped between Fremont on the north and Shields's Tyler on the south. Carroll soon realized he was facing Jackson's entire army. Fremont was nowhere to be seen. Carroll saw rebel soldiers forming behind stone fences and other barriers; artillery was being wheeled into place. Main Street became a battle scene, with bullets whizzing by in every direction. Greatly outnumbered, Carroll decided to retreat across the South River and rejoin General Tyler, who was in Lewiston, two miles northeast of Port Republic. Retreat meant giving up control of the bridge over the North River and abandoning the South River at Port Republic.

Stonewall had planned to fight both Fremont and Shields separately, not together. The arrival of Carroll caused a change of plans. He sent General Winder against federal troops at Lewiston. During the night, Jackson built a footbridge using wagon parts to take his infantry across the South River. General Tyler successfully fended off Winder and his reinforcements. Jackson's losses were 816. Federals lost 832.

Captain Davenport arrived at what had been the Port Republic bridge early on June 9. All that remained of the once beautiful covered bridge over the North River were a few charred timbers lying on each shore. There were no signs of Confederates in the village. Battle was taking place on hilly terrain east of the South River. Alfred returned to Fremont's headquarters to give this report. Fremont ordered long-range guns east along the north shore of the Shenandoah, where they began shelling rebels fighting Tyler and Carroll. Union men east of Port Republic, faced with an overwhelming number of Confederates, were forced to retreat to a mountain plateau known as the Coaling.

Jackson moved his army late the next day to a cove at the foot at Browns Gap in the Blue Ridge Mountains, which permitted his escape from the valley. On June 10, Shields—under presidential orders—returned to Luray. Fremont was ordered by Lincoln to return to Harrisonburg. Confederate colonel Munford's cavalry was harassing a retreating Union army, causing Fremont to leave for Strasburg on June 14. Year 1862's battle for the Shenandoah Valley was finished.

Washington announced on June 28 that General Fremont was superseded in command by General Pope. Fremont left for Washington; his staff was broken up. Alfred was transferred to an army post at Middleton on July 4, reporting to Quarter Master Maj. Charles N. Goulding. Captain Davenport was now in the Quartermaster Corps. July 13 found Alfred at Quartermaster Headquarters in Washington, DC. He met with Surg. Gen. W. A. Hammond and his staff, where he was assigned the responsibilities of a supervisor of hospital construction in the western theater of the war, providing status reports for Washington. He returned to Circleville on July 30, waiting for orders to begin his western tour.

Major Goulding was not so fortunate. While visiting Major General Pope's supply headquarters at Catlett Station, Virginia, on August 21, the post was attacked by 1,500 Confederate cavalry troops led by Jeb Stuart. The Union lost 300 men, Major General Pope's dress uniform, and several hundred thousand dollars in U.S. currency. Goulding was taken prisoner and sent to Richmond.

Civil War military leaders had diverse training. Generals Lee, Jackson, and Johnston enjoyed the advantage of training in military strategy and tactics as graduates of U.S. military academies. The valley campaign during the spring of 1862 was led by President Lincoln, Secretary of War Stanton (both trained lawyers), and Generals Banks, Fremont, and Shields, political appointees. Results of clashes in the Shenandoah Valley demonstrated differences between leaders with military training and those without. Both sides made mistakes that spring; however, many of the North's problems began with Washington. Were Union generals "more concerned about not losing a battle than filled with a desire to win"?

PART V

Quartermaster Department

Chapter 37

Alfred's New Assignment

    Alfred brought a wealth of experience to the Quartermaster Department. His role as manager of Fremont's Pine Tree Mine in Mariposa, California, provided skills for working with people, production, and finance. The next twelve months would find Davenport traveling extensively in the West as the Quartermaster Department raced to construct new hospitals. Military successes in the western states in Kentucky, Tennessee, and Mississippi meant more troops, more battles, and an increased need for hospital facilities. All aspects of developing, constructing, and equipping new hospitals had to be approved by the quartermaster general's office. Invoices to pay vendors needed approval in Washington, endorsement by the secretary of war forwarded to the Treasury Department for payment. All paperwork was processed by hand.

    The Army Quartermaster Department in the Civil War became an immense, far-reaching organization necessary for the success of any military campaign. The department was structured into three major sections. Section one handled clothing: knapsacks, haversacks and canteens for all enlisted men and uniforms, tents, and garrison equipment for officers.

    Section two covered transportation. Sailing ships, steamboats, railroads, wagons, ambulances, horses and mules to pull wagons, and forage for animals fell under this domain. Six mules or four horses were needed to pull a wagon. Twelve pounds of hay (forage) and 10 pounds of grain were needed daily for each animal at a cost of thirty cents per day. Railroads, operated by the quartermaster, carried 300 tons of supplies each day. Steamboats carrying men and materials were owned or chartered by the quartermaster.

Section three included all regular and contingent supplies of all departments—hospitals, barracks, quarters, fuel, stationary items, and incidentals used by the army. The section built and furnished houses at each post. Fuel costs: fifteen cents for a bushel of coal, Four dollars for a cord of wood. In three and a half months, January 1 through April 20, 1863, 150,000 bushels of coal and 18,000 cords of wood were delivered to supply depots. Two hundred miles of board fences were taken from the countryside to be used for bunks, cots, and coffins Major distribution centers gathered supplies and shipped them to regional depots for sending to frontline locations serving armies in the field.

Henry Varwig, a baker in Cincinnati, Ohio, contracted to produce 3 million pounds of hard biscuits (hardtack) for the army. He used 200 barrels of flour a day to make 800 boxes of hardtack. Boxed hardtack were shipped to a supply depot in Columbus, Ohio, combined with other goods and sent by railroads to major supply depots in Washington DC, Baltimore, and Louisville. These centers would forward hardtack to locations supporting field armies.

The Commissary Department was responsible for feeding the army. The cost of a daily ration was twenty cents per man. Quartermasters provided transportation, collecting food from vendors for distribution to supply depots. Troops received fresh bread three out of each five days. Hardtack was supplied when fresh bread was not available or when troops were on a march or in battle. Quartermasters supplied each brigade with portable bake ovens and equipment, kneading troughs, baking pans, and other items needed for bread. Alfred learned that regiments with the best cooks were the healthiest and most effective troops.

Labor needs by the war effort were immense. Quartermasters, commissaries, provost marshal's, judges, and policemen hired nonmilitary citizens paid $75 to $100 a month to handle required paperwork for quartermaster headquarters in Washington. Over 3,000 men were hired as mechanics and laborers. They shoed horses, repaired wagons and gear (harnesses), were used as teamsters, or were hired to bury the dead. The responsibility of burying war dead and care of national cemeteries belonged to quartermasters.

Controlling costs and preventing fraud in purchase contracts required vendors to submit bids advertised in local newspapers. A new law in June of 1862 required all contracts to be signed by a vendor and certified by a magistrate. Civilian contractors were subject to U.S. Army regulations, enforced by a court-martial. The law helped limit overcharging and fraudulent contracts.

Care of a wounded soldier began at a dressing station at the edge of a battlefield. Wounds were packed with lint; tourniquets were applied to halt or slow bleeding. Men with chest or abdominal wounds were given opium to get relief from pain. Wounded soldiers in stabilized condition were transferred to a field hospital, a large tent located at the rear of a battle area, for secondary care. Hospital tents provided poor protection from the elements. They were hot in the summer, cold and wet from rain and snow in the winter. Wounds were sewn; amputations of mangled limbs were performed at field hospitals. The aftermath of intense battles would find piles of amputated limbs stacked outside a field hospital, awaiting burial details.

During a battle, there were never enough surgeons to attend massive numbers of wounded men. Surgeons were forced to operate well beyond sunset, using only the light of candles to perform their duties. Today's sterile procedures followed in hospital operating rooms were unknown. Mornings found surgeons visiting sick and wounded men, changing dressings, treating fevers, and preparing men to be removed to a general hospital for convalescence.

Kentucky, a border state, began 1862 with rebels controlling a large part of the state denoted by a line stretching east from Columbus on the Mississippi River through Bowling Green, the Confederate state capital, east to Cumberland Gap. Columbus was fortified with 143 pieces of artillery. Rebels constructed a heavy iron chain across the river connecting Columbus to Belmont, Missouri, an effort to deny Union use of the river south of the barrier.

A combined force of the Union army and navy led by Gen. Ulysses S. Grant and navy commodore Andrew H. Foote took Fort Henry on the Tennessee River in northern Tennessee on February 6. Ten days later, a second combined operation gained a strategic location in Tennessee, taking Fort Donelson on the Cumberland River. The Confederate army lost over 14,000 men, 20,000 rifles, 65 pieces of artillery, and significant supplies. This was the first major win in the Civil War for the Union and the first capture of a rebel army. The way was open for the North to take Tennessee's state capital, Nashville, on February 23. The city had been an important Confederate manufacturing and munitions center.

Grant moved to southwestern Tennessee, camping at Pittsburg Landing near Shiloh Church on the Tennessee River. Confederate general Albert Sidney Johnston surprised Grant on the morning of April 6, attacking with a force of 30,000 troops from his base in Corinth, Mississippi. Confederate general Johnston was killed during the battle. Grant was able to establish a defensive line around his landing despite the surprise attack. Heavy Union artillery from river gunboats throughout the day held off rebels.

Gen. Don Carlos Buell's Army of the Ohio, camping at nearby Savannah, Tennessee, raced into battle, increasing Grant's army strength to 40,000 men. Grant launched a fierce attack at six in the morning on April 7, forcing Confederates to lose initiative. Running low on food and ammunition, rebels retreated to Shiloh Church. Well-placed rebel artillery supported by 5,000 men held off Union troops while the bulk of Beauregard's army escaped to their base at Corinth.

The Confederate's attack on April 6 caused the Union army to lose its field hospitals and equipment. Wounded men had to be left where they fell; stretchers, ambulances, and medical supplies for field hospitals were lost during early hours of battle. A few fortunate wounded souls were taken to the rear by friends. Volunteer women nurses on the battle's perimeter, lacking supplies, tore up their skirts for dressings. Dr. B. J. Irwin, arriving with Buell's Army of the Ohio, commandeered enough tents from the infantry to accommodate 2,500 wounded men. He hastily constructed a field hospital to care for the wounded until they could be evacuated north by a fleet of medical riverboats on the Tennessee River manned by members of the Western Sanitary Commission based in Saint Louis.

Union major general Halleck started for Corinth on April 29. Seventy thousand rebels hiding behind an earthwork protecting the town were suffering from dire straits. The town's water supply was contaminated. Thousands of once effective troops suffered from typhoid fever, dysentery, and diarrhea. That night, Confederate general Beauregard loaded his army on flat cars of the Mobile and Ohio Railroad and escaped. Union troops arrived to face dummy guns mounted like cannons on the earthworks. The only troops remaining were buglers and drummers, who continued to play Confederate fight songs after the arrival of Union soldiers.

A Mississippi River naval battle lasting for two hours on the outskirts of Memphis was fought on June 6. The Confederate navy's deep draft vessels lacked adequate protection from Union naval guns. Systematically, the Union navy sunk Confederate boats in a two-hour battle. Only the

CSS *General Earl Van Dorn* escaped to New Orleans. The city surrendered at noon the same day.

Confederate generals Braxton Bragg and Kirby Smith met on July 31 in Chattanooga, drafting plans for a campaign to retake Kentucky. A newly created Confederate Army of Kentucky was planned. They would clear Union troops out of Cumberland Gap and destroy Buell's Army of Ohio. Kentucky would become a Confederate state. Battle began on October 7, 1862, near Perryville, Kentucky, with 20,000 men fighting on each side. The fight was basically a draw, with the Union giving up about one mile of real estate. Confederates soon realized they were not going to capture badly needed Union stores. Contrary to the Confederate commander's belief, the local population had no desire to join the Southern cause. Rebel troops were forced to retreat through Cumberland Gap to Knoxville. Casualties for both sides were high; the Union lost 4,276 men, the Confederates 3,401.

The Army of Ohio lacked a field hospital or ambulance system at Perryville. In the race to reach the Confederate Army of Kentucky, Buell ordered medical equipment and hospital wagons left behind. His army maintained few regular army surgeons. Without tents, the 2,800 wounded were forced to occupy every farmhouse in a ten-mile radius around Perryville. Men suffered for days, not having their wounds dressed. Perryville was experiencing a drought. The town's wells were dry; wounded men were dirty and remained dirty. The only available food was field rations consisting of hardtack and salt pork not digestible by wounded men. Relief came only when trains ordered from the Army Medical Department and the Western Sanitary Commission arrived in Perryville.

Abraham Lincoln replaced Buell with Maj. Gen. William S. Rosecrans, feeling Buell spent too much time preparing to fight and not enough time fighting the enemy. The combined armies of Buell and Rosecrans became the Army of the Cumberland. Rosecrans departed from Nashville on December 16, 1862. President Lincoln wanted Confederate forces out of middle Tennessee and Union control of eastern Tennessee. The English Parliament was meeting in January. Lincoln feared Confederate control of middle and eastern Tennessee would strengthen an argument that the South was winning the war. England's Parliament might vote for England to join the war on the Confederate side.

Union and Confederate armies clashed on December 31 at Stones River near Murfreesboro, Tennessee. A surprise early morning charge by rebels caught Union troops at breakfast. The Union army was pushed back five miles. The Confederate attack was blunted by Union general Philip Sheridan, whose men had prepared for a surprise attack. His troops fought hard, slowing the rebel charge. Regrouping and employing effective artillery and reinforcements allowed Union counterattacks to save Rosecrans's line of communication, the Nashville Pike.

The next day, January 1, 1863, saw little activity as both sides celebrated the new year. A rebel assault on January 2 was repulsed by Union artillery. Forty-five cannons pounded rebels with withering fire, causing 1,800 casualties in the first hour, followed by a counterattack ending with a Confederate retreat. Confederate general Bragg withdrew his army during the night of January 3 to Tullahoma, Tennessee, thirty-six miles south. The Battle of Stones River (also called the Second Battle of Murfreesboro) involved 78,400 men—12,906 Union casualties and 11,739 Confederate. The battle took the lives of 4 brigadier generals. The armies fought again on June 24 to July 3. Rosecrans defeated Bragg at Tullahoma, securing central Tennessee for the Union.

Congress expanded the Quartermaster Department in July 1862, adding 100,000 new men. Alfred was part of this group. He spent most of July in Washington learning new responsibilities and his role in the Quartermaster Department. He returned home to Circleville, Ohio, in mid-August before assuming duties in the western theater of the war.

The Army Medical Department was not prepared for war. Senior officers realized suitable hospital facilities were unavailable when thousands of wounded and sick men flocked North after the First Battle of Bull Run. Each army regiment maintained a field hospital, the traditional unit of medical treatment. Field hospitals were small and inadequate. They lacked supplies and were found, upon inspection, to be filthy. Fourteen army regiments had no hospitals. Maj. Gen. Don Carlos Buell, like some of his contemporaries, considered medical departments a tolerable but unpleasant necessity. Visits by Army Medical Department officers in July of 1861 to Cairo, Illinois, and supply depots in Ohio and Missouri found no ambulances or stretchers. A feeble effort to remedy the situation was begun. Cairo, one of the West's major supply and distribution centers, received only two ambulances and two stretchers by November 1861. No guidance nor instructions about the use of ambulances and care for the wounded were performed.

The Quartermaster Department was responsible for transporting wounded men using ambulances and boats. Hospital ships lacked provisions, medicines, and medical supplies. The Battle of Fort Donelson brought to the forefront the army's inability to properly care for wounded troops. Men in field hospitals (tents) suffered through cold and wet weather, sleeping on the ground due to a lack of hospital beds. After four to five days, a wounded soldier was sent to a regional hospital. In the West, they were carried by steamers to Paducah, Mound City, Cairo, or Saint Louis. The war had gone on for a year when on April 16, 1862, Congress, addressing deficiencies in medical care, passed a bill reorganizing the Medical Department to care for sick and wounded men. Surg. Gen. William A. Hammond became head of the department on April 25, establishing a general hospital system.

In early autumn 1862, Captain Davenport was sent to Nicholasville, Kentucky, to visit a newly planned quartermaster supply depot and hospital called Camp Nelson, where he reported on the status and needs of the new camp's hospital to Washington's Quartermaster Department. Later in the war, the camp became a refuge for escaped slaves and their families and a recruitment center for African American soldiers.

Alfred's diary shared the report of his journey to Nicholasville. He traveled by train, using a ferry to cross the Ohio River between Cincinnati and Covington. He was required to keep a detailed log of all expenses—railroad tickets, ferry, meals, and lodging—to obtain reimbursement from the Quartermaster Department. Early in his travels, he had adequate funds for his expenses. Longer trips and extended stays soon depleted his savings. He was forced to borrow funds from his brother Charles while he awaited reimbursement from the Quartermaster Department. Alfred's army income was $70 per month.

An expense report submitted in December contained expenses for an extensive two-week trip. His journey was by train to Cincinnati and Danville, Kentucky; horse-pulled carriage to Lebanon; and train to Bowling Green with a return through Danville. Alfred's train segments were short. Each segment of the rail line had a different owner even though railroads segments were connected to one another. This meant multiple tickets needed to be purchased for a long trip. He spent $33.10 in transportation costs.

Hospital care continued to be a critical problem in the western theater of the war as the number of battles increased. Upon termination of hostilities in Perrysville, Danville's new courthouse and many town buildings were appropriated for use as hospitals. Alfred's visit provided a detailed update on the status and condition of Danville hospitals. Included in the report were details of medical inventories and supply requirements for hospitals. His report detailed the suffering of wounded men caused by inadequate hospital care.

Alfred was ordered to Memphis in December 1862. Memphis was an important agriculture center of the antebellum South. Slave labor in cotton fields made possible the South's financial success. Cotton was the financial king in Memphis. Shipping on the Mississippi River opened doors for cotton exports worldwide through New Orleans. Memphis was Alfred's introduction to Deep South culture. It was an unusual town. Streets were paved in rotting creosoted wood planks giving off a damp, musty smell. Trash and raw sewage plagued the city. Saloons and brothels were a large visible part of the bustling business of Memphis.

Generals Grant and Sherman selected Memphis as a regional military headquarters. Memphis was strategically located on the Mississippi River between New Orleans and Saint Louis, Missouri, and the military supply center at Cairo, Illinois, located at the mouth of the Ohio River. Memphis was served by two important railroads. The Mobile and Ohio Railroad stretched north to the Ohio River and south to Mobile, Alabama. The Memphis and Charleston Railroad connected Memphis with the East Coast. Both the river and railroads were critical to move men and supplies for the U.S. Army's western campaign. Alfred was soon surprised by the discoveries he made after his arrival in Memphis.

Chapter 38

Alfred Visits Western Hospitals

Initial estimates of Civil War deaths were 620,000. The count had been revised upward to include deaths of emigrants who volunteered to join the conflict. Eight hundred thousand emigrants came to the United States between 1861 and 1865. Large numbers arrived from Ireland, Scotland, Wales, England, and Germany. The United States population was 31 million at year-end 1860.

Two million recruits under the age of twenty-one joined the Union army. Most recruits were between eighteen and nineteen years old; some signed on as musicians. The youngest, a drummer, was thirteen. Two-thirds of Civil War deaths were caused by disease. Cholera, typhoid, malaria, measles, diarrhea, and dysentery were major causes. Men joined from farms and rural communities. They never had been ill and were susceptible to childhood and other diseases. In the first year of the war, 640 out of every 1,000 recruits suffered from intestinal ailments. During the next twelve months, this number grew to 995 out of every 1,000. Illness was caused by several factors. Poor diet, unclean and unsuitable clothes, a lack of decent shoes, filthy quarters, unsanitary latrines, contaminated water, and no baths were common for the army. Fresh, clean water was not available at most camp locations.

Men cooked their own meals. Young recruits had no experience cooking. The easiest method for preparing food was to use a frying pan. Everything consumed, often limited to salt pork and beans, was fried. Vegetables and sweets were not provided by the army's Commissary

Department. It was late in the war before the value of fruit and vegetables was recognized when potatoes, onions, turnips, and dried apples were added to a soldier's diet, creating a notable improvement in their health.

Surg. Gen. W. A. Hammond began revamping the military's hospital system, which was to become a worldwide standard. Each military hospital was designated a military post with a surgeon in command. Cities with multiple hospitals had off-site hospital command centers. Reforms instituted by Hammond vastly improved military hospitals. General hospitals were built with new and innovative designs. Roof ventilation and circulating, fresh, clean air among the sick and wounded lessened the transmission of airborne diseases. Private vendors hired to remove waste from hospitals were replaced by army-led detailing groups. Hammond banned the use of medical compounds containing mercury, which he felt were not safe nor effective. A new system of career promotion for the medical war department was established based on performance and competence, not on rank or political connections.

Constructing and equipping new hospitals fell on the Quartermaster Department. Building a new hospital was time consuming and slow; as a result, a variety of buildings in many locations were used as hospitals. Warehouses, railroad stations, a girl's school, jails, a coach manufacturing facility, and a silk mill were converted to hospitals. Administration and bookkeeping for general hospitals were centralized. Wards for patients were separated from kitchens, laundries, and supply areas, leading to efficiency in discharging duties. Changes helped reduce mortality rates.

Pavilion hospitals emerged with a newly created design. Wings, looking like spokes of a wheel, spread out from a central core provided good ventilation for patients. Men with wounds were separated from those suffering with diseases. Size of hospitals ranged from "giant" with 3,000 beds to "pigmy" with 102 beds. Specialty hospitals were constructed in multiple locations. Saint Louis had an eye and ear hospital. Nashville had two hospitals for venereal disease. Memphis had a hospital for those suffering from gangrene, one for smallpox patients, and a third for those with measles. Under the orders of the surgeon general, 182 general hospitals were in use by the end of 1863. Only 8 additional general hospitals would be built by the war's end.

Capt. Alfred Davenport's duties required visits to general hospitals in the western theater of the war. He forwarded reports evaluating construction progress, staffing, and operational readiness to quartermaster headquarters.

Memphis was his busiest stop. The city become a hospital town with over 5,000 beds used for the military. Ten buildings, formerly housing businesses and warehouses in Downtown Memphis, were converted into hospitals. They were located on streets ending at the Mississippi River, providing ease of access for steamboats and barges bringing scores of wounded and sick men to the city for medical treatment.

Hospitals needed immense stores of material and food to supply their needs. High levels of planning, organization, and job execution were needed to make the hospital system work. Innovations abounded. The Gayoso Hospital pumped water from wells to storage tanks on its roof, providing water for use on each floor. This allowed patients access to a bath. Mary Ann Bickerdyke, a highly regarded Union nurse working with Dr. Irwin, established steam laundries for Memphis hospitals. Hospital were traditionally staffed with male nurses. In Memphis, women from the Western Sanitary Commission and nuns from the Catholic Sisters of Charity were added to hospital staffs. Several hospitals established libraries for convalescing patients. New patient treatments developed. Cases of gangrene, treated with a mild bromine solution, dropped mortality rates from over 60 percent to less than 3 percent.

Wounded officers had separate care. Officers were treated in private hospitals and returned home on sick leave to convalesce. They were not sent to general hospitals. Memphis opened a small officers' hospital staffed by Sanitary Commission nurses who provided food, beds, and clothing. It was an army custom for officers to pay for their own food. Major support for all wounded men was provided by the United States Sanitary Commission, a predecessor of the American Red Cross. The commission was started in Saint Louis to provide aid for the wounded in the western theater. Gen. U. S. Grant hired steamboats for the Western Sanitary Commission to be used as floating hospitals to transport wounded men to general hospitals.

During a visit to Jefferson General Hospital, the tragedies of war came home to Alfred. He learned that many wounded were from his hometown. The 114th Regiment, Ohio Voluntary Infantry, one of 260 Ohio regiments, mustered into the army at Camp Circleville, Ohio, on September 11, 1862. The camp, located on land donated by Jacob Ludwig, was an army recruiting post, two miles from Circleville. Recruits came from Pickaway, Fairfield, Fayette, Perry, Hocking, and Vinton Counties.

The regiment's first major battle was fought at Chickasaw Bayou (Walnut Hills). The battle began on December 26, 1862. It was the start of the Union army's attempt to remove Confederates from Vicksburg, Mississippi. Seven gunboats escorted fifty-nine transports led by Gen. William T. Sherman up the Yazoo River north of Vicksburg, landing at Johnson's Plantation. Naval-artillery-initiated action pounded Confederate troop positions. Soldiers waded through knee-deep cold water, fiercely assaulting rebels. Initial efforts pushed the enemy from the river's edge across the Chickasaw Bayou (swamp).

The main fight, an attack on the Confederate's strong point, Walnut Hills, began on December 29. A four-hour artillery barrage was followed by a line charge. Unfortunately, Sherman's naval and land artillery did little to destroy entrenched enemy positions located on an Indian mound at the center of the Confederate line. Repeated attempts to take the hill were repulsed, creating heavy casualties. After five unsuccessful attempts, Sherman ordered Union troops to withdraw. A flanking move upriver was called off due to heavy fog.

Sherman's report to General Halleck stated, "I reached Vicksburg at the time appointed, landed, assaulted and failed." Grant's attempt to take Vicksburg was stalled. Sherman was greatly chastised by Northern newspapers for his December failures. His army of 30,720 suffered over 1,800 casualties. Ohio provided eleven infantry regiments and three artillery units for the action. The wounded were taken to the nearest general hospitals, located in Memphis.

Alfred slowed his work in Memphis to visit sick and wounded men from Ohio's 114th Regiment. The youngest was a fourteen-year-old musician, a drummer in the regiment band. Music by army bands was an important part of both Union and Confederate armies. Mid-1862 recorded over six hundred regimental bands in the Union army. Officers used bands to invigorate soldiers before beginning a battle. Emigrant band members were a favorite, especially music from German musicians.

Alfred discovered that men in the 114th were from all companies; the largest group came from Company E. Alfred's examined hospital records, seeking additional information about the men he visited. Hospital records were incomplete, poorly maintained, and of little help. He learned that soldiers who survived minor wounds or disease were returned to their regiment. In many instances, they were assigned to a "new" company, making it difficult to track the service history of missing or deceased men. Seriously wounded men who lost limbs or were permanently crippled, deaf, or blind were given a certificate of discharge by a surgeon and sent home.

Alfred offered to write letters for a few men unable to write family or loved ones. One letter was to the parents of Jacob Basil, notifying the family that their son would soon be discharged. The letter asked them to "please send someone to Memphis to help their son return to Fairfield County, Ohio." Another letter was sent to Joseph Asbury. It reported that his son, wounded in battle, was convalescing at the Jefferson Hospital in Memphis. "Would his father please send him a letter and tell him about his family."

Alfred listened to survivors tell stories of heroics, bravery, and the horror of a man next to a soldier in a line charge, seeing a buddy cut down by enemy fire. "Captain Lynch was perfectly cool in battle. He stood like a rock facing a hail of bullets directing his men's fire at enemy positions until taken down by a Minie Ball." Minié balls were hollow bullets sent down a rifled gun barrel by an explosive charge. Shots were accurate to 250 yards. Minié balls shattered bones and shredded internal organs. Easy to load, minié balls made bayonet charges obsolete. Lieutenant Wilson lost a leg from a cannister shot. Cannisters replaced grape shots during the Civil War. Cannisters, fired from artillery cannons, broadcast a wide pattern of steel or lead bullets with an accuracy of 400 yards. A well-placed cannister shot would effectively take out an entire line of charging enemy soldiers.

Men who recovered returned to their regiments. Pvt. John W. Hearn's luck ran out when he was killed on May 27 at the Battle of the Black River, Mississippi. Nathan Cokeley returned to Company H and died of wounds at Van Buren Hospital in Lykens-Bend, Louisiana. Survivors returning to their regiments faced death and disease before their enlistment ended.

Alfred was visiting hospitals in Cincinnati when he received his next assignment, Nashville, Tennessee. He departed on April 23 aboard the steamboat *Imperial*, the grand dame of steamboats plying western rivers. A fast side wheeler, she was a showpiece gliding through the Ohio and Cumberland Rivers to Nashville. Decks were high, allowing Alfred to enjoy fresh springtime air. Army officers traveled first class, meals an upgrade over army rations. No guerrilla incidents nor interruptions occurred on the voyage to Nashville. The *Imperial* was the first steamboat from Saint Louis to arrive in New Orleans after the fall of Vicksburg opened the Mississippi River to the Union in August 1863.

Nashville had twenty-five hospitals with over 7,000 beds. It was the second-largest federal military hospital network, exceeded only by Philadelphia, Pennsylvania. When Union troops captured Nashville in

February 1862, the Confederacy lost about 30 percent of the Confederacy's hospital capacity. Hotels, churches, schools, a carriage factory, Masonic buildings, and private homes had been converted into hospitals. More men suffered from disease than from battle wounds. Hospital Number 16 took care of African American soldiers. Nashville's old military college housed convalescing Confederate soldiers. The "Pest House" was a specialty hospital for treating soldiers with venereal diseases.

Alfred discovered Nashville's hospitals were crowded and dirty. Disease was rapidly spreading among Union soldiers even though the wounded were segregated from men with illnesses. Alfred completed his Nashville report for the surgeon general in May. He was due in Louisville to visit the Brown General Hospital, the largest of six military general hospitals, a regional center for treating ophthalmic wounds and disorders. While in Louisville, Alfred noted in his diary that he needed a new watch, acquiring one at G. Wolf Watch Makers. Next were visits to Cincinnati and Cairo, Illinois.

Cairo was maintained as an important military center throughout the war because of the town's strategic location at the confluence of the Ohio and Mississippi Rivers. Men and supplies arrived at Cairo by steamboat and railroads. Cairo began the war with an inadequate, miserable hospital system. In the summer of 1861, Mary Ann Bickerdyke brought the U.S. Sanitary Commission to Cairo. Her efforts and those of a local lady, Mary Jane Safford, greatly improved the state of hospital care in Cairo. Quarters for wounded and sick men were cleaned, improved, and upgraded. Men were provided with a healthy diet. The steamboat *City of Memphis* was converted into a hospital ship managed by the Sanitary Commission. Cairo war her home port.

In June 1863, Surgeon General Hammond completed his military hospital construction program. Alfred's duties in the department were about to change. When visiting Belleville, a manufacturing center in southern Illinois across the river from Saint Louis, an advertisement appeared in in a Saint Louis newspaper dated June 27. It stated that an important letter was waiting for Capt. Alfred Davenport at the Saint Louis U.S. Post Office. He sent a telegraph asking the letter to be forwarded to him in Belleville, Illinois. Soon after its receipt, Alfred was on a train heading East.

Chapter 39

A Brief Trip East

Captain Davenport's new assignment was in Greencastle, Pennsylvania, an eight-day trip from Saint Louis, Missouri, traveling on a series of railroads. Early in the war, private and military railroads came under the Quartermaster Department, which was given responsibility for all rail transport of men and supplies needed for the war effort. The department wisely selected seasoned and experienced railroad executives to supervise and manage Union railroads.

Year 1861 began with ten thousand miles of railroads in the North concentrated in mid-Atlantic states and New England. American railroads were operated by four hundred different companies. Railroads companies were local businesses, each controlling fifty to one hundred miles of track. Not all railroad gauges (widths) were the same. Standardized rail gauge was not set until well after the war. Long-distance travel meant multiple transfers between rail companies at major rail junctions, most likely located at or near a city. Trains hauling freight stopped at the end of a company line; freight was transferred to a line owned by a different company. Passengers followed the same routine. Some transfer points were over a mile apart. Only a few cities had a Union station where all rail lines came together in one location. One city, Columbus, Ohio, was among the first cities to have a Union station, completed in 1851.

Steam engine's requirements for water meant frequent stops to refill engine boilers. A cord of wood was consumed by an engine's firebox every fifty miles. Stops for wood and water created delays on every journey. Coal, a more efficient fuel to burn, was not used universally by railroads until after 1865. The speed of a passenger train was slow, averaging twenty miles an hour on a level ground. Climbing inclines, rounding bends, and crossing bridges necessitated slower than average speeds. Tracks were iron or steel rails secured to wood ties placed on the ground. No wood preservatives nor gravel ballast was used, resulting in deterioration of wood ties in a short time span. Railroads used by the military had a limited number of passenger cars. Open, flat cars and freight cars fitted with crude wood benches transported most troops. Doors on freight cars remained open for ventilation. Freight cars had no toilets. A hole cut in the corner of a car served the purpose.

Alfred reported to Brig. Gen. Fitz Henry Warren, commander of the Department of the Susquehanna, upon his arrival at Greencastle, Pennsylvania on July 22. Warren, a Massachusetts native, was editor of a Burlington, Iowa, newspaper in 1844. Politically active in the Whig Party, he was the first to promote Gen. Zachary Taylor for president at the party's convention in 1848, landing Warren an appointment as first assistant postmaster general, a job he kept until President Taylor's death. Warren rose in the Whig Party, becoming secretary of the party's National Executive Committee. A split in the party at the National Whig Convention of 1846 created a new party, the Republican Party. Warren, a principal organizer of the new political party, selected John Charles Fremont as the Republican presidential candidate in the 1856 election. Fremont lost to James Buchanan, a Democrat, who served as president until Abraham Lincoln, a Republican, was elected to the office beginning March 4, 1861. Warren was the chief editor of the *New York Tribune* when the First Battle of Bull Run occurred. He covered the battle, writing a controversial article, "On to Richmond." He left New York for Iowa, joining the military as a colonel, where he helped recruit the First Regiment Iowa Volunteer Cavalry for the Union army. President Lincoln appointed Warren as brigadier general on July 18, 1862.

In the spring of 1863, President Lincoln—realizing Confederate commander Gen. Robert E. Lee was headed into Maryland and Pennsylvania—called for 100,000 volunteers from Pennsylvania, Ohio, New Jersey, and New York to stop a Confederate invasion of the North. Two military departments were created in Pennsylvania, the Department of the Monongahela and the Department of the Susquehanna. The latter established headquarters in the Cumberland Valley at Chambersburg, commanded by Maj. Gen. Darius N. Couch. Both departments were to be filled with volunteer militia recruits charged with defending Pennsylvania from a Southern invasion. Unable to fill both departments after recruiting 33,000 volunteers, the United States provost marshal, under instructions from Secretary of War Stanton, used the Civil War Military Draft Act of March 3, 1863, to draft men aged twenty to forty-five into the army. Draft quotas were based on the number of eligible men living in a congressional district.

Enforcement of the act by federal agents created civil unrest. In New York City, four days of draft riots occurred; a barrel containing the names of 1,200 men selected for the army was torched. Strikes broke out in Pennsylvania's coal mining counties; miners opposed the draft and the war. Anthracite coal production, critical for war materials, was slowed or stopped, with mobs taking over mines in some areas. Governor Curtain refused to use state militia to enforce the draft. General Couch recommended using the federal army to stop draft riots.

Early skirmishes between the militia's Department of the Susquehanna against Confederate cavalry occurred on June 20 at Greencastle, Pennsylvania. A large rebel army invaded Cumberland Valley on June 24. General Couch abandoned Chambersburg, moving his headquarters to Harrisburg, where he began constructing fortifications to defend the state capital from invaders. General Lee advanced across Maryland, establishing headquarters in Chambersburg, Pennsylvania, on June 27. Confederates raided U.S. Quartermaster Department storage facilities in Chambersburg, taking medical supplies, ordnance, clothing, food, and other items for their supply trains. Federal warehouses were burned; farms in the area were ransacked. Farmers suffered losses of hams, bacon, salted beef, vegetables, stored wheat and grains, cattle, and horses. Southern troops were amazed at the abundance of farms in the valley, especially trees filled with ripe cherries.

A company of Pennsylvania militia soldiers captured by Confederates were instructed to form a line and told to remove their socks and shoes. The militia was sent on its way barefoot minus weapons. Most Confederate soldiers had worn out their shoes; their army lacked replacements. On June 29, Lee ordered his corps east of the mountains toward a small town called Gettysburg to protect his communication lines to Virginia. General Ewell, who had taken Carlisle, reluctantly headed south and east to join Lee. On the same day, Brig. Gen. Fitz Henry Warren received an order to report for a command in the Department of Susquehanna. On July 1–3, 1863, Gettysburg, Pennsylvania, suffered the bloodiest battle of the Civil War, incurring between 46,000 to 51,000 casualties. Both sides claimed victory. Lee—running short of ammunition, supplies, and manpower—was forced to leave Pennsylvania and return to Virginia. The tide had turned for the North.

Problems persisted in Pennsylvania's coal mining counties after the Gettysburg campaign. Miners continued to resist orders to be drafted into the army. Forty U.S. Army dragoons (cavalry troops) arrived in the village of Hackersville, where they were met and surrounded by a mob of over 100 angry miners. Army officers, explaining the recruiting needs of the army, moved on to other locations without incident. Three thousand men in Mineville, Pennsylvania, planned to attack the Forty-Seventh Pennsylvania but backed off when the militia field artillery and infantry troops arrived at the scene. Col. James B. Fry, U.S. provost marshal general in Washington, ordered Pottsville's provost marshal to complete his draft recruiting, using federal troops for enforcement. J. W. Bomford, provost marshal of Pennsylvania, notified Fry that Scranton and parts of Luzerne and Columbia Counties' coal regions needed larger numbers of troops to guard lines of communications, bridges, and railroads for protection against destruction by rioters.

Secretary of War Stanton's answer to Pennsylvania's draft resistance was an army directive ordering protesters to be rounded up with force. The orders specified the use of bayonets to take rioters to an induction center. Substitution, a practice where a wealthy man would pay $300 for a man to take his place on a draft role, was a widely used rich man's tool, hotly despised by miners. Hysteria was spread by local papers with reports of disruptions, violence, and inflammatory comments. "The drafts is as welcome as a pack of mad dogs." Immigrant miners had no loyalty to the North or South. Many who spoke little English lacked understanding of the war nor why they had become involved. They were trying to earn a living under difficult conditions. Work hours were long; working conditions in mines were not safe. Company towns and stores kept mining families poor.

Secret societies arose, dominating county politics, influencing judges and jurors. The societies, referred to as Molly Maguires, were active antiwar clubs dedicated to the disruption of coal production in anthracite coal fields. Miners voiced demands for better mining conditions, higher wages, and no draft. Scranton's vital war industries—manufacturing iron and steel for armaments, railroads, and ships—were dependent on the production of anthracite coal to maintain the needs of military for the war and became targets of protesters.

Alfred reached General Warren in Pottsville on July 29. August 1 found Alfred making his way to Scranton, a growing city with a population of 12,000 (as reported in the 1860 census). Half the population was foreign born. Labor demands were high in Scranton, home to two of the country's major war industry suppliers. The Dickson Company manufactured railroad locomotives and large steam-powered engines used to pump water out of coal mines. Lackawanna Iron and Coal Company produced Iron T rails for railroads.

In Scranton, Alfred learned that local provost marshals had the power to administer the draft without approval from state or local authorities. Provost marshals represented the interests of major coal and manufacturing companies, often owning a financial interest in these companies. War had blurred the lines between job-related labor strife and draft resistance. Strike activities had become viewed as a resistance to draft, unpatriotic, and an act of terrorism.

Davenport's reports for the Quartermaster Department in Washington found no major disruption in the supply chain for products shipped to the army from Scranton. No major labor incidents occurred requiring use of troops from the Department of the Susquehanna during his visit. General Warren received orders on September 29 to report to the Department of the Gulf in New Orleans, Louisiana. Alfred left Scranton the next day for Cairo, Illinois, and a Mississippi River steamboat that would take him to New Orleans.

Naval Combat off Fort Wright in the Mississippi River, May 8, 1862

Timberclad

Hospital Tree at Fair Oaks

Second Try

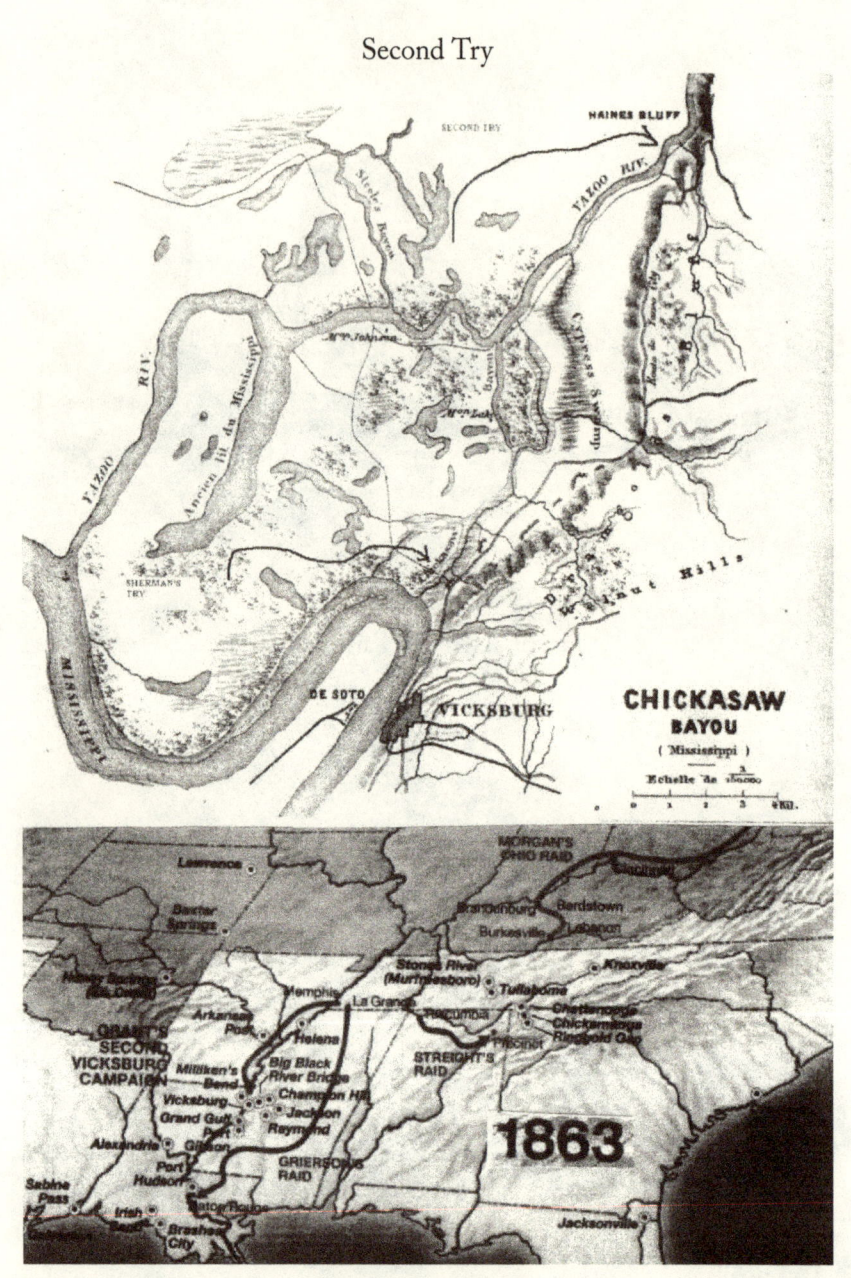

Chickasaw Bayou
(Mississippi)

Chapter 40

Mississippi River

Two remaining Confederate strongholds on the Mississippi River were taken by the federal army and navy in the summer of 1863: Vicksburg, Mississippi, on July 4 and Port Hudson, Louisiana, on July 9. Immediately after capture, Port Hudson was improved by the Seventh Regiment, Corps d'Afrique, composed of former slaves. Colonel Zelensky reported that the corps' work, repairing and strengthening the fort, made it stronger than when rebels held it. African soldiers worked hard from six in the morning until six at night. They were a happy group with an interest in advancement. Their greatest desire was to learn to read and write.

Two thousand miles of river under Union control permitted water transport from the Midwest to the Gulf of Mexico. Saint Louis–based captain Lewis B. Parson, assistant quartermaster in charge of steamboat transportation, established an efficient and well-functioning system of transport to serve federal military operations in the western theater. The first challenge he faced, demand for steamboats to carry men and materials on the Mississippi River, greatly surpassed the supply of available boats. A partial answer was to employ barges to transport troops and materials. Barges created a new set of problems. A towed barge traveled slower than a steamboat, making it a target for guerrilla attacks. The navy answered these challenges by establishing convoy systems. Gunboats were used as escorts. A convoy was composed of ten to twelve vessels, both steamboats and barges. Gunboats did not stop rebel guerrillas who continued to be active, attacking Union shipping.

Convoys used a system of whistles to communicate with one another announcing distress, an enemy sighting, landing, or a fuel stop. Fuel stops for steamboats were needed twice a day. Ideally, cut wood would be stacked and waiting for a steamboat's arrival at a woodlot. An empty woodlot meant a boat crew must go ashore and cut timber to fuel a boat's boiler for the next leg of a journey. Woodcutters, freed slaves called contrabands, were hired by woodlot owners to cut and size logs for steamboat boilers. Contrabands worked hard long hours to keep up with constant growing demands for steamboat fuel.

Alfred, part of General Warren's regiment, joined a brigade departing from Cairo, Illinois, on October 19 in a convoy bound for New Orleans. Boats and barges were loaded using a system created by Captain Parson. Alfred's duty as a quartermaster officer was to inspect and enforce loading regulations. He checked each vessel in his convoy before departure to ensure they were not overloaded and safe for carrying men, animals, and supplies. Steamboats in river service were limited to carrying 1,500 people. This resulted in the splitting of army brigades for river travel. Despite rules and regulations enacted for safe travel, vessels loaded with horses, mules, wagons, artillery, weapons, and supplies made for crowding and cramped travel conditions. There were few places for an enlisted man to sit, sleep, or cook a meal. Men complained; discipline often became a problem.

Passage to Memphis was without incident with one exception. Exceptionally heavy rains in the spring and early summer created massive flooding in the Mississippi River valley. Flooding made navigation difficult. Old channels became filled with sand and silt; new channels unknown to boat pilots took their place. The river took a sharp turn a northwest direction at Island Number Ten, flowing toward New Madrid, Missouri, where it turned south. Island No. 10 had been the major Confederate fort located between Columbus, Kentucky, and Memphis, Tennessee. The combined forces of the army and navy took the island after a three-week siege on April 8, 1862.

Alfred was standing along the port rail, viewing the remains of Confederate fortifications on the island, when his boat seemed to shudder, followed by a scraping sound. Alfred instinctively grabbed a deck rail next to where he was standing. A few seconds later, the ship came to complete stop with a sudden jerk. Alfred's firm grip on the deck railing allowed him to remain upright.

The ship's pilot had missed a submerged sandbar that had shifted the river channel close to the island during spring flooding. The steamboat's captain called for all engines to be run full astern to back the ship off the obstruction. This effort did not work. His next step was to transfer freight on the lower deck to the stern, taking weight away from the front of the vessel, and to move as many passengers as could be aft. New weight distribution permitted the ship to slip back from the sandbar, allowing the boat to proceed on its way.

Conversation drifted among the passengers, questioning the skills of the ship's pilot. Pilots were local men trained to learn about every turn, ripple, and obstruction in the water. Certain pilots were known Southern loyalists wanting to delay or cause problems for Union military transport. Was the sandbar stoppage a deliberate misreading of currents to delay the arrival of men and materials fighting Southern armies? Nothing could be proven; the topic soon was forgotten.

Enlisted men cooked their own meals. They were charged with the responsibility of keeping their quarters clean. In most instances, the lower deck remained dirty. A stop at night allowed soldiers traveling on the crowded lower deck to sleep onshore. During this time, the boat crew scrubbed the boat, shoveling residue from meals and animal waste into the river. Officers traveled on a steamboat's upper deck. Captain Davenport and other members of General Warren's staff enjoyed comfortable sleeping quarters with meals prepared by the ship's galley.

The navy's fleet of gunboat and mortar barges continued to break up Confederate artillery batteries and subdue guerrilla attacks after the Mississippi River was open. On October 1863, riverboats faced a growing number of renegade attacks by guerrillas whose plans were to disrupt troop movements and commerce. Seasonably low water in autumn saw convoys navigating around sandbars and obstructions not found in the spring when the river levels were higher. Maneuvering a barge around a multitude of *S* curves in the river, especially south of Memphis, was filled with danger, for slow-moving vessels created tempting targets for guerillas. Rebels hid in thick groves of trees bordering the river or behind a multitude of levees built to keep water from flooding farm fields. The packet boat *Eugene* was fired on by rebels from Randolph, Tennessee. Union general William T. Sherman answered by sending the Forty-Sixth Ohio Regiment to burn Randolph. Sherman implemented a program in Memphis where he forced thirty to forty prominent Southern sympathizers to line top decks of steamboats traveling through known guerrilla territories. They became unwilling targets during guerrilla attacks. After an attack, Sherman employed a scorched earth policy where rebels lived. Cabins, barns, plantations, and towns suspected of housing guerrillas were torched and leveled by his troops.

Steamboat losses continued high due to fires, accidents, navigational errors, and rebel attacks. Steamboats *Continental* and *Dickey* took rifle fire from rebel artillery; two civilians on the *Gladiator* were shot and killed by rebel sharpshooters. Its crew valiantly fought, saving the ship from a fire ignited during the fight. Instructions from the Confederates in Richmond urged attacks on Union ships throughout the war, but after the loss of Mississippi River forts, the Confederacy lacked resources to mount a major river campaign. On August 1863, a rebel-set fire aboard the steamboat *Ruth* in Columbus, Kentucky, destroyed $2.5 million in cash belonging to the paymaster in the Quartermaster Department. The *Champion* was torched while moored at a berth on a Memphis levee. Four steamboats docked in Saint Louis were burned in September, followed by another three in October. The perpetrators in October were Confederate agents disguised as black contrabands assigned to work details in the shipyard.

Admiral Porter responded with tough new regulations for the navy. New sentries were posted for each boat traveling on western rivers. A small craft approaching a vessel that failed to follow sentry demands would be fired on. Two tugboats in every convoy were on patrol twenty-four hours a day. Steamboats stopping for the night in areas with questionable safety would lie with steam up, ready to leave at the first sign of hostilities. A company of armed soldiers were posted at key landings in Columbus, Memphis, Vicksburg, and the mouth of the Yazoo River. Steamboats posted twenty-five armed troops, marines, behind a barricade at the bow of each boat. Admiral Porter insisted that locals must pay for damages to steamboats. In the absence of cash, payment would be extracted by taking horses, mules, and crops, especially cotton. Levees used by guerrilla fighters were destroyed, flooding large acreage used for crop cultivation. Construction of new levees was forbidden until the war ended.

Guerrilla muskets erupted from shore in patches of thick cane as Alfred's convoy neared Hutchins Landing. Gunboats escorting the convoy replied with a withering broadside of artillery, muskets, and mortars. When shoreside firing ceased, a detachment of troops landed to discover that the perpetrators had departed. A wooden shack was burned. Sugarcane and brush hiding guerrillas was destroyed. Troops landed to "clear" areas bordering the ambush site. Confederate schemers continued sporadic attacks on federal ships plying the Mississippi River, hoping to take back captured real estate. These ideas turned into pipe dreams, largely abandoned by early 1865.

Alfred reached New Orleans on October 30. New orders sent him to Baton Rouge on November 3. The same day near Grand Coteau, not far from Baton Rouge at Bayou Bourbeau, Lt. Col. Theodore E. Buehler, commander of Indiana's Sixty-Seventh Regiment, was surprised and sacked by Texas cavalry. He lost 700 men. Buehler was taken prisoner. Buehler's unfortunate defeat and surrender caused other army regiments in the bayou to retreat. Rebels pursuing a routed enemy halted their advance to allow near-starved troops to feast on the bounty of the federal army camp. Union general Carencro arrived with five infantry and one cavalry regiment causing Confederate commander General Green started to rethink his position. Greatly outnumbered, he chose to slowly withdraw in the face of Carencro's new and superior force. Buehler's defeat raised questions. "Was his defeat honorable, or was it a case of incompetency under fire?" Buehler was exchanged in a POW exchange on Christmas Day 1863. A military court convened at the Odd Fellows Hall on Camp Street in New Orleans in February 1864. The court reviewed Buehler's performance. Buehler was found guilty of incompetence and misbehavior. He was dismissed from the army.

Alfred was the quartermaster supply officer in Baton Rouge. He arranged for the replacement of materials lost and destroyed in the November Battle of Bayou Bourbeau. On November 19, Davenport was ordered to return to New Orleans and report to the Department of the Gulf, where he was informed that General Warren and his adjutant would be departing for Texas. His new assignment was to the customhouse as a special agency aide of the Internal Revenue Department.

Chapter 41

New Orleans

New Orleans, claimed as the South's most hedonistic city, in many ways reminded Alfred of San Francisco. Its heritage was one of the most fascinating in the country. Founded in 1682 by French explorer La Salle, Nouvelle-Orleans became a city in 1718. During 1763, French colonies west of the Mississippi River and New Orleans were ceded to Spain. A treaty between Spain and France in 1800 returned New Orleans to France. Napoleon, emperor of France, sold Louisiana to the United States in December 1803.

Alfred discovered a unique social structure upon arrival at this Southern city. White planters were the top of society. African slaves were at the bottom. Creoles made up a large diverse group in the middle. Creoles included whites, freeborn blacks, and mixed-race people whose ancestors came to Louisiana during French and Spanish colonial times. Creoles enjoyed a café lifestyle, different from life experienced in the American North. Opera, minstrel shows, festivals including Mardi Gras, masked balls, gambling, drinking, prostitution, horseback racing and cockfights were parts of a Creole man's life. Cuisine was a blend of many cultures and tradition, which became one of the highlights of Alfred's stay in the city. Prostitution and gambling, legal in New Orleans, was tolerated by the occupying military. Union soldiers arriving in New Orleans sought the company of "horizontals." Brothel owners paid off corrupt politicians, police and government officials. Basin Street was the main artery containing brothels. New Orleans had unique religious practices. Voodoo, an African-inspired spiritual belief, was actively practiced in the parish (county). Over the years, it had become part of New Orleans, influencing Catholic traditions and French culture.

Alfred loved Creole cuisine; jambalaya and gumbo, a thick shellfish soup seasoned with okra or filé (made from dried sassafras leaves) and other spices. Alligator, turtle, wild boar, crayfish, shrimp, and oysters were enjoyed when his budget permitted. He loved sweet pastries, especially beignets and *oreilles de cochons*.

Captain Davenport reported to George Stanton Denison, acting collector of customs of the United States Treasury Department, in New Orleans on November 21, 1863. Denison, a Northerner, moved from Vermont to San Antonio, Texas, in 1854. In Texas, he had no preconceived dislike of Southerners or Southern institutions. He gradually came to disapprove the power and terror of the South's secessionist movement, which was bankrupting the Texas economy. He returned to Vermont in early 1861, where he published articles in the *Burlington Free Press*, describing how most Texans had been conned into joining the Southern secessionist movement.

Denison wanted to serve the U.S. government. His second cousin Salmon P. Chase, secretary of the U.S. Treasury, assisted him in receiving appointment as customs collector in New Orleans in July 1862. Chase needed an ear in this controversial Southern city. He instructed Denison to provide biweekly confidential reports of military and Union government activities in the Department of the Gulf. Some reports were military secrets, not official department communications.

Alfred was assigned work as an agent of the U.S. Treasury, overseen by the quartermaster general. It was reported that revenue agents in New Orleans collected over a million dollars in the autumn of 1863. Sources of funds came from penalties assessed by the provost marshal's court. Confederates not willing to take a loyalty pledge to the Union were subject to having their assets seized and liquidated by the court. Proceeds of sales were sent to the federal Treasury Department in Washington. Not everyone was happy with this arrangement. Nathaniel Banks, commander of the Department of the Gulf, learned of the large amounts of revenue leaving New Orleans for Washington. Banks interceded, redirecting collected funds to his department.

The provost marshal's court, originally established as a military court, evolved into a court handling civil as well as military cases. New Orleans district courts handling civil cases ceased to exist after federal occupation. Provost court judges were selected from a pool of private citizens and government officials. All appointments had to be approved by the provost marshal general of the Department of the Gulf. A local newspaper reported that the court "was a fat place with salaried officials who were generally opposed by our citizens."

General Banks appointed a civilian friend, Alexander A. Atocha, judge of the court, in August of 1863. Atocha's knowledge of the law was greatly lacking. In March of 1864, it became apparent that his sentencing records were filled with inequities. He was unable to account for funds passing through the courts during his tenure, forcing him to promptly resign in disgrace.

General Banks offered the judge's post to his secretary, Capt. James Tucker. Tucker declined the offer, saying he thought the court was illegal, unconstitutional, and filled with prejudice. It was a tool for creating wealth benefiting a few insiders. Court decisions were sadly inconsistent. A verdict for a keeper of a bawdy house and four of his "girls" brought a sentence of two months in the workhouse. Instead of jail time, the owner and his girls were ordered to pay a fine of $50 each. When the group raised only $175 in required fees, the court accepted cash, releasing the offenders. In another case, a soldier who stole a watch chain was sentenced to ten years in prison. A German coffee house owner, accused of receiving two bags of stolen government-owned oats that he denied receiving and were never found or seen on his property, was found guilty of theft of government property. He was sentenced to two years in prison.

Alfred became uncomfortable with Treasury Department operations not long after his appointment as a revenue agent. Graft and corruption were a personal concern in which he would have no part. Abuses in the department were glaring. Director Denison was shipping boxes of books, merchandise, and household furnishings seized from Southerners at provost court auctions to family members in Vermont. Davenport was anxious to leave the department.

In early January 1864, he was appointed superintendent of construction for the new Sedgwick Military Hospital at the Greenville Encampment located between New Orleans and Carrollton. Greenville Encampment was a training ground for 2,641 cavalry men including members of the Corps d'Afrique. The hospital, constructed in a pavilion style, was composed of fifteen units or wings for sick and wounded men. Separate buildings, connected by covered walkways, were a kitchen, dining facility, and a two-floor administration building. The military's need for a new hospital was critical due an increase in diseases, especially smallpox, cholera, yellow fever, and malaria.

Provost Marshal Col. James Bowen, in April 1864, renewed a program initially begun by General Butler in 1862 to clean up the city. Buildings were whitewashed; canals and drainage ditches were cleaned of trash, allowing water to flow out of the city. Yellow fever cases began to decline after these efforts. Spring of 1864 found the economy of New Orleans improving from the depressed conditions of 1863. Speculators continued to drive up the prices of sugar, coffee, meat, and, butter, translating to high prices paid for food. Alfred reported that the cheapest dinner at the Saint Charles Hotel cost over $2. Two slices of toast and coffee cost thirty-two cents. A full day's meals could cost $4 to $5. Business recovery began in late 1863, continuing throughout 1864. A flood of entrepreneurs and opportunists arrived from the North, filling gaps in the local economy left vacant by locals who remained loyal to the Confederacy. Locals were prohibited by the occupational government from practicing their trade unless they pledged loyalty to the Union.

Alfred noted with great concern the condition of refugees and poor arriving in New Orleans. War widows whose husbands and fathers were gone found their families without support. Impoverished survivors left small towns and farms, hoping to find a way to get a meal and housing and earn a living in New Orleans. In January 1864, the parish of Orleans reported that over 1,000 destitute adults and orphans were being supported by the city's charitable organizations. In May of the same year, the Odd Fellows Lodge reported that the depletion of its relief funds used to support Confederate soldiers' families. In June, General Banks's chief quartermaster, Holabird, reported that his department and the Commissary Department contributed $41,676 to the city's orphan asylums during 1863 and 1864. General Banks asked the state government (responsible to occupational forces) to provide $35,000 to local charities. Union society leaders raised $8,500 at a fair held at the opera house in the fall of 1864. Despite all efforts, the needs of the poor and destitute greatly surpassed revenues from fundraising.

On a happier note, Alfred thoroughly enjoyed his stay in New Orleans, especially the festivities of Mardi Gras held before Ash Wednesday, signaling the beginning of Lent in Christian churches. Streets were jammed, full of people wearing masks and costumes, displaying a variety of characters created for the moment. Men dressed as women, women as men. Every theatrical costume in the city found its way into the festivities. People from all classes and races mixed, enjoying the revelry; all were considered equals. Revelers carried small pouches of either flour or bonbons. Each could be tossed on an opponent depending on the wishes of the thrower. The height of the day was a torchlit evening parade by the Mystic Krewe of Comus, followed by masked balls extending to the wee hours of the next day.

Alfred frequently visited the French opera house or one of the many theaters open from November to May. Summertime picnics at Lake Pontchartrain or a circus held at Congo Squares was not to be missed. The famous restaurants Antoine's and Café Du Monde and Mardi Gras activities remained on the top of his favorite places to visit while in New Orleans.

Construction of the hospital in Greenville was completed in late October 1864. Captain Davenport was ordered to report to the provost marshal general on November 1. He received a new position in the Quartermaster Department, special officer of military detective, an assignment that caused Alfred a considerable amount of grief.

CHAPTER 42

Military Detective and a New Assignment, 1865–1866

Hostilities starting in April 1861 enveloped the nation's capital in a fog of bewilderment, confusion, and disorganization. Large numbers of people departed from Washington. Government employees, cabinet members, legislators from both houses of Congress, judges, and members of the military, both officers and enlisted men, loyal to the South resigned their posts to join the Confederacy. Northerners living in the South were forced North, losing their homes, businesses, and property. The federal government was unprepared for a war between the states.

Congress trusted no one. It established an oversight body, the Committee on the Conduct of the War, with authority to supervise plans of military commanders. Findings were sent to the secretary of war and the president, recommending discipline for generals who met with the committee's disapproval. Lincoln needed to bring order to Washington's chaos. He began using executive privilege to create regulations and laws needed to fill government requirements and demands created by war.

Part of the president's challenge was monitoring and controlling information flowing in and out of Washington. Political organizations and secret societies reported names of people in the North sending money and materials to their Southern brethren. Military sources gathered information on Confederate resources and military plans, but this data fell short of tracking money, materials, and supplies headed South.

Secretary of State William H. Seward embarked on a program to keep foreign European powers out of America's Civil War. Allan Pinkerton's National Detective Agency was hired to provide surveillance for the Washington government. Gen. U. S. Grant appointed Gen. Grenville Dodge as chief of intelligence services for western operations in October 1862. Dodge created an intelligence department different from Pinkerton's. One program recruited a cavalry company composed of Southern unionist who spoke local dialects. They wore Confederate uniforms and carried Confederate weapons while operating behind rebel lines. Data was gathered on troop size, deployments, and plans. He created a network of men and women spies to pass through enemy lines for the collection of information vital to federal war efforts. Spies and couriers were identified by numbers; no names were used. Dodge's favorite spies were two Mississippi women, covertly known as Jane Featherstone and Molly Malone.

Hostile antiwar secret political societies developed and spread in Midwestern lodges located in what was then called "the northwest." Territory included states west of Pennsylvania, north of the Ohio River to the border of Canada, and east of the Mississippi River. Antiwar societies opposed the draft and wartime taxation. They became antiwar activists, pacifists, or Southern sympathizers. Names of the lodges included New Democrats, Copperheads, Butternuts, Knights of the Golden Circle, and Sons of Liberty. The latter claimed to have a membership of four hundred thousand.

Antiwar societies became increasingly militant as the war dragged on during 1863 and 1864. They actively opposed military draft, offering protection for army deserters. Plots were made to seize arsenals and interfere with railroad and telegraph service. A Confederate Secret Service agent Capt. Thomas Henry Hines operated out of Toronto, Canada. Funded with a million U.S. dollars, he developed close ties with groups wanting to disrupt federal war efforts. Hines established a base for the creation of a "Northwestern Confederacy." A proposed leader for a new Confederate state was a former congressman, Clement L. Vallandigham from Ohio. Offsetting anti-Union secret societies were "loyalty leagues." Their members unconditionally supported the Union and the war. Washington broke up pro-Confederate societies by secretly inserting federal spies into antiwar lodges. Members were arrested; leaders were charged with treason.

Treasury department's power and scope of operations were expanded in New Orleans by the provost marshal general's staff. Secret service agents in the Department of the Gulf infiltrated Masons, Independent Order of Odd

Fellows, and similar service organizations. They befriended business and society leaders. They found work as domestics and laborers. Information of all kinds was gathered about all citizens, locals or occupational forces. Reports of political activities were noted and forwarded to the provost marshal general.

Gaining Union loyalty was a continuing challenge facing each commanding general of the Department of the Gulf. General Butler, the first commander, closed Protestant churches whose preachers insisted praying for the Confederate president and rebel soldiers. General Banks, his successor, learned that loyalty was not taught in over half the area's 150 private schools. Catholic school administrators refused to discuss the issue. He closed noncomplying schools.

Provost Marshal James Bowen learned that local police were not effective; crime, graft, and lack of loyalty were rampant. He weeded out officers with questionable loyalty. This move created a staffing problem. His answer was to bring fifty police recruits from New York City. Twenty signed on to the position of detective. They became the base of Banks's intelligence network.

Problems soon developed. New York City recruits lacked detective training and discipline. Under the expanded force, arrests surged. Wives and children of U.S. soldiers were detained as vagrants. Police would not release a detainee until a fee was paid to the arresting officer. Other problems surfaced; drunkenness, failure to pay for lodging and board, payoffs from gamblers, and prostitutes plagued the department. A whole new type of difficulty facing provost courts surfaced in the summer of 1864. Loyalty arrests were made by special police agents without orders or authorization from a judicial body, creating terror among citizens, loyal and not loyal.

Questionable characters arrived in New Orleans claiming to assist the occupational government by cleaning out hidden pockets of dissenters. Dr. Issachar Zacharie entered the city proclaiming he was the "confidential agent" of President Lincoln or the "Chief of U.S. Detectives." A fancy dresser with oil-slicked hair and a waft of perfume, he moved comfortably through the highest levels of society. In Louisiana and throughout the South, he crossed over enemy lines, traveling as an itinerant Jewish peddler, collecting intelligence that he claimed he forwarded to the president. General Banks liked Zacharie; others thought differently. George Denison considered him a fraud.

Davenport's new assignment as a military detective began in early November 1864, moving his career into controversial territory. Initially, he envisioned his post as a thrilling and exciting opportunity. He would act clandestinely, posing as a government clerk to discover Southern spies working for the occupational government posing as loyal Union supporters. However, the system was porous. Word of his true responsibilities leaked to all he knew or met.

Quickly, he learned that the status of a military detective was held in low regard. Detectives were considered dishonest men. They were called "sneaks" who spied on everyone and could not be trusted. Suddenly, Captain Davenport had no friends. He wanted no part of detective work. Alfred requested transfer to another section of the Quartermaster Department.

New duties began on January 1, 1865, at Fort Pickens in Pensacola, Florida. He remained assigned to the Treasury Department in Florida and Alabama until discharged in May of 1866. The Department of the Gulf remained active into 1866 due to threats of a Texas invasion by Austrian archduke Ferdinand Maximilian, installed as emperor of Mexico by French emperor Napoleon III in 1864.

Fort Pickens, Florida

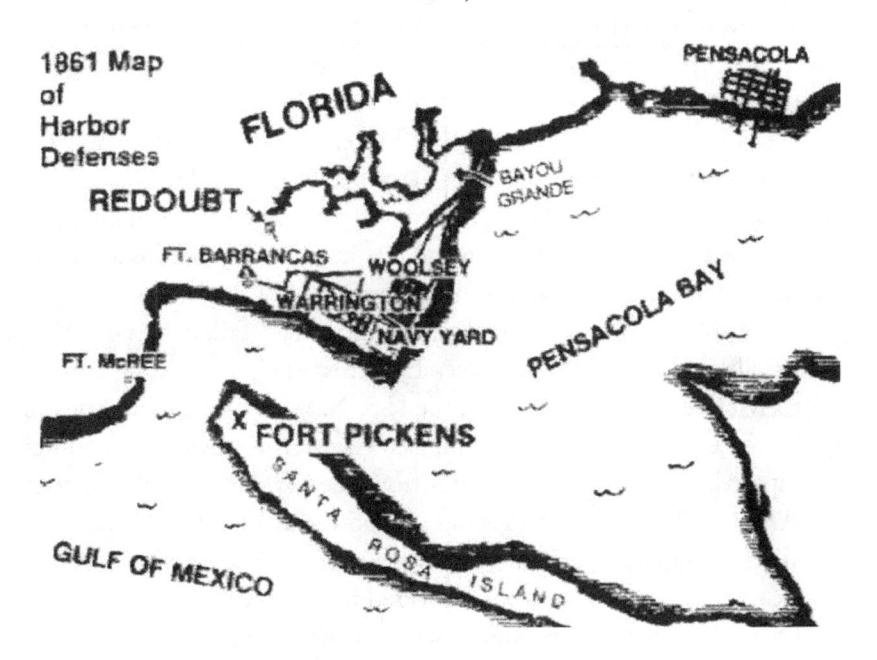

Chapter 43

Louisiana, Florida, and Alabama

Ft.Pickens, located in Santa Rosa Island at the entrance of Pensacola Bay, remained in federal hands throughout the war. The fort was heavily armed. Seven batteries containing thirty-five heavy guns were found within the fort walls. Five additional batteries with twenty-two guns were strategically placed outside its walls. Fort McRee protected the land entrance of Pensacola Bay. It faced Fort Pickens. East of McRee was Fort Barrancas and Warrington, a small village between Fort Barrancas and a large U.S. Navy shipyard. The shipyard was the home of a million-dollar dry dock used for ship construction and repairs. The city of Pensacola was six miles beyond the shipyard on the eastern shore of the bay.

On October 1861, a Confederate land attack failed to take Fort Pickens, although rebels were successful across the bay, gaining control of Forts McRee and Barrancas and the U.S. Navy shipyard. A few weeks later in November, a successful U.S. Navy action regained its lost forts and shipyard, removing Confederates from the bay. Combined efforts of U.S. Army artillery at Fort Pickens and powerful broadsides from two United States ships, *Niagara* and *Richmond*, silenced Fort McRee and Fort Barrancas artillery. McRee never recovered from punishing navy guns.

U.S. Army successes in Tennessee and the taking of New Orleans caused Confederate military planners to move troops from Florida to northern theaters of war. Confederate troops left Pensacola in May of 1862, destroying miles of railroad tracks on the Alabama-Florida line. They burned wooden structures at Fort Barrancas and the navy shipyard.

Hurrying their departure, they failed to destroy brick and stone structures, the armory, a large storehouse, and an important navy wharf located at the shipyard.

Alfred's new home in January 1865 was at Fort Barrancas. The post, a significant military facility, was the headquarters of the local government. It housed thirteen thousand soldiers including a regiment of recently arrived black troops. The Quartermaster Department was large, containing many departments, though not as large in volume as Alfred found in New Orleans. Quartermasters continued bringing clothing, food, ammunition, and medical items for the military. It provided materials and staffing to rebuild forts and the shipyard.

The Treasury Department's special agents scoured the countryside, collecting taxes. The provost marshal investigated and enforced loyalty oaths required for Southerners to reclaim property lost during the conflict. It operated courts enforcing martial law. Departure of Confederates left Pensacola and Florida without a civil government, courts, and legal systems. Banks were closed; businesses were shuttered. Confederate currency was worthless.

U.S. military officers arriving in the summer of 1862 discovered many stately, grand residences in Pensacola empty after their owners, senior Confederate military officers, departed. United States brigadier general Richard Arnold moved his headquarters into the mayor's office and resided in the home of Confederate colonel William Chase. Col. William Wilson of the Sixth New York Volunteers took over the house of the Confederate secretary of the navy Stephen Mallory.

Change orders came from Washington. New instructions arriving in March 1863 ordered the military to leave Pensacola and return to offices and quarters at Forts Barrancas and Pickens and the navy yard. This was done as a cost-saving measure, not because of a Confederate threat. Pensacola became a ghost town.

Alfred found grand old Pensacola in a state of deterioration. After two years of vacancy, stately old houses badly needed repairs. Ravages of summer heat, tropical storms, and a lack of maintenance had taken its toll. Streets were filled with weeds. Wooden sidewalks were falling apart. The city's population was not static; it was growing. Black refugees, freed men and women escaping from former lives on Southern plantations, were settling in Pensacola, seeking food and work. Confederate soldiers of all types—deserters, disabled, antiwar, and pro-unionists—flocked to

Pensacola. The U.S. military supplied rations to refugees to stop starvation. A few refugees found limited employment serving the military.

Congress passed a new law in the spring of 1865. It created the Bureau of Refugees, Freedmen, and Abandoned Lands. Known as the Freedmen's Bureau, it was established to assist black people in their adjustment to freedom and to maintain peace between former rebels and freedmen. Freedmen's Bureau agents were dispatched to all areas of the South. They were responsible for issuing rations, starting hospitals, organizing courts, administering loyalty oaths and processing land claims. Pensacola became a regional center for the bureau, working closely with the military to provide services and to keep peace in the town and Escambia County.

During April of 1865, the Treasury Department initiated a program to seize Southern cotton from owners who failed to pay taxes. (Most cotton remained in the hands of plantation owners, who kept it in a bonded warehouse for the Confederacy.) Treasury agents scoured Florida, finding over 5,400 bales in the first five months after hostilities ceased, with a value of $800,000 in gold.

The Treasury Department handled abandoned property but lacked the staff to process loyalty claims and distribute land to returning Southerners. Freedmen's Bureau agents took over these duties. Newly established guidelines for the bureau greatly simplified the process of administering loyalty oaths and handling property transfers. One bureau goal was building schools to teach former slaves how to read and write. Education helped freedmen negotiate contracts, find employment, and function in society.

Florida's economy was stimulated by the recovery of the lumber industry. Harvesting long needle pine trees for lumber was northern Florida's major industry before the war. Mills reopened in 1865, providing jobs and greatly needed lumber supplies. The presence of army forts, the navy shipyard, and a general return of business from the mills improved life in the western panhandle of Florida.

Rear Admiral David Farragut was commander of the navy's West Gulf Blockading Squadron. Mobile, Alabama, was the only remaining Confederate port east of the Mississippi River. A combined operation by Farragut and the army's major general Edward R. S. Canby, commander the Military Division of West Mississippi, was planned to neutralize Mobile Bay's three forts and destroy the Confederate's sea power. Early in the Battle of Mobile Bay on August 5, 1864, ironclad *Tecumseh*—steaming through a mine field—hit a torpedo (as mines were called) and quickly sunk. Ship commanders asked Farragut if they should turn back and cancel the attack. He famously answered, "Damn the torpedoes. Full speed ahead." Smoke from ship guns filled the air like a dense fog. Farragut climbed his ship's rigging. Lashed to the mast of his flagship, he directed the battle, resulting in Confederate loss of the bay and its three forts. Blockade runners were denied access to the city of Mobile. The city remained loyal to the Confederacy, surrendering on April 12, 1865, three days after Confederate general Lee's surrender in Virginia.

Cessation of hostilities prompted Southern states to create new constitutions and laws to reestablish local governments and courts. Florida's new constitution became effective in November 1865. New laws written without federal direction or guidance created antebellum practices. Black codes were written to restrict freedmen's rights and activities. Freedmen were prohibited from voting. Codes created severe penalties for minor infractions of simple rules of law. Black codes were designed to make former slaves second-class citizens.

The role of the military government in Pensacola began to sharply decline after Lee's surrender. Governing roles and responsibilities were taken over by the Freedmen's Bureau. Changes affected officers in the Quartermaster and Treasury Departments. Treasury needed people in Alabama. Alfred received orders to report to Mobile.

Chapter 44

Winding Down

Upon hearing of General Lee's surrender at Appomattox Courthouse, Alfred shared his thoughts about the end of hostilities. Writing in his diary, he "thanked brave people whose heroic efforts and suffering crushed the great rebellion. He was pleased in his own small way to have been able to serve his country and felt fortunate to survived to the end of the conflict. He never once lost faith, always believing our people would protect the constitution framed in the time of George Washington, which now provides freedom for all future generations of Americans."

Captain Davenport arrived in Mobile to find a once proud Southern city suffering greatly from the war. The city of thirty thousand was in far worse shape than New Orleans had been upon his arrival in late 1863. On May 25, 1865, a disastrous explosion at a federal ammunition depot killed three hundred people, sunk ships on the Mobile River, and destroyed a large portion of the city's dock and warehouse space. Before the beginning of the war, Mobile had been the third largest United States port exporting half the cotton crop produced in the South's "Black Belt." Cotton, the great economic engine of Mobile, was no longer king. A disastrous drought in the summer of 1865 left hundreds without adequate food supplies. Salt, critical to one's diet, was in short supply. Medicine and drugs were no longer available. They had necessarily been replaced by homemade remedies. Quinine, used to treat malaria, disappeared from pharmacies. Fine clothes, once the pride of a prosperous community, were replaced with homespun, homemade materials. Before 1861, the city's dry goods stores acquired fabrics and clothes from the North or imported them from foreign countries. With sources gone, carpets were taken apart; reusable fibers were woven into blankets. Window coverings were turned into women's clothes. Bark, roots, and berries were used to dye fabrics. Groups of women formed spinning and sewing bees to make clothes and provide uniforms for soldiers.

After the war, Confederate currency was worthless, Southerners had no funds for life's most essential items. A federal "button order" prohibited Southern men from wearing Confederate military buttons. Men could not afford to purchase new buttons, which were expensive and difficult to locate. Fines for wearing a Confederate button ranged from $5 to $50.

The attitude of citizens was better than Alfred had expected. People were somewhat friendly, but he would never be invited into a local's home. Residents of Mobile, deeply hurt by war and losses of family and friends, did not want to start a friendship with anyone who might have been responsible for the loss of a loved one. Young ladies in Southern towns wore veils in public to keep "blue coats" from starting a conversation.

Large portions of Alabama, after the removal of Native Americans in the 1830s, were settled by people from Georgia, South Carolina, and other Southern states. Newcomers moved to Alabama to raise cotton. Twenty percent of the population was African slaves residing on plantations and farms to provide labor for agriculture. Citizens of Alabama never grew close to the North before the state's secession due to Northern antislavery movements, threatening the state's livelihood and way of life. Reports of Northern Christian churches proclaiming the South was infected with a "leprosy of slavery" were widely spread by the Southern press before the start of the war.

The year before the war ended, prices of food became unreachable in Mobile. A bushel of corn sold for $13. A Confederate soldier's pay was $11 per month. At the end of hostilities, Confederate currency was worthless. Wealthy people were ruined. Land retained little value. Animals and farming implements were gone. Landowners lacked funds to purchase seed or to pay laborers. Many young men who had tended farms never returned from the war. Owners of fine homes sold furniture, pianos, furnishings, silver, gold, jewelry, and paintings to live, often facing starvation. Household items, purchased by federal occupying troops, were sent North to soldiers' families, causing widespread resentment around the state. The only government in Alabama for the first six months after the cessation of hostilities was the U.S. military.

Federal soldiers and sailors, at the urging of President Johnson, began leaving the military. Farm boys were anxious to return home for the spring planting season. The thinning of United States troop ranks meant more work for Alfred at the Treasury Department.

Federal occupational forces arrived at plantations, seeking bloodhounds. Rumors in the North had spread; antebellum landowners used bloodhounds to "manage" their slaves. In truth, most slaves had been entirely dependent on their plantation masters. Older freed men and women were confused and unable to cope on their own after President Lincoln's Emancipation Proclamation.

Andrew Johnson desired to punish former slave owners. All trade was to be handled by agents of the U.S. Treasury Department. Cotton and produce were to be purchased at a 25 percent discount to market prices; the discount was a "tax" sent to the Treasury. Agents resold cotton at the prevailing market price. Treasury agent impostors purchased cotton at government discounts, pocketing the tax. Group of planters, not trusting agents, formed partnerships with federal officers to ship cotton out of state, paying a $5 or $10 per bale commission to the officers who set up the deal. The Treasury Department did not have enough agents to halt tax avoidance schemes. Sales of cotton, produce, and personal property as well as land transfers continued to remain controversial transactions throughout the South during the early years of reconstruction. Wayne Swayne, commissioner of the Alabama Freedmen's Bureau, implemented a labor system to maintain agricultural production. It served freedmen until 1870.

Alfred received discharge papers on May 26 on a visit to New Orleans. He returned on May 29 to Pensacola, where he collected his last pay of $20 before heading North to Milton, Alabama, near Mobile. He was able to find limited work as a carpenter in Milton. Sparse work prospects convinced Alfred to take the steamboat *Lucy Blossom* to Montgomery in hopes of finding more work. A search for work in June was a bust; he worked for only three days. He was becoming hungry. Most of his savings were gone. On July 4, the black community of Montgomery celebrated Independence Day with a grand parade celebrating their newfound freedom, an entertaining break in Alfred's days of searching for nonexistent jobs. On July 16, Alfred found employment working to rebuild a railroad.

He wrote home on the July 17, asking for money for passage back to Ohio. Alfred's health was breaking down, aggravated by the heat and humidity of a southern Alabama summer. He received $50 from relatives toward a long journey home.

Alfred's return home introduced the shocking state of a broken-down, decayed Southern rail system. During the last year of the war, Confederate railroads were close to a complete collapse. Little improvement in rolling stock had been made by the summer of 1866. Railroad funding was earmarked to replace major rail infrastructure, trestles, bridges, culverts, roundhouses, and nonexistent rails. Worn-out tracks, poorly maintained railroad ties, and outdated, barely running equipment caused trains to creep at speeds of less than ten miles per hour. Stops for wood and water were frequent. When wood was not available, trainmen would be forced to scour nearby woods and cut timber for fuel. Water for boilers frequently had to be drawn from rivers and creeks near a rail line.

Travel was uncomfortable, especially when one was ill. Railroad coaches were old, rickety, and filthy. Seats were broken, often replaced with roughly made benches. Windows in coaches failed to open. Window glass was cracked or more likely missing and covered with boards. Trains were crowded and expensive, costing Alfred more than ten cents per mile. When coach seating was not available, Alfred rode in boxcars or open freight cars. Passengers were forbidden to ride on the tops or platforms of cars because of frequent accidents and derailments. Every section of rail travel encountered workers, shoring up track, repairing bridges, and rebuilding local depots.

Davenport's journey began in Montgomery early on August 16. He traveled on the Atlanta and West Point Railroad to the city of Atlanta, Georgia. There was no terminal. It had been burned during the Battle of Atlanta in 1864. Alfred used his brief time in Atlanta to purchase a local weekly newspaper. The paper was filled with articles of interest. Court-ordered property sales filled the paper. This told him that business was not good. Former wealthy people were bankrupt. Large plantations were offered for sale. Cotton production had fallen to one-quarter of its prewar level.

The paper carried a section reporting political news. An editorial discussed a dislike of the federal governments approach to reconstruction. Its target was the Freedmen's Bureau. A bureau-appointed "judge" in Savannah sentenced two black men, who had pleaded guilty to stealing two horses, to thirty days on a chain gang. The paper noted that if the men were white, they would have been sentenced to several years in the state penitentiary or would have been hanged.

Alfred quickly left Atlanta; a cholera epidemic had broken out at a U.S. Army barracks. The Western Atlantic Railroad took him to Chattanooga, Tennessee. The line was in a good state of repair, for it was the major supply line for General Sherman's march through Georgia. Rail lines carried Alfred from Chattanooga to Nashville, Louisville, Cincinnati, and Columbus. A hired cab took him twenty-seven miles south to his family in Circleville, Ohio. Alfred recorded thar his trip home cost $175. He remained in Circleville at the home of his sister Harriet Wilkes, regaining his health during the fall and early winter of 1866. New adventures were ahead in 1867.

Part VI

Army Warrant

Chapter 45

Kansas

Kansas was named by French explorers after a Dakota Sioux Indian word, *kanze*, meaning "south wind." Located on America's Great Plains, Kansas began attracting European and American settlers in 1850. Congress passed a Homestead Act in 1862 opening the Great Plains to settlers. The act granted 160 acres of public land to settlers for a small filing fee with a requirement of five years of continuous residence to gain title. Post–Civil War found people flocking West for free land. Most newcomers emigrated from Eastern and Southern states. They included veterans, businessmen, speculators, African Americans, foreigners, and convicts. Newspapers carried stories of great opportunities to own land in Western states. Fears that newly opened land would soon be gone filled Eastern newspapers, creating a race to acquire land.

Christmas in 1866 found Alfred in good health, fully recovered from his summer health problems. Year 1867 began with a great surprise. Alfred received from the army a warrant for 120 acres of land in the state of Kansas for his participation in Fremont's California Battalion in the 1846 war with Mexico. Acreage issued in a warrant was based on the number of days a volunteer soldier (not an officer) served in a war. Alfred's warrant was the only compensation he received for service in the California Battalion.

Alfred was not the only person in Circleville to become excited about the prospects of owning land in Kansas. A group of businessmen eyed acquiring newly opened lands in Kansas for wheat production. Kansas, they were told, would become the "breadbasket of the world." Before leaving

Circleville, Alfred met with a group of leading citizens, agreeing to work as their agent in a search for Kansas farm properties. In 1867, 1,292,775 acres of public lands became available for sale by the U.S. Treasury. Almost 900,000 acres were ceded to the government by a treaty with Osage Indians removing the tribe from Kansas to Oklahoma. The Morrill Act of 1862, known as the Land Grant College Act, provided 30,000 acres of public lands, based on the number of each state's representatives to Congress, to be sold to fund the establishment and maintenance of colleges and universities teaching agricultural, mechanical, veterinarian, and other disciplines. The act was designed to provide higher education for farmers and working-class people.

Alfred left Ohio in early February 1867. He stopped for a couple of days in Cincinnati before boarding a steamboat to Saint Louis. Two days after arriving in Saint Louis, he took the Northern Missouri Railroad for Chariton County, stopping at Glasgow. He was anxious to see his old friend and fellow captain William C. Heryford, who served with him in John C. Fremont's Missouri Body Guard. Heryford's farm reminded him of the fine farms his family owned in Pickaway County, Ohio. William's wife, Elizabeth, was a gracious and educated lady. Alfred spent the next few weeks investigating business opportunities in Kansas. Weather turned bad during his stay with Heryford. An intense winter blizzard blew in from the Great Plains on March 8, followed by three days of below-zero temperatures. Conversations with Heryford, a farmer and state representative, gave Alfred a working knowledge of locations of good farmland in Kansas. He used this information to correspond with G. L. Harris, government land commissioner in Hannibal, Missouri, to learn about available farm sites in Kansas.

On March 25, days were becoming longer; it was time for a visit to Kansas to investigate newly opened public lands. At Glasgow, Alfred discovered that his departure for Kansas City was delayed for two days while he waited for the first available steamboat. Near noon on a rainy morning, the steamboat *Yellowstone* came into view, slowly docking at town's quay. Fuel, freight, and passengers were loaded. The Big Muddy, as the Missouri River was called, was in a wild and angry state. Davenport's small stern-wheeler, the second to carry the name of *Yellowstone*, churned away from the dock, struggling to make headway against strong and frothy currents. Progress was slow, about 2 miles per hour. Because of difficulties finding the river's main channel, Alfred questioned if he had made a mistake traveling aboard the *Yellowstone*. Early in the morning of March 28, running with a full head of steam in a newly uncharted channel, the boat slammed into a hidden snag where she held fast. Shifting freight and passengers, the crew worked feverously until midday to free the steamboat and get underway.

Departure from Lexington, Missouri, was at four the next morning. Alfred enjoyed an early morning eastern sky filled with streaks of brilliant orange. He felt invigorated by a new day with a glorious sunrise. The *Yellowstone* continued its winding journey upstream, eventually passing rows of hills crowded with houses on the approach to Kansas City. Landing was midday on March 30.

Davenport spent the next six days waiting for a letter from Attorney McCrae, representing Circleville investors Ruggles, Turney, Brown, and Dowden, with instructions to locate one-third of a section of land for farming in newly opened public lands located in southeastern Kansas. McCrae's instructions told Alfred to meet Mr. Gerhardt from Circleville at the U.S. land agent's office in Humboldt. Alfred left Kansas City for Lawrence, riding on the Southern Kansas Stage Line. The trip was long and slow; weather was wintery and cold. Mules pulling the stage needed to be changed every 10 miles. Eight scheduled stops in small towns, discharging and taking on passengers and freight, made the trip seem to never end.

Sunset was long past when Alfred stopped for the night in Garnett. Lodging was at Garnett House Hotel, also called the Lighthouse Hotel for a lantern placed in a second-floor window. Hotel rooms were limited. Alfred shared a bed with two other men. Coach travel was no panacea. Kansas dirt roads had not been improved like macadam roads in the East. In dry times, they could be relatively smooth, albeit dusty. Winter weather left roads full of holes with pools of water, ice, and mud. On occasion, Alfred, along with other passengers, was asked to assist in extracting an immobile coach trapped in mud.

Gerhardt was late to arrive at Humboldt. He appeared on April 16, carrying dispatches from McCrea and Turney, instructing Alfred to choose land in Butler County for investors. Davenport spent the next week visiting suitable sites recommended by the land agent. In Humboldt, he confirmed availability of federal land with the U.S. agent and mailed a report detailing his findings to McCrea. His project ended on May 6 in Humboldt. A contract to purchase land and a certificate of location from the U.S. land office were prepared and sent to Circleville. Having finished his work in southeast Kansas, Alfred returned to Glasgow and Heryford's, staying until July when he returned in Kansas to locate 120 acres fulfilling his warrant. Finding nothing to suit his needs, he returned to his friends in Missouri late in October.

Early in April 1868, Alfred returned to Greenwood County, Kansas, where he sold his warrant, investing in lots where he would use his carpentry skills to help build Eureka.

Texas-Kansas Cattle Trails

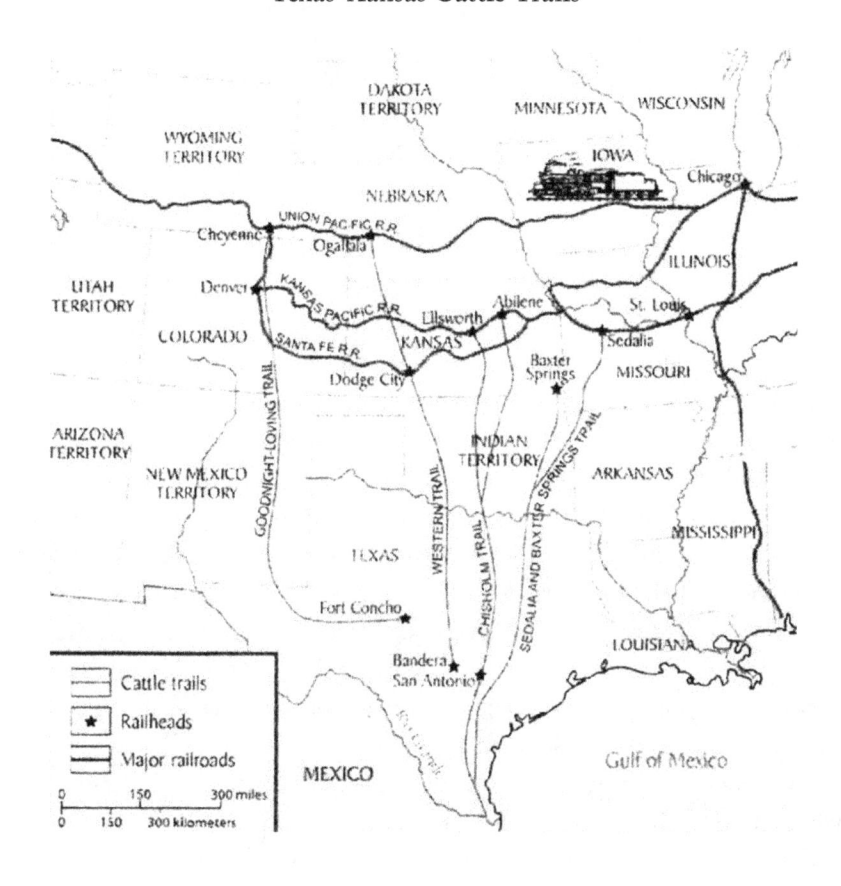

Chapter 46

Eureka, Kansas, 1868–1875

Alfred's October 1867 decision to return to Missouri was fortunate. He missed a cholera outbreak that rapidly spread throughout southern Kansas in late December. The epidemic had passed by the time he returned in 1868. Traveling from Heryford's to Eureka in Greenwood County permitted Alfred time to reflect on what he had seen and learned about Kansas resulting from 1862's Homestead Act, opening neutral (Indian) lands, and the rush of settlers to acquire farm land in the Great Plains of Kansas. On any April day, Alfred watched long lines of immigrants traveling in white canvas-topped wagons snaking westward, searching for homesteads in southern Kansas counties. Settlers were from diverse backgrounds, cultures, and religious beliefs; all had one goal—acquire 160 acres of land, build a house, and settle as quickly as possible, for the most desirable locations would soon be gone. Land was a good investment; prices were accelerating 50 to 100 percent a year.

Living on the prairie faced new types of challenges. Unlike the East, where pioneers found ample supplies of timber, 5 percent of Kansas land had timber. Newcomers needed to cut heavy thick bricks from prairie sod to construct a house for their family. A typical house of 16 × 20 feet required three thousand sod bricks. Sod needed to be cleared from fields so a farmer could plant wheat, corn, oats, and vegetables. Shallow wells of 15 to 25 feet were dug to supply a homestead's water needs. Most families kept a cow for milk to supplement their diet. Farming tools and household equipment were expensive and difficult to purchase. Shortages prompted pioneers to share. One item, a griddle for cooking corn cakes or wheat cakes, was known to be shared between six families.

During a visit to Lawrence, Kansas, Alfred learned about Jayhawkers, the name given to antislavery bands of Kansas men who fought proslavery bushwhackers along the Missouri-Kansas border in the 1850s. The New England Emigrant Aid Company (NEEAC), with strict rules of governance and strong antislavery beliefs, developed in early Kansas. NEEAC was predominant in establishing Lawrence, Manhattan, Topeka, and other towns. NEEAC's efforts helped Kansas enter the Union in 1861 as a free state.

The first newspaper in Greenwood County was published in Eureka during August 1866, carrying the motto "Be sure you are right, then go ahead." Alfred looked forward to its weekly publication, the only news source for Eureka. It carried articles describing development of railroad towns or railheads.

Texas provided large numbers of cattle to the Confederacy during the Civil War. Eighteen sixty three's closing of the Mississippi River to the Confederacy stopped eastern flow of livestock to the Old South from west of the Mississippi River. The number of cattle raised on Texas 'open range grew to a large surplus. Prices for beef collapsed. Year 1866 found Texas cattlemen receiving $1 to $2 per head at livestock sales. Ranchers learned that Chicago and other Eastern cities had cattle markets where an animal sold from $8 to $11 per hundred pounds. Butchers in Eastern cities sold beef for forty cents a pound. Reaching lucrative markets required driving cattle from Texas north to Kansas railheads. Cattle drives originated at multiple locations: Brownsville, San Antonio, and Fort Worth. Driven north on the Chisholm Trail, trails crossed the Red River, passing through Indian territories on ancient paths to Kansas railheads. Marshalling yards loaded livestock for Eastern shipment. A typical cattle drive contained 2,500 to 3,000 Texas longhorns. A drive took three to four months. Cattlemen brought 35,000 cattle to Abilene, Kansas, in 1867; 75,000 in 1868; and 350,000 in 1869, growing to 600,000 in 1870. Major railheads developed in Kansas cities: Wichita, Newtown, Ellsworth, Junction, Caldwell, and Dodge. Five million head of cattle were shipped East from Kansas between 1867 and 1871. New rail lines connecting Texas to the East during the 1870s diminished the need for cattle drives from Texas to Kansas.

Cowboys and Kansas homesteaders mixed like oil and water. Texas cowboys were free spirited; many were ex-Confederate soldiers. They believed and followed traditions of the Old South. Most were young, idealistic, and hardy. Living on the open range created self-reliance and individualism. Cowboys thrived on new adventures. Homesteaders looked on a cowboy as a wild roughneck who preferred to settle disputes with a gun. Cowboys were not fond of farmers, who they considered weak, taking handouts of land from the government while maintaining strict anti-South views. Controlling skittish animals, especially during thunderstorms on open, unfenced Kansas prairies, challenged cowboys. A loose herd of rogue cattle wandering on homesteaders' land caused severe damage to crop and farm buildings. Diseases carried by Texas cattle infected and killed homesteader cows, causing additional grief and loss.

The end of a cattle drive was eagerly anticipated after a long and dangerous journey across the prairie. Drovers arrived in Kansas dusty, dirty, unshaven, unkempt, and hungry for entertainment and a drink of whiskey. Celebrations began soon after cattle were delivered to stockyards when cowboys were paid. Towns were crowded; lodging was inadequate. Waiting in towns for the arrival of hundreds of cowboys were saloons, often owned by outlaws, gamblers, and prostitutes, all anxious to help cowboys spend hard-earned cash. Lawlessness in railheads became a problem. Murders, thefts, and crime were common. Abilene, described as the wickedest Kansas town, hired William "Wild Bill" Hickok as town marshal. Wichita, where every third building was a saloon or gambling house, employed Wyatt Earp as a policeman. J. H. Runkle, a prosecutor from Ellsworth, Kansas, reported in October 1867, "A homicide had been committed in the area every day for the past ninety-three days." Most residents in Kansas towns were law-abiding conservative citizens, yet local law enforcement and courts lacked the ability to protect citizens when cattle drives were at their peak.

Small towns answered, replacing traditional law and order with a variety of extralegal organizations that became the norm for handling disputes. Real estate matters were handled by claim clubs that employed violence or threats of violence to settle disputes. Some organizations rewrote laws governing economic or political rivals. Vigilantes targeted horse thieves, confidence men, swindlers, prostitutes, and murderers who they removed from their communities by a gun or hangman's noose. A group known as White Caps demanded upgrades of community morals, enforced by beatings and whippings. Extralegal societies dominated Kansas efforts at local law enforcement during the post Civil War era into the 1870s.

Alfred wrote describing newcomers and settlers he had met during the past years. Settlers worked to adopt life and ways established in their new community. Over time their attitudes would change. They began doing what they thought was important or correct, not what was dictated by law. He experienced similar changes wherever he lived—Ohio, Oregon, California, or Missouri. When it came to what is the lawful or what is right, Davenport followed the law. He was critical of people who chose to do "what is right." He had no interest in joining an extralegal organization.

Social banditry was an illegal criminal activity in Kansas and Missouri, yet some felt it morally acceptable. Gangs of social bandits developed in former pro-South communities. Gang members were often ex-Confederate soldiers or ex-guerrillas fighting against institutions that they thought were opposed to their beliefs. Law officers viewed social bandits' robbing of banks, railroads, and stagecoaches as criminal violence. It had been said that social bandits used some of their ill-gotten funds to aid poor, less fortunate citizens. Sympathetic town leaders were known to support or turn a blind eye to gangs in shocking and infamous ways. Jesse and Frank James and the Younger brothers' gang were social bandits. They committed a wide swath of robberies from Texas to Minnesota. Banks in Missouri and Kansas were hit hard by this group.

A frequent topic of conversation among friends and acquaintances was about horses. Popular lore in the Old West stated that a horse was worth more than a man's life. This was evidenced by the treatment of a horse thief. If a man stole your cow, he was jailed. If he stole your horse, he was hanged. The horse was a universal means of communication. A man's horse pulled his wagon, plowed his fields, and carried him to neighbors or church or into town. Cattle were herded using horses. Indians fought battles and wars from horseback. In 1870, a civil war almost started in Kansas because of horses. Theft of horses began to rise in the spring, accelerating as summer reached Greenwood County and its neighbors. Butler County was especially hard hit. Unable to get satisfactory help from local law enforcement, citizens formed vigilance committees to solve horse theft problems. Eight hundred people signed up as vigilantes to track down horse thieves.

Late in autumn, vigilantes stopped at the home of longtime resident Lewis Booth. Booth, his brother, and a friend, Jack Corbin, were dragged from their house, charged as horse and cattle thieves. The men were ordered to be hanged from a large tree in the front yard. Corbin was first to go. Before dying, Corbin fingered fifty men in the county as horse thieves. Two men were executed by gunfire when they attempted to escape. In the ensuing days, more suspects were rounded up and executed. Law-abiding citizens became outraged at executions performed without the benefit of a judge, trial, and jury. The state governor sent his adjutant general, David Whittaker, and one thousand armed militiamen to El Dorado, Butler County seat, to confront the vigilantes. A tense negotiation occurred. Vigilantes, desiring no bloodshed, backed down. Eighty-eight men and one woman were turned over to the militia. Eight-five were dismissed. A judge dropped charges on the three remaining men.

Alfred's plans for Eureka in April of 1868 were exciting. The town had been laid out the previous year; construction skills and experience were needed. Soft limestone was the most abundant building material. Limestone bricks were left in the sun to weather hardened, making them a desirable building material. Alfred constructed a house for his residence and invested in town lots, hoping to profit from the boom in real estate. He theorized; skilled immigrants would settle in towns, need housing driving up housing prices.

Life on the prairie had its good moments. After Sunday church services, church congregations gathered to share and discuss topics of common interests. Gatherings lasted for several hours. Eureka's favorite party was held on July 4. Tables were set on a vacant town lot, filled with food brought by attendees. First on the day's agenda was the singing of "The Star-Spangled Banner." A preacher read the Declaration of Independence. Local officials began a litany of endless speeches. Food was served: roast pork, prairie oysters, fried chicken, breads, dried apple pie, and gingerbread cakes. Games, horse races, and a tug-of-war ended afternoon festivities. In the evening, a dance was held with a fiddler providing music. Year 1868 had been a full and busy year for Alfred. November's mail brought him an invitation from the Heryford's to join them for the winter in Missouri. He bid farewell to friends, telling them he would return in April.

In April 1869, Davenport offered his Eureka properties for sale but found no buyers. He would stay in Eureka until the next year, hoping to sell his land. Year 1870 was a growth year for Eureka. Alfred continued to work on town building projects. In February, he joined the local lodge of the Independent Order of Odd Fellows. The town's first bank opened in August by a man named Quackenbush. Year 1871 saw Eureka's population double to over 500 from 250 the prior year. Not everyone was prosperous.

Quackenbush's bank failed and closed in January. It was replaced by the Eureka Bank during the summer. Alfred worked on the construction of a county courthouse. It was a three-floor structure built with limestone bricks located 1.5 miles west of the town center. Plans were made for the construction of Eureka Mills that could process 100 bags of flour a day.

World and national events in the 1870s brought changes that would filter down to Eureka, Kansas. War in Europe between France and Prussia resulted in unification of German states into a modern Germany. Germany, needing troops, initiated universal conscription, forcing all men of military age into the army. Men of draftable age immigrated to North America. Worldwide prices for agricultural and nonagricultural products doubled from early 1861 levels to a peak in 1873. Farmland under cultivation grew 50 percent between 1870 and 1880, aided by cheap trans-Mississippi land, improved farming machinery, and the use of steam-powered threshers to harvest grains. United States wheat production in 1870 was 250,000 bushels. It doubled to 500,000 by 1873.

Newspaper reports in 1872 suggested that southern Kansas had been "filling up rapidly." Alfred noted that immigrants bypassed Greenwood County, choosing to settle in locations farther west because most of eastern Kansas's most desirable farmland was no longer available. Eureka's town fathers vetoed an opportunity to have a railroad in 1871. Lack of rail service put Eureka at a competitive disadvantage to neighboring railroad towns. The U.S. economy received a jolt when Jay Cooke's Northern Pacific Railroad failed in September 1873, resulting in a financial panic and depression lasting across the nation until 1879. At the same time, President Grant returned the dollar to a gold standard. The move restricted credit, taking much-needed cash out of circulation, and dampened trade. Eighteen thousand businesses, eighty-nine railroads, ten states, and hundreds of banks went bankrupt. Railroads had been granted 6,400 acres of federal land for every mile of a completed rail line, a government designed program to stimulate Western settlement and development. In some areas, after the crash in 1873, there were no buyers for vacant railroad land. Before the September panic, railroad companies had completed three lines across Kansas east to west and four north to south. Alfred wrote that world and national economic problems arrived in Eureka, Kansas.

Alfred Davenport wrote that southern Kansas endured the worst weather he had ever seen in the winter of 1873. He was very "dissatisfied with the climate at this latitude." Cold winter days were long and very uncomfortable. He spent many days at the Odd Fellows Lodge, saying it was a "good place and would be better if every member lived up to the teachings of the order." He recognized that some men were "weak, not able to control their passions. A few lodge members who got beyond rules, felt they should be pardoned when their passions get the best of them." Alfred's comments were directed toward men who consumed excessive amounts of alcohol. He listed twelve members of his lodge "whose hearts were paced by our creator in the right positions, were good friends" but needed help.

On January 7, 1874, on his fifty-fourth birthday, Alfred wrote that he was happy with his life, but "Eureka was dull, all kinds of businesses are stagnant," especially real estate. Lots were not selling; demand had dwindled. Despite these sentiments, the year was not a bore. Year 1874 brought unique surprises for Alfred. At the end of spring, weather became exceedingly hot and dry, remaining for weeks without a drop of rain. A never-ending wind blew from the south. Tree leaves shriveled and dropped. Fields of crops wilted and died in scorching heat. Day after day, the sun burned a bright blue; not a cloud was seen in the sky. Heat caused great suffering for man and animals.

Suddenly, without warning, in early August, the sky turned black. The sun was hidden by a dark cloud. Wind sounded like a tornado. Millions of vibrating, rasping insects fell to the land, devouring everything in sight. Known as locusts or grasshoppers, they stripped leaves from trees. Fields where crops had been growing were laid bare; only plant stubble remained. Animals were victims. Poultry and hogs gorged on insects and died. Sheep were shorn of wool. Horse harnesses were devoured, paint stripped from wagons. Insects invaded houses, destroying everything not in barrels and boxes. In some locations, locusts covered the earth to a depth of four feet. Farmers, hoping to protect crops, raced into fields, spreading recently threshed straw that they burned as a deterrent with limited success. Food supplies became exhausted. Crops waiting to be harvested for the upcoming winter were gone. Housewives pulled wings and feet off grasshoppers to make a soup or to fry in butter. Settlers became discouraged, packed up belongings, and returned East. Kansas lost one-third of its homesteaders. In the spring of 1875, grasshopper eggs began to hatch. A late snow and a sudden deep frost killed grasshopper larvae, ending the insect plague.

Alfred needed a change. He planned a trip to visit the Rocky Mountains. He would spend the next two months traveling and sightseeing using railroad. Railroads were the means of fulfilling Manifest Destiny.

In 1845, a belief promoted by the press and religious groups suggested that the North American continent was predestined to be settled by Americans who would bring political, religious, and social order to wild, unclaimed territory. The United States government promoted Western development with grants of 130 million acres of land to the nation's railroads. Progress in expansion across the Great Plains was rapid; one report stated that two miles of track was being laid every thirty minutes. Bridges and culverts were built, mountains graded, tunnels built. Poles beside rails carried telegraph wires, tying communities together with the latest information and news.

Railroad companies in 1875 remained short of cash for construction. Needing more passenger traffic, they initiated a marketing campaign glorifying the benefits of leisure travel. Destinations became quicker and more easily reached. Long-distance travel took less time. Standardization of track width, or gauge, eliminated time-consuming transfers between competing railroad lines. One could travel from the East Coast to Denver in four days by the mid-1870s. Pullman's latest design of railroad cars enticed travelers: dining cars, hotel cars, lounge cars with swivel chairs, and sleeping cars. Safety improved with the inventions of air brakes and automatic couplers. Atchison, Topeka, and Santa Fe's line offered discounted ticket prices to potential investors who would travel West to visit land offered for sale.

Alfred saw this as an opportunity to investigate available land in Colorado Territory before it became a state on August 1, 1876. He began a rail journey in Wichita in May, stopping in Granada, Colorado. Arrival of rail service in 1873 made Granada a boom town. Three restaurants and a hotel were completed in eight weeks. Granada, for many years, had been known as an important stop on the Santa Fe Trail, offering travelers good supplies of water and wood from tall cottonwood trees growing along the Arkansas River. The trail, founded in 1822, was the southern route for merchandise to reach Santa Fe, New Mexico, and California.

Alfred enjoyed Granada, where he met a mixture of people—railroad employees, gamblers, buffalo hunters, and cowboys. The town was known for famous people. Calamity Jane, a former pony express rider; Ed Masterson, known as a buffalo hunter, lawman, and scout for General Custer; and Ben Thompson, an ex-Confederate gunslinger hired to defend the railroad in land disputes. Alfred found no real estate of interest during a visit to Granada's land office.

The next 100 miles traversed dry Colorado scrubland with sparse vegetation. He left the train at Fort Lyon, originally called Bent's Fort (rebuilt after a disastrous flood in 1866). The fort brought back memories of forts he visited on prior cross-country journeys. It was a supply center providing travelers and settlers protection from ongoing hostilities from Cheyenne and Arapaho Indians. Alfred had seen enough fighting in his life. He left for Pueblo, Colorado, a growing city he later would consider as a replacement for his home in Eureka.

Pueblo's growth was an example of changes brought by Western expansion. Originally a trading post on the Santa Fe Trail at the confluence of the Arkansas River and Fountain Creek, it provided travelers with an excellent source of water before heading south to Santa Fe. Pueblo's 1870s census showed 666 residents. Ten years later, it had grown to 3,217. The population was over 1,550 when Alfred arrived. It was becoming a major rail center. The Denver and Rio Grande Railroad reached the city in 1872. Year 1876 saw the completion of the Atchison, Topeka, and Santa Fe Railroad to Pueblo. Visiting the town brought Alfred memories of Sacramento during early gold rush days. Both cities were located near mountains on a river and served as a major transportation center. Alfred planned to use Pueblo as a basis for exploring mining country.

Early morning found Alfred aboard a Denver and Rio Grande train bound for Rosita, west of Pueblo. The route snaked along the banks of the Arkansas River, which became a fast-moving mountain stream. Three bridges and several culverts were crossed as the railroad wound through a valley with spectacular mountain vistas. Tall mountain peaks along the route were capped with winter snow. Soon after arriving in Canyon City, he visited a nearby natural wonder, the Arkansas River's Royal Gorge. Walls of the gorge dramatically rose 1,259 feet above swirling river waters. The base of the gorge was narrow, only 50 feet wide. Alfred thought the scene was impressive, though not comparable to what he saw as a youngster in Niagara Falls, New York.

The next morning, Alfred continued to Rosita, named by Spanish explorers for small wild roses blooming in the valley floor surrounding the town. A typical Colorado mining community, Rosita's 1,500 residents lived at an altitude of 8,800 feet. It was located on a mountain plain along the Hardscrabble Creek at the base of conical-shaped mountains named Wet Mountains. West of the plain ran the Sangre de Cristo Mountain Range. Horn Peak, not far from Rosita, reached a height of 13,450 feet. Businesses in the town included several hotels, one saloon, a cheese factory, a brewery, and a smelter to recover copper and silver ore from mines working Rosita's Pocahontas Vein. The vein produced $900,000 in precious metals during its fifteen-year life. Alfred's visit to Rosita was a nostalgic reminder of years spent in the pursuit of California gold before the Civil War brought him East. Slowing of mineral production in Rosita mines meant fewer jobs and less income for businesses supported by mining. Rosita eventually became a ghost town.

Denver was Alfred's last visit before returning to Kansas. In November 1858, William Larimer—a land speculator from Pittsburgh, Pennsylvania—staked out one square mile of land at the confluence of the South Platte River and Cherry Creek that he named Denver City in honor of Colorado's territorial governor James W. Denver. The site located on the front range of the Rocky Mountains became a service and supply center for a Colorado gold rush. Gold was discovered in 1858 near Pike's Peak, 70 miles south of Denver. Placer recovery ended more quickly in Colorado than in California. It was replaced by deep shaft mines. Expensive smelting operations were required for producing gold, silver, and copper. Colorado's mining industry developed slowly, with the Civil War diverting attention from mining. When the conflict ended, people slowly began to migrate to Colorado. Denver reported a population of 4,759 in 1870, almost the same as reported in 1860. This soon changed.

During the 1870s, Denver experienced 22 percent growth a year. Census in 1880 counted 35,629 residents. Mining and railroads became a major contributor to Denver's growth. One of most important developments in the nineteenth century was the completion of a railroad across the continent. Congress chartered two railroad companies for the work. California's Central Pacific began construction in Sacramento, California. It crossed the Sierra Nevada and passed Reno and northern Nevada into Utah. The Union Pacific began in Chicago. It crossed Iowa, Nebraska, and Wyoming, extending into Utah. The two railroads met at Promontory Summit, north of the Great Salt Like. A grand celebration was held at eleven o'clock on May 10, 1869. Leaders of each company took turns driving a golden spike into the last railroad tie, signifying a unification of a nationwide railroad. Denver's leading citizens, concerned about losing railroad related business in Colorado, raised $300,000 for the Denver Pacific to build a line to connect with the transcontinental railroad at Cheyenne, Wyoming, 100 miles north of Denver. Service began in June of 1870. August of the same year, the Kansas Pacific Railroad completed a line from Kansas City to Denver. Connections between Denver and Pueblo were completed in 1872. Multiple railroads made Denver a premier transportation center. The state government, railroads, mining, and land development helped accelerate the city's growth.

A visit to the U.S. land office in Denver enlightened Alfred about land ownership in the new state. Claim clubs dominated many of Colorado rural land transactions. Land purchases were controlled by the clubs. Small 160-acre farms were often not profitable due to weather issues. Frequent dry spells hurt grain and corn production in eastern counties of the state. Range-fed cattle were profitable if you owned or had access to thousands of acres of land. Farms located on high mountain plateaus had short growing seasons. Barley, oats, wheat, and peas were successful high-altitude crops when growing seasons were short. Breweries had a healthy appetite for barley. Bakers and horses loved oats. Colorado intrigued Alfred, though he thought he would be better off remaining in Kansas. He enjoyed the amenities in Denver, especially restaurants. Theaters and opera brought popular entertainers to Denver. Alfred enjoyed both before returning to Kansas.

Chapter 47

Kansas, 1876–1879

Life on the prairie was not all work. On rare occasions, Alfred took time off for a special celebration. One occurred in Baxter Springs with the opening of the Missouri River, Fort Scott, and Gulf Railroad in May of 1870. The governor, mayors of nearby towns, newspaper reporters, and guests gathered for a celebration. Songs were sung, speeches were given by the governor and local dignitaries, cheap whiskey flowed freely. After supper, entertainment was provided by an Indian war dance held in front of a bonfire on the town square. Twenty Indians danced around the fire; continuously emitting howls led by a leader pounding on a single drum. Another fifty danced, circling the twenty. Dancing men and boys were clothed in a single loincloth dropping to six or inches above their knees held in place by a rope around the waist. Each dancer carried an item—blanket, sword, spear, or old gun—all were painted with ribbons of paint, vermillion, black, yellow, and red. Suddenly, they were joined by women wearing loose dresses with bright colors, most notably orange. Whirling, stamping of feet, yelling, and patting their mouths continued until a predetermined time, when they melted away. The next venue was a grand ball that lasted until the wee hours of the next morning.

Business in Eureka during 1876 and 1877 was slow. Farmers complained about the time needed to take crops to towns with railroads. Commodity prices for grain crops had declined. Wheat was priced 50 percent below levels reached early in 1873. Real estate was in a slump; land values were in a slow decline. Alfred's investments did not generate enough income to cover his expenses. He was concerned he would have little income for old age.

Awareness of social problems became a national issue. Consumption of alcohol was blamed on the country's problems. Immigrants in crowded Eastern cities were targeted for their drinking habits. Alcohol consumption was part of an immigrant's daily life. Germans were beer drinkers. Frenchmen and Italians enjoyed wine. Antisaloon groups created images of working-class men finding their way to local watering holes wasting hard-earned wages on drink, leaving their families destitute. Drunkenness and solutions to cure the "evils of drink" became a focus of Christian church pulpits across the land. Fire and brimstone sermons were published and spread by the press. The national temperance movement came to Eureka in 1878.

Alfred, who rarely used alcohol, became amazed by friends who were former drinkers. He said, "The old temperance excitement is repeating itself. Men who have been users of liquor all their lives are now fanatics in the cause of temperance, losing all sense of reason." The church preaches that "one should follow his [God's] commands and be forgiving." Reformed drinkers criticized and condemned old friends who would not give up drinking. Alfred saw them in a new light. They were hypocrites; he would never again trust their word. He questioned why he felt this way. After consideration, he thought maybe this criticism was part of his getting older.

Good news came to Eureka in January 1879. The Kansas City and Southern Railroad was extending a line through Eureka from Fort Scott to Wichita. Alfred's health suffered through a hot summer and autumn. Malarial fevers, a constant concern from the time he spent in the South, returned. If he wanted to live to old age, he would need to move away from the Kansas climate. He celebrated his sixtieth on January 7 in good health and spirits, writing he was physically weaker. He thought about moving to the West Coast, but his roots were now in Eureka; he would re-consider a move later in the winter.

Congress again was discussing a pension for the few remaining veterans who fought Mexico in 1846. It would not be a large amount of money, $8 a month. However, unpaid funds for the past thirty-four years would be a welcome check. He disliked men currently in the U.S. Congress who ignored veterans' services and sacrifices. He felt Washington politicians were a group of selfish demagogues.

Alfred sold his house on March 17. He had enjoyed many "happy and pleasant days in Eureka, but the town had become dull and tame." He planned to leave for the mountains of Colorado.

Chapter 48

Alfred Returns to California

Alfred decided to visit the West in April 1880 with no planned agenda. He would investigate Pueblo, Colorado, a city he thought might be his next home. Twenty days into his visit, he "became very much dissatisfied and restless." He left for California "with the intention of taking up his old business of managing a gold mine." Sacramento, his first visit in twenty years, was a different city. A gold rush frontier town had been replaced by a thriving state capital. The first item on his agenda was to locate old friends. These efforts brought on heartache when he discovered many of his old friends had passed away. A few he met were old, suffering from poor health. Alfred continued to San Francisco in hopes of enjoying a city he had grown to love, now considered the Paris of the West.

San Francisco's 1880 population was 234,000 up from 21,200 in 1860. Immigrants lived in ethnic neighborhoods. Italians resided in North Beach, French in the Western Addition. San Francisco rivaled large Eastern cities with restaurants, markets, and all types of entertainment. Landfill had enlarged the city's waterfront. Dolores Mission was part of the city, no longer a rural outpost. Neighborhoods were identified by distinctive architecture and decorations featuring Empire, Romanesque, Queen Anne, and Italianate homes. Some things had not changed. China's large immigrant population of about 21,200 people lived in the segregated Chinatown. Chinese were not permitted to live outside their quarter unless they were employed as domestic servants or were laundry owners who must live at their place of business.

Men from San Francisco, always risk-takers, thrived in an ever-changing business environment. Mining, agriculture, fishing, finance, and timber became leading industries, bringing success and profits. Wealthy citizens lived in a grand style with fancy clothes and opulent houses, enjoying fine dining, arts, and social and sporting events. They established private membership clubs, symbols of power, prestige, and privilege. One club, the Bohemian Club, founded in 1872 by journalists for members of their trade craft, included artists and musicians. By 1880, the club welcomed businessmen. Alfred discovered that the city had three distinct business districts: finance, wholesaling, and retailing.

A search for friends netted only two old men. Disappointed in not finding old comrades, he boarded the SS *Oregon*, a cargo-passenger steamship for a two-day trip to Portland, which he had not seen since his departure in 1844. Alfred's was impressed with Portland. The city's population growth was rapid. Arising from a single log hotel and a weekly newspaper, the *Oregonian*, in 1850, the city featured a deep-water port, making it a major center for commerce, agriculture, and trade with a population of 17,500. Portland dwarfed Oregon City. Shipyards loaded timber, furniture, and agricultural products for export to San Francisco and world markets. The city was clean and fresh with many new buildings. A disastrous fire in August 1873 destroyed twenty city blocks along the Willamette River. Horse-drawn carriages served pedestrians. Heavy industry was coming to Portland. Alfred walked on a newly graded path north of the city created for a narrow-gauge railroad line leading to an iron foundry under construction. It was built to provide iron rails for West Coast railroads. The landscape around Portland had changed. Deep, thick forests with giant trees had been replaced with large farms and orchards. Success and prosperity were everywhere. Missing were the Clatsop, Klamath, Cayuse, Umatilla, and other Indians who had been a major problem for settlers in 1844.

Alfred returned to San Francisco and Sacramento in early June to visit Jerome C. "JC" Davis. Alfred "Alf" Davenport first met JC on a chilly night in the Mayacamas mountain range in June 1846, when he stumbled on a group of armed men led by Zeke Merritt headed to Sonoma. Alfred, with a young man's spirit of adventure and a feeling of invincibility, eagerly joined Merritt's band. Davis, one of Merritt's volunteers, became a lifelong friend. Both men signed on to John Charles Fremont's California Battalion in the war against Mexico. Davis—from Perry County, Ohio—found employment running Joseph B. Chiles's ferry across the Sacramento River in Yolo County. A quick venture in the gold fields netted few profits. He married Mary Chiles, Joseph's daughter, purchasing farmland along Putah Creek. Eventually, he owned 13,000 acres. He was always looking for a means to improve business, pioneering the use of horse-powered treadmills to thresh grain and bale hay.

Noting the weakness of Mexican cattle, Davis returned East, bringing superior breeds of cattle over the California Trail from Ohio and Missouri to California to strengthen his herds. He built a slaughterhouse, a flour mill, and a dairy to supply products from his farm, serving explosive population growth during California's gold rush. In 1872, he sold 773 acres to the state for a university in Davisville. The name was shortened to Davis in 1907.

Alfred and Jerome spent evenings reminiscing, reliving life and adventures as young men in early California. During days, they visited old mining communities and mining sites. A train carried them to Placerville. Its population had declined from 2,466 in 1860 to under 1,950 in 1880. Deep shaft gold mines continued to operate in nearby areas, replacing placer mining. A visit to the Middle Fork of the American River took Alfred to the abandoned and forgotten site of the famous Murderer's Bar gold mine.

Late in June, the two men boarded the Central Pacific Railroad for a visit to the mining and railroad center Rocklin and its nearby Secret Ravine. The ravine was unrecognizable. It had been heavily mined by placer and hydraulic mining, creating a scarred landscape marred with mine tailings and little vegetation. Later, granite found in the ravine was mined for use in constructing the state capitol in Sacramento.

June weather turned extremely hot and dry. Heat in the Secret Ravine seemed excessive to Alfred. His vision began to blur; he had a headache and felt he was losing his sight. The men returned home. Mary put Alf in bed; JC went for a doctor who examined Alfred, diagnosing he had experienced a sunstroke. Over the next few days, Alfred's health continued to decline. His sickness remained for two months. Days "brought on feelings of gloom and despondence he had never before felt." Recovery always seemed far away. Alfred "hoped for death but it did not come." He became sad and distressed. He had "no way to repay Mary and Jerome for the kindness and care they had given him."

Alfred's strength improved so he could return East. He bid adieu to his wonderful friends on August 26, traveling by rail to his sister in Circleville, Ohio. During the journey, his sickness began to return; he was almost blind. He stopped traveling to rest when he reached Kansas City. After a few days, he felt strong enough to resume his trip to Ohio, arriving on September 8.

Alfred's hometown had changed. Population grew from 4,380 in 1860 to 6,556 in 1880. The Ohio and Erie Canal and two railroads helped the town become an important manufacturing and agricultural center. Its meatpacking, cannery, tannery, and milling operations were recognized throughout the Midwest. Circleville was known worldwide for its production of broomcorn. Alfred looked forward to visiting family and getting to know nieces and nephews.

The care and kindness received from his sister Harriet Wilkes and her family deeply touched Alfred. He lamented having never adequately verbalized his strong feelings and the depth of his appreciation for all she had done for him. Writing in his diary, Alfred exclaimed, "God knows the love I have for her."

Two months of recuperation permitted Alfred to feel that his health had recovered. The old bachelor started to become restless. Suddenly, his mind was filled with an urge to return to Kansas.

John Charles Fremont

Jerome C. Davis

Fitz Henry Warren

Chapter 49

Alfred in Kansas and Ohio, 1880–1886

Alfred thought long and hard about returning to Kansas, where he spent fourteen years with little to show for his effort, yet Kansas was pulling him like a magnet. It had become his home. He "felt he should follow his instincts, bidding adieu to Harriet and his nieces on a cool November day, he boarded a train bound for Kansas."

Five days after arrival, he began the construction on one of his Eureka lots. The new house was tiny, twelve by fourteen feet. Work was difficult for Alfred, compounded by an early arrival of winter, freezing rain, sleet, and snow. His house was not ready to occupy until late January 1881. Alfred wrote in March, "I continued to recover from last summer's sunstroke, however any physical exertion seemed to bring back illness." Later in the month, he resumed work as a real estate agent, realizing it could provide a livelihood, but he did not expect to become wealthy from the endeavor.

A heat wave in June brought Alfred much discomfort. He needed to stay in the shade to avoid headaches. Life improved when summer heat broke in September. Parties and gatherings of friends and neighbors used to be highlights of Alfred's life. Now he was content to stay by himself, although he enjoyed watching young people having a good time. Memories of adventures over the past fifty years remained strong; however, names and dates began to leave him. Alfred worried that his savings were too small to pay for his funeral. He neglected to consider the value of his house and vacant lots in Eureka when mentioning these concerns.

October 1884 was a bad month for Alfred. He was "taken down with the bloody flu." The local chapter of the Odd Fellows Lodge employed a nurse to provide care for Alfred. Thanks to good nursing and a strong constitution, he recovered but was not strong enough to work. In January 1885, his sixty-fifth birthday, Alfred wrote, "Life of a carefree bachelor was great when you are young and in good health." His health had become poor. Suffering from general weakness and frequent headaches since his sunstroke, he blamed chronic headaches for losses of memory.

Visitors were the highlight of any day. Hours were spent reminiscing about his rich and fulfilling life for which he was very thankful. "Pains in his head, weakness of body and feebleness" made Alfred think he should be with his family, especially his sister. He wrote, "Friends here did all in their power to cheer me in my declining days, but no one can provide the warmth, comfort and kindness provided by family." Realizing his time was near, he returned to Ohio in November 1885 to live with his sister Harriet Wilkes. Capt. Alfred "Alf" Davenport died shortly after his sixty-sixth birthday. It was February 20, 1886.

Special Thanks

Roger Hamernik, Phd.,Plattsburgh State University for his assistance in editing the original manuscript.

Darlene Weaver, director, and Carolyn Weigand at the Pickaway County Historical and Genealogical Society, 210 N. Court Street, Circleville, Ohio 43113

Amy Lucadamo, college archivist, Gettysburg College, Musselman Library, 300 Washington St. Gettysburg, Pennsylvania 27325 for Special Collection, Col. Wm Brisbane papers containing military orders of Brig. Gen. Fitz Henry Warren.

Michael Harrell for books about Union Spies, Civil War (see bibliography).

Weldon Svoboda, director, U.S. Army Quartermaster Museum, 1201 22nd Street, Bldg. 5228, Ft. Lee, Virginia, USA.

John Winston, Liverpool Museum, UK, for merchant ship *Thomas Dickerson*, sailed winter 1831, ref. Chas Davenport diary.

Sources

Diary: "My Life" by Capt. Alfred Davenport, 1820–1886. Owned by John Gardner Wilder

Diary: Capt. Alfred Davenport, 1862–1867, Mountain Department, Quartermaster Dept., Visit to Kansas. Owned by John Gardner Wilder.

Diary: Charles Davenport's journal from February 24, 1831, to June 30, 1831. Description of travel from Eccleshill, England, to Circleville, Ohio. Copy of Charles Davenport's journal from the archives of Miss Mary Emily Wilder (a niece of Harriet Davenport's daughter, Martha Ann [Wilkes] Wilder). She was head librarian of Circleville, Ohio's public library and keeper of Davenport-Wilkes-Wilder family archives. She died in 1954. Her archives are now held by the Pickaway County Historical and Genealogical Library, 210 N. Court St., Circleville, Ohio 43113.

Copy of newspaper story from the *Herald*, October 31, 1845, "Letter from Oregon," written by Alfred Davenport, mailed from Oregon City on April 1, 1845, provided by Mary Emily Wilder's family archives.

Ohio History Central's online histories of the Ohio and Erie Canals and Circleville, Ohio: www.OHC@ohiohistory.org.

Jstor.org, an online library providing journals covering Civil War and California gold rush topics, www.jstor.org.

Wikipedia, an online encyclopedia, www.wikipedia.org.

Wilder, John Gardner, *The Mover*, online, Xlibris-item 133133, 2013.

Bibliography

Early Years, 1820–1844

Atwater, Caleb. *The Writings of Caleb Atwater.* Columbus, Ohio, 1833.

Burke, Thomas. *Travel in England.* New York: Charles Scribner's Sons, 1946.

Chapman brothers. "Portrait and Biographical Record, Fayette, Pickaway and Madison Counties, Ohio." Chicago, September 1892.

Dana, Richard Henry Jr. *The Seaman's Friend.* Boston: Thomas Groom Publisher, 1847. Online, Gutenberg Project.

Davenport, Alfred. "My Life," 1830–1887. Diary.

———. Untitled diary.

———. Alfred Davenport to his family in Circleville, Ohio, from Oregon. Mary E. Wilder Archive, Pickaway County Hist. and Genealogical Library, Circleville, Ohio.

Davenport, Charles. Travel journal, February 24, 1831, to June 30, 1831. Mary E. Wilder Archive, Pickaway Co. Hist. & Genealogical Library, Circleville, Ohio.

Druett, Joan. *Hen Frigates.* New York: Simon & Schuster, 1998.

Dunlop, M. H. *Sixty Miles from Contentment*. New York: Basic Books, 1995.

Hawthorne, Nathaniel. "The Canal Boat." *New England* no. 9 (Dec. 1835): 398–409.

Henderson, Robert. *Salty Words*. New York: Hearst Marine Books, 1984.

Howe, Henry. *Historical Collections of the Great West*. Cincinnati, 1855.

———. *Historical Collections of Ohio*. Cincinnati, 1846.

Kilbourne, John. *The Ohio Gazetteer*. Columbus, Ohio, 1831.

Mansfield, J. B., ed. *Great Lakes Maritime History*, vol. 1, no. 1. Chicago J. H. Beers, 1849.

Morehead, Blanch Morehead. "Ohio Canals." Hocking County Historical Society, 1976.

Nogle, Mac. "Pig Trouble." *Pickaway Quarterly*. Pickaway County Historical Society, 2007.

Ohio Central History. "Circleville, Ohio," "Ohio and Erie Canal," "Agriculture and Farming in Ohio," "Zoar Village."

Ohio Memory. "Daily Life in Ohio 1803–1903." https://ohiomemory.org.

e

Paul, Marco. "Marco Paul's Travels on the Erie Canal." https://www.eriecanal.org/texts/abbott/abbott.html.

Trollope, Fanny. *Domestic Manners of the Americans*. New York: Penguin Books, 1997.

Union College. "Mirror for America," "West Central # 2," "Engineering the Erie," "The Need-for-a-Canal," "Tour of the Erie Canal,"

"Bank-Walk Views of the Canal," "Making It Work," "Aqueduct," "Piers," "Locks." Erie Canal. https://eriecanal.org./texts.

Wilder, Laura Ingalls. *Farmer Boy*. New York: Harper Reprint, 1994.

Wyld, Lionel. *Low Bridge: Folklore and the Erie Canal*. Syracuse University Press, 1977.

Oregon Trail, 1844; Hawaii, 1845

Barmac, Jean. *Hawaiian Journal of History* 2 (October 1922).

Bryant, Edwin. *Rocky Mountain Adventures*. New York: Hurst and Co., Arlington edition, 1885.

Clyman, James. *Diaries*. Edited by Charles L. Lewis. New Delhi, India: Isha Books, 1928, reprint 2013.

Davenport, Alfred. Letter from Oregon. Mary E. Wilder Archive, Pickaway Co. Hist. and Genealogical Society.

Dary, David. *The Oregon Trail*. New York: Oxford University Press, 2004.

Devoto, Bernard. *Across the Wide Missouri*. Cambridge, Mass.: Riverside Press, 1947.

Gagnon, Gregory O. *Culture and Custom of the Sioux Indians*. Lincoln: University of Nebraska Press, 2012.

Guthrie. A. B. Jr. *The Way West*. New York: Houghton Mifflin, 1949.

Holmes, Kenneth L., ed. *Covered Wagon Women 1840–1849*, vol. 1. Lincoln: Univ. of Nebraska Press, 1983.

McLynn, Frank. *Wagons West*. New York: Grove Press, 2002.

Oregon Trail. "Reminiscences of Experiences of the Oregon Trail in 1844, Ch 6, Ft. Bridger to Ft. Hall." *Oregon Historical Society Quarterly*.

Parkman, Francis, Jr. *The Oregon Trail*. New York: Caxton House, Inc.

Sage, Rufus B. *Rocky Mountain Life*. Lincoln: Univ. of Nebraska Press, original printed in 1846, Bison Books, ed. 1982. Like original edition, omitted are pages 15–26.

Spoher, Alexander. "Fur Traders in Hawaii: The Hudson's Bay Company in Hawaii 1829–1861." *Hawaiian Historical Society Journal* 5, no. 20 (1986).

Stewart, George R. *The California Trail*. Lincoln: Univ of Nebraska Press, Bison Books, 1983.

Webber, Burt, ed. *The Oregon Trail Diary of Edward Evans Parrish in 1844*. Medford, Oregon: Webb Research Group, 1928.

Hawaii

Kuykendall, R. S. *The Hawaiian Kingdom*. Honolulu: University of Hawaii Press, 1938.

California, 1846–1847
Bear Flag Rebellion, California Battalion

Altrocchi, Julia Cooley. *The Old California Trail*. Caldwell, Idaho: Caxton Printers, Ltd, 1945.

Boule, Mary Null. *Mission San Francisco Solano*, book 21. Vashon, Washington: Merryant Publishers, Inc.

Bryant, Edwin. *What I Saw in California*. New York: D. Appleton & Co., 1849.

Dellenbaugh, Frederick S. *Fremont and '49*. New York: G. P. Putnam Knickerbocker Press, 1914.

Egan, Ferol. *Fremont*. Reno: Univ. of Nevada Press, 1977 and 1985.

Fremont, John Charles. *Memoirs of My Life, 1842, 1843, 1844, 1845–1847.* New York: Cooper Square Press, 2001.

Giffen, Guy J., and Helen S. Giffen. "Tracking Fremont's Route with the California Battalion from San Juan Bautista to Los Angeles, Nov. 1846–Jan. 1847." Online.

Hittell, John. *History of the City of San Francisco.* Columbia, SC: First Rate Books.

Nevin, David. *Dream West.* New York: Forge Books, 1983.

Nevins, Alan. *Fremont, Pathfinder of the West,* Vols. I and II. New York: Frederick Ungar Publishing Co., reprint 1961.

Rosenus, Alan. *General Vallejo and the Advent of the Americans.* Berkeley, CA: Heyday Books, 1999.

Sides, Hampton. *Blood and Thunder.* New York: Doubleday/Random House, 2006.

Spoher, Alexander. "Fur Traders in Hawaii: The Hudson's Bay Company in Hawaii 1829–1861." *Hawaiian Historical Society Journal* 5, no. 20 (1986).

Stewart, George R. *Ordeal by Hunger.* Lincoln: University of Nebraska Press, Bison Books, 1983.

Upham, Charles Wentworth. *The Life, Exploration and Public Service of John Charles Fremont.* Boston: Ticknor and Fields, 1856.

U.S. Army, "California Battalion of Mounter Riflemen, Master Rolls 1846–1847, Commanded by Lt. Col. J. C. Fremont," Vol I [15 leaves]. Berkeley, Ca.: Univ. of Calif. Bancroft Library, MSS C-A 126. http://osicat.berkeley.edu/record=b11233448-s1.

Gold Rush 1849–1861

Borthwick, J. D. *The Gold Hunters.* New York: Outing Publishing Co., 1917.

Bristow, Gwen. *The Calico Palace.* Amazon.com. Kindle.

Browne, J. Ross. *Mule Back to the Convention: Letters of a Reporter to the Constitutional Convention, Sept.–Oct. 1849.* San Francisco: The Book Club of California, 1950.

Bancroft, K. M., ed. *Bret Harte's Gold Rush.* Berkeley: Heyday Books, 1997.

Delano, Alonzo. *On the Trail to the California Gold Rush.* Lincoln: Boson Books, 2001.

———. *Life on the Plains and among the Diggings.* Lincoln: Bison Books, 2005.

Dellenbaugh, Frederick S. *Fremont and '49.* New York: G. P. Putnam, Knickerbocker Press, 1914.

Egan, Feral. *Fremont.* Reno: University of Nevada Press, 1977, 1985.

Fremont, Jessie Benton. *Mother Lode Narratives.* Edited by Shirley Sargent. Mariposa, Ca.: Mariposa Heritage Press, 1996.

Holliday, J. S. *The World Rushed In.* New York: Simon and Schuster, 1981.

Jackson, Joseph Henry. *Anybody's Gold.* New York: D. Appleton-Century Co., 1941.

Marryat, Frank. *Mountains and Mole Hills.* London: Longman, Brown, Green and Longmans, 1855; Time Life Books, reprint 1989.

Monahan, Jay. *Australians and the Gold Rush.* Berkeley: University of California Press, 1966.

Potter, David Morris, ed. *Trail to California: Overland Journal of Vincent Geiger and Wakeman Bryarly*. New Haven: Yale University Press, 1945, third printing March 1967.

Twain, Mark. *Roughing It*. Los Angeles: University of California Press, 1942.

Civil War, Missouri, 1861

Feree, Rev. P. V., MD. *The Heroes of the War for the Union and Their Achievements*. Cincinnati: R. W. Carroll Co., 1864.

Beckenbaugh, Terry. "First Battle of Lexington, Mo. or the Battle of Hemp Bales, Sept. 18–20, 1861." Kansas City Public Library. https://www.civilwarinthewest.org/encyclopedia/first-battle Lexington.

Fremont, Jessie Benton. *The Story of the Guard: A Chronicle of the War*. Boston: Ticknor and Fields, 1863.

Nevins, Alan. *Fremont*, Vols. I, II. New York: Frederick Ungar Publishing Co, reprint 1961.

Wikipedia, "Missouri in the American Civil War."

———. "Action at Springfield or the Battle of First Springfield/Zagonyi's Charge Oct. 25, 1861."

Civil War Mountain Department, War in the West (Mississippi Valley), 1862, 1863

Allen, William. *Stonewall Jackson's Campaign in the Shenandoah Valley of Va. Nov. 4, 1861–June 17, 1862*. London: Hugh Rees, Ltd., 1912.

Adams, George Worthington. *Doctors in Blue*. Baton Rouge: Louisiana State University Press, 1980.

Catton, Bruce. *Glory Road*. Garden City, NY: Doubleday & Co. Inc, BCE.

Catton, Bruce. *Mr. Lincoln's War*. Garden City, NY: Double Day & Co., BCE.

Davenport, Capt. Alfred. Unnamed diary, 1863. "A Special Messenger for Maj-Gen. John Charles Fremont While Serving in the Mountain Dept. 1862." Author's family papers.

Farragut, David Glasgow. "The Life of David Glasgow Farragut." In *Blue and Gray at Sea*, edited by Thomsen, Brian. New York: Tom Doherty Assoc., 2003.

Freeman, Douglas Southall. *Lee's Lieutenants*, Vols. I, II, & III. New York: Charles Scribner's Sons, 1944.

Fremont, John Charles. *Report of the Operations of Maj-Gen Fremont While in Charge of the Mountain Dept. Spring and Summer 1862*. New York: Baker & Godwin, 1866, reprint.

Henderson, Col. G. F. R., "Stonewall Jackson and the American Civil War": New York: Longman's Green & Co., Inc. 1961

Krick, Robert K. *Conquering the Valley, Stonewall Jackson at Port Republic*. Baton Rouge: Louisiana State University Press, 1996.

Lang, Theodore F. *Loyal West Virginia, 1861–1865*. Baltimore: Deutsch Publishing Co., 1895. Reprint, Charleston, WV: Blue Acorn Press, 1998.

Mareen, Karissa A. "Guerrilla Warfare in Western Virginia 1861–186: Garden City Publishing Co. Alfred A. Knopf 19385." Thesis, Lynchburg, Va, Liberty University, Masters of History.

McKinney, Tim. *Civil War in Greenbriar Co., W. Va*. Charleston, WV: Quarrier Press, 2004.

McPherson, James M. *Battle Cry of Freedom*. New York Oxford: University Press, 1998.

Nevins, Alan. *Fremont*, Vols. I, II. Reprint, NY: Frederick Ungar Publishing Co., 1961.

Ohio Civil War Central. "Battle of Princeton Court House, a.k.a. Battle of Pigeon Roost May 15–17, 1862." https://www.ohiocivilwarcentral.com/entryphp?rec=729.

Porter, David Dixon. "The Siege of Vicksburg." In *Blue and Gray at Sea*, edited by Thomsen, Brian. New York: Tom Doherty Assoc., 2003.

Reed, Rowena. *Combined Operations in the Civil War*. Annapolis, MD: Naval Institute Press, 1978.

Tanner, Robert G. *Stonewall in the Valley*. Garden City, New York: Doubleday & Co., 1976.

Schley, Winfield Scott. "The Port Hudson Campaign." In *Blue and Gray at Sea*, edited by Thomsen, Brian. New York: Tom Doherty Assoc., 2003.

Styple, Wm. B., ed. *Writing and Fighting the Civil War: Soldier Correspondence to the New York* Sunday Mercury. Kearny, NJ: Belle Grove Publishing Co., 2000.

Wiley, Bell Irwin. *Life of Johnny Reb*. Baton Rouge: Louisiana State Univ. Press, 1943.

———. *Life of Billy Yank*. Baton Rouge: Louisiana State Univ. Press, 1952.

Williams, T. Harry. *Lincoln and His Generals*. New York: Alfred A. Knopf, 1952.

Quartermaster Department, 1862–1866
Pennsylvania, Ohio-Mississippi Valley

Avary, Myrta Lockett. *Dixie after the War.* New York: Doubleday, Page & Co., 1906.

Adams, George Worthington. *Doctors in Blue: The Medical History of the Union Army in the Civil War.* Baton Rouge: Louisiana State University Press, 1952.

Brisbane, Col. William. *Col. William Brisbane Papers*, series 3, M-S-162. "Conversations between Brisbane and Brig-Gen. Fitz Henry Warren, Commander, Dept. of the Susquehanna, Pa., U.S. Army 1863." Gettysburg College, Musselman Library.

Brown, Patrick. "Scranton Business, Industrial Pioneer, and the Transformation of America 1840–1902." Thesis, Georgetown, University, May 4, 2009.

Edmunds, David C. "Surrender on the Bourbeau. Honorable Defeat or Incompetency under Fire." *Journal of Louisiana History Assoc.* 8, no. 1 (1977): 63–85. https://jstor.org.

Edmunds, Emma. *Nurse and Spy in the Union Army*, 1st ed. Hartford: W. C. Williams & Co., 1865.

Gereman, David J. "Island Number 10." https://www.essentialcivilwar.com/island-no-10.

Gillett, Mary C. "The Army Medical Department 1818–1865." Washington, DC: Center for Medical History, U.S. Army, 1987.

Hess, Earl J. *Civil War Logistics.* Baton Rouge: Louisiana State University Press, 2017.

Lackey, Rodney C. "Noted on Civil War Logistics: Facts, Stories-Transportation Corps." https://www.transportation.army.mil/history.

La Pointe, Patricia M. "Military Hospitals in Memphis 1861–1865." *Tennessee Historical Society Quarterly* 42, no. 4: 325–42. https://jstor.org.

Miller, Francis Trevilian, and Robert Simpson Lawler. *Photographic History of the Civil Was, Prisons and Hospitals*. Stanford, Ca.: Stanford University Library.

O'Harrow, Robert, Jr. *The Quartermaster, Montgomery C. Meigs*. New York: Simon and Schuster, 2016.

"Official Roster of Soldiers of the State of Ohio in the War of Rebellion 1861–1865, 110–140 Voluntary infantry Regiments." U.S. Archive Office, sec. 1309, Vol. VIII. https://archive.org.

Palladino, Grace. "Another Civil War, Labor, Capital and the State of Anthracite Regions of Pennsylvania 1840–18."

Patterson, Benton Rand. *Mississippi River Campaign 1861–1863*. Jefferson, NC: McFarland & Co., 201.

Reed, Rowena. *Combined Operations in the Civil War*. Annapolis: Naval Institute Press, 1978.

Rodenbaugh, Bvt. Brig. Gen. Theodore F., and Maj. Wm. Haskins, eds. *Historical Sketches U.S. Army Staff and Generals-in Chief*. Reprint, New York: Maynard & Merrill, 2010.

Ryan, Joseph. "Union Control of the Mississippi River April 1862–July 1863." https://joeryancivilwar.com/union-controlmississippi.

Stewart, Charles W. "Admiral David D. Parson, May 18, 1863–Feb 29-1864." Official Records of the Union and Confederate Navies in the War of Rebellion, U.S. Navy Department, 1912.

Shankorn, Arnold. "Draft Resistance in Pennsylvania in the Civil War." *University of Pennsylvania Press*, no. 2 (April 1927): 190–204.

Styles, Edward H. "Fitz Henry Warren." *Annals of Iowa* 6, no. 7 (1904): 401–44.

Welter, Franklin H. "The American Civil War: A War of Logistics." Thesis, Bowling Green State University, 2015.

Wooten, Franklin H. *Johnsonville*. Dorado Hills, Ca.: Savas Beatie, 2019. Special thanks to Timothy M. Gilhool, Dept. of Civilian Command, Lascom History Office, U.S. Army, Ft. Lee, Va.

New Orleans

Brackett, John Matthew. "The Naples of America, Pensacola During the Civil War and Reconstruction." Master's thesis, Florida State University, 2180005. https://jstor.org.

Callender, William. *A Union Spy from Des Moines: An Autobiography June 15, 1881*. Edited by J. M. Dixon. Big Byte Books, 2016.

Casamajor, George H. "The Secret Service of Federal Armies." https://www.civilwarsignals.org.

Central Intelligence Agency. "Intelligence in the Civil War." Public Affairs, Washington, DC. https://www.CIA.gov.

Davis, William Watson, PhD. *The Civil War and Reconstruction in Florida*. New York: Columbia University, 1913.

Doyle, Elizabeth Joan. "Civilian Life in Occupied New Orleans 1863–1865." PhD thesis, Louisiana State University, 1955. https://jstor.org.

Fishel, E. C., *The Secret War for the Union: The Untold Story of Military Intelligence in the Civil War*. Boston: Houghton Mifflin, 1996.

Fisher, Margo. "Secret Political Societies in the North during the Civil

War." *Indiana Magazine of History* 4, no 3: 187–286. https://jstor.org.

Fleming, Walter, PhD. *Civil War and Reconstruction in Alabama*. Spartanburg, SC: Repeat Co. Publishers, 1928.

Markel, Donald E. *Spies and Spymasters of the Civil War*, rev. ed. New York: Hippocrene Books, 2004.

Marten, James. "The Making of a Carpetbagger, George S. Denison and the South 1854–1866." *Louisiana Historical Assn.* 34, no. 2 (1993). https://jstor.org.

Person, William Whatley, Jr. "The Committee on the Conduct of the War." *American Historical Review* 23, no. 3 (550–576). https://jstor.org.

Stover, John F. "Georgia Railroads during Reconstruction." *Railroad History*, no. 134: 58–65. https://jstor.org.

Kansas 1867-1880

Andreas, A. T. *History of the State of Kansas*. Chicago: 1883, various online sources.

Bunkowski, Lisa Miles. "Butler County War 1870." Doctoral thesis, Dept. of History, University of Kansas, 2003. https://jstor.org.

Cortwright, David T. "Disease, Death, and Disaster on the American Frontier." *Journal of the History of Medicine & Science* 46, no. 4: 452–92. https://jstor.org.

Dale, Edward Everett. "Those Kansas Jayhawkers, a Study of Sectionalism." *Agricultural History* 2, no. 4 (1923). https://jstor.org.

Garfield, Marvin H. "A Journal of the Central Plains, Defense of Kansas Frontier 1868–1869." *Kansas History Quarterly* 5 (Nov. 1932): 541–473.

Giddens, Paul H. "Eastern Kansas, 1869–1870." *Kansas History* 9, no. 8 (November 1940): 371–83. https://jstor.org.

Mead, S. G., publisher. *Eureka Herald*, August 1869, online.

Humboldt, Kansas. "A Letter by an Unknown Person Concerning the Character of Eastern Kansas 1869–1870, Written in the Kansas City, Missouri, *Spectator*." *Kansas History* 1 (Nov. 1940).

Kirby, Russell. "Nineteenth Century Patterns of Railroad Development on the Great Plains." *Great Plains Quarterly* 3, no. 3 (1883): 157–70. https://jstor.org.

Risser, C. C. "Outlaws and Vigilantes of the Southern Plains 1865–1885." *Missouri Valley Historical Review* 19, no. 4 (March 1933): 534–54. https://jstor.org.

Veblen, Thorskin B. "The Price of Wheat since 1867." *Journal of Political Economy* 1, no. 1 (Dec. 1892): 68–104. https://jstor.org.

Trost, Brent. "Rails of Destiny, Early Development in Kansas City 1840–1870." Doctoral thesis, Missouri State Univ., Maysville, Mo., April 2014. https://jstor.org.

White, Richard. "Outlaws in the Idle Border, American Bandits." *Western Historical Press Quarterly* 12, no. 4. https://jstor.org.

Weiser, Kathy, compiler. "Legends of Kansas, Greenwood County, Eureka, Garnett, Humboldt." https://www.legends of Kansas.com/Kansas History.

Wells, O. V. "The Depression of 1873–1879." *Agricultural History* 11, no. 2 (July 1937): 182–219. https://jstor.org.

Yost, G. "History of Lynchings in Kansas." *Kansas History* 2, no. 2 (May 1933): 182–219. https://jstor.org.

Colorado, 1875, 1880

Andrews, Thomas G. "Made by Toile, Tourism and Labor in the Construction of the Colorado Landscape 1856–1971." *Journal of American History* 92, no. 3 (Dec. 2005): 842–917. https://jstor.org.

Ambrose, Stephen E. *Nothing Like It in the World, Transcontinental Railroad 1863–1869.* New York: Simon and Schuster, 2003.

Levine, Brian. *A Brief History of Hard Scrabble Area and Wetmore, Colorado.* Crested Butte, Colorado: Wetmore-Hard Scrabble Geological and Historical Society, Mt. Gothic Tones and Reliquary Rare Books.

Kirby, Russell. "Nineteenth Century Patterns of Railroad Development on the Great Plains." *Great Plains Quarterly* 3, no. 3 (1883): 157–70. https://jstor.org.

Morgan, Lewis H., Leslie A. White, and Lewis H. Moor, eds. "Journal of a Trip to Southern Colorado and New Mexico June 21–Aug. 7, 1878." *American Antiquities* 8, no. 1 (July 1942): 3–8. https://jstor.org.

Thompson, Gerald, "Henry De Grout and the Colorado Gold Rush of 1862." *Journal of Arizona History* 32, no. 2: 131–40. https://jstor.org.

California, 1880

Burchell, Robert A. "The Faded Dream: Inequality in Northern California in the 1860s and 1870s." *Journal of American Studies* 23, no. 2 (Aug. 1989): 215–34. https://jstor.org.

Vaught, David. "After the Gold Rush, Replicating the Rural Midwest in the Sacramento Valley." *Western Historical Quarterly* 34, no. 4: 446–87. https://jstor.org.

Wikipedia. "San Francisco," "Portland," "Oregon."

Chapter Notes

Early Years, Oregon Trail

Chapters 1–10

Two diaries were written by Alfred Davenport. "My Life" covers 1830–1867. An untitled diary describes Civil War experiences and life in Kansas after the war. A letter from Oregon sent to relatives in Circleville recaps his Oregon Trail experience in 1844. A journal from Alfred's brother Charles partially covers Charles's February 24, 1831, to June 30, 1831, journey to America. Samuel and his family departed from Liverpool, England, on August 16, arriving at New York City in mid-October 1830.

The early history of Samuel Davenport's family in America was reported in *A History of Fayette, Madison and Pickaway Counties, Ohio* by Chapman brothers (Sept. 1892) with a reference to Samuel Davenport and his family's immigration to Pickaway County, Ohio. Various independent sources identify the Davenport family's arrival in 1830 (page 444, N. G. Davenport; page 624, S. G. Davenport). The publication reported that Alfred's father, Samuel, was a member of an elite business group in England, British Crown Surveyors.

Charles Davenport, Alfred's elder brother who sailed from Liverpool in 1831 after completing his education to become a medical doctor, reported that he sailed to America on a merchant vessel, the *Thomas Dickerson*. Charles practiced medicine and farmed in Circleville, Ohio. British Customs' historical records (bills of lading) show the *Thomas*

Dickerson arriving at Liverpool on February 19, 1831. Shortly after arrival, she returned to New York.

Hen Frigates offers pictures of rigging and types of nineteenth-century ships (pp. 47–48), describing ship routines and watches (pp. 56–58).

Nautical terms were provided from *Salty Words* (pp. 39, 84, 92).

Early impressions of New York and its harbor and nineteenth-century maritime experiences provided data gathered during many visits to New York's South Street Seaport Museum.

A Mirror for Americans: The Great Water Highway through New York State, 1829 begins with steamboat passage to Albany and mentions types of canalboat, locks, and a trip to Utica, whose beauty Alfred enjoyed.

A description of early steamboats is provided in *Sixty Miles from Contentment* (deck passage, pp. 160–162; gender division, pp. 143, 165–68; meals and fixings, pp. 125–27; spitting, p. 157; smoking, p. 158; wooding, p. 161; no protection around machinery, p. 161).

Low Bridge! Folklore and the Erie Canal describes the following: construction (pp. 9–10); packet boats (pp. 13, 22); lock keeps (p. 17); sleeping (pp. 29–30); canallers' culture (pp. 51–53); canal laborers (pp. 56–57); gambling, liquor, and entertainment (pp. 62–63); and right-of-way (pp. 70–73).

Richard Palmer's two-page essay covers the role of Irish laborers in constructing the canal through the Montezuma Swamp.

Nathaniel Hawthorne's four-page article speaks of line boats; canal scenery; a description of Utica, New York; and his inability to sleep due to an uproar of snoring in canal boats' small cabin.

Ohio History Central provided articles about Ohio and Erie Canal, Cleveland, Canal Fulton, Coshocton, Hopewell Indians, Newark, Newcomerstown, Pickaway County, and Circleville and Zoar, Ohio.

Sixty Miles from Contentment by Dunlop describes national highway (p. 37); earthworks (p. 82); Cincinnati, "the Empire City of Pigs" (p. 123); speed eating (p. 127); dinner table silence (p. 129); restrained behavior between sexes (p. 184); and the use of tobacco.

Alfred's 1844 travels to Oregon were mentioned in notes written by group leader Nathaniel Ford. A reprint of James Clyman's diary is presented as four books. In book 1 (Independence, May 14, 1844, to Little Blue River, June 30, 1844), on pages 71–72, the Clyman diary lists "members of the train in account with Clyman" including Alf Davenport. Alf was Alfred's childhood nickname. Clyman's book 2 continues West from the Little Blue River, July 1, 1844, to Red Buttes near the mouth of the Sweetwater, August 14, 1844. Book 3 is about August 15, 1844, to the Blue Mountains in Oregon, September 30, 1844. On September 4, Clyman and three men left Ford's train with packhorses for Oregon City. Alfred remained with Ford until Fort Hall, where he and three others departed on foot for Fort Boise. A diary by Edward Evans Parrish, traveling with Cornelius "Neal" Gilliam, covers the same period as that mentioned by Clyman, including the combining of Ford's and Gilliam's wagon trains.

Wagons West by Frank McLynn, chapter six, "Through Flood and Famine" (pp. 177–228), presents a broad view of emigrants and their reported stories on the Oregon Trail in 1844 including the Sager family's misfortunes on pages 188–89, 208–11, 215–16, 219–20, referenced in this book.

David Dary's *The Oregon Trail, An American Saga*, chapter 7, "Self-Rule and More Emigrants" (pp. 109–27) furnishes an entertaining view of the migration on the Oregon Trail in 1844.

"Emigrants to Oregon in 1844" compiled by Stephanie Flora (OregonPioneers.com) lists Davenport from Circleville, Ohio.

Oregon-California Trails Association's Octa-Trails.org provides studies of traveling to Oregon and California in the 1840s, listed by categories.

"The Oregon Trail in the Columbia Gorge, 1843–1855: The Final Ordeal" by G. Thomas Edwards provides a summary of challenges to emigrants in the Columbia River valley.

Two Wikipedia studies ("John McLoughlin" and "Ft. Vancouver") led to the understanding of what Davenport encountered in Oregon City.

"Sandwich Island" discusses English and American rivalries in commercial development in the Hawaiian Islands in the mid-nineteenth century at the time Davenport visited the islands.

California, 1846–1847

Chapters 11–20

Alfred's arrival in California brought two surprises. First, the Hudson's Bay Company's large warehouse in San Francisco (Yerba Buena) was closed. Second, the edict from the Mexican governor directing all Americans to leave created events that would forever change the life of Alfred Davenport.

His joining the Bear Flag Revolt and the friendship he developed with John Charles Fremont would influence the next fifteen years of his life. Alan Nevins in *Fremont*, Vol. I, provided explanation of the developments in California leading to its war with Mexico, a history of the conflict, and the establishment of California as state in 1849. Chapter XVI begins on December 10, 1845, with Fremont's topographical bureau mapping tour of central California and Monterey and his clash with Mexican general Jose Castro (pp. 215–33).

On May 8–9, 1846, Lt. Archibald Gillespie delivers instructions from the president to John C. Fremont, telling him to stand down as an explorer and serve as an officer of the U.S. Army, suggesting the president's desire for Fremont to be the president's eyes and ears in California (Nevins, *Fremont*, pp. 244–48). Zeke Merritt, an American settler, was in Fremont's camp when it was reported that Mexicans (Castro) dispatched Lieutenant Arce to gather 170 horses to be used by Mexican troops against settlers. Coached by Fremont, Merritt surprised Arce, captured his horses, and took them to Fremont's camp (Ferol Egan, *Fremont*, pp. 342–43). Merritt, leader of a band of settlers calling themselves *Osos* or Bears, planned to take the northern Mexican fortress in Sonoma with guidance and planning provided by Fremont. Traveling with Merritt was William Todd, a cousin of Mrs. Abraham Lincoln. They stopped for the night in Pope Valley at the home of Elias Barnett, where they picked up more volunteers (Alfred Davenport) (Egan, *Fremont*, p. 344).

The Bears captured Vallejo and his fortress with 250 arms (Alan Rosenus, *General Vallejo*, chapter 9, "The Revolt Begins," pp. 105–19). Todd, who had been sent to Bodega for supplies, was missing, reported to have been captured by De la Torre at Olompali. Lt. Henry Ford, second-in-command, took nineteen volunteers, including Davenport, to find Todd. American sharpshooters hidden by trees faced Mexicans armed with lancers and old short-range muskets, no match for Americans with an accurate long rifle. Mexicans departed; Todd escaped his captors during the battle, returning with Ford to Sonoma (pp. 149–50).

Nevins, *Fremont*, p. 280. The Bear Flag Revolt was over. Alfred joined Fremont's 160 handpicked men in the newly formed California Battalion, authorized by U.S. Navy commodore John Sloat, replaced by Commodore Robert Field Stockton. Maj. J. C. Fremont was to command all military forces in California, increase his battalion by 300 men, and establish garrisons of 50 men in Pueblo de Los Angeles, Monterey, and

San Francisco. Stockton ordered Fremont to meet him in San Francisco on October 25. Fremont would be appointed governor of California (Egan, *Fremont*, p. 369). On October 1, Stockton learned that Mexicans revolted in Los Angeles and San Diego. Fremont's plans to sail to San Diego were aborted when he learned that rancheros' horses were not available for his army in San Diego. Fremont, now a lieutenant colonel stationed in Monterey, raced to fill the ranks of his battalion to 450. He contacted Ned Kern at Sutter's and Edwin Bryant, a Kentucky journalist, asking for volunteers to join his battalion. One of the volunteers was Hell Roaring Thompson (Egan, *Fremont*, pp. 377–84). Fremont's incident with Don Jose de Jesus Pico in San Luis Obispo from Egan, *Fremont*, pp. 397–99.

The Historical Society of California's "Tracing Fremont's Route with the California Battalion from San Juan Bautista to Los Angeles from Nov. 1846 until Jan. 1847" by Larry J. and Helen S. Giffen, online from the Bancroft Library of the University of California, is the primary source for a study of the battalion's trip South, including the harrowing Christmas Eve and Christmas Day crossing of the San Marco Pass to Santa Barbara. While in Santa Barbara, Fremont was wooed by Senora Bernarda Ruiz, who pleaded to end hostilities. She outlined goals that pleased Fremont. This led to the end of hostilities and the articles of capitulation with Gen. Andres Pico. See Egan, *Fremont*, pp. 402–5, and A. Nevins, *Fremont*, pp. 299–300.

Kearny's battles, detailing his army's participation in the Mexican War in 1846, were found online at Wikipedia, "Battle of San Pasqual," "Battle of San Gabriel."

Alfred resigned with other soldiers in the California Battalion when Fremont was dismissed by U.S. Army general Kearny. Davenport joined Fremont's small group of followers for Fremont's return East in the summer of 1847.

California, 1849–1861

Chapters 21–31

Alfred's return to California traveled lightly, quickly stopping in Sacramento for supplies before heading to Hangtown to find the best prospects for employment and the search for gold.

The *Columbus Dispatch* reported on April 2, 1849, that sixty men from Columbus, including physician Charles E. Boyle, departed for California gold fields. Unlike the Columbus group, Alfred traveled alone, unaffiliated with any group that would slow his trip.

Boyle's diary was mentioned in David Dary's *The Oregon Trail*, pp. 212, 215.

Wagons West by Frank McLynn says that "4,000 people in St. Louis died of cholera in 1849" in the search for gold (p. 432).

The Oregon Trail, David Dary: "East coast publishers were scrambling to print California guidebooks" (p. 201).

L. S. Tichenor, "Life of John A. Sutter 1803–1880," pp. 1–6, http://score.rims.k12-ca.us/activity/suttersfort/pages/sutter.html.

"History of Sacramento, California," Wikipedia, pp. 4–6, https://en.wikipedia.org/wiki/"History-of-Sacramento-California".

"California Gold Rush," Wikipedia, pp. 4–6, https://wikipedia.org/wiki/"California-Gold-Rush".

Michael. D. Jackson, "Old Hangtown, Small Town Tales," pp. 1–5. Hangtown was first called Dry Diggings, later named Placerville.

J. D. Borthwick, "Looking for Gold," in *The Gold Hunter*, ed. Horace Kepart, pp. 49–53, provides a view of life in Hangtown in 1849–1850.

Over 89,000 gold seekers descended on California in 1849, creating extraordinary demands for goods and services, pushing prices greatly more than the technology boom of 2019. Coffee was today's equivalent of $4.20 per pound; a shovel in today's dollars cost $1,007.00, a dozen eggs $90.00.

"Egg War," Wikipedia. Farallon Islands provided murre seabird eggs for hungry miners.

September 1849 was the last month to work in gold fields. Seasonal rains beginning in October kept miners out of gold fields until the next dry season in 1850. Alfred spent the winter in San Francisco.

An excellent source is the San Francisco digital archive www.foundsf.orqindex.php. The index provides a section of a primary source of San Francisco history describing San Francisco in the 1850s. Each chapter averages 3–5 pages. Of note were chapters covering the following topics: conditions in 1850 and 1851; immigration of Chinese, French, and Italians; fires; forty-niners; monetary crises in 1851; financial depression of 1854; the Hounds in 1849; vigilance committees; gambling frenzy; prostitution; theater and opera; and performances by Lola Montez. Individual studies cover the development of specific neighborhoods. The 1850s online archive contains 181 pages.

Frank A. Marryat in "Mountains and Molehills", chapter XIX pp. 341-351 provides an English man's whimsical view of San Francisco: firemen, barbers, oysters and places of amusement.

J. D. Borthwick's *Gold Hunters* chapter 3 describes San Francisco in 1851: "A city in the making," pp. 25–41.

Anybody's Gold, Joseph Henry Jackson, on "the importance of transportation and mail delivery to miners" in chapter 5, "The Concord Was a Lady," pp. 141–67.

Wells-Fargo by Edward Hungerford traces early commerce, commercial transport, and the development of mail delivery in California and the gold country in the 1850s, pp. 1–44.

In "Shirley Letters from the California Mines in 1851-52," Dame Shirley (Mrs. Louise Amelia Knapp Smith Clappe) sent 23 letters to her sister in Massachusetts (reprinted from *Pioneer* magazine of 1854–55), providing a lady's view of '49ers.

Alfred joined Zeke Merritt at Murderer's Bar after the disastrous flood of 1850. The mines at the bar generated $75 million in gold in 1851 and $81 million in 1852. Thereafter, gold production declined.

"Hydraulic Mining," Wikipedia, https://wikipedia.org/wiki/hydraulicmining.

"Greenwood Mining District," https://www.edgov.us/landing/Living/Stories/pages/greenwood-minimg-district.aspx.

"Hardrock Mining in Grass Valley," https://www.150. Parks. ca.gov/?page-id-27652.

"Columbia, California, 1850," https://www.columbiacalifornia.com/history.

Snowy Range Reflections staff, "Mining Techniques of the Sierra Nevada and Gold County," https://www.sierracollege.edu/journal.

In *Mother Lode Narratives*, Jessie Benton Fremont mentions the building of Camp Jessie on Mount Billion 4,000 ft. above sea level (pp 89–93). "Mr. Davenport, one of Mr. Fremont's party from '45 to '49 took great part in making all right for us up here. He gave it my [the camp] name." (note 4). On page 93, in 1860, Ohio-born Davenport was a mine manager for Fremont (U.S. Census, Bear Valley enumeration).

The Civil War

Missouri, Department of the West
Chapters 32–36

"Major Charles Zagonyi's Guard was one of the best trained U.S. Cavalry armies in the Civil War." Jessie Benton Fremont, in *The Story of the Guard*, noted on pages 87–88, "The men were put through a hard drilling and riding school, each man equipped with Beale's revolvers, a Colt carbine and a saber."

Captain Davenport's western experiences were helpful to Zagonyi's cavalry recruits, teaching riding and shooting skills. Captain Davenport rode with Zagonyi in the Battle of Springfield, Missouri, October 24, 1861 (*The Guard*, pp. 133–47).

Fremont fought incursions in his Missouri operation by the powerful Saint Louis Blair family supported by President Lincoln. Blairs won their fight against Fremont, persuading Lincoln to remove Fremont from Missouri after one hundred days of service (Allan Nevins, *Fremont*, pp. 503–28).

Nevins, *Fremont*, p. 550. "Zagonyi Guards were mustered out [of the army] without, quarters, pay or rations." Captain Davenport returned home to his family in Circleville, Ohio.

The Mountain Department

Pressure grew from the press both East and West and from political supporters in Washington for Fremont to receive a new command (Nevins, *Fremont*, pp, 554). Lincoln assigned Major General Fremont to command the newly created Mountain Department on March 29, 1862. His headquarters was in the McLure Hotel in Wheeling, (West) Virginia. Captain Davenport received orders from Major General Fremont to report to headquarters in Wheeling to serve as an aide-de-camp with duties as the commander's special messenger. Davenport's unnamed diary discussed his assignments as a messenger and the pursuit of Stonewall Jackson in the Shenandoah Valley.

Three Sources for Mountain Department

1. Reprint of the *Report of the Operations of Maj-Gen. Fremont While in Command of the Mountain Department Spring and Summer of 1862* (New York: Baker and Godwin, 1866).
2. William Allan, *Stonewall Jackson's Campaign in the Shenandoah Valley of Virginia,*" 1st ed. With maps (London: High Rees, Ltd., 1912).,
3. Robert Tanner, *Stonewall in the Valley* (Garden City, NY, 1976); T. Harry Williams, *Lincoln and His Generals* (New York: Alfred A. Knopf, 1952), pp. 33–40, 70, 77, 98.

Articles

"The Battle of Princeton Court House," Wikipedia. Davenport carried dispatches to Brig. Gen. Jacob Cox, commander of the Kanawha District, when Cox was in Charleston, West Virginia, and in Princeton.

A. Newman, "The Civil War Battle of Pigeon Roost, Princeton," West Virginia Public Broadcasting, May 17, 1862.

Scott M. Kozelnik, "Camp Piatt," a U.S. military camp and hub for steamboats on the Kanawha River, visited by Davenport on tours to Kanawha District headquarters, *The West Virginia Encyclopedia*.

Mary Elizabeth Kincaid, "Fayetteville, W.Va. during the Civil War," *West Virginia Archives and History* 14, no. 4 (July 1953), Part III, Activities in 186. A town visited by Captain Davenport on his trip to Princeton.

Source unknown, "Walkie-Talkie the Messenger," tales of people and places in Civil War history, August 8, 2013, on role and dangers facing Civil War messengers.

Fremont's Report of Operations

"Milroy's brigade repeatedly attacked and charged a greatly superior force, exhibiting a courage and tenacity worth of highest praise. The Ohio troops behaved with gallantry and suffered severely. After several hours of fighting, our troops, outnumbered, reluctantly yielded portions of the field" (p. 11). Davenport returned from Princeton, catching up with Fremont in Moorfield.

On May 28, ten miles east of Moorfield, a halt was called for the twenty-ninth. Hundreds of stragglers and broken-down men from the Blenker division "were encountered. The number fit for duty was below 6,000" (p. 17).

"Fremont's advance, under Lt-Col Cluseret, touched the pickets of General Ewell's brigade" (outside Strasburg) (pp. 18–19).

Fremont describes his inability to stop Confederates' destruction of the bridge over the North Fork of the Shenandoah River on pp. 22–23 of his report. The burning of the bridge gave Jackson a thirty-hour advantage in escaping from the Union (p. 25).

Despite an early start, it was near eight thirty when the enemy was discovered near Union Church (Battle of Cross Keys) (pp. 27–31). "One of his [Fremont's] aides-de camp, Captain Nicholas Danka, was killed by a rebel musket ball while carrying orders to a field general during this [Cross-Keys] battle" (p. 31). Allen in *Stonewell Jackson's Campaign* reported, "Ewell repulsed Fremont so decisively [Cross Keys] on one wing as to paralyze his army and secure victory."

Wm. Allen Notes

"Cluseret occupied Strasburg" (*Stonewall Jackson's Campaign*, p. 169). "Cluseret without guides passed the town of Strasburg contacted Ashby's cavalry two miles beyond Strasburg" (Fremont, *Report of Operations*, p. 19).

The battle and death and funeral of Confederate general Ashby was reported by Allen in *Stonewall Jackson's Campaign*, pp. 175–83.

"Jackson escaped taking a road through the forest to Brown's Gap [in the Blue Ridge Mountain] to avoid Fremont's guns" (*Stonewall Jackson's Campaign*, note 115).

Colonel Henderson's *Stonewall Jackson* summed up the spring 1862 war in the valley. "Lincoln and Stanton learned nothing from the valley campaign. They had not yet learned the best defense is a good offence" (p. 305).

Lincoln replaced Fremont with General Pope. Fremont resigned from the army. Captain Davenport was assigned to the Quartermaster Department.

Quartermaster Department

War in the West
Chapters 37–40

"The Quartermaster Department 1861–1864," *Quartermaster Review* (September–October 1928): pp. 1–6. The study describes three departments of the Quartermaster Department during the Civil War: (1) clothing, camp, and garrison; (2) transportation, land, and water; and (3) regular and contingent supplies for the army with a special section on the Commissary Department.

Rodney C. Lackey, "Notes on Civil War Logistics Facts and Stories," logistical demands of each army company, brigade, and corps from the Quartermaster Department.

Earl J. Hess, "Civil War Logistics," an analysis of Civil War transportation systems and operational logistics.

Robert O'Harrow Jr., *The Quartermaster, Montgomery C. Meigs*, quartermaster general of the Union army whose logistical genius created a supply system permitting a Union victory during the War of the Rebellion.

Franklin M. Walters, "The American Civil War, A war of Logistics," Part II, "The Bakery" (Master thesis, Bowling Green State University, 2015, pp. 19–24). Walters cleverly traces an important army food source, hardtack, from a German immigrant baker in Cincinnati, Ohio, through the Quartermaster Department.

Rowena Reed, *Combined Operations in the Civil War*, pp. 84–88, Union capture of Fort Henry and Fort Donaldson.

Oscar F. Long, "July 17, 1862, Congress Authorized [Quartermaster Dept.] the Acceptance of Service of 100,000 Additional Volunteers for 9 Months' Service," Quartermaster Dept., U.S. Army Headquarters, Washington, DC, Nov 15, 1895.

Captain Davenport provided detailed reports of his travel expenses. His untitled diary (diary no. 2) listed days, type and cost of transport, lodging, and meals. Visiting Memphis, Tennessee, December 1862–January 1863, Davenport shared his meeting with wounded soldiers from the 114th Ohio Infantry Regiment, mustered into the army at Camp Circleville, Ohio. See appendix A.

Patricia M. La Pointe, "Military Hospitals in Memphis 1861–1865," *Tennessee Historical Quarterly* 42, no. 4 (Winter 1983): 326–42.

George Washington Adams, *Doctors in Blue*, chapter 8, "The General Hospitals": pavilion hospital program, pp. 153–58; hospital morale, pp. 162–73; chapter 10, army sanitation and hygiene, pp. 194–221.

"Ohio Civil War Central, 114 Regiment Ohio Voluntary Infantry 1862–1865."

"Official Roster of Soldiers of the State of Ohio in the War of the Rebellion, 1861– 1865, 114 Regiment Ohio Voluntary Infantry."

"Battle of Chickasaw Bayou December 26–29, 1862," Wikipedia.

On July 22, 1863, Captain Davenport was ordered to report to Brig. Gen. Fitz Henry Warren, commander of the Department of the Susquehanna, Greencastle, Pennsylvania.

Bruce Catton, "The Army of the Potomac: Glory Road," pp. 220–24, antiwar riots and strikes in anthracite coal areas along the Susquehanna River in Pennsylvania.

Patrick Brown, "Scranton Business in 1863" (Thesis, Georgetown University, History Dept.), pp. 409–11.

Arnold Shankorn, "Draft Resistance in Pennsylvania in the Civil War," *University of Pennsylvania Press* 2 (April 1927): 190–204.

Gen. Fitz Henry Warren and Capt. Alfred Davenport were transferred to New Orleans, Louisiana.

Earl J. Hess, *Civil War Logistics*, chapter 9, "Targeting Steamboats," pp. 215–34.

"Battle of Island No. 10., February 28–April 8, 1862," Wikipedia. Defeat of Confederate stronghold opened the Mississippi river to Memphis, Tennessee.

David C. Edmunds, "Surrender on the Bourbeau, Honorable Defeat or Incompetence under Fire," *Louisiana History Journal* 18., no. 1 (1977): 63–85 (Captain Davenport in Baton Rouge).

New Orleans and the Gulf States

Chapters 41–44

Herbert Asbury, *The French Quarter: An Informal History of the New Orleans Underworld*, a basic primer on a diverse, hedonistic city that digs deeply into the soul of New Orleans.

James Marten, "The Making of a Carpetbagger: George S. Denison and the South 1864–1866," *Journal of Louisiana History* 34, no 2: 133–60.

Denison was acting collector of customs in New Orleans. As a high-ranking federal official, he was the personal spy for Secretary of Treasury Salmon P. Chase, his cousin.

James Marten, "A Glimpse of Occupied New Orleans, the Diary of Thomas Duval of Texas 1863–1865," *Louisiana Historical Quarterly* 30, no. 3 (Summer 1983): 303–16.

Edward McMillan, "Military Medicine in New Orleans, 1863," *Louisiana History* 8, no. 2: 191–204.

Elizabeth Joan Doyle, "Civilian Life in Occupied New Orleans, 1862–1865" (PhD thesis, Louisiana State University, Dept. of History, 1955), pp. 238–39. "The Provost Marshall's Court was a fat place providing grinding oppression of citizens, [Judge] Alexander Atocha unable to track his fines departed in a cloud of scandal." Food prices, pp. 30–41; charity donations by Chief Quartermaster Holabird, pp. 161–12.

Captain Davenport's diary provided details of his work supervising the military hospital in Greenville (now part of Downtown New Orleans).

Donald E. Markle, *Spies and Spymasters of the Civil War*, Allen Pinkerton, pp. 4–7; Grenville Dodge, pp. 7–11; Thomas H. Hines, p. 110; chapter 3, "Secret Organizations," pp. 29–31.

Bruce Catton, *Army of the Potomac, Glory Road*," Clement Vallandigham, pp. 228–33.

George H. Casamajor, "The Secret Service of the Federal Armies," Signal Corps Assn. (1860–1865), Marley Creek Archives, pp. 1–10, https://www.civilwarsignale.org/pages/spy/fedsecret/fedsecret.html.

Doyle, "Civilian Life." Provost Marshal James Bowen, under Major General Banks, ordered fifty to one hundred men to infiltrate New Orleans to locate pockets of disloyalty (p. 126). Dr. Issachar Zacharie calling himself the confidential gent of President Lincoln, pp. 130–31.

Emma S. Edmunds, *Nurse and Spy in the Union Army*, 1st ed. (Hartford, Ct.: W. S. Williams & Co., 1865).

William Whatley Pierson Jr., "The Committee on the Conduct of the War," *American Historical Review* 23, no. 3: 550–76.

Wikipedia provided the following outlines, each six to eight pages long. Military forts in Pensacola Bay: Fort Pickens, Fort McRee, Fort Barrancas, and the Battle of Pensacola and the Battle of Mobile Bay.

William Watson Davis, PhD, *The Civil War and Reconstruction in Florida*, facsimile reproduction of the 1913 edition (Gainsville: University of Florida Press, 1964), "Freemans Bureau and Public Opinion," pp. 377–82; "Clash of Authority, Freeman's Bureau vs. the Courts," pp. 405–6.

John Matthew Brackett, "The Naples of America, Pensacola during the Civil War and Construction," (Thesis, Dept. of History, Florida State University, Spring 2005).

Myrta Lockett Avary, *Dixie after the War* (New York: Doubleday, Page & Company, 1906), p. 109. Ladies wore veils to shield their faces Blue Coats.

M. L. Avary, *Button Orders*, p. 123. Ex-Confederates were prohibited from wearing military buttons on their clothes or receive a dine of $5 to $50.

Lt. Gen. Richard Taylor, Confederate army (son of Pres. Zachary Taylor), *Destruction and Reconstruction*, a Project Guttenberg e-book, #323747 (December 5, 2007). "The government undertook to own all cotton that could be exported, therefore all cotton, as well as naval stores, were ordered burned so as not to fall in the enemy's possession" (p. 235). "Loss of slaves destroyed the value of land. The land was filled with widows and orphans, all accumulated wealth had disappeared" (p. 236). "Treatment of Northern Men [in Alabama]," pp. 318–21.

Walter L. Fleming, PhD, *Civil War and Reconstruction in Alabama* (Reprint of 1905 edition, Spartanburg, SC: Repeat Company Publication, 1978).

Pete S. McGuire, "Railroads of Georgia 1860–1880," *Georgia Historical Quarterly* 16, no. 3 (Sept. 1932): 179–212.

John T. Stover, "Georgia Railroads during Reconstruction," *Railroad History* no. 134: 56–65.

Kansas and Colorado

Chapters 45–47
Alfred's diary:

Travels Saint Louis to Glasgow, Missouri, 181 miles; Glasgow to Kansas City, 134 miles.

Captain Davenport represented the following Circleville, Ohio, investors in their search for farmland in Kansas: L. K. Ruggles, A. McCrea, Geo McCrae, W. F Brown, Louden, Gearhart, Turney, and Dowden.

Capt. William C. Heryford served with Davenport in Fremont's

Body Guard in Missouri. A farmer, Heryford served in the Missouri state legislature after the war and introduced Davenport to G. L. Harris, government land commissioner of Missouri who advised Davenport about farmland available in Kansas.

Alfred traveled to the U.S. Land Office for southeastern Kansas from Lawrence to Humboldt, Kansas, where Davenport negotiated land purchases for the Circleville investment group.

Kathy Weiser, "Legends of Kansas, Greenwood County and the town of Eureka," https://legendsofkansas.com/Kansashistory, provides a thumbnail sketch of Eureka and Greenwood County.

Marvin H. Garfield, "Kansas History: A Journal of the Central Plains, Defense of the Kansas Frontier, 1868–1869," *Kansas History Quarterly* 5 (Nov. 1932): 451–73.

Alfred's diary:

Davenport in Kansas City on April 6 received a letter from Geo McRae to meet a Mr. Gearhart from Circleville at a Humboldt, Kansas, law office. Gearhart brought a letter from Turney instructing him to proceed to Butler County to find land for Circleville's investors. Description of suitable land was sent to N. J. Turney on April 4. The land deal was certified. Davenport returned to Glasgow, Missouri, on May 10, where he stayed until July. Searches in Kansas to satisfy his warrant found no land suitable to meet his needs; he returned to Missouri in October.

On April 1868, Alfred returned to Eureka, Kansas, investing in local properties and assisting in town development. In December, he returned to Heryford's in Missouri. In 1869, he attempted to sell land in Eureka, found no buyers, and thought property sales would improve in 1870. Eureka was incorporated in 1870. Town founders declined to permit a railroad to travel through their newly incorporated town. Davenport joined the Eureka IOOF lodge.

Paul H. Giddens, "Eastern Kansas in 1869–1870," *Kansas History* 9, no. 4 (November 1940): 371–83.

Thurskin B. Veblen, "The Price of Wheat since 1867," *Journal of Political Economy* 1, no. 1 (Dec. 1892): 68–104.

O. V. Wells, "The Depression of 1873–1879," *Agricultural History* 11, no. 2: 237–51.

Brent M. S. Campney, "Ever since the Hanging of Oliphant, Lynching and the Suppression on Mob Violence in Topeka, Ks.," *Great Plains Quarterly* 33, no. 2: 71–86.

Richard White, "Outlaw Gangs of the Middle Border: American Social Bandits," *Western Historical Quarterly* 12 no. 4: 387–408.

C. C. Riser, "Outlaws and Vigilantes of the Southern Plains, 1865–1885," *Mississippi Valley Historical Review* 19, no. 4 (March 1933).

Edward Everett Pale, "Those Kansas Jayhawkers, a Study of Sectionalism," *Agricultural History* 2, no. 4 (October 1928): 167–84.

Vol P. Mooney, *History of Butler County, Kansas* (Lawrence: Standard Publishing Company, 1916), p. 78. "July 4th Celebration," p. 79, grasshopper year.

Louis Reed, "Railroads in Kansas," Kansas Heritage, https://kansasheritage.org,/research/rr/history.html.

Russell Kirby, "Nineteenth-Century Patterns of Railroad Development on the Great Plains," *Great Plains Quarterly* 3, no. 3: 157–70.

Thos G. Andrews, "Made by Toile, Tourism, Labor and the Construction of Colorado Landscape 1858–1917," *Journal of American History*, pp. 37–63.

Lewis H. Morgan and Leslie H. White, "Journal of a Trip to Southwestern Colorado June 21–August 7, 1878," *American Antiquities* 8, no. 1 (July 1942): 1–26.

John E. Dillavou, "Ghost Towns Going under Development Takes Over," *Landscape Architecture* 7, no. 4: 292–93.

Brian Levine (Mt. Gothic Tomes and Reliquary, Rare Books). Box 3048 Creste Butte, Co. 81224. Views of mining town Rosita, Colorado.

California

Chapters 48–49

John Hittell, *A History of San Francisco* (Reprint, First Rate Publishers, October 1, 1878). Chapter 7 discusses generalities, changes in San Francisco from 1856 to 1876.

M. Louisa Locke, "What San Francisco Looked Like in 1880," Wikipedia, 5 pages.

David Vaught, "A Tale of Three Land Grants on Northern California Borderlands," *Agricultural History* 78, no. 2: 140–54.

David Vaught, "After the Gold Rush, Replicating the Rural Midwest in the Sacramento Valley," *Western History* 34, no. 4: 446–67.

Jerome C. Davis, biographical sketch of Davis, Wikipedia. (Davenport met Davis during the Bear Flag Revolt while attacking Sonoma, visited Davis in 1880).

Leslie M. Scott, "Early Portland Contrasts," *Oregon Historical Project* 32, no. 2 (Dec. 1931): 313–15.

William Toll, "The Making of a Market Town; Religion, Social Clubs, Education; Early Portland: Portland as a Market Center," Oregon History Project.

Map 299591, printed in 1893, shows the Pacific Railroad line from Sacramento to Roseville, Rocklin, and the Secret Ravine, https://oldmapsonline.org.

https://www.sacramentohistory.org/resourcestimeline.

Aver Auerbach, "San Francisco's South of Market District 1850–1950: The Emergence of Skid Row," *California Historical Society Quarterly* 52, no. 3: 197–223.

Carl Abbott, "From Urban Frontier to Metropolitan Region: Oregon Cities 1870–2008," *Oregon Historical Quarterly* 110, no. 1: 74–95.

Index

A

Adirondack Mountains, 17
Ahwahnechee Indians, 196
Akron, 21
Albany, 8, 10–11, 14, 17, 336
Alderman (Hudson's Bay employee), 39
Allegheny Mountains, 3–4, 17, 20, 22, 27
Alta California. *See Daily Alta California*
Alvarado, Juan Bautista, 75, 78, 141, 152
antiwar activists, 274
Armour, Philip, 149
Arnaz, Jose, 115–16
Arnold, Richard, 279
articles of capitulation, 91, 339
Ashby (brigadier general), 225–26, 230–32
Aston-Johnson percussion pistols, 134
Astor, John Jacob, 46

B

Bale, Edward Turner, 88–89
Banks, Nathaniel, 27, 198, 223–27, 231, 238, 269–71, 275
Bannock-Shoshone Indians, 56
Bartell, Thomas, 156–57
Bates, Edward, 203
Battle of Natividad, 106
Bayard, George D., 230–32
Bayley, Alden, 142
Bear Mountain, 11
Bear Valley, 180, 190, 193, 195–96, 198, 341
Beauregard (Confederate general), 244
Bella Union, 156–57
Bennett, Elias, 88
Benton, Thomas Hart, 76, 85, 131, 192, 203
Benton Dam and Stamping Mill, xi, 191, 194
Bent's Fort, 131
Berryessa, Jose de los Santos, 92–93
Bickerdyke, Mary Ann, 251, 254
Bidwell, John, 77, 145
Big Sandy River, 52–53, 125
Birch, James, 179–80
Black codes, 281
Blacks Fork, 53–54
Blair, Frank, 204, 207–9
Blair, Montgomery, 203, 208
Blenker, Louis, 223–25, 229, 234
Blue Mountains, 55, 58–59, 61–62, 337
Blue River, Big, 39
Blue River, Little, 41

Body Guard (a.k.a. the Guard), xiv, 206, 212, 290, 349
Bohlen, Henry, 235
Boudin Bakery, 157
Bowen, James, 271, 275, 347
Boyle, Charles, 132, 340
Bragg, Braxton, 245
Brant house, 207
Brennan, Sam, 142, 159
Bridger's trading post, 54
Brown, J. H., 153
Brown, John Henry, 76
Brown Hospital, 254
Buell, Don Carlos, 244–46
buffalo chips, 41, 51, 53
buffalo people, 47
Bull Tail (Lakota chief), 46
Burnt River Canyon, 59
Burruss, Charles, 103–4
Burton Farm, 23
Butler, Benjamin Franklin, 271, 275

C

Californian, the, 142
Cameron, Simon, 209
Campbell, Robert, 46
Camp Jessie, 195, 341
Canby, Edward R. S., 280
Cannon, Joe, 172
Cape Clear (Ireland), 4
Carencro (general), 267
Carrillo, Carlos, 116
Carroll, S. S., 236–38
Carson, Kit, 77–78, 85–86, 92–93, 99–100, 111–12, 114, 131
Castro, Jose, 75, 79, 87, 94, 99, 102–3, 112, 338
Castro, Manuel, 103
Catskill Mountains, 11
Cayuse Indians, 60
Chase, Salmon P., 269, 347

Chase, William, 279
Chavez, Jose, 80
Chickasaw Bayou, 251–52
Chiles, Mary, 310
Chillicothe (Ohio), 27, 29
Chimney Rock, 45
Chisholm Trail, 295
Christian, 182
Cincinnati (Ohio), 27, 31, 247, 253, 290
Circleville (Ohio), 22–23, 26–27, 30, 190, 212, 238, 246, 286, 290–92, 311
Cleveland (Ohio), 19, 21, 25, 336
Cluseret, Gustave Paul, 229–30, 235
Columbia (town), 61–63, 187
Columbia and Stanislaus River Water Company, 186
Columbia Plateau, 58
Columbus (Ohio), 26–27, 218, 243, 255
Concord coach, 179
Cook (colonel), 122
Cooke, George, 119
Cooke, Jay
 railroad failure in 1873, 299
Corbin, Jack, 297–98
Corwine, R. R., 217
Couch, Darius, 257
Courthouse Rock, 126
Cowie, Thomas, 92–93
Crocker, Charles, 149
Cross Keys Battle, 234–36, 344
Cuyahoga River, 25

D

Daily Alta California, 158, 160, 167
Dalles, 62–64
Dana, William Godwin, 108
Danka, Nicholas, 234
Davenport, Alfred, xiii–xiv, 30, 51, 68, 88–89, 205–6, 250, 254, 299, 317, 319, 335, 337–38, 346

Davenport, Samuel, 28, 169, 335
Davis, Jefferson, 204
Davis, Jerome, 28, 169, 190, 335
De la Torre (owner of house in San Rafael), 92–94, 338
Denison, George Stanton, 269
Dennison's Exchange, 156
Denver (Colorado), 301–4
Deschutes River, 62
Dewell, Benjamin, 91
Digger Indians, 138
Dobbs Ferry, 10
Dodge, Grenville, 274
Dolores Mission, 308
Donner-Reed party, 123
Doty (N. R. Dougherty), 58–62

E

Earp, Wyatt, 296
East River (New York), 6
El Camino Real, 116
El Dorado Hotel, 149
Elzey, Arnold, 235
Emory, W. H., 112, 118
Enclosure Act in England, 3
Erie (lake), 14, 19, 27
Erie Canal, 14, 17, 19, 21, 26–27, 124, 190, 311, 320
Eureka (Kansas), 292, 294–95, 298–300, 302, 305–7, 313
Ewell, Richard S., 225, 229, 232, 234–36, 257

F

Fallon, William "Le Gros," 78, 122, 124
Fargo, William, 162
Farragut, David, 280–81
Fayetteville (West Virginia), 219
Featherstone, Jane, 274

Federal Indian Removal Act of 1830, 283
Feliz, Tomas, 116
financial panic and depression on 1873–1879, 163, 180, 299
Fitzpatrick, Thomas "Broken Hand," 34, 111
flood, Sacramento, 152
Flores, Jose Maria, 101–2, 114–16, 118
Fool Chief (Kaw Indian), 38
Foote, Andrew H., 243
Ford, Henry, 92, 338
Ford, Nathaniel, 34, 37, 39, 43, 54
Fort Boise, 55–56
Fort Hall, 54, 56, 122–23, 137
Fort Kearny (Nebraska), 135
Fort Laramie, xi, 37, 40, 45–46, 49–50, 52, 54, 57, 126, 133, 136
Fort Nez Perce, 61
Fort Vancouver, 63–64, 68, 76
Fort Walla Walla, 54, 60–62
Fowler, George, 92–93
Fox, Douglas, 193
Freedmen's Bureau, 280
Fremont, John Charles, 76–78, 80–81, 85–87, 91–94, 97–103, 105–11, 115–16, 118–27, 131–32, 155–57, 192–99, 203–18, 224–26, 229–32, 234–38
Fremont family camp, 80–81, 87, 338
Fry, James B., 258
Fulton Fish Market, 8

G

Galvin mountains, 81
Garcia, Four Finger, 92
Gaviota Pass, 108
Genesee River, 18
Gerhardt (Circleville land agent), 291
Gillespie, Archibald H., 85, 87, 98–102, 112–13, 119–20, 338

Gilliam, Cornelius "Neal," 34–35, 39, 43, 51, 134
Gilliam, Martin, 35
Godey, Alex, 77, 102, 114, 131
Goulding, Charles, 238
Granada (Colorado), 301
Grant, Ulysses S., 208, 223, 243–44, 248, 251–52, 274, 290, 299
Great American Desert, xi, 40, 50
Green (general), 267
Green River Mormon Ferry, 54
Greenwood (California), 170, 173–74, 292, 294–95, 297, 299
Grigsby, John, 90–91
Gwin, William M., 156

H

Halleck (major general), 244, 252
Hammond, William A., 238, 247, 250, 254
Hangtown (a.k.a. Dry Diggings, Placerville), 146–50, 152, 158, 160, 163, 168, 174
Harney, William S., 204
Harris, G. L., 349
Harris, Moses "Black," 34, 52
Hartnell Ranch, 78, 80–81
Haskell (major), 231
Hawken rifle, 42, 94, 134
Hawk's Peak, 81
Hayes, Kate, 182
Hayes, Rutherford B., 219–20
Hell Gate, 6
Heryford, William C., 290, 292, 294, 298, 348–49
Heth, Henry, 219
Hickok, William "Wild Bill," 296
Hines, Thomas Henry, 274
hoggy, boys driving animals pulling canalboat, 14, 16
Holabird, S. B., 271

Hopkins, Mark, 149
Hornitos League, 192–93
Hotchkiss, Jedidiah, 225–26, 231
Hounds, 6, 154, 340
Hudson (town), 11
Hudson River, 8–9, 11, 17, 236–37
Hudson River sloop, 10
Hudson River Valley, 10
Hudson's Bay Company, 39, 54, 58, 60–61, 63–65, 68, 76, 138
Hudspeth's bypass, 138
Humboldt River, 123–24, 138
Hunter, David, 209, 212
Huntington, Collis, 149

I

Ide, William B., 89–94
Independence (Missouri), 31, 33–35, 37, 39, 41, 46, 135
Iron Shell (Lakota chief), 46
Irwin, B. J., 244, 251
Island No. 10 (Mississippi River), 264

J

Jackson, Claiborne, 204
Jackson, Thomas J. "Stonewall," 223
Jailhouse Rock, 45
James, Frank, 297
James, Jesse, 297
Jefferson General Hospital, 251
John Day River, 62, 122
Johnson, Abraham, 112
Johnson, Andrew, 284
Johnson, Edward "Allegheny," 223
Johnson's Ranch, 62, 122, 139, 143
Johnston, Albert Sidney, 244
Johnston, Joseph E., 222
Josselyn, Amos Piatt, 132
Journado, "journey without water," 137

K

Kansas Indians, 38
Kansas River, 36–38, 41, 135
kanze, 289
Kaskaskia River, 26
Kaw Indians, 38
Kearny, Steven Watts, 111–16, 118–22, 124–26
Kelsey, Nancy, 91
Keogh, Miles W., 236
Kern, Edward M., 207
Knight, William, 87, 100

L

Lajeunesse, Basil, 86
Lakota chiefs, 46
land warrant, 289
Larkin, Thomas O., 75, 103
Lee, Robert E., 223, 256
Licking River, 25
line boat, 14
Liverpool (England), 1, 5, 7, 20
Lockport, xi, 13, 19
locks, 14, 17, 19, 21
locust plague, 189, 300
long knives, 46
Los Osos, Rancho, 107
Louisville (Kentucky), 31, 242, 254, 286
Ludwig, Jacob, 182, 251
Lyon, Nathaniel P., 204–5, 208–9

M

Malakoff Diggins, 180
Malheur River, 58
Mallory, Stephen, 279
Malone, Molly, 274
Manifest Destiny, 300
Mariposas, 155, 192, 194, 198–99, 205
Mark Twain Plaza, 164
Marshall, Humphry, 219
Marshall, James, 141
Mason, Richard, 119–20
Matteson, Edward, 180
Maxwell, Thomas, 206
Mayacamas Mountains, 90, 309
McCready, Irene, 157
McKim, 152–53
McKinley, William, 220
McLoughlin, John, 337
McLure Hotel, 217
Merced Mining Company, 192
Merritt, Ezekiel, 87–91, 169, 309, 338
Mervin, William, 101
Methodist mission near Lone Elm, 36
Michigan merchants, 175
Milroy, R. H., 224–25, 235–36
miner's lynch law, 171
Mission Dolores, 74, 176
Mission San Buenaventura, 115
Mission San Fernando, 116
Mission San Juan Bautista, 98, 108
Mission San Luis Obispo, 107
Mission San Miguel, 106
Mission San Rafael, 82, 93
Missouri Republican, 36
Missouri State Guard (Confederate), 204, 207–8
Missroon, John S., 92
Miwok Indians, 141
Molly Maguires, 258
Montez, Lola, 182
Montezuma Swamp, 18, 336
Montgomery, J. B., 87, 91–92, 203, 285
Mormon Ferry, 54
Morrill Act of 1862, 290
Morrison, Robert, 35, 52
Mound Builders, 26
Mule Hill, 114
murre eggs, 163

N

national road, 26, 218
Nevada City, 168, 179–82
Newark (Ohio), 21–22, 30
Newburgh (New York), 11
Newcomerstown (Ohio), 22
New York City, 6–10, 14–15, 17–18, 20, 164, 182, 256
New York Herald, 142, 160
Niagara Falls, 19, 302
Nidever, George, 109
North River. *See* Hudson River
Nueva Helvetia, 75

O

Ogden, Peter Skene, 138
Ohio and Erie Canal, 19, 21, 26–27, 190, 311
Ohio Voluntary Infantry 114th Regiment, 251
Old Dry Diggings, 145–46
Olompali, Rancho, 92–93, 338
Osos (Bears), 88, 90, 92–94, 338
Owen, Dick, 78
Owyhee (Hawaiian), 58

P

packet boats, 1–2, 8, 14
Padilla, Juan, 92
Palace Hotel, 156
Papins ferry, 38
Parrish, E. E., 54, 59
Parson, Lewis B., 263–64
Parting of the Ways, 57
Paso de Robles, Rancho, 106
Patton, James, 236
Pawnee Indians, 44, 126, 135
Pawnee versus Sioux, 44
Payette, Francois, 58

Pensacola (Florida), xiv, 276, 278–81, 284
Peralta, Sebastian, 80
Pickaway Plains, 23, 25–26, 30, 251, 290, 315, 317, 319–21, 335–36
Pico, Andres, 112, 114, 116, 118
Pico, Javaela Villavicencio, 107
Pico, Jose de Jesus, 106–7
Pico, Pio, 75, 99, 102, 106
Pierpont, Francis H., 217
Pigeon Ridge, Battle of, 220
pigs, 6, 17, 27
Pine Tree Mine, xiii, 193, 197, 206, 241
Pinkerton, 274
Piqua, 26
Placer, definition of, 147
Plateau Indians, 59
pocket mines, 185
Polk (president), 76, 78, 85, 100, 111, 126–27, 142
Pope, John, 208
Porter, David, 266
Portsmouth (Ohio), 30
Poughkeepsie (New York), 11
Powder River, 59
Prentiss, Benjamin, 205
Price, Sterling, 204
Pueblo (Colorado), 302, 304, 308
Purdon, Victor, 90–91

Q

Quackenbush (Eureka, Colorado's first banker), 298–99
Quakers (Society of Friends), 22
Queen of the Southern Mines, 185

R

Raft River, 57, 137–38
Red Butte, 51, 53
Reed, William, 106
Regulators, 154

Reid, John, 58
Revere, J. W., 95
Ridley, Robert, 76, 82, 94, 153
Robidoux, Antoine, 54
Rochester (New York), 18
Rocky Mountains, 31, 34–35, 45, 49, 51–52, 58, 124, 136, 143, 300, 303
Rosecrans, William S., 214, 218, 245–46
Rosita (Colorado), 302–3
Royal Gorge (Colorado), 302
Ruiz de Rodriguez, Bernarda, 110
Runkle, J. H., 296
Russ, Christian, 182
Russell, William H. "Owl," 118

S

Sacramento in 1849, xiii
Sager family, 49
Sagundai, James, 77, 86
Saint Francis Hotel, 153
Saint Louis, xiii, 30–31, 33, 36, 77, 126–27, 131–33, 161, 196, 199, 203–4, 206–7, 209–10, 218, 250–51
San Bernardo Pass, 116
Sandhills, 41
Sandwich Islands, 58, 64, 67, 99
San Francisco fires, 154
San Marco Pass, 108, 339
Santa Barbara, 100, 103, 105, 108–10, 115
Saunders, Allen, 35
Scammon, E. P., 219
Schenectady, 14
Schofield (general), 205
Scioto River valley, 26, 29
Scott, Winfield, 119, 205
Scotts Bluff, 45
Sears, John, 91

Secret Ravine in California's gold country, 168, 310
Sedgwick Military Hospital, 270
Segovia, Juanita, 172
Semple, Robert, 90–91, 94
shaman lead an Indian sun dance, 47
Shaw, William, 35, 49–50, 52
Shawnee Indians, 36
Sheridan, Philip S., 246
Sherman, William Tecumseh, 248, 252, 265–66, 286
Shields (brigadier general), 224, 226, 231–32, 236–38
ships used to build San Francisco, 73
Shoshone Indians, 54, 57
Shubrick, William B., 119–20
Sigel (colonel), 205
Sioux Indians, 46–47
Slide Mountain Peak, 11
Sloat, John D., 94, 97–98, 338
Smith, Jedidiah, 30, 34
Smith, Kirby, 245
Snake River, 50–51, 55–59, 137
social bandits, 297
Soda Springs, 54, 137
Sonora, 100, 112, 184–86, 203
South Street Seaport, 7
Spalding, Elizabeth, 58
Spalding, Henry, 58
Springfield, Battle of, 204–5, 210–11
SS *California*, 142
Stahel, Julius, 235
Stanton, Edwin, 217, 223, 226, 238, 257–58
steamboat losses, Mississippi River, 266
Stevens, Frank, 179
Stockton, Robert, 98–102, 105, 111–12, 114–18
Stony Point Lighthouse, 10
Storm King Mountain, 11
Streeter, William, 109

Studebaker, J. M., 149
Sturgis, Samuel, 205, 208
Sublette, Andrew, 39
Sublette, William, 46
Sublette Cutoff, 54, 137
Sweetwater River, 51, 122, 136
Sydney Ducks, 154
Syracuse (New York), 17–18, 162

T

Tadich Grill, 157
Talbot, Theodore, 76, 78
Tappan Zee, 10
Taylor, Zachary, 256
theaters in San Francisco, 164
Thomas, Lorenzo, 209
Thompson, Buford "Hell Roaring," 102–4
Three Buttes (Sutter Buttes), 86
Three Island Crossing, 57
Todd, Alexander, 162
Todd, William, 88, 91, 338
treaty of capitulation, 116
Treaty of Guadalupe Hidalgo, 110, 116
Trimble, Isaac, 235–36
Trinity Church, 8
Tucker, James, 270
Turner, Henry, 113, 119
Tuscarawas River, 25
Tyler, Erastus, 236

U

Umatilla Indians, 62
Umatilla River, 60
Umtippe (Cayuse Indian chief), 60
United States Military Academy, 11
Utica, 16–18

V

Vallandigham, Clement L., 75, 90–91, 274

Vallejo, Mariano, 75, 90–91, 274
Vallejo, Salvador, 90–91
Varwig, Henry, 242
Vasquez, Louis, 137
Vermillion River, Black, 39
Vermillion River, Red, 39
vigilance committee, 154
vigilante justice, 296–98
Vioget's survey, 76
von Humboldt, Baron Alexander, 138

W

Wakarusa, 36–37
Walla Walla Indians, 102–3, 122
Walnut Township (Ohio), 23, 25
Ware, Joseph E., 132
Warren, 154
Warren, Fitz Henry, 154, 256–57, 259, 267
water shortages in 1852, 53
Weber, Charles, 145
Wells, Henry, 162
Western Expositor, 35
West Point, 11, 219, 285
Westport (Missouri), xiii, 34, 36, 132–34, 143
White Buffalo Calf Woman, 47
White Caps, 296
Whitman, Marcus, 60
Whitman, Narcissa, 50
Whittaker, David, 298
Wyndham, Percy, 232

Y

Yerba Buena, 73, 337
Yonkers, 10

Z

Zacharie, Issachar, 275

CPSIA information can be obtained
at www.ICGtesting.com
Printed in the USA
LVHW110147220422
716940LV00004B/56